LONG ISLAND LANDSCAPES

and the Women Who Designed Them

LONG ISLAND LANDSCAPES

and the Women Who Designed Them

CYNTHIA ZAITZEVSKY

SOCIETY FOR THE PRESERVATION OF LONG ISLAND ANTIQUITIES
IN ASSOCIATION WITH
W. W. NORTON & COMPANY • NEW YORK AND LONDON

For

N I C K

my companion in this

and all the projects of my career

For information about permission to reproduce selections
from this book, write to Permissions,
W. W. Norton & Company, Inc.
500 Fifth Avenue, New York, NY 10110

For information about special discounts for bulk purchases,
please contact W. W. Norton Special Sales at
specialsales@wwnorton.com or 800-233-4830

Manufacturing by Friesens
Book design by Abigail Sturges
Production manager: Leeann Graham

Library of Congress Cataloging-in-Publication Data

Zaitzevsky, Cynthia.
Long Island landscapes and the women who designed them / Cynthia
Zaitzevsky ; foreword by Robert B. MacKay. — 1st ed.
p. cm.
ncludes bibliographical references and index.
ISBN 978-0-393-73124-8 (hardcover)
1. Landscape architects—New York (State)—Long Island--Biography.
2. Women landscape architects—New York (State)—Long Island—
Biography. 3. Landscape architecture—New York (State)—Long Island—
History—20th century. I. Title.
SB469.9.Z35 2009
712.09747'21—dc22

2008018539

ISBN 13: 978-0-393-73124-8

W. W. Norton & Company, Inc.
500 Fifth Avenue, New York, N.Y. 10110
www.wwnorton.com

W. W. Norton & Company Ltd.
Castle House, 75/76 Wells Street, London W1T 3QT

0 9 8 7 6 5 4 3 2 1

CONTENTS

Foreword by Robert B. MacKay / **6**

Preface and Acknowledgments / **7**

CHAPTER 1   A New Profession for Women / **10**

CHAPTER 2   Beatrix Jones Farrand 1872–1959 / **32**

CHAPTER 3   Martha Brookes Brown Hutcheson 1871–1959 / **60**

CHAPTER 4   Marian Cruger Coffin 1876–1957 / **76**

CHAPTER 5   Ellen Biddle Shipman 1869–1950 / **108**

CHAPTER 6   Ruth Bramley Dean 1889–1932 / **136**

CHAPTER 7   Annette Hoyt Flanders 1887–1946 / **162**

CHAPTER 8   The Second Generation, I / **192**

CHAPTER 9   The Second Generation, II / **226**

CHAPTER 10   A Look Backward and Forward / **256**

APPENDIX   Projects on Long Island by Women Landscape Architects / **265**

Notes / **271**
Index / **299**

FOREWORD

"COUNTRY HOMES, with their mile-long driveways, are continuous for hundreds of miles," reported the *New York Herald* in 1902, which found that "Long Island was rapidly being divided up into estates of immense acreage . . . beyond all precedent of American country life." Referring to the sea change that was reshaping the region, the *Brooklyn Daily Eagle* commented that it was as if Long Island had been "touched by magic, a new version of the sleeping princess." What had in fact touched Long Island was New York's ascent as the nation's financial and media capital, which in the age before reliable air travel made having a residence in its environs a requisite for many of the nation's captains of industry and finance. Over a thousand estates were to be built east of the city line on Long Island in the late nineteenth and early twentieth centuries in a phenomenon that was to transform an agrarian landscape that had remained little changed since the seventeenth century.

When the Society for the Preservation of Long Island Antiquities surveyed this phenomenon in *Long Island Country Houses and Their Architects, 1860–1940*, published by W. W. Norton in 1997, the editors, Anthony K. Baker, Carol A. Traynor and I, were particularly surprised by one statistic. For the approximately 150 houses whose landscapes were then known to have been designed by landscape architects, half were by women while only a couple of the country houses had been designed by architects of the same gender. We also noticed that while Olmsted Brothers, James L. Greenleaf, Guy Lowell, Innocenti and Webel, and a few other landscape firms of note were active on Long Island, many of the men were not well known, yet the women landscape archi-

tects were among the most famous practitioners in their field, and their work on Long Island had not been limited to country houses. It appeared that landscape architecture was one of the first areas in the design fields where women really made their mark, and that Long Island had been central to these developments. Could this have been due to influence of Long Island's 1,931 prominent garden clubs, such as the North Country Garden Club, whose tour of North Shore estate gardens in conjunction with the Garden Club of America's annual meetings in New York had brought thousands out to see the greatest concentration of landscaped estates in the nation? Might this be a subject for further study? Carol A. Traynor was an early advocate of such a project, Anthony K. Baker thought it would be an interesting sequel to the country house book, and Nancy Green of W. W. Norton also saw the possibilities and has been unwavering in support of this project for nearly a decade. After interviewing a number of landscape scholars to commence such a study, we were delighted when Cynthia Zaitzevsky accepted the challenge.

I first met Cynthia when she was a graduate student in 1970, during the formative years of the Boston Chapter of the Society of Architectural Historians. A historian of both architecture and landscape architecture, she received her doctorate in fine arts from Harvard in 1975 and is a well known Olmsted scholar. Her book *Frederick Law Olmsted and the Boston Park System* was published in 1982 and was followed by several cultural landscape reports for the National Park Service and her chapter on the Olmsted firm's work on Long Island for our own country house study. One of the first scholars to give serious attention to

PREFACE AND ACKNOWLEDGMENTS

landscape architecture, Cynthia has been at the forefront of the effort to document the field and its practitioners. A meticulous researcher, she has spent eight years compiling this study, tracking down leads not only on Long Island, but traveling coast to coast to examine archival holdings.

For SPLIA, *Long Island Landscapes and the Women Who Designed Them* is the latest title in a publication program that dates back to 1960 and includes biographies, teaching manuals, illustrated histories and exhibition catalogs, landmark guides, and architectural histories and has included such studies as *Long Island Is My Nation—The Decorative Arts & Craftsmen 1640–1830, Long Island Windmills, Useful Art—Long Island Pottery, Woven History—The Technology and Innovation of Long Island Coverlets, 1800–1860, AIA Architectural Guide to Nassau and Suffolk Counties, Long Island* and *Long Island Country Houses and Their Architects, 1860–1940*. We hope that Cynthia's book will soon be joined by three other publishing projects now in the works as we continue to focus on salient aspects of Long Island's remarkable past with particular emphasis on architecture and the decorative arts.

Finally, the Society would like to offer particular thanks to Anthony K. Baker and the George F. Baker Trust for their generous and long-standing support of this project, as well as to Patricia P. Sands and the members of our Publications Committee and W. W. Norton & Company, Inc., our partner in the publication of three of our studies.

ROBERT B. MACKAY, PH.D., *Director*
Society for the Preservation of Long Island Antiquities
November 2007

WHEN ROBERT B. MACKAY suggested this project to me a number of years ago, I was at first somewhat ambivalent: brilliant landscape architects, spectacular gardens, but why separate the women from the men? After all, one cannot tell by looking at a landscape whether it was designed by a woman or a man.

The answer did not come to me all at once but evolved over time as I worked on the book. I decided to divide my emphasis more or less equally between the landscapes on Long Island and the designers, who turned out to have much more in common than their gender. So this book became, in part, a series of capsule biographies, each followed by a discussion of the Long Island landscapes, but giving the women equal weight with their work. Initially, I took this approach because only a few had been the subject of book-length studies. Gradually, a larger picture began to emerge. When the family backgrounds, education, and careers of the women were compared—six in detail and twelve more briefly—a fascinating story unfolded about the almost meteor-like entrance of women into a new profession. Even men had been practicing for only about forty years, since the advent of Frederick Law Olmsted, his partner Calvert Vaux, and their joint creation Central Park in New York City, begun in 1857.[1] The phenomenon of successful women landscape architects as it played out on Long Island has ramifications well beyond this slender finger of land off the East Coast. In the development of landscape architecture in the first half of the twentieth century, Long Island was a microcosm of the country.[2]

I have included all of the women known to me who designed landscapes on Long Island, not just for the sake of comprehensiveness but also because of the exceptionally high quality of their work.[3] Most of the landscapes discussed date from the first four decades of the twentieth century; some are later, since many of the women remained active into old age and also managed to ride out both the Depression and World War II.

In general, work on this book became more difficult the further I progressed. The first four women—Beatrix Jones Farrand, Martha Brookes Hutcheson, Marian Cruger Coffin, and Ellen Biddle Shipman—had been studied closely, although not necessarily with special reference to their work on Long Island. Books had been published on Farrand, Coffin, and Shipman, and Hutcheson's own book, *The Spirit of the Garden*, had recently been reissued with a biographical and critical introduction. There were entries in biographical volumes on both Ruth Bramley Dean and Annette Hoyt Flanders, but more extensive work had been frustrated by the lack of Dean archives and the apparent lack of Flanders archives.[4] Excitingly, two caches of Flanders materials turned up in the course of preparing this book. Both are now in the Sophia Smith Collection at Smith College in Northampton, Massachusetts. Few of the twelve women in chapters 8 and 9 had been studied at all, and most died after the periodical *Landscape Architecture* had abandoned its practice of publishing "Memorial Minutes" or other obituary notices of members of the American Society of Landscape Architects.

This dearth of biographical information led me to search through the vital records of various states, the censuses of 1880, 1900, 1910, and 1920 in the National Archives, microfilmed newspapers or newspaper clipping files, city directories, and similar repositories. (The 1890 census for all but a few states burned.) At this point, I had to do genealogical research to establish the most basic facts, moving, unfortunately, at the glacial pace characteristic of such work. In the case of Isabella Pendleton, a summer resident of Martha's Vineyard in Massachusetts, I hit paydirt in the form of the library of the *Vineyard Gazette*, a distinguished local daily that published numerous articles on the activities of Pendleton and her husband, Ezra Bowen.

Why is this kind of information important at all? If I had studied only one woman, especially a relatively well-known one, such basic digging would have been less necessary. But this technique was fruitful: in the course of comparing the careers of eighteen women, a number of interesting patterns became apparent, which are discussed more thoroughly in chapter 1 but can be mentioned briefly here. First of all, they came from upper-middle-class families (hardly a surprise). Beyond this, the two most important patterns were that nearly all of the women had a family member who shared their landscape interests and encouraged them, and nearly all also had a male mentor.

Education in landscape architecture is an important theme of this book. Transcripts were sought, and generally located, from all of the educational institutions still in existence today where these women studied. These records led to several surprising discoveries, including the fact that programs at some institutions such as Massachusetts Institute of Technology and the University of Illinois at Urbana-Champaign had diametrically different views on what a prospective landscape architect needed to learn. The information garnered from registrars' offices and college catalogs is discussed in more detail in chapter 1 as well as in context in the chapters treating the individual women.

Occasionally, in the course of working on this book, I stumbled into areas where I don't usually venture. For example, Marjorie Sewell Cautley suffered from a debilitating and ultimately career-ending mental illness. In order to understand much of the correspondence in the Cautley collection at Cornell University and to gain insight into this greatly gifted but tragic woman, I attempted to educate myself in the history of mental illness and its treatment in America. Fortunately, some excellent publications are available, and discussions with friends in related professions proved fruitful.

Pictorial sources are abundant for much of the work of these women, including photographs from the Mattie Edwards Hewitt Collection at the Long Island Studies Institute, Hofstra University; the Samuel Gottscho photographs at the Drawing Collection, Avery Architectural and Fine Arts Library, Columbia University; and the American Memory Collection (a digital catalog only); as well as plans for projects by Beatrix Jones Farrand and Mary Rutherfurd Jay in the Archives of the College of Environmental Design, University of California, Berkeley, and plans or specifications for projects by Ellen Shipman, Nellie B. Allen, and Helen Elise Bullard at the Carl Kroch Library, Cornell University. For the Long Island projects of some of the women, however, negatives or original photographic prints were sparse and plans practically nonexistent. Most of the photographs of work by Ruth Dean and some of those of Annette Hoyt Flanders, as well as many of Isabella Pendleton, come from the yearbooks of the Architectural League of New York and the American Society of Landscape Architects, New York Chapter. While valuable sources, these yearbooks apparently limited contributors to one photograph per project, making detailed analysis of these landscapes very difficult, since it is impossible, in the absence of a plan, to tell whether a single photograph shows all of a project or only a part.

Finally, in accordance with my decision to emphasize the women as well as the work, I am including portraits of them as well as quotations from their writings and interviews. I want readers, in addition to enjoying plans and photographs of their distinguished landscapes on Long Island, to be able to see their faces and hear their voices.

IN THE COURSE of this project, I have incurred numerous debts: first of all to Robert B. MacKay, director of the Society for the Preservation of Long Island Antiquities, whose idea it was and who has been unfailingly supportive since. I am also grateful to the able staff at SPLIA, who have been patient and friendly through all of my frequent requests, especially Charla Bolton, formerly of SPLIA, who frequently undertook fieldwork and photographic research.

I am also indebted to numerous scholars in the field of the history of American landscape architecture, some of whom are old friends while others are new and valued colleagues. These include: Diane Kostial McGuire, Eleanor M. McPeck, and Jane Brown (Beatrix Jones Farrand); Virginia Lopez Begg, Rebecca Warren Davidson, and Lauren Meier (Martha Brookes Hutcheson); Kimberly S. Alexander (Guy Lowell); Nancy Fleming (Marian Cruger Coffin); Judith B. Tankard (Ellen Biddle Shipman, Rose Standish Nichols, and Nellie B. Allen); Eve F. W. Linn (Ruth Bramley Dean); Patricia L. Filzen and R. Terry Schnadelbach (Annette Hoyt Flanders); Patricia M. O'Donnell and Eleanor M. McPeck (Mary Rutherfurd Jay); Elizabeth Igleheart (Louise Payson); Nell Walker and R. Terry Schnadelbach (Marjorie Sewell Cautley); Susan E. Schnare (Isabella Pendleton); J. Winthrop Aldrich (Mary Deputy Lamson Cattell); and Thaisa Way (Helen Elise Bullard).

Perhaps my greatest debt in this regard is to Joseph W. Tyree, who generously shared with me the products of his many years of research on gardens in the Hamptons.

More general advice has also been gratefully received from Judith B. Tankard, as well as from Phyllis Andersen, Leslie Rose Close, John Furlong, Mac Griswold, Robin Karson, Daniel W. Krall, Thaisa Way and Eleanor Weller. Charles A. Birnbaum, formerly of the National Park Service, and Diane Kostial McGuire also made helpful comments. Their input has been invaluable.

In addition, Fred Hicks of Hicks Nurseries in Westbury was kind enough to let me study his nursery archives. I am grateful to Richard Weir for many fruitful horticultural conversations and to Huyler Held for his encyclopedic knowledge of Long Island people and places.

My debt to various institutions, repositories, and libraries is also great. The staffs of my local standbys, the Frances Loeb Library of the Harvard Graduate School of Design, the Library of the Arnold Arboretum of Harvard University, and the Fine Arts and Microtext Departments of the Boston Public Library have been unfailingly helpful.

I owe sincere thanks to Catha Grace Rambusch and Chris Panos, formerly of the Catalog of American Landscape Records at Wave Hill, the Bronx, New York, and to Mildred De Riggi, formerly of the Long Island Studies Institute, Hofstra University, Hempstead, New York.

Eugene Neely of the Adelphi University Archives has been most helpful in unearthing the involvements of Helen Swift Jones at this campus.

I am also grateful to the staffs of other institutions, including Janet Parks and Louis Di Gennaro of the Drawings Collection, Avery Architectural and Fine Arts Library, Columbia University; Joyce Connolly of the Archives of American Gardens, Smithsonian Institution, Washington, DC; the staff of the Prints and Photograph Collection, Library of Congress, Washington, DC; and Waverly Lowell and Carrie McDade of the Archives, College of Environmental Design, University of California, Berkeley. Renée Nisivoccia, formerly of the Martha Brookes Hutcheson Collection, Morris County Park Commission, Morristown, New Jersey; the curators of the Geneva Historical Society, Geneva, New York; the Marian Coffin Collection, Henry Francis du Pont Winterthur Museum, Wilmington, Delaware; and the Rare Book and Manuscript Collections of the Carl A. Kroch Library, Cornell University, Ithaca, New York, have been generous and responsive, as have the staffs of the Smith College Archives and the Sophia Smith Collection at Smith College, Northampton, Massachusetts.

I am most grateful as well to Lou Jones, photographer, of Boston who did all of the copy work from periodicals owned by the Loeb Library, and to the staff at Boston Photo Imaging, who did the copy work from material at the Boston Public Library, Fine Arts Department, and from various other sources.

CHAPTER 1

A New Profession for Women

THE TITLE OF THIS BOOK is no exaggeration. Records at the Society for the Preservation of Long Island Antiquities indicate that half of all the gardens laid out on Long Island during the Country Place era (ca. 1890–1940) were designed by women landscape architects. The fine, though admittedly few, public landscapes designed by women on Long Island during this same period also form a significant group, because, during these years, women were rarely offered even small-scale public work.

Although all the landscapes discussed in this book are on Long Island, the designers were among the most prominent female landscape architects in Boston, Connecticut, New Jersey, and New York City. Many had national practices, with projects spread widely across the country; others concentrated on the Northeast. Eighteen notable women are included here: Beatrix Jones Farrand, Martha Brookes Brown Hutcheson, Marian Cruger Coffin, Ellen Biddle Shipman, Ruth Bramley Dean, Annette Hoyt Flanders, Mary Rutherfurd Jay, Rose Standish Nichols, Louise Payson, Marjorie Sewell Cautley, Isabella Pendleton, Eleanor Roche, Mary Deputy Lamson, Nellie B. Allen, Helen Elise Bullard, Helen Swift Jones, Janet Darling Webel, and Alice Recknagel Ireys.

Because they designed a large number of projects on Long Island, the first six women have been given chapters of their own, while the other twelve are discussed together in chapters 8 and 9. The chapters on individual landscape architects are arranged chronologically, according to the date when each began practicing, whether independently or in someone else's office.

When the lives and careers of the women discussed in this book are compared, interesting patterns emerge. A surprising number were first-born or only children, indicating, possibly, parental investment that might otherwise have been channeled toward a son. Virtually all had a relative—a parent, grandparent, aunt, or uncle—who shared their interest in gardens and plants and encouraged them in their choice of career.

These women were born into privilege but not into great wealth. Their fathers were doctors, lawyers, businessmen, clergymen, and military officers. For at least four—Farrand, Coffin, Shipman, and Dean—professional income was a necessary supplement to reduced private means. For Farrand and Coffin, this was the result of the separations and divorces of their parents, which left the two young women either partly or wholly responsible for supporting not only themselves but also their mothers. In Shipman's case, her own divorce forced her to support herself and her children. Dean's family was apparently intact but seemed to have limited resources. These women might have become nurses, teachers, or secretaries without causing controversy, but the arts were where their interests lay.

Many of these eighteen women were unusually long lived. A notable exception was Ruth Dean, whose sudden death was untimely. Annette Hoyt Flanders died of cancer in early middle age. Mammograms, pap smears, and other screening procedures did not exist then.

The first three designers, Farrand, Hutcheson, and Coffin, are really in a class by themselves, beginning their practices, respectively, in 1896, 1903, and 1905. In 1908, when they were the only female landscape designers in the country who had anything other than small local practices, Mary Bronson Hartt, a reporter from *The Outlook,* wrote them requesting advice for young women aspiring to the profession.[1] In 1932, it was again these three pioneers whom Clarence Fowler approached for stories of their beginnings.[2] Fowler, a landscape architect himself, published their reminiscences in the Alumnae Bulletin of the Cambridge School of Domestic and Landscape Architecture for Women, an institution that began informally in 1915 but was put on a somewhat more formal footing the following year. The Cambridge School provided professional training for women in both architecture and landscape architecture. Farrand, Hutcheson, and Coffin, and their immediate successors Shipman and Dean, broke into the male-dominated world of landscape architecture around the turn of the century. Each of them showed extraordinary resourcefulness, and each, whether by choice or because of life circumstances, took a different path of entry into the profession. As Farrand recalled to Fowler: "It seems almost funny to look back on the haphazard way in which we forerunners of the army of women landscape architects got our education."[3]

Farrand, then Beatrix Jones, began her studies at the renowned Arnold Arboretum in Jamaica Plain, Massachusetts. Hutcheson and Coffin both studied in the landscape architecture option, established in 1900 as part of the Department of Architecture at Massachusetts Institute of Technology. Neither received a degree and only Coffin took a substantial number of courses. Nichols took a few single courses in architecture at MIT with Professor Desiré Despradelle just before the landscape option was introduced. Jay seems to have been tutored by MIT professors. Her private studies, like those of Beatrix Jones at Columbia, left no record in MIT's registrar's office. Harvard's program in landscape architecture, also established in 1900, did not admit women until 1942. Hutcheson and Coffin also took field courses at the Arboretum and, like Farrand, traveled widely in Europe.[4] In contrast, Shipman's proving ground in landscape design was her own garden in Cornish, New Hampshire.[5]

A generation earlier, nearly all professions were closed to women, yet the mothers of many of the women landscape architects, including those of Farrand and Coffin, strongly supported their daughters' career choices. Hutcheson's mother, herself a gardener, was initially aghast at her daughter's decision, but Hutcheson was strongly self-motivated and persevered.[6] She reported to Fowler that, after conferring with professors at MIT "and with Mrs. Farrand, who was then practicing alone in the field, I was fired with the desire to enter the Institute in spite of the fact that, at the time, it was considered almost social suicide and distinctly matrimonial suicide for a woman to enter any profession."[7]

According to her sister, Ruth Dean first studied music, and then turned to landscape architecture: "At a time when even to become a 'musician' caused lifted brows, to aspire to the profession of landscape architecture created panic in well-ordered breasts." The well-ordered breast apparently belonged to Dean's father, because, as her sister continued, "A family rupture was only avoided by maternal tact and encouragement when this one child firmly refused to follow the beaten track, and with stubborn determination clung to her choice of landscape architecture as a profession. . . . Despite family opposition, Ruth Dean entered the University of Chicago in 1908 to begin the formal preparation for her career."[8]

With the exceptions of the programs at the Lowthorpe School of Landscape Architecture, Gardening and Horticulture for Women in Groton, Massachusetts, founded in 1900, and the Cambridge School, generally only land-grant public institutions and universities such as MIT, Cornell, and the University of Illinois, opened their doors to women in the early years of the twentieth century. Annette Hoyt Flanders received the most complete formal education of any of this group. She graduated from Smith College in 1910, then earned a degree in landscape gardening from the University of Illinois and pursued further professional studies at Marquette University and the Sorbonne.[9]

In accordance with the conventions of the time, when women with careers rarely married, a number of the eighteen women remained single. Those who married, with the exception of Shipman and Annette Hoyt Flanders, tended to marry considerably later than was customary in the era. Only seven of the eighteen had children. Shipman and Flanders were both divorced, or at least separated, before their careers were really underway. After the birth of her daughter in 1912, Martha Brookes Hutcheson closed her office but continued to consult and to lecture widely on landscape-related subjects. By contrast, Ruth Dean blithely took care of her office, husband, and daughter, seemingly without effort.[10] Marjorie Sewell Cautley met her husband while both were studying at Cornell. Their daughter was born not long after, but Cautley does not appear to have interrupted her career until the onset of her mental illness in 1937.[11]

In spite of the generally hostile environment in which these women entered their profession, a surprising number had male mentors—either landscape architects or men in related professions.[12] Beatrix Jones's mentor was Professor Charles Sprague Sargent, director of the Arnold Arboretum, where, in the early 1890s, she went, at Sargent's invitation, to study horticulture. One day Sargent suggested to his startled protegée that she continue her studies with a view to becoming a landscape architect. After taking some time to think over Sargent's "wild scheme," she continued with private studies in architecture and civil engineering and a European study trip.[13]

Hutcheson and Coffin both started their studies at MIT as "special" students, meaning that they took many of the courses but, unless they were later readmitted as students in full standing (which these two were not), they could not receive a degree. Hutcheson took every lecture in horticulture given by Professor Benjamin M. Watson at the Bussey Institute, then the School of Agriculture at Harvard. She was also coached by the "celebrated Professor Jones" of the University of Vermont in the trees and shrubs of that state.

Coffin, while initially terrified by the course work at "Tech," as it was then called, nevertheless persevered largely because of the encouragement and support of architect Guy Lowell, who led the MIT program, and that of Professor Sargent.[14]

MIT was founded in 1861 and opened in 1865 at the conclusion of the Civil War. An architecture school, modeled on the École des Beaux-Arts in Paris, was initiated there in 1868 by William Robert Ware, who later began a similar program at Columbia University. MIT, like Cornell and the University of Massachusetts in Amherst, was a land-grant institution; most of these admitted women to their programs relatively early.[15]

MIT began admitting women students to some of its programs in 1883, and, two years later, the architecture department followed suit. The first woman architecture graduate was Sophia Hayden (1890), who in 1893 won the design competition for the Woman's Building at the World's Columbian Exposition in Chicago. Another early MIT graduate was Marion L. Mahony (1894), who became one of Frank Lloyd Wright's principal designers in his Oak Park, Illinois, studio. The landscape architecture option at MIT was gradually phased out, apparently on the grounds that two landscape programs were not necessary in the Boston area. The full undergraduate program was offered only from 1900 through 1904, although a graduate curriculum continued until 1909. Lowell offered instruction until 1912—probably single courses—turning over his salary to the architecture department for fellowships.[16]

For the first three years, students in landscape architecture and architecture followed the same curriculum. As many as ten courses were offered per semester; the average course load of special students, such as Hutcheson and Coffin, seemed to be four or five courses per term, although the degree candidates, whether men or women, seem to have taken many more than that. Hutcheson and Coffin both seem to have been exempted from the language requirement (French or German), probably because they had already been adequately tutored in these subjects. The first year emphasized mathematics and science, as well as freehand and mechanical drawing, military science (which none of the women took), English, history, highway engineering, business law, and so forth. In the fourth year, landscape students took horticulture, and, for the first time, landscape architecture and landscape design, as well as preparing a thesis.[17] (It is not clear how MIT differentiated between landscape architecture and landscape design courses.) The Beaux-Arts–influenced curriculum dominated American architectural schools until it was replaced by more modernist and functionalist approaches in the late 1930s and early 1940s.[18]

Cautley and Bullard both studied at Cornell, graduating in 1917 and 1919, respectively. Like MIT, Cornell University was a private educational institution that obtained some of its financial backing from funds made available under the Morrill Act of 1862. The Act provided that each state would receive 30,000 acres of federal land for each congressional representative from that state, to be sold to provide an endowment for "at least one college where the leading object shall be . . . to teach such branches of learning as are related to agriculture and the mechanical arts . . ."[19] The land was bought primarily by speculators, and, because of the large supply, most states received very little money for their land. Cornell, however, had other sources of income and was able to hold onto its land until it could be sold for $5.50 per acre, eleven times more than Kentucky, which had to sell its land during the depressed period following the Civil War. The purpose of the Act was to make higher education available to students who could not afford elite private colleges and universities, which, at the time, still emphasized the classics and the liberal arts. These students also needed to be able to make a living in a practical field.[20]

MIT was, of course, Massachusetts' school of "mechanical arts," while the University of Massachusetts in Amherst, founded in 1863, was its agricultural school.[21] Landscape programs often found a home within these agricultural schools.[22]

Cornell University was begun in 1865 by Ezra Cornell, founder of the Western Union Telegraph Company, and Andrew Dickson White, a scholar and politician. As its motto, the university adopted these words by Cornell: "I would found an institution where any person can find instruction in any study." His words proved prophetic, since Cornell now comprises fourteen colleges and schools. Cornell also meant what he said by "any person": the first woman was enrolled in the university in 1872.[23]

Established in 1904, the landscape architecture program at Cornell went, for its first few years, by the delightful sobriquet "Out-Door Art." After making brief detours through the titles "Rural Art," "Landscape Art," and "Landscape Design," it settled permanently in 1922 on "Landscape Architecture." Housed for some time in the School of Agriculture, it then went into the School of Art, Architecture, and Planning. This shift had an impact on students' finances, since the Agricultural School was free, while the School of Art, Architecture and Planning was not.[24] Thus, Cornell was in the unique position of being a private university in which there were some programs that were public. (MIT is, and always has been, private.)

The first woman to study landscape architecture at Cornell appears to have been Elizabeth Leonard Strang, who graduated in 1910 but who designed no landscapes on Long Island. Because Cornell was a land-grant institution and because of the eventual renown of Strang, Cautley, and Bullard's work, Cornell's landscape program acquired the reputation of being welcoming to women. But this was far from the case.[25]

Instead, women applicants to Cornell, or their advocates, met responses that ranged from unenthusiastic to downright withering. At the gentler end of the spectrum, Professor E. Gorton Davis in 1914 responded to the father of an applicant: "This is a co-educational university and the girls have an equal chance with the boys . . . but it is an experiment . . . ."[26] In a more severe tone, Bryant Fleming, a distinguished landscape architect who then headed the landscape program at Cornell, wrote to an administrator at Lake Erie College in Painesville, Ohio, "I would not urge your girls to follow landscape as a profession. . . . they are in many ways physically unfit to do the work. We cannot send them through the rough work in the College of Civil Engineering . . . ."[27]

As will be seen in chapter 10, Bullard and her surveying class, in 1918, braved cold winter weather in inadequate clothing to do just that. Fleming also told the Lake Erie College administrator that women "do not grasp the larger conceptions of the work and in the classes retard the progress of the men."[28] Marian Coffin instead found at MIT a congenial atmosphere of mutual support between the men and women. The teachers in the Cambridge School found that their women students had no problem grasping the larger conceptions of the work. At Cornell, Bullard, who came from the small town of Schuylerville, New York, ran into some academic trouble in design courses; she explained that she was hampered because she had never seen any examples of executed landscape architecture.[29] This is the equivalent of expecting someone to compose music who has never heard music.

By contrast, a very positive recommendation came from Professor Ralph Curtis supporting the application of Marjorie Sewell (later Cautley) for a summer job with Massachusetts landscape architect Warren Manning. In 1917, he wrote Manning that not only was Sewell well fitted in landscape planting but very determined to succeed in the profession.[30]

Cautley's transcript could not be located in the Cornell Registrar's Office, but Bullard's reveals that, in contrast to MIT's curriculum, the Cornell landscape program required almost no math. (Bullard, however, had been very well prepared in math at the Schuylerville High School.) Each year, she took at least one course in "Landscape Art," probably landscape architecture or landscape design; however, Cornell distinguished between these two subjects. Over the course of her career at Cornell, she also took three courses in architecture. She took several science courses, as well as courses in such subjects as "The Farm" and "Rural Engineering," which were unknown at MIT.[31] There were some parallels, however, with Flanders' graduate courses at the University of Illinois, described in chapter 7.

In 1919, Bullard received a B.S. degree in the School of Agriculture, as Cautley undoubtedly had two years earlier.

A few years after Cautley and Bullard graduated, students, both male and female, in Cornell's landscape program acquired a supportive friend in the person of Daisy Farrand, the wife of President Livingston Farrand and sister-in-law of Beatrix and Max Farrand. Livingston Farrand assumed the presidency of Cornell in 1921. Mrs. Farrand, herself a talented gardener and horticulturist and the apparent possessor of a dynamic personality, frequently dropped into the architecture and landscape architecture studios and invited classes that had problems due that night to the president's house for a late supper of oyster stew. On these occasions, as many as forty students might attend.[32] At this time, there were about sixteen women in the landscape program out of a total of 120 students.[33] For a period, Daisy Farrand was among their ranks, actively pursuing the discipline of landscape design as a special student in the School of Architecture.[34]

Shipman did not study landscape architecture at any school, college, or university, but her mentor was the noted artist, architect, and landscape designer Charles Platt, with whom she later collaborated on a number of projects.[35] Platt probably had some knowledge of Shipman's financial situation, as Sargent, no doubt, had of Farrand's.

During the years that the three "pioneers" began practicing, the press seemed fascinated by them. In 1908, Mary Bronson Hartt prefaced her *Outlook* article on "Women and the Art of Landscape Gardening" with this statement:

> Collectors of novel occupations for women—how many they are to be sure, and how conscientiously they scour the earth for things a woman might supposedly be able to do!—are lightly holding out the profession of landscape gardening as a congenial, soothing, out-of-doors pursuit to which a woman of taste . . . cannot do better than turn her hand. . . . Landscape architects tell me that they are continually besieged with letters from fair aspirants seeking advice how best to arm themselves for careers in the garden.[36]

In the first few years of her practice, Beatrix Jones was the subject of at least ten newspaper articles, most of them in New York City or Bar Harbor, Maine, newspapers. In 1897, after she had been practicing for only a year, the *New York Sun* published a long article, which included several lengthy quotes from an interview with Jones.[37] In Bar Harbor, where Jones and her mother had a summer home and where many of her early commissions were located, the press literally followed her around. In 1904, the *Bar Harbor Record* published an article about her first design project "Chiltern," on which she had then been working for eight years:

> Miss Jones was for many years one of the leaders of Bar Harbor society and the germans and cotillions were stale without her. A few years ago she decided that society in its upper circles was a frothy farce and being a lover of nature and a natural artist decided to turn her attention to landscape gardening. Her mother . . . encouraged her. . . . This society girl, clad often in a suit resembling a fisherman's on a rainy day, with rubber boots and minus a society umbrella, moved about in the soggy soil directing the movements of over a hundred men.[38]

Why so many articles on a twenty-five-year-old novice landscape designer? As Hartt noted, at this period, there was a great interest in women who were doing unusual things. Right beside the interview with Jones, the *New York Sun* published an article on a woman who ran a theatrical agency, managing, among other actors, her husband. This was entitled: "Mrs. Mansfield's Office: She's President and a Manager, Yet Lives in Peace." On the previous page of the *Sun* was a story about a sixteen-year-old San Francisco girl who helped run her father's butcher shop, entitled: "Here is the Butcher Girl. Lillie Kanitz, a Successful Assistant to Her Father in His Shop."[39] Some larger social phenomenon was clearly at work aiding the emergence of women in the professions and business.

Around the turn of the twentieth century, there was indeed such a phenomenon, known as the "New Woman," a concept that flourished between about 1890 and 1920 and was widely disseminated in the popular press. A typical New Woman might study such "male" subjects as science or classics, adopt occupations or professions traditionally held by men, take up athletic activities such as bicycling, golf, or hunting, generally considered the domain of men, and dress in less restrictive clothing than women of the period customarily wore.[40] Although none of the women in this book described herself as a New Woman, at least one of the articles about Beatrix Jones did.[41] All of these women, of course, took up a new profession; most of them were athletic as well. As Jones cautioned "fair aspirants," the presumed readers of Hartt's 1908 article: "robust health is an essential to a woman who wishes to build up more than a small practice in landscape gardening. The physical fatigue in this perpetual travelling is very great. . . ."[42]

In spite of such widespread public interest, it was still all but impossible for a woman to apprentice or find employment in the offices of male landscape architects. Marian Coffin found this out when, after completing a four-year course of study at MIT in three years, she expected that the world would welcome her. Instead, she was greeted at offices by the repeated query, "My dear young lady, what will you do about supervising the work on the ground?," coming from men who were obviously unaware that Beatrix Jones had been doing just that for nine years. Coffin's response was that "the only thing seemed to be for me to hang out my own shingle and see what I would do about it."[43] Only three years into her profession, Coffin wrote that not only was there a prejudice in many offices against hiring women but also that starting alone was a handicap in other ways: "A woman has to solve many problems and learn the ropes entirely by herself, while a man has the advantage of long office training and experience."[44]

By the time Dean and Flanders entered the field, the situation had improved somewhat. After finishing her studies at the University of Chicago, Dean worked for approximately two years in the office of Chicago landscape architect Jens Jensen, initially as his unpaid apprentice. She then moved to New York where she worked in the offices of several architects, including Aymar Embury II, whom she later married.[45] During the years after Dean's employment with Embury and before their marriage in 1923, Embury was Dean's frequent collaborator and mentor, steering clients her way and asking her to write a book. After completing her education and serving with the American Red Cross in France in 1918 and 1919, Flanders also went to New York City. There she was associated with Vitale, Brinckerhoff & Geiffert, where she was in charge of design and supervision of planting. She opened her own office in 1922.[46]

Louise Payson, Nellie B. Allen, and many others in the "second generation" took a different route. By the time they began their careers, there were several well-established women landscape architects, as well as the educational opportunities offered by the Lowthorpe School and, later, the Cambridge School. Farrand, Shipman, and others maintained women-only offices, and many of their employees eventually established firms of their own. By this means, the little band of pioneers at the beginning of the century had, by 1932, grown exponentially into what Farrand called an "army."[47]

Many of the "second-generation," discussed in chapters 8 and 9, studied at either the Lowthorpe School or the Cambridge School. Payson, Pendleton, Roche, and Allen graduated from the Lowthorpe School; Lamson, Jones, and Webel graduated from the Cambridge School. Neither school could offer degrees to those who fulfilled its requirements, although students could earn certificates instead.

In 1900, the Lowthorpe School for Landscape Architecture, Gardening and Horticulture for Women opened its doors in Groton, Massachusetts, under the leadership of Mrs. Edward Gilchrist Low, an alumna of the Swanley College in England. Although always hampered by shaky finances, low enrollment, and its distance from Boston, the Lowthorpe School had a superb reputation in horticulture and placed its graduates in many fine women-owned offices during its approximately four decades of existence.[48] One of the early instructors was Elizabeth Leonard Strang, who, as we have seen, was the first woman graduate of Cornell's "Outdoor Art" curriculum. When Strang arrived at Lowthorpe, she found that there was just a course (probably meaning a curriculum, not a single course, as we generally use the term today). Strang established a broader "course" on the basis of her studies at Cornell, which included history, theory, landscape design, engineering, and planting design.[49] At a later date, however, Lowthorpe was denied membership in a group of landscape architectural educational institutions.[50]

In 1910, Jane Browne Haines, a graduate of Bryn Mawr, founded the Pennsylvania School of Horticulture for Women in Ambler, Pennsylvania. The school offered some courses in landscape design, but its focus was on horticulture and practical gardening.[51] Unlike the Lowthorpe and Cambridge Schools, the Pennsylvania School of Horticulture survived the World War II period, eventually becoming Ambler Junior College. In 1958, it began an association with Temple University, and its programs were made available to men. Three years later, it formally became the Ambler Campus of Temple University.[52] It is difficult, however, to identify successful women landscape architects who graduated from the Pennsylvania School in its early days. Certainly, no such women have emerged who designed landscapes on Long Island.

The casual beginnings of the Cambridge School have already been mentioned, and its history is more thoroughly explored in chapter 10.

Interestingly, many of the eighteen women landscape architects discussed here were talented in arts other than their own. According to her later client and friend Mildred Bliss, Farrand "was profoundly sensitive to music" and had a fine voice. For a time, she considered a career as a classical singer.[53] Dean was also a musician and during World War I entertained troops by playing the piano.[54] Mary Deputy Lamson was a pianist as well.[55] While at Smith College, Annette Hoyt Flanders studied piano and voice and excelled in dramatics.[56]

Martha Brookes Hutcheson spent approximately two years at the New York School of Applied Design for Women, learning mechanical drawing, "tooling designs for book covers, learning the rudiments of historic ornament and applying it to patterns for wall papers, chintzes, or anything which came into my head."[57] As a young woman, Marian Coffin somewhat naively dreamt of becoming a great artist but found that she did not have talents for the only arts then considered appropriate for women: music, writing, painting, or sculpture.[58] After finding her métier in landscape design, she later discovered that she also had ability as a painter of still life and botanical subjects in oil and pastel. Some of her paintings were exhibited in New York City in 1942.[59]

Ellen Shipman's facility for design emerged early. In her teens, she was given to drawing house and garden plans in her notebooks at Miss Sarah Randolph's school in Baltimore, Maryland. As a history prize, the perceptive Miss Randolph gave her an architectural dictionary. Charles Platt recognized her drawing skills soon after they met in Cornish.[60]

Until relatively recently, there was an assumption that women were good only at designing private gardens, and commissions for parks or other large-scale public projects eluded them. Garden design was seen by some people as an outdoor extension of housekeeping and interior decoration, accepted spheres for women. John Nolen, the Cambridge-based landscape architect and town planner, pointed out to Mary Bronson Hartt that, in justice to women, they were not likely to get a chance to show what they might do with public projects. Hartt expanded on the subject:

> In other arts there is nothing to restrain a woman from making a deliberate display of her powers. If she wants to paint a Last Judgment, or model a Pieta, no one can stop her. But in landscape architecture success waits on invitation. A woman might map out the most ambitious plans for an imaginary park. But even supposing she could get any one to look at them, they would be valueless. For the essence of success in such designing is that the plans shall fit specific conditions.[61]

Beatrix Jones, who by 1908 had already designed some small squares and parks, confirmed this view: "So far as I can learn from the present trend of things, it seems likely that for some time to come women's work will be almost entirely limited to that of a domestic character."[62] Hutcheson thought that women might cooperate with men in planting schemes for public parks, but, if they had to work alone, private estates were better suited to them.[63]

Shipman stayed above the fray. In 1938, she told a *New York Times* reporter: "Before women took hold of the profession, landscape architects were doing what I call cemetery work. . . . Until women took up landscape gardening in this country [it] was at its lowest ebb . . . The renaissance of the art was due largely to the fact that women, instead of working over their boards, used plants as if they were painting pictures and as an artist would. Today women are at the top of the profession."[64] Harsh words for men—especially since Olmsted Brothers, Warren Manning, James L. Greenleaf, and other male landscape architects were then doing some of their best work, and it was not cemetery work.

Guy Lowell, who taught women at MIT, noticed that, "A woman will fuss with a garden in a way that no man will ever have the patience to do. If necessary, she will sit on a camp-stool and see every individual plant put into the ground. I have no hesitation in saying that where the relatively small garden is concerned, the average woman will do better than the average man."[65] As a parting shot, Lowell advised aspiring women landscape architects: "Don't go into it unless you simply can't keep out!"[66]

By the mid-1930s, women finally started to get some public work. As part of a plan to put seventy thousand unemployed people to work, Park Commissioner Robert Moses installed forty landscape architects in the loft of the Madison Square Garden building and assigned them projects for rehabilitating the city's parks. Many of these landscape architects were women, including Helen Swift Jones (see chapter 9). As an observer noted, "The pay scale set up for the landscape architects on this project was somewhat lower than that for bricklayers, but enthusiasm for their job seemed to more than compensate for the lack of financial gain."[67]

Ironically, by the time women were regularly considered for public commissions, most cities in the country were already well endowed with large parks, thanks to the legacies of Frederick Law Olmsted Sr., his successor firm Olmsted Brothers, and their contemporaries. However, the task of rehabilitating or restoring America's large urban parks has gone on for some time and will probably continue indefinitely, at least in good economic times. In recent years, opportunities, for men or for women, to design new urban parks have generally been limited to small public spaces, frequently on "found" land.[68]

In spite of their perceived exclusive talents for residential work, many of the women in this book eventually attracted institutional clients. Farrand had long-term consultancies at both Princeton and Yale Universities, as well as projects at the University of Chicago, Oberlin, and Vassar Colleges, Occidental College in Los Angeles, and the California Institute of Technology in Pasadena. In the early 1930s, Hutcheson prepared plans for Bennington College in Bennington, Vermont. Between 1918 and 1952, Coffin was the landscape architect for Delaware College (later the University of Delaware), working on plans for both the men's and women's campuses. In the 1930s, Shipman had a number of public and institutional clients: the Women's

Advisory Council for the New York Botanical Garden, New York City; the Alger Museum in Grosse Pointe Shores, Michigan; the Fine Arts Center in Colorado Springs, Colorado; and the Sarah P. Duke Gardens at Duke University, Durham, North Carolina.[69] Many of the "second-generation" women also had institutional clients.

A glance at the birth and death dates of these eighteen women landscape architects reveals that many of them had strikingly long life spans for their era. A number lived into their eighties, a few, including Nellie B. Allen and Helen Elise Bullard, into their nineties. It is difficult to know what to attribute their longevity to: heredity? a healthy life style? lots of fresh air? Given their comfortable socioeconomic status, the women would have had good nutrition and health care through their lives. But these advantages would not have protected them from the many infectious diseases, such as tuberculosis and polio, that were still prevalent and frequently could not be effectively treated. They would also not have been protected from degenerative diseases.[70]

However, it appears that women landscape architects were not the only women professionals who enjoyed exceptionally long life spans. A recent study demonstrates that many "entrepreneurial" women born during the late eigh-teenth and nineteenth centuries had similarly long lives.[71] In this study, "entrepreneurial" does not refer exclusively to women with business careers but includes those with a wide variety of professional careers as well.[72] With the exception of Bullard, who worked almost exclusively in the public sector, the eighteen women discussed here set up landscape design offices of their own and thus were necessarily business women as well as professional women and artists.

Perhaps the most important characteristic that these women shared was a passion for excellence. They seemed to realize that, in order to succeed at all, they had to sustain an exceptionally high level of quality. As professionals, there was no room for mediocrity, and even just being "good" would have meant a return to dilettantish expectations for women in the arts. In 1960, the author of Martha Brookes Hutcheson's biographical minute wrote of Hutcheson, as well as of her contemporaries Coffin and Farrand:

> Martha Brookes Hutcheson was an exemplar of a race that is now passing. . . . These women entered the profession out of deep conviction that this was the career they wanted. Nice young ladies did not undertake careers unless they had an overpowering drive to do so. The weak ones did not even try.[73]

ROSE ARBOUR IN GARDEN FOR
PERCY CHUBB ESQRE DOPORIS L.I.
BEATRIX JONES, LANDSCAPE GARDENER

C.1 *Beatrix Jones,*
Landscape Gardener. Rose
arbour in garden, Percy
Chubb Residence, Dosoris.
Watercolor, undated.
Berkeley

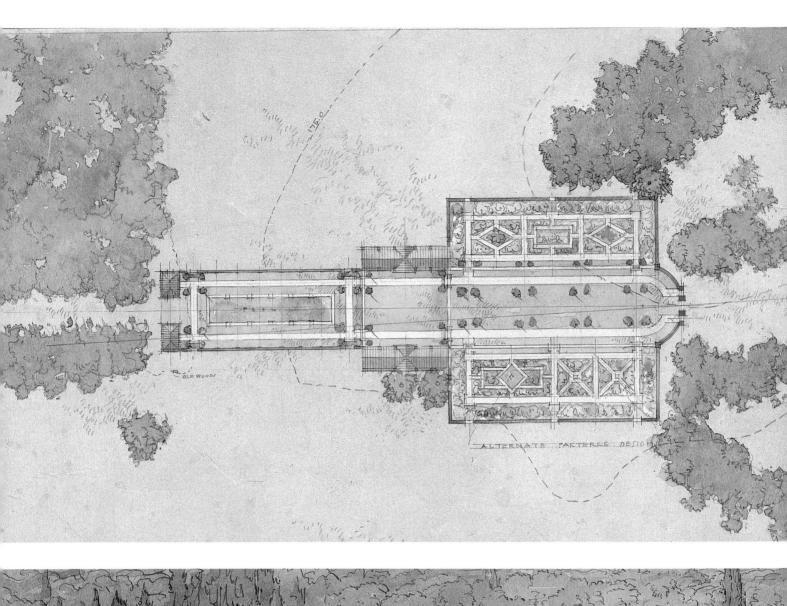

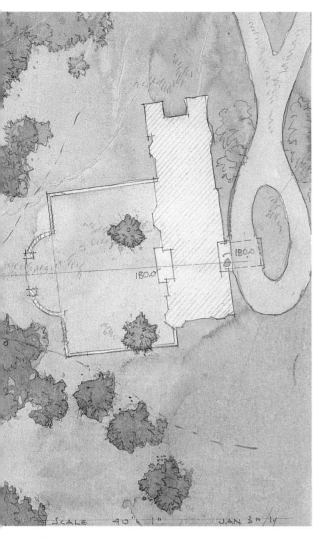

C.2 *Beatrix Farrand, Landscape Gardener. Plan of the Chinese garden, Applegreen, Mrs. Willard D. Straight Residence, Old Westbury. Pencil, ink, and watercolor on cardboard, January 1, 1914.* Berkeley

LEFT
C.3 *Beatrix Farrand, Landscape Gardener. Perspective of the Chinese garden, Applegreen, Mrs. Willard Straight Residence, Old Westbury. Pencil, ink and watercolor on cardboard, ca. 1914.* Berkeley

ABOVE
C.4 *Beatrix Farrand, Landscape Gardener. Alternative sketch for summer house, S. Vernon Mann Residence, Great Neck. Pencil and color on tracing paper, undated.* Berkeley

19

C.5 *Ruth Dean. Garden,*
G. Arthur Schieren
Residence, Great Neck.
Color perspective, ca. 1917,
rendered by Birch Burdette
Long. From *House and*
Garden, May 1932

C.6 *Annette Hoyt Flanders,*
landscape architect. J. Floyd
Yewell. Garden, Vincent Astor
Residence, Port Washington.
Pastel drawing, ca. 1932.
From *Country Life in America*,
August–September, 1932

C.7 *Annette Hoyt Flanders, landscape architect. Dogwood allée, Mrs. Charles McCann Residence, Oyster Bay. 1980s 35-mm color slide of a ca. 1930s tinted glass slide.* Annette Hoyt Flanders Papers, Sophia Smith Collection, Smith College, Northampton, Massachusetts (See also fig. 7.13)

C.8 *Annette Hoyt Flanders, landscape architect. Perennial-bordered pathway, Mrs. Charles McCann Residence, Oyster Bay. 1980s 35-mm slide of a ca. 1930s tinted glass slide.* Flanders Papers, Smith

C.9 *Annette Hoyt Flanders,*
landscape architect. Swim-
ming pool and bath houses,
Mrs. Charles McCann
Residence, Oyster Bay.
1980s 35-mm color slide
of a ca. 1930s tinted glass
slide. Flanders Papers, Smith

23

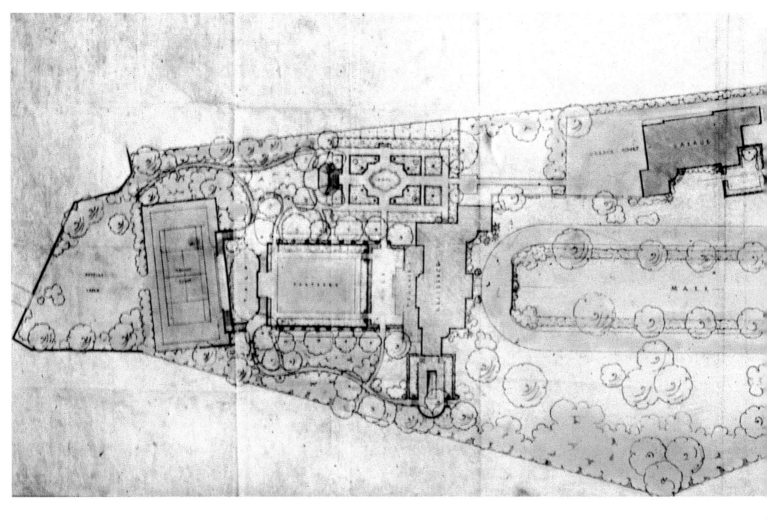

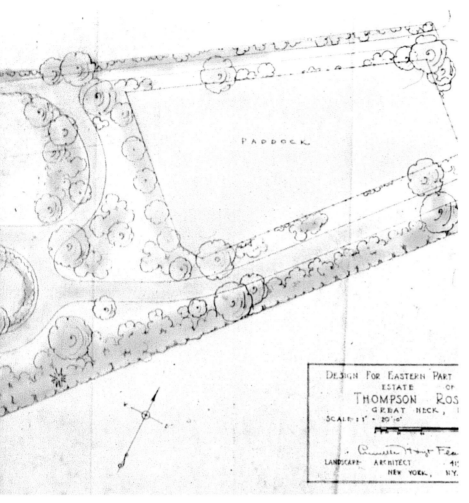

C.15 *Annette Hoyt*
Flanders, landscape archi-
tect. Detail of Kiser garden,
Southampton. 1980s 35-mm
color slide from a 1930s
tinted glass slide.
Flanders Papers, Smith

C.16 *Annette Hoyt Flanders, landscape architect. Rose and heliotrope garden, Valmay Cottage, the Mrs. Patrick A. Valentine Residence, Southampton. 1980s 35-mm color slide from a 1930s tinted glass slide.* Flanders Papers, Smith

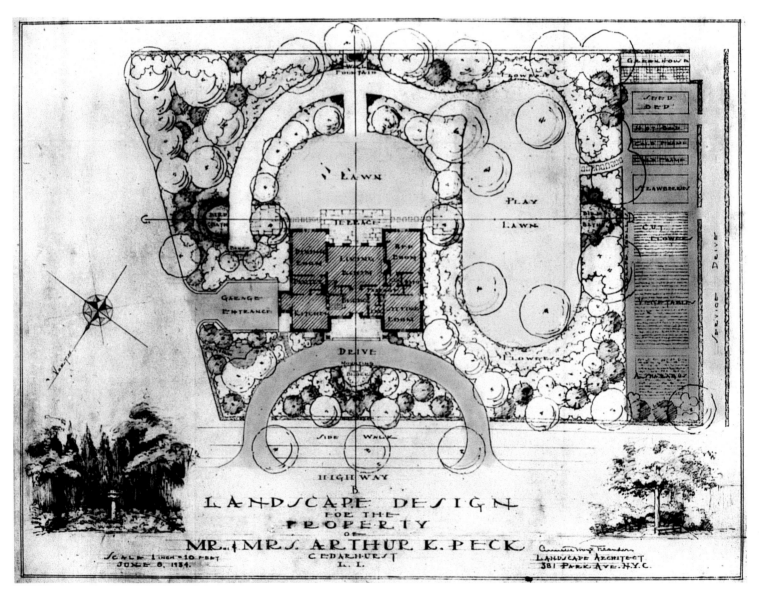

C.17 *Annette Hoyt*
Flanders. General Plan,
ca. 1934, Mrs. Arthur Peck
Residence, Cedarhurst.
1980s 35-mm color slide
from a 1930s tinted glass
slide. Flanders Papers, Smith

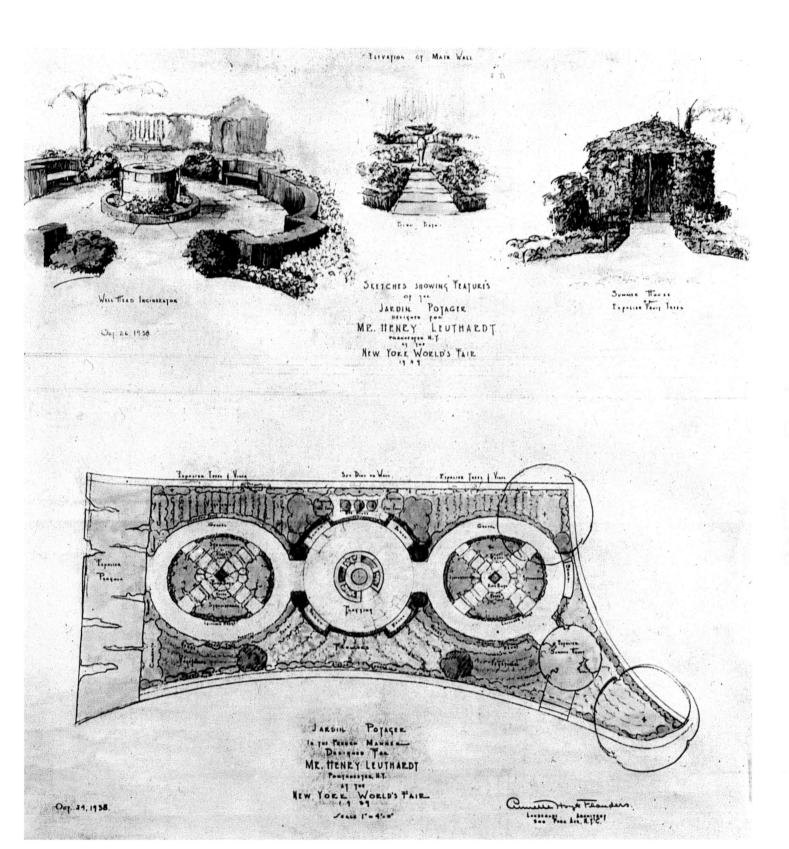

C.18 *Annette Hoyt Flanders. Sketches for a "Jardin Potager in the Period Manner" for Mr. Henry Leuthardt, 1938. 1980s 35-mm color slide from a 1938 tinted glass slide.* Flanders Papers, Smith

CHAPTER 2

Beatrix Jones Farrand

1872–1959

BEATRIX CADWALADER JONES (fig. 2.1) was born in New York City on June 19, 1872, the only child of Mary Cadwalader Rawle and Frederic Rhinelander Jones. She was also the niece of the novelist Edith Wharton, who was only ten years her senior. In 1913, already well established in her career, Beatrix married Max Farrand, chairman of the history department at Yale University.[1]

The Joneses were an established New York family, and the Philadelphia Rawles and Cadwaladers were similarly well connected. Like other "old" families, the Joneses suffered financially from the devaluation of currency and the depressed real estate values that followed the Civil War. After their marriage in 1870, Frederic and Mary Jones acquired a comfortable, although not lavish, town house at 21 East Eleventh Street, which Mrs. Jones filled with books, pictures, and antique family furnishings. In 1896, Beatrix set up her first office in an upper-floor room there, and her mother lived in the house until her death in 1935. The Jones's summer home was Reef Point, located on a promontory overlooking the ocean in Bar Harbor, Maine. As a child and young woman, Beatrix busied herself with rearranging the plantings there. The Joneses were divorced in 1896 but had probably lived apart since 1887. At some point after the separation, Mr. Jones went to live permanently in France, and father and daughter seem to have had no further contact.[2]

On her father's side, Beatrix came from a family of five generations of garden lovers. As a small child, she helped her grandmother Lucretia Jones in the garden at Pencraig,

her summer home in Newport, Rhode Island, where Beatrix learned the names of many old roses.[3] Beatrix shared a passion for plants and flowers with her aunt and, in 1901, designed portions of the grounds at The Mount, Wharton's summer residence in Lenox, Massachusetts.[4] After she moved to France, Wharton carried on a spirited, plant-centered correspondence with her niece about her triumphs and trials in her two French gardens.[5] Mary Cadwalader Jones, on the other hand, although always supportive of her daughter's career, was a thoroughly urban person. Her inability to identify even the simplest flowers sometimes amused friends and relatives.[6]

Aside from her mother and aunt, the person closest to the young Beatrix was her mother's first cousin John Lambert Cadwalader, a New York lawyer and a founder of the New York Public Library. Probably around the time that she was first considering a shift of focus from her early interest in music to landscape design, Cadwalader told Beatrix's mother, "Let her be a gardener, or, for that matter, anything she wants to be. What she wishes to do will be well done."[7]

Beatrix's entire primary and secondary education was provided by private tutors, as was the case with many similarly situated girls and young women.[8] From the time Beatrix was in her late teens, her mother gave literary and artistic Sunday luncheons, often attended by artists, including John La Farge, Augustus Saint-Gaudens, and John Singer Sargent and the popular novelist F. Marion Crawford.[9] For houseguests, Mrs. Jones set aside a two-room

"author's suite," where the expatriate novelist Henry James stayed during parts of his two extended trips to the United States in 1904–5 and 1910–11.[10]

In 1893, Beatrix met Mrs. Charles Sprague Sargent, who invited her and her mother to stay at Holm Lea, the Sargents' residence in Brookline, Massachusetts. Professor Sargent quickly recognized the young woman's intense interest in plants and suggested that she study horticulture and landscape gardening at the Arnold Arboretum under his direction.[11] After she had worked with him for some months, Sargent noticed that she had developed a strong sense of design but was moving away from her earlier single-minded absorption in plants. When she showed him a carefully prepared plan for a garden, he snapped, "Don't waste time on what you call design. You must hybridize and propagate."[12]

Sargent was sad to see his "beloved pupil" leave the Arboretum, but he gave her the names of people who could help her reach the professional goals she had chosen.[13] One of them was Professor William Robert Ware, who was then dean of the School of Architecture at Columbia University. Ware helped her identify the academic subjects she needed to prepare for what she later described as "this nebulous profession."[14] She was tutored by instructors in the School of Architecture and in mathematics and surveying.[15] Farrand never recorded exactly what she had studied, but it almost certainly included drafting. When she told a colleague many years later that she regretted never having learned to draw, she probably meant freehand drawing.[16] Then, as she wrote to Clarence Fowler in 1932: "After two or three years coaching and grinding, more or less manufacturing my own curriculum with Mr. Sargent's advice, I went abroad with my patient mother and together we visited, measured, photographed and noted a considerable number of the gardens in France, England, Italy and Germany."[17] Farrand's gardening notebook from this journey is among the documents that she gave to the University of California, Berkeley, in 1955.[18] Farrand's acknowledgment of her mother's active participation in these field studies is important. For one thing, two people are needed to measure a garden or building. Some of the photographs from this trip may have been taken by Mrs. Jones, who seems to have been a more adept photographer than her daughter.[19]

When she returned from Europe, Beatrix Jones had "private tutors supplied me from Columbia University in such branches of civil engineering as I should need."[20] This training allowed her, very early in her career, to undertake large-scale civil engineering projects such as draining fields and clearing forests. That phase of her education completed, she went back to the Arboretum and, in 1896, she received her first commission: "I was terrified and excited by being told that Mr. Sargent had found a client venturous enough to give me a trial. When I asked him in some excitement what I should do in this first piece of work about which I knew practically nothing, he said with his pleasant and yet grim smile, 'Do what your client wants.'"[21]

Farrand described the job as some tree thinning and the remodeling of a small planting on a garden slope, but did not give the name of the client.[22] That description does not fit either of the two projects she started almost simultaneously in the summer of 1896, both in Bar Harbor, Maine. One was the grounds of Chiltern, the summer residence of Edgar Scott, a friend and distant relative of the Jones family, who would have contacted her directly.[23] Farrand later described the other job—a civil engineering project for Mrs. William H. Bliss, mother-in-law of her future client Mildred Barnes Bliss—as her first work.[24] In 1913, she wrote to her then fiancé Max Farrand that the Bliss project had been a "useless piece of extravagance, though I didn't realize it at the time."[25]

Farrand's next project seems to have been designing the grounds of the William R. Garrison property in Tuxedo Park, New York (1896). The following year, she supervised the moving of a cemetery in Seal Harbor, Maine, and designed a lych gate, a sheltered resting place for the coffin, for it.[26] Other early projects include gardens for two brothers, Dr. E. K. Dunham in Seal Harbor (1898) and Dr. Carroll Dunham in Irvington-on-Hudson, New York (1899).[27]

In 1898, Henry Y. Satterlee, Bishop of the Diocese of Washington, recommended to the Cathedral Board "a young lady who had been named to me as the most skilful [sic] landscape gardener in America, Miss Beatrix Jones" to report with the architect on the best site for the Girls' School within the Close of the National Cathedral.[28] At that time, construction had not yet begun on the Cathedral, and only an approximate site had been selected. In 1900, Bishop Satterlee arranged to have some stones from Glastonbury Abbey (then privately owned) in England donated to form the cathedra, or bishop's chair, at the Cathedral. Beatrix Jones supervised this operation, and the Glastonbury cathedra is in the main sanctuary of the National Cathedral today.[29] In addition, she worked with the Cathedral Park Board, a women's group, to lay out paths and roads and to plant trees within the Close.[30] The Cathedral Close in its present form was designed by Olmsted Brothers between 1907 and 1928, and the ultimate site of the Cathedral was not the one Jones had recommended. Almost fifty years later, she told Mildred Bliss that she had wanted the Cathedral to be raised on a "great high crypt or further basements and to have nothing between the Cathedral and the road, so that it would soar up from its ravine as Laon towers over the countryside."[31]

In 1900, the fourth year of her practice, Jones was invited to become a charter member of the American Society of Landscape Architects, which had been founded a year earlier. The other ten charter members were men.[32]

The busy years of Beatrix Jones's early practice were punctuated by further European study trips and by regular vacations in Scotland. In August and September of most years, John Lambert Cadwalader rented Millden Lodge, a hunting lodge on a grouse moor in the Highlands, and Mary Cadwalader Jones served as his hostess for many house parties. The guests frequently included Henry James, who did not ride or shoot. Beatrix, on the other hand, was an expert horsewoman, and the gillies called her "as guid as the best shot of a man."[33] James, astonished by her shooting prowess, once wrote to Mary Jones that "Beatrix is probably now a confirmed murderess, in spite of which I embrace her. "[34]

Among the guests at the grouse moor was Charles Follen McKim, cofounder of the distinguished architectural firm McKim, Mead & White, whose buildings Farrand frequently landscaped. In 1907, McKim hired a "machine," and he and Beatrix spent three weeks scouring "the good Scotch roads in every direction."[35] A grouse moor may seem a peculiar place for a landscape architect to find clients, but this happened to Beatrix Jones more than once.

A meeting with Mrs. Moses Taylor Pyne took Jones to Princeton, New Jersey, in 1912, and the next year she began her campus work at Princeton University.[36] In 1913, she was also asked to design gardens for the residential colleges at Yale University. At the same time, she received an honorary Master of Arts from Yale. Yet another fortunate meeting—at a dinner party at Yale—led to her marriage to Max Farrand.[37] As she later wrote of her marriage in her autobiographical account: "They were neither of them young and each had attained some distinction in their work, consequently they agreed to go ahead with their professional careers and the years of marriage enriched both their lives."[38] On hearing of her engagement, Henry James wrote: "This is a grand showing & I am greatly touched at seeing the curtain so generously drawn for me by your fair hand. I congratulate you without reserve, for I think a married lady is in a much better situation, even more . . . than the most free-ranging single. . . . Kindly assure him [Mr. Farrand] of my consideration and confidence. He sounds most interesting, nay remarkable. . . . It's jolly that you have so big & beautiful an asset as your delightful profession to contribute to the concern, & I seem to see that the union of your so perfectly individual & sovereign states will make for a tremendous strength & a most striking frontier."

Beatrix worried about what would happen to her mother when she married, but James dismissed that concern: "I sacrifice Mummy . . . without wincing. . . .Mummy wasn't . . . made the most intelligent & sympathetic woman in the world for nothing. . . . Besides, at the worst, Mummy can come over & live with *me*, & that strikes me indeed as a very natural arrangement."[39] Mrs. Jones did not take him up on this offer.

The Farrands were married on December 17, 1913, at 21 East Eleventh Street by the Right Reverend Philip Rhinelander, a relative and the bishop of the Episcopal Diocese of Pennsylvania, assisted by the Reverend Charles Lewis Slattery, rector of Grace Church, probably the Joneses' parish church. Beatrix was given away by John Cadwalader, who died a few months later.[40] Perhaps because of his frail health, the Farrands did not delay the ceremony until Edith Wharton could arrive from France and Mrs. Jones recovered from surgery. After Wharton returned to France, she wrote to Beatrix: "Blessedness gives such a bloom even to chairs and tables—and how the sunlight strikes on a bowl of flowers, when one looks at it through a haze of happiness! Fasten with all your might on the ines-timable treasure of your liking for each other and your understanding of each other—build your life on its serene foundations, and let everything you do and think be a part of it." Surprisingly, the childless Wharton added, "And if you have a boy or girl, to prolong the joy, so much the better. Be sure it's worthwhile."[41] The Farrands had no children.

Farrand's career continued to be both prolific and distinguished, and, increasingly, she received large-scale commissions characteristic of the era. Many of her Long Island projects date from 1913 or later. She continued to design gardens and a few small public spaces on Mount Desert Island in Maine; her projects there ultimately accounted for about a quarter of her life work. There were also further clients in the Berkshires. Among her very few extant designs are Dumbarton Oaks in Washington, DC, for Robert Woods and Mildred Barnes Bliss, begun in 1922, and the Eyrie in Seal Harbor, Maine, begun in 1926 for John D. Rockefeller Jr. and Abby Aldrich Rockefeller. Her gardens at Eolia (1919–32) in New London, Connecticut, designed for Mr. and Mrs. Edward S. Harkness, benefactors of Yale University, have recently been restored.[42]

Farrand's list of college and university clients continued to grow. While keeping up with a busy practice, she wrote numerous articles on landscape matters and lectured from time to time. Farrand's colleague and friend Robert W. Patterson characterized her personal landscape style: "Beatrix Farrand gardens had always a subtle softness of line and an unobtrusive asymmetry. No surface was completely flat, no object balanced with another of exactly equal weight and position. Brick and pavement patterns, once established, must be laid not with tape and straightedge, but by eye." He also revealed that she thought of planting plans only as general guides and instead chose to "fuss" in the way that Guy Lowell thought only women would: "She preferred to prepare a planting when alone in her sitting room, a landscape clear on her inner eye, arranging her palette by writing plant names on a half-bushel of white sticks. Sorted into bundles, the labels were taken to the job, parceled out to gardeners and assistants, and the picture painted on the spot in a forest of white sticks. The pictures that she composed—in her later years, seated on a campstool and swathed in rugs—grew to a perfection that could be preserved only by constant care."[43]

As her 1932 letter to Clarence Fowler indicates, Farrand's standards of excellence and professional commitment never wavered:

Naturally, three years' study as scattered and disjointed as mine was only the foundation for later work, which I have tried to carry on to this day, feeling that the profession is as endless in its need for study as it is in its power to give interest and joy to life. I do, however, feel most strongly and increasingly that women should not enter the profession as a taste which they mean to gratify, but that it must be an absorbing passion with them if they really are to throw themselves into the work with the enthusiasm and interest demanded by the art.[44]

Max Farrand became as devoted as Beatrix to Reef Point, the Joneses' summer place in Bar Harbor. Always an outdoorsman, he became greatly interested in landscape gardening. In 1927, he resigned from Yale to become the first director of the Henry E. Huntington Library and Art Gallery in San Marino, California. While keeping her primary New York office and the office at Reef Point, Farrand set up a third in a large studio attached to the Director's House at the Huntington. In the late 1930s, the Farrands began planning for their retirement in Maine, and they eventually formed Reef Point Gardens, an educational and philanthropic foundation.[45] In 1941, Max Farrand retired from the Huntington, but the Farrands continued to spend the winter months in California, staying in a cottage at the Valley Club in Montecito.[46]

Max Farrand died in 1945. After that, Beatrix, whose practice was winding down, devoted the next ten years to advancing Reef Point Gardens as a future educational center for prospective landscape architects, establishing the Max Farrand Memorial Fund for this purpose. The house was completely remodeled, and her garden prints, library, and herbarium cases were arranged for study. The combined effects of World War II, a disastrous fire in Bar Harbor in 1947, and the decline of the town as a summer resort made the whole project seem less viable. The final blow came when Bar Harbor refused to grant Reef Point Gardens tax-exempt status. (Bar Harbor's tax base had been greatly eroded by the destruction of the numerous expensive summer homes in the 1947 fire.) In 1955, Farrand gave the Reef Point Gardens Collection, which also included the drawings of Gertrude Jekyll and drawings, plans, slides, and other materials relating to Mary Rutherfurd Jay, to the landscape architecture department of the

University of California at Berkeley and demolished Reef Point and its gardens. Farrand's own drawings seem to have been a last-minute addition to the gift.[47] She wrote: "Installed in much smaller quarters in Bar Harbor, Farrand looked back: She felt her life had been a happy one, she was grateful for what it had given her. She was ever thankful for the affection and help of her friends and associates during her long life, and attributed much to having had the privilege of their guidance."[48]

BEATRIX JONES FARRAND designed twenty-five landscapes and a headstone on Long Island, as well as three landscapes and another headstone for Long Island clients in Europe or other parts of the United States. Some of the projects for which there are only a few drawings at Berkeley may never have been carried out. Unlike Olmsted Brothers, Farrand did not assign job numbers to her projects, or, if she did, these records have been lost. Plan numbers, enclosed within a circle, are visible at the bottom right of some of her drawings. There are few complete sets of numbered plans for projects in the Berkeley archive, which indicates that, in spite of Farrand's meticulous nature, many plans must have been lost or discarded. Of her three offices, the one in New York City produced the bulk of the drawings. We know the names of a few of her New York draftswomen. However, for her later work in Maine, she had the assistance of Robert Whiteley Patterson, a Mount Desert Island resident who was both an architect and a landscape architect.[49] Patterson would have been Farrand's consultant, not an employee.

Beatrix Jones Farrand's first Long Island client was Percy Chubb.[50] In 1882, Chubb, with his father, Thomas Caldecot Chubb, founded a marine underwriting business in

2.2 *Plan for the garden, Percy Chubb Residence, Dosoris, Glen Cove. Ink on linen, March 15, 1900.* Berkeley

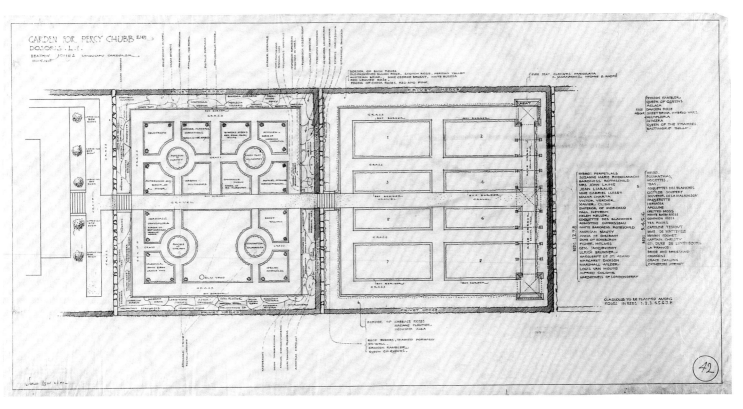

New York City. In 1900, Farrand designed a terraced garden for Rattling Spring (formerly Rolling Stone), in Dosoris, part of Glen Cove. How did Jones, then twenty-seven years old and only four years into her career, gain her entrée into Long Island patronage? The answer is straightforward: in the case of this and most of her early projects, she garnered her clients through family connections. Like John Lambert Cadwalader, Percy Chubb spent the autumn months grouse hunting in Scotland, and the two men must have known each other from this, and probably other, common interests.

Jones's plan for the Chubb garden was complex and highly sophisticated. Steps from a grass terrace adjacent to the rear entrance of the house led to the upper level (to the left in fig. 2.2), with further steps directly into the garden. Flanking a central gravel path were eight (top) and four (bottom) more-or-less square planting beds filled with a variety of annuals and perennials, including heliotrope, coreopsis, and calendula. There were also four circular beds with flowers like alyssum, candytuft, pansies, and California poppies planted "as carpet." The lower garden, reached by more steps, contained eight beds of mixed types of roses, most of which are no longer grown. At the far end, an arbor covered with several kinds of climbing roses extended across the entire width of the garden. Jones also directed that gladiolus be planted among the roses in the beds to take over from them in late summer.[51] The rose garden also had an arbor (see fig. C.1). This was a most

2.3 *Percy Chubb Residence, Glen Cove. Aerial photograph, ca. 1925.* Avery Architectural and Fine Arts library, Columbia University, New York

impressive achievement, especially for such a young and relatively inexperienced designer.

An aerial photograph of the Chubb garden (fig. 2.3), taken about 1925, conveys a good sense of its scale, its relationship to the house, and its general character. The photograph also reveals that a number of changes had already been made to the garden and that more alterations were planned for its surroundings. In the lower terrace, Farrand's rose beds and arbor had already been replaced by an evergreen garden, with massed evergreens at its far end and on the left. In the upper terrace, Jones's configuration of beds had been retained on the right, but to the left the existing elm shown in fig. 2.2 has apparently become so large that flowers could be planted only in a bed beside the central path. Much grading had recently been completed on two sides of the garden and extending considerably beyond it, possibly in preparation for an additional garden to the right of the house.

Jones's next four Long Island commissions were among the twelve projects she described in a brief but astonishingly candid account sent to Max Farrand. Written in the spring or summer of 1913, during the couple's engagement, this remarkable document seems to have escaped the notice of previous Farrand scholars. Although the account is undated and has no salutation, there are many internal references to dates and to dated or datable projects. The tone is relaxed and informal, with self-deprecating humor, referring to clients as "victims." Her collaborative method of working with her clients is also very evident. Once, she admits the client's idea for the garden was better than her own. She also assessed the quality of two marriages, one negatively and another very positively. Toward the end of the document, she revealed that Max Farrand called her, at the age of forty-one, his "girl."[52]

All twelve projects appear to have been in progress (some for as long as ten years) during the Farrands' engagement, and she several times promised to take Max to see them. Completed projects like the Percy Chubb property were not mentioned.[53]

The earliest Long Island project Jones described was for Roswell Eldridge and his wife in Great Neck. Louisa Udall Skidmore Eldridge was a most progressive and unusual person. After the legislature of the State of New York authorized the first village on the Great Neck peninsula in 1911, Roswell Eldridge, who bred toy spaniels, became the acting mayor of Saddle Rock, as the new village was called. In 1920, women won the right to vote, and, in the State of New York, they also gained the right to be elected to office. In that year, Mrs. Eldridge became the first woman mayor of Saddle Rock (and the first woman mayor in the country), holding the office until she died in 1947 at the age of eighty-seven—still running for office.[54]

At Mrs. Eldridge's property, Jones found: "an old farmhouse rebuilt or enlarged fairly well, standing on the northern bluff & looking down into the cove that makes one side of Great Neck. The place is an old one & has been in Mrs. Eldridge's family for three or four generations. It has its charm, just as she has, of real kindliness & unselfishness & shows all of her sweetness of character & complete lack of head."[55]

Mrs. Eldridge asked Jones for some redesigning of plantations around the house, some terraces, and a rose garden. Then, "bang," as Farrand wrote, she fell ill with appendicitis.[56] To her dismay, the work "had to be finished by the architect & it is an abomination in my eyes." Of the three terraces, she felt that the top one, a rose garden, was rather nice (fig. 2.4). There was, however, "great trouble with the maintenance as out of the kindness of her heart she keeps on an aged & perfectly incompetent gardener, who is bone lazy, thoughtless & colour blind. The result is that it is always in heart breaking condition."[57]

All of the drawings for this property at Berkeley, including the arbor (fig. 2.5) postdate the 1903 appendicitis attack. Farrand continued to do work for Mrs. Eldridge until 1930. A small public park is now on the site of the Eldridge property.

Between 1906 and 1914, Beatrix Jones Farrand created a walled garden for Edward Farley Whitney in Oyster Bay. Originally from Boston, Whitney moved to New York in

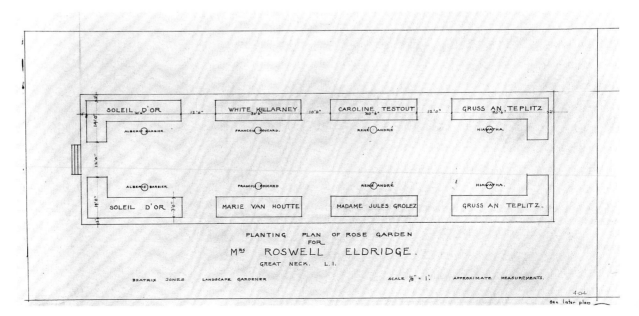

2.4 *Planting plan of rose garden. Mrs. Roswell Eldridge Residence, Great Neck. Ink on linen, undated.* Berkeley

ARBOUR for Mrs. Roswell Eldridge

Beatrix Farrand - Landsc Gardener

8/30
2.10

2.5 _Sketch of an arbour for Mrs. Roswell Eldridge Residence, Great Neck. Ink on linen, undated._ Berkeley

1901 and joined the banking firm of J. P. Morgan. He was a member of many clubs and active in racing and yachting circles. A bachelor, Whitney lived with his niece, Margaret Sargent Whitney, who encouraged him to contact Farrand.[58]

In her 1913 notes for Max, Jones described the Whitney property:

This place eight years ago was a sandy bare spot on which there were about ten apple trees in one corner, three or four shade trees on a little natural bluff between the house and the water . . . and a little group of oaks on a sandy knoll is on another corner of the six acres. A bare house stood stark on the knoll, vainly pretending that three trees to the north gave shade, the apple trees were dying & the high tides washed through the broken sea wall & seeped up through the soil. The low ground to the wall west of the house was all "made" land, leaving the dredged out (soil) of the beach to fill a swampy estuary. That was the condition when I was called in. The niece of the victim, who was the one who wanted me, said quite firmly that she wanted a naturalistic garden. But I said at the outset, that it was impossible as there was no possibility of escaping the domination of the house & its formality & of the rigid line of the sea wall, on so small a place.[59]

An Oyster Bay engineer surveyed the property in 1901, and the document was updated on March 19 and April 10, 1906, probably at Jones's request.[60] As a survey, it is atypical, since there are no contours, only intersections showing grades at 50-foot intervals. There were no great variations in grade on the site. While no photographs of the Whit-

ney house have been located, its footprint on the survey shows that it was, just as Jones wrote, very large and symmetrical. The only trees shown are quite small, probably indicating that the house had been built shortly before the survey was made.

Jones persuaded Miss Whitney that the naturalistic approach was not feasible and proceeded to lay out a formal garden:

So she reluctantly consented to a formal arrangement. It was difficult as there were but the two strong lines, the rectangle of the house & the angle of the sea wall—& after fussing over it for a long time, I came to the conclusion that the [illegible] line was the strongest—the line of the sea & that of the house must be subordinated. So the bordering lines of the garden were made parallel to the sea, & it was [knit?] to the house by a flight of steps leading down the grass terraces to a round pool, where the two angles meet & lose themselves. It makes a sort of hinge or pivot. The garden had to be protected from wind & as hedges would be very slow, a high wall was necessary. & in order to break its stiffness two arbours, one on each side were poked up above the top of the wall to get some relief in the varied heights. The grades in the garden plot did not make terracing reasonable, so all the light & shade & change of surface had to be simulated by planting & masses, such as the arbours, & the screen separating the main garden from the rose garden, which leads out of the main garden like the apse of a church, a part of it, but separate. The garden was as bare as a box set down in the desert & had to be framed with shrubs to make walls get down in their places. Now it begins to look well & it pleases me to see her pleas-

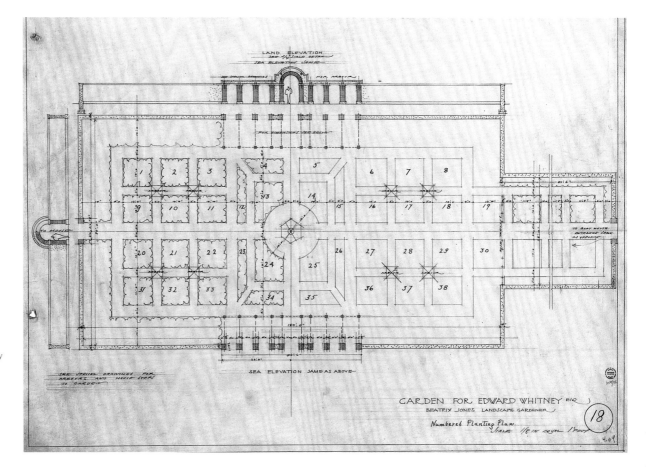

2.6 *Planting plan for garden, Edward F. Whitney Residence, Oyster Bay. Ink on linen, undated.* Berkeley

2.7 *Garden, Edward F. Whitney Residence, Oyster Bay. Photograph, undated.* Berkeley

ure in it. It is one of the best things I have done & you will like to see it, & I shall like to show it to you. The rest of the place has developed & now the thinning out & destroying of the temporary plantations has begun, in order to detach the masses & leave the peaceful openings where nothing happens, except that one's eyes rest. A great deal of the credit of the place is due to Miss Whitney who has been of great help with her intelligent criticism & suggestions. If it looks well, I'll show it you in October.[61]

The general layout may be seen in an undated planting plan (fig. 2.6). While this is a numbered planting plan, the key has unfortunately been lost. Nevertheless, it does reveal the overall concept and the garden's relationship to the house. The "apse" of the rose garden is clearly delineated, although species and varieties are not known. Undated photographs in the Berkeley archive give some clues to plant choice, one showing tulip foliage and blooming hyacinths and others, white lilies (fig. 2.7). Although Farrand was deeply interested in and knowledgeable about plants, she seldom went in for rarities. In addition to this garden, the Whitney property included an informal iris garden interlaced with grass paths.[62]

The Whitney house was replaced in the late 1920s by a new one constructed for Joseph Kerrigan, built apparently on the same site.[63]

Two other Long Island projects described in the notes to Max Farrand must have been started in 1913, although all of the plans for both projects date from 1914.

Jones described the C. Oliver Iselin property, Wolver Hollow, near Glen Head as: "an old farmhouse remodeled very attractively. . . . There is to be a large garden, more or less modelled on the French one in the Bois in Paris, called Bagatelle, where the city of Paris has a rose garden. Bagatelle is very well known to horticultural tourists & is exceedingly good, but it is going to be too big and too important for the place."[64]

Despite its name, the Bagatelle rose garden in the Bois de Boulogne is very large. Jones initially fought this concept for Iselin, but then agreed when she found that it would be possible for her to design what is now known as a "therapeutic garden." (As she explained to Max: "I would not have yielded if I had not realized that it was going to be perhaps a way of curing Mr. Iselin. He has been a nervous invalid for years & this place & its garden interest him & he is perhaps going on with its development himself & that will give him an occupation & probably get him all right again."[65]) The drawings at Berkeley for the Bagatelle rose garden show beds but again no indication of rose varieties. It was probably not carried out, and we do not know whether Iselin became "all right again."

Also in 1913, Jones began some work for Mrs. George D. Pratt in the Pratt family compound in Dosoris, Glen Cove. There, at Killenworth, she found a stone house "Tudorish" in period. As she wrote to Max:

James L. Greenleaf, a colleague, was given charge of the place, roads, & general lay-out. It was a bare field when he tackled it a few months ago. Mrs. Pratt wanted a garden, & came to

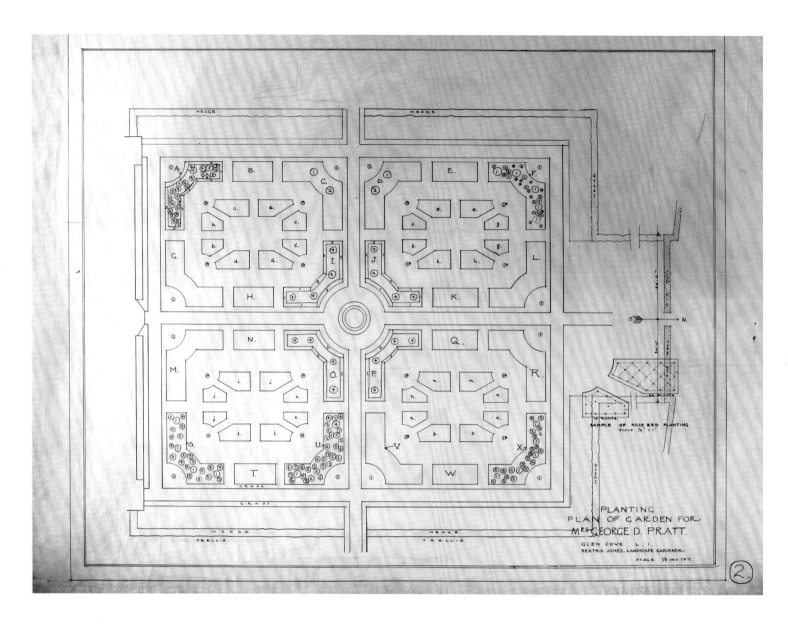

PLANTING
PLAN OF GARDEN FOR
MRS. GEORGE D. PRATT.
GLEN COVE L.I.
BEATRIX JONES, LANDSCAPE GARDENER.
SCALE ⅛ IN = 1 FT.

2.8 *Plan of garden, Mrs. George D. Pratt Residence, Glen Cove. Ink on linen, undated.* Berkeley

2.9 *The garden wall. Chinese garden, Applegreen, the Mrs. Willard D. Straight Residence, Old Westbury. Photograph, ca. 1923.* From P.H. Elwood, *American Landscape Architecture,* 1924)

me. I was horrified & wrote Greenleaf at once. He answered that it was all right, that his work stopped at the planting & roads, & was most civil & nice. So I started on a gridiron kitchen garden below the house & near the service wing. On one side is rather a bad rustic arbor—not to be allowed—on the north a stucco retaining wall for the service road & on the east there will be a tennis court divided from the garden by a lattice screen—not very good. The plan of the garden is fairly good, but it needs relief, some lead figures or good vases; it is all too flat & dull. The hedges too, need height as they are now imperceptible except with a magnifying glass. This place won't be any good till after it has had about five years growth; then it will drop down into its place, it now stands out too much.[66]

There are eight plans at Berkeley for the Pratt property, two of which are dated (March 1914). An undated plan that Jones indicated was her first for Mrs. Pratt (fig. 2.8) shows a very symmetrical garden, although not exactly a gridiron. There is no indication whether this was supposed to be a flower garden or a vegetable garden. Including hedges and paths, the garden measures 177 by 90 feet, dimensions roughly comparable with the two-level Chubb

flower garden. On the other hand, it was right next to a projected tennis court. There is a pool at the center. If this is in fact the kitchen garden, Farrand seems to have chosen the pool rather than vases or statuary.

An exceptionally important landscape was that which Farrand designed for Willard D. and Dorothy Whitney Straight in Old Westbury. Straight, an international banker and partner in J. P. Morgan, and his wife spent their extended honeymoon in Europe and Russia, ending with six months in China. After this trip, they continued to maintain close intellectual ties with China and with Asia generally.[67] The house, called Applegreen, was originally a small eighteenth-century Quaker farmhouse, which was greatly enlarged and remodeled by Delano and Aldrich around 1913.[68]

Farrand worked on the Straight property for eighteen years, beginning in 1914. Although the project included plans for a tennis court, tea house, playhouse, and some suggested road changes, its central feature was a walled Chinese garden, which incorporated a decidedly western element: a swimming pool. Two stunning watercolor drawings—a plan and a perspective (see figs. C.2 and C.3)— are among the 127 plans for this project at Berkeley. The

2.10 *Pool in lower section of Chinese garden, Apple-green, the Mrs. Willard D. Straight Residence, Old Westbury. Photograph, ca. 1930.* From American Society of Landscape Architects, *Illustrations of Work of Members*, 1931

symmetrical Chinese garden was laid out slightly off-axis to the house. The site was completely flat, or graded to be so, with informal groupings of existing trees just outside it at either end. From a semicircular forecourt with handsome gates, a visitor could walk onto a broad grass panel with elaborate parterre flower gardens on either side (fig. 2.9) and continue onto a central turf section with a Chinese-style arbor on either side. Finally, there was a narrow rectangular pool, where the Straight children sometimes sailed toy boats (fig. 2.10). Farrand created an artificial perspective by making each section smaller and narrower than the one that preceded it (see fig. C.2). The double paths that extend the length of the garden terminated in Chinese-style bath houses. Chinese moon gates were inserted in the side walls; the far end was left open to create a vista through the woods.[69]

The watercolor plan is dated 1914 and the perspective was probably done at the same time, suggesting that the Chinese garden may have been completed fairly rapidly.[70] Surrounding areas were landscaped over the next several years. Anne Baker, who had joined Farrand's office as an

assistant in 1924, took on a supervisory role with the Straight project, field-checking plantings there.[71] In 1924, for example, she recorded that early spring bulbs had been planted along the lilac walk. Willard D. Straight died in 1918, and, in 1925, Dorothy married Leonard Elmhirst, a Yorkshireman. For most of the year, the Elmhirsts lived in Devonshire, England, where they established a progressive school at Dartington Hall in Totnes. Farrand worked on those grounds in the mid 1930s. The Long Island property was subdivided in 1951, but the foundations of the Chinese garden are said to remain.[72]

Farrand's largest project on Long Island was for S. Vernon Mann at Grove Point in Great Neck. Between 1918 and 1930, her office produced 248 drawings for Grove Point; there are also twenty-three supplementary drawings at Berkeley but only one photograph, which is in bad condition and yields no useful information.[73] Farrand laid out the grounds in the immediate vicinity of the house, siting the tennis court and swimming pool, designing the service entrance gates, as well as a terraced garden with an arbor, a knot garden, a cutting garden, fountains, a summer house (see fig. C.4), a boat house, and more. Most of these areas were to the north of the house (fig. 2.11). A 1920 topographical map shows that this was an extremely large property, extending well beyond Farrand's gardens and even including salt marshes. This job was carried out in at least two stages, the second beginning in 1927, when Farrand did a sketch plan for "new development." In fact, most of the drawings at Berkeley for the Mann project date from between 1927 and 1929. Hicks Nurseries supplied the plants.[74] The Mann grounds have been subdivided, although the house (apparently) survives.

In 1919, Farrand began a group of gardens for Mr. and Mrs. Otto H. Kahn at Oheka in Cold Spring Harbor. The German-born Otto Hermann Kahn was an investment banker who was then a partner in the New York firm of Kuhn, Loeb. An art collector and chairman of the board of the Metropolitan Opera, he has been described as "the most influential patron of the arts ever known to America."[75] Kahn felt that his profession was "outrageously overpaid" and was deeply convinced that he must "atone" for his wealth.[76] In addition to his support of the opera, he brought Vaslav Nijinsky and Sergei Diaghilev's Ballets Russes to the United States in 1915. Even more remarkably, Kahn helped to advance the careers of at least three of the country's most important early twentieth-century artists: stage designer Norman Bel Geddes, singer and actor Paul Robeson, and poet Hart Crane, who dedicated his long, multipart poem "The Bridge" to Kahn. While ever the prudent businessman, Kahn was extraordinarily generous and patient, especially to the perennially insolvent Crane.[77]

Kahn's personal interests lay primarily in the performing arts and poetry. Addie Wolff Kahn, a sculptor, selected most of the paintings and sculptures for the family's collection. In addition, Mrs. Kahn was responsible for the day-to-day supervision of architects and designers.[78] Beatrix Farrand specifically listed her as the client, and, undoubtedly,

2.11 *Sketch plan, portion of property, Grove Point, the S. Vernon Mann Residence, Great Neck. Pencil on tracing paper, October 1929. Berkeley*

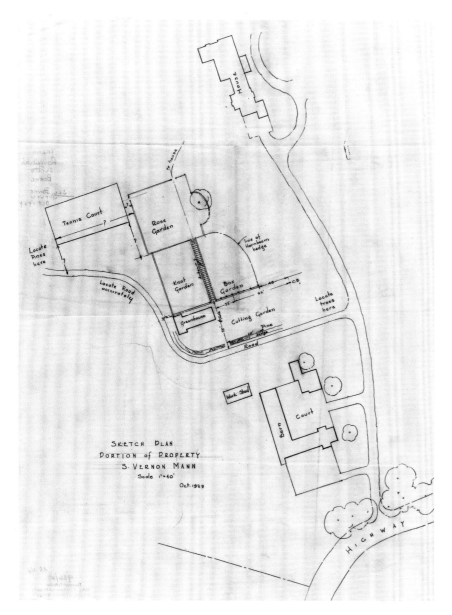

Delano and Aldrich and Olmsted Brothers reported to her as well.

Between 1915 and 1917, Delano and Aldrich designed a huge chateauesque house atop an artificial mound in the Kahns' 500-acre property in Cold Spring Harbor. Sweeping down on axis with the principal facade of the house was a formal landscape in the French baroque style (fig. 2.12).[79] Olmsted Brothers were involved in this design, but Delano and Aldrich kept a firm upper hand. Grand as it was, this scheme offered few spaces for quiet sitting, reading, or talking, and flowers played no role. This is presumably why Mrs. Kahn engaged Farrand in 1919 to create a series of interconnected garden rooms at the foot of the formal water gardens. The Kahn project was carried out over nine years, and 159 drawings were produced by Farrand's office.

Delano and Aldrich were probably no longer on the site when Farrand began her work, but they left her with a schematic plan for the area to the south of the water gardens (fig. 2.13). She adhered to it fairly closely, although the arrangement was more symmetrical and rigid than she would have created on her own.[80] To some extent, however, she played with the shapes prescribed by the architects, reconfiguring the large square flower garden into a slightly more rectangular "Dutch" garden and the small circular garden on the lower right into a greatly enlarged octagon, thus transforming the ensemble into an imaginative sequence of garden spaces that flowed seamlessly into each other (fig. 2.14). Following the Delano and Aldrich scheme, she designed an amphitheater, but its shape was rectangular rather than circular.

2.12 *House and formal landscape at Oheka, the Mr. and Mrs. Otto H. Kahn Residence, Cold Spring Harbor. Aerial photograph, Aiglon Aerial Photos, ca. 1923.* From Elwood, American Landscape Architecture

47

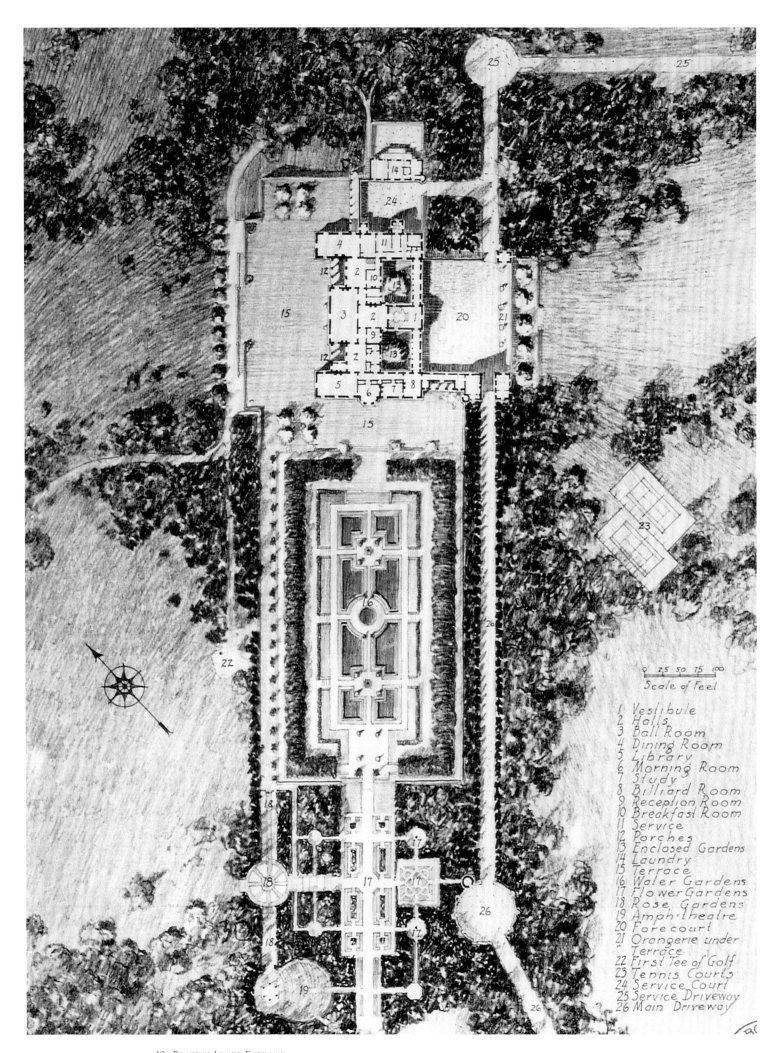

1 Vestibule
2 Halls
3 Ball Room
4 Dining Room
5 Library
6 Morning Room
7 Study
8 Billiard Room
9 Reception Room
10 Breakfast Room
11 Service
12 Porches
13 Enclosed Gardens
14 Laundry
15 Terrace
16 Water Gardens
17 Flower Gardens
18 Rose Gardens
19 Amphitheatre
20 Forecourt
21 Orangerie under Terrace
22 First Tee of Golf
23 Tennis Courts
24 Service Court
25 Service Driveway
26 Main Driveway

Scale of Feet
0 25 50 75 100

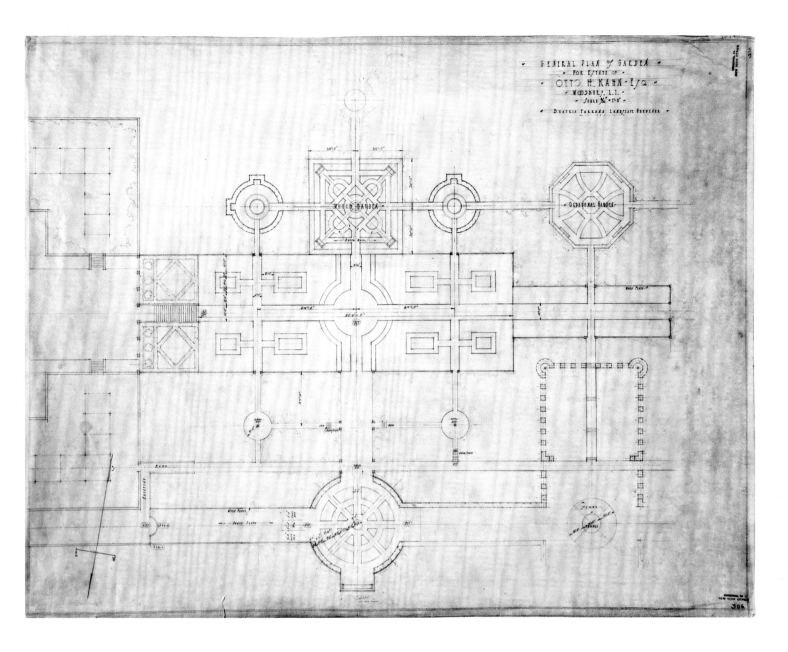

FACING PAGE

2.13 *Delano and Aldrich.
General plan for the Estate
of Otto H. Kahn, ca. 1917.*
From *Portraits of Ten Country
Houses Designed by Delano and
Aldrich,* 1922

ABOVE

2.14 *General plan of
garden for Estate of Otto H.
Kahn, Westbury, L.I. Ink on
linen, undated.* Berkeley

The pool garden was planted with perennials and annuals, including peonies and irises (fig. 2.15), and the Dutch garden with tulips (fig. 2.16). For the Dutch garden, Farrand prepared a planting plan and numerous plant order lists for thousands of tulip bulbs to allow a succession of bloom from early to middle to late spring. The early single tulips were in subtle shades of yellow and orange, while the Darwin tulips included some pink, white, and purple varieties. Among the May-flowering cottage tulips, the greatest number were "Inglescombe Pink." There were also quantities of "breeder" tulips, mostly in shades of bronze, orange, and yellow. In addition, Farrand ordered a thousand blue hyacinths for the entrance to the rose garden, as well as numerous narcissus, grape hyacinths, snow drops, and crocuses. Most of these bulbs were ordered from Segers of Holland. An undated memo notes that "Mrs. Kahn wants (she says) 'millions' of columbines in the garden. It is spring! So we'll have to get her a few." They ended up ordering about a thousand.[81]

Sometimes the gardens were connected by flagstone paths (fig. 2.17), sometimes by grass paths. Since the land for the most part sloped steadily downward, the gardens were frequently connected by stone or grass steps as well. Within the gardens, there might be herringbone brick paths and such garden features as sundials (fig. 2.18). Notes made by Farrand's principal assistant, Margaret Bailie, reveal that she and Bailie frequently had scale models made of garden furniture—benches, fountains, and so on—to study their effect before the actual elements were fabricated. By varying the sizes and shapes of the gardens, their levels, their focal sculptures or garden structures, as well as their paving and plant materials, Farrand avoided repetition and accomplished a tour de force of spatial planning within a confined site.

In addition to this series of gardens, Farrand added topiary trees (type unspecified, but some sort of compact evergreen) to punctuate the water gardens. Box plants were also added to the Delano and Aldrich/Olmsted Brothers gardens.

Oheka is extant, and the Delano and Aldrich water gardens have been restored. The land that Farrand's gardens occupied is now owned separately and shows no evidence of her designs.[82]

49

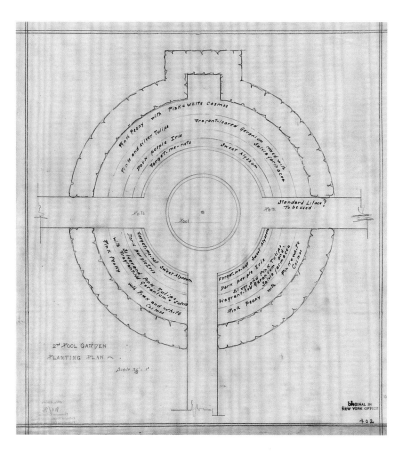

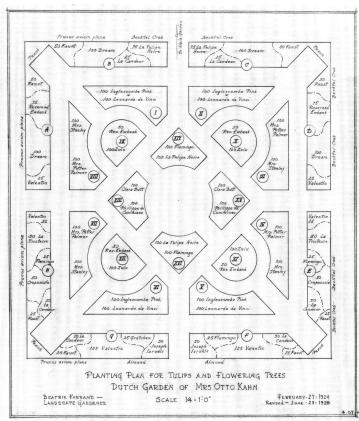

2.15 *Planting plan for pool garden, Oheka, the Mrs. Otto H. Kahn Residence, Cold Spring Harbor. Pencil on tracing paper, undated.* Berkeley

2.16 *Planting plan for tulips and flowering trees, Dutch garden, Oheka, the Mrs. Otto H. Kahn Residence, Cold Spring Harbor. Pencil on tracing paper, February 27, 1924, revised June 29, 1928.* Berkeley

2.17 *Garden steps and walks, Oheka, the Mrs. Otto H. Kahn Residence, Cold Spring Harbor. Photograph, Mattie Edwards Hewitt, 1928.* Long Island Studies Institute, Hofstra University, Hempstead, Photograph 5687.65

Shortly after former President Theodore Roosevelt's death in 1918, his widow, Edith Kermit Roosevelt, commissioned a joint headstone for him in Youngs Memorial Cemetery, not far from Sagamore Hill, the family house in Oyster Bay (fig. 2.19). Farrand prepared three schemes for this stone, offering alternate treatments for the fluting of the pilasters framing it. This restrained, classical, and elegant design is Farrand's only extant project on Long Island. Farrand also designed a headstone for the Roosevelts' son Quentin and his friend Hamilton Coolidge, who both died in World War I, at an unknown location in France.

Around 1921, Farrand laid out drives and a garden for Mr. and Mrs. Edward S. Harkness in Manhasset. The house was designed by Cross and Cross, and the place was called Weekend.[83] This was apparently a small project with only five drawings. How much was carried out is unclear.

Between 1922 and 1932, Farrand designed two small public landscapes in Great Neck: the Great Neck Green and the Great Neck Green Public Library, with thirty-seven and sixteen drawings respectively. She probably owed both commissions to Mrs. Roswell Eldridge, who was the founder of the library and also in charge of the Great Neck Park District.[84] The Great Neck Green seems to have been an existing open space, which Farrand relandscaped. Her designs included a garden, fountain, bandstand, gate, wall, and planting plans for the whole area (fig. 2.20). In April 1927, plant orders were sent out to eight nurseries, including Cottage Gardens Company, Queens Village, Long Island, and Hicks Nurseries, asking that plants arrive at the site by May 2.[85] Farrand, through Anne Baker, also ordered fencing from the Anchor Post Iron Works.[86] There seem to be no photographs of what must have been a very visible public landscape. While portions of the Green are still vaguely suggestive of Farrand's design, there are intrusions, especially a large, relatively recent apartment building on one corner. The planting plans and lists are extensive enough that the rest could be restored.

The Great Neck Green Public Library was a very interesting project that was not realized. Architect George S. Chappell of New York City made plans to enlarge the library, located on Arrandale Avenue at one end of the Green. Farrand designed gardens at each end of the new building and an outdoor reading room for children (fig. 2.21). Since the library was never enlarged, Farrand's plan could not be carried out. In the 1960s, a new library was built in another location and the one on Arrandale Avenue has been converted to a community center called Great Neck House.[87]

Another large project (201 drawings and 70 supplementary drawings) was that for Percy R. Pyne II at Rivington House in Roslyn, which Farrand designed between 1925 and 1929. As is frequently the case, projects for the Pyne family form a cluster within Farrand's work. Mrs. Percy R. Pyne was an early benefactor of the National Cathedral, one of Farrand's first projects. Farrand also designed a garden for Mrs. Moses Taylor Pyne, who was instrumental in bringing Farrand her first campus job, at Princeton University. The architects of the Roslyn house were Cross and Cross, many of whose supplementary drawings are in the

files for this job at Berkeley. Since the files at Berkeley include many plant orders, most of them marked "planted fall 1927," this job obviously was executed. Although Farrand ordered a number of trees and shrubs, including oaks, maples, crabappples, cherries, pines, viburnums, various shrub roses, hawthorns, mountain laurel, dogwood, and so on, from Hicks Nurseries, there were also large rose and flower gardens with beds surrounded by low box hedges (fig. 2.22).[88]

In 1928 and 1929, Farrand designed two gardens for Oak Point, the Harrison Williams property in Bayville. The house was built in 1901 for Winslow Pierce from designs by Babb, Cook and Willard and was altered in 1927 for Harrison Williams, a lawyer, by Delano and Aldrich. This was a large project for which Farrand's office produced seventy-five drawings and also vertical files. The original plan for the gardens was done by Delano and Aldrich in January 1928.[89] It shows five different formal gardens and an abbreviated allée of unidentified trees. The gardens included an octagonal rock garden, a round Chinese willow garden, an oval garden consisting apparently of concentric flower beds, a rectangular garden containing two cedar of Lebanon, and a large octagonal flower garden centering on a lily pond. All of these were located between the main house and the play house, which contained an indoor swimming pool and an indoor tennis court.

Farrand's drawings are limited to the rock garden and the Chinese willow garden. While the hulking massiveness of the rock garden (fig. 2.23), which was planted in part with dwarf evergreens, seems to lack Farrand's usual refinement, the Chinese willow garden (fig. 2.24) is more in character.[90] It is a pity that Farrand was not brought in earlier, since her approach would have been quite different. Unlike the elegant sequences of the Straight Chinese gar-

2.18 Sundial in garden, Oheka, the Mrs. Otto H. Kahn Residence, Cold Spring Harbor. Photograph, Mattie Edwards Hewitt, ca. 1928. LISI, 5687.87

2.19 Headstone, Theodore and Edith Roosevelt grave, Youngs Memorial Cemetery, Oyster Bay. Photograph, ca. 1945. LISI, 3004

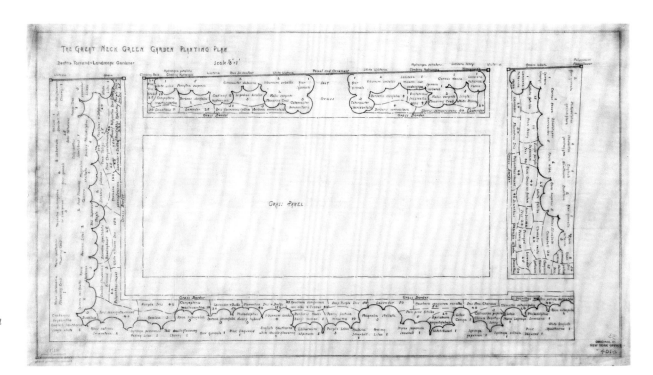

2.20 *Planting plan, Great Neck Green, Great Neck. Pencil on tracing paper, undated.* Berkeley

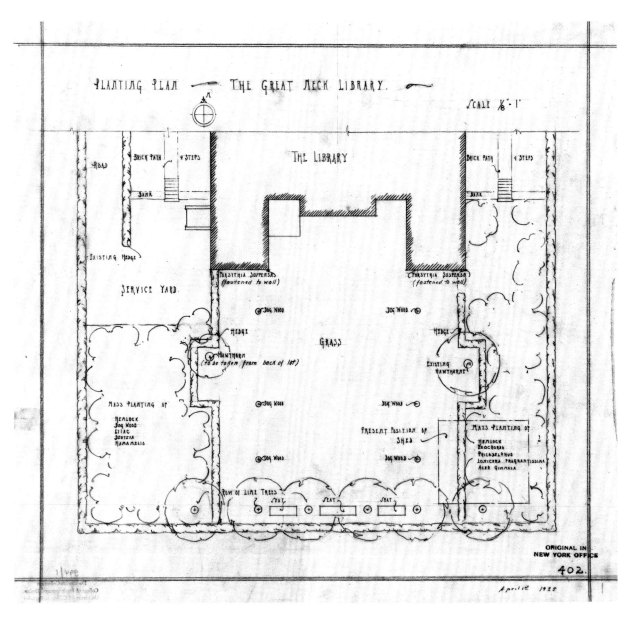

2.21 *Planting plan, Great Neck Green Public Library. Pencil on tracing paper, April 1, 1925.* Berkeley

2.22 *Garden, Rivington House, the Percy R. Pyne Residence, Roslyn. Photograph, Mattie Edwards Hewitt, 1929.* LISI, 5867.294

2.23 *Octagonal rock garden, Oak Point, the Harrison Williams Residence, Bayville, Photograph, undated.* Berkeley

2.24 *Chinese willow garden, Oak Point, the Harrison Williams Residence, Bayville. Photograph, undated.* Berkeley

den or the flowing garden rooms at Oheka, the gardens at Oak Point seem arbitrarily placed and visually unconnected, although short paths run between them.[91]

The group of gardens took up a relatively small part of the 94-acre site, which fronted on Long Island Sound. (Fig 2.25 is a map of the whole property from an undated real estate brochure.[92]) On the map, the first and second gardens to the left in the upper tier are Farrand's rock and willow gardens. The rock garden is either incorrectly drawn or had deteriorated beyond recognition. As may be seen at the lower left of the map, a farm group, separated by belts of woods from the house, was located near the southwestern part of the property. In 1933, Olmsted Brothers worked on this area (job #9342), but their involvement seems to have been minimal.[93] The house at Oak Point was demolished in 1968, and the gardens are gone as well.

Between 1933 and 1938, Farrand redesigned and replanted parts of the grounds of Dartington Hall in Totnes, Devonshire, England, for Dorothy and Leonard Elmhirst. Dartington was not an ordinary educational institution: rather, its mission was to create "nothing less than the furtherance of the Good Society—of happy, responsible, creative living—through education, the study and practice of the arts, and the development of new methods of farming and industry on a sound economic basis, in a decaying rural area."[94]

In September 1926, the school opened, its students consisting of the three Straight children and fourteen local youngsters. Manual labor was stressed, but the academic curriculum was highly unstructured. Frankness and permissiveness were the order of the day, to the extent that some mornings began with an instructor interpreting the

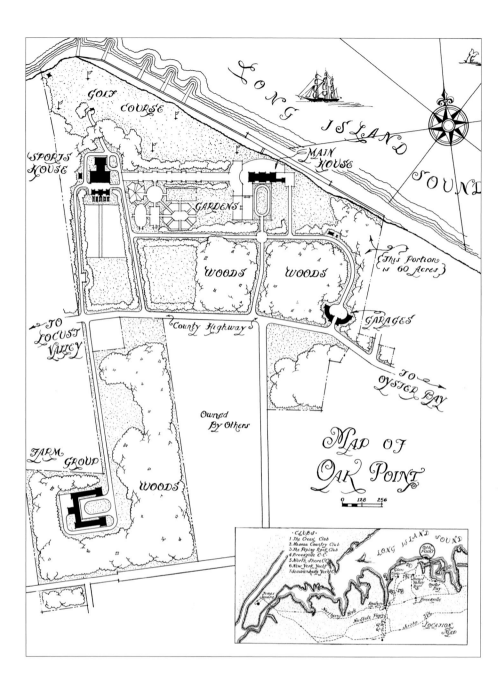

2.25 *Map of Oak Point, the Harrison Williams Residence, Bayville, undated.* SPLIA

students' dreams. With the aid of intensive tutoring, the two Straight boys entered Cambridge University. Ultimately, a more conventional preparatory curriculum was introduced at Dartington.[95]

The house at Dartington Hall, which dates back to 1559, was in a near ruinous condition when the Elmhirsts acquired it. During the first years of their ownership, much rubbish was cleared, and restoration of the fabric of the medieval building was carried out by the American architect William Weir. With the help of an able garden superintendent, R. S. Lynch, some work had been done on the grounds, but Dorothy Elmhirst was not satisfied. In September 1932, she wrote Farrand urging her to advise them on landscape developments. Farrand agreed and arrived in February 1933, happy to see Dorothy and eager to begin work. After visits to Kew and Oxford, she spent several days studying the Dartington grounds.[96] Dorothy Elmhirst has left us a vivid description of Farrand at work: "She worked incessantly—scrutinizing every corner and angle, setting up her stakes, taking meticulous notes, planning,

planning every hour of the day and night."[97]

The meticulous notes that Farrand took, neatly typed by her secretary, are in the files for this project. Ranging in date from February 4, 1933 to February 27, 1933, they minutely record the conditions she found, what she proposed to do, and plantings that she recommended for each part of the grounds. There is a list of "Plants liked by Mrs. Elmhirst," which contains nothing especially arcane—magnolia, lemon verbena, Forsythia suspensa, weeping cherry, lilacs, wisteria, among others.[98] In the some parts of the grounds, Farrand recommended native British plant material. In the Wilderness, she planned four walks: a lower walk, emphasizing rhododendrons and white evergreen azaleas; a middle walk, with camellias as the main plantation; a high-level walk, with mixed plantations, including holly and myrtle; and an upper (hedge) walk, consisting of a formal laurel hedge underplanted on one side with clumps and drifts of early bulbs of various sorts.[99] As she wrote to Dorothy Elmhirst, she did her work mainly in the field, finding that planting plans were often unsatisfactory, and preferring that the "actual conditions on the ground should be the governing ones."[100]

Once back in her office, she set her staff to work making plans for the projects she had outlined in her notes. Forty-three plans were ultimately produced, and there are numerous supplementary plans. Strangely, there are no planting plans among them. The courtyard of Dartington Hall is widely regarded as Farrand's finest achievement at this property, yet all of the drawings for the courtyard were produced by the Gardens Department, Dartington Hall, Ltd.[101] Some are annotated by Farrand and by her senior draftswoman, Ruth Havey.

Early in her career, Farrand, who was not skilled at free-hand drawing, initiated a system of having her drafts-women prepare sketches, frequently of garden furniture, which she would comment on, sometimes writing directly on the plan. She would then send the drawing back for further development and refinement. Later, she often delegated the annotating to assistants.[102] The plans for Dartington Hall include a series of sketches for the Darting-ton Bench, or Bench #3. It is difficult to tell how many of these studies were originally prepared. Some are numbered, some are lettered, and there are breaks in both sequences. In the files today, there are twenty-three sketches for this bench. In some cases, the comments are written directly on the plan in a hand that is not Farrand's, possibly that of Havey. Astonishingly, the series of numbered plans have brief typed critiques attached to the plan with a straight pin or paperclip (fig. 2.26). The voice is unmistakably Farrand's. About one study, she commented, "perhaps we could get a little more movement to the arms."[103] Attached to another is a critique that reads in part, "I again fear that the back may be a little too wide for comfort. I fear one's bulginess would be likely to slip in between the slats, as the spaces seem to me to be about 5-1/2" wide."[104] The dated studies were all drawn on January 31, 1934. Someone in Farrand's office was very busy that day,

turning out a drawing about every fifteen minutes or so; in between Farrand would dictate her comments, which her secretary would transcribe, insert the pin, and bring it back to the draftswoman.[105]

In 1934, Farrand also worked on the Churston Development Co., Ltd., a project for the subdivision of part of the 1,000-acre Dartington Estate.[106] In 1942, Farrand did a sketch plan for a property belonging to Michael Straight, son of Dorothy and Willard D. Straight, in Alexandria, Virginia.[107]

Early in her career, Farrand commented to an interviewer: "Society? Yes, it is very agreeable. . . . But this grand art of mine is a noble art."[108] She was perhaps thinking of the famous song by Franz Schubert, "An die Musik," which begins "Du holde Kunst, in wieviel grauen Stunden" (Thou noble art, in how many gray hours). In an act of unprecedented courage, this gently brought up young woman shifted her focus from one noble art—music, specifically singing—to another, and left an indelible mark on the art and profession of landscape architecture as its first female practitioner.

It is appropriate to let Dorothy Elmhirst have the last word on Farrand as a professional and a human being:

No one who worked with Beatrix Farrand could fail to be impressed by her professional attitude to her job. Always the first to be out in the morning, she was the last to come in at night. Her energy seemed able to surmount any obstacle—even the worst onslaughts of rain and cold. In her tweeds and Mackintosh, we could see her tall, erect figure conversing—in all weathers—with architects, builders, gardeners, tactfully collaborating with them all and slowly winning them to her ideas. . . . Her finely chiseled face and dignified bearing seemed . . . the personification of royalty. Her clear incisive mind was greatly enriched by her wide cultural background. Both in her professional capacity and as a friend and companion, she was in every way a remarkable woman.[109]

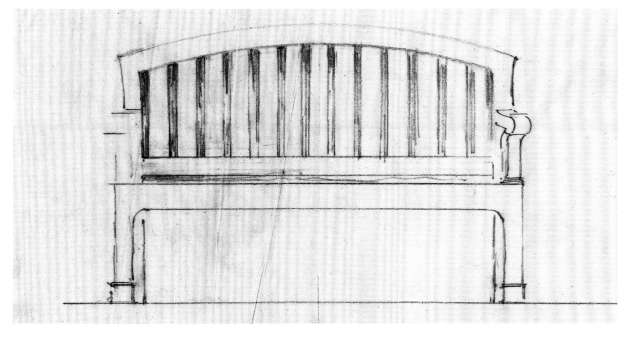

2.26 *Sketch for Bench #3, Dartington Hall, Devon, England. Study #13, Pencil and colored pencil on tracing paper, undated.* Berkeley

Martha Brookes Brown Hutcheson

1871–1959

MARTHA BROOKES BROWN HUTCHESON was born in New York City on October 2, 1871, the daughter of Joseph Henry Brown, a merchant, and Ellen Douglas Brookes.[1] She was the second of five children.[2] As with Beatrix Farrand, Brown's primary and secondary education appears to have been provided by private tutors, and she may also have attended a private school. In 1910, she married William Anderson Hutcheson, a vice president of Mutual Life Insurance Company.[3]

In 1932, Hutcheson described the genesis of her professional life to Clarence Fowler: "Since earliest childhood, everything which grew absorbed me. . . . From early youth the leading interest of my summers was always in my garden on my mother's summer place, doing all the work, and, incidentally learning its hidden lessons."[4] The family summer home, Fern Hill, originally developed by Hutcheson's great-uncle John Norton Pomeroy, was on the outskirts of Burlington, Vermont, overlooking the Winooski River, which flows into Lake Champlain. Pomeroy was a lawyer, who received a large inheritance on the death of his father in 1844 and subsequently devoted most of his time to his agricultural interests. Hutcheson described him as "an alert, scholarly, genial, practical and public spirited man with a flare [*sic*] for astronomy, chemistry, poetry, farming and architecture."[5] Pomeroy designed the house at Fern Hill, which was completed around 1850, orienting it to the points of the compass, with the west and east doors framing magnificent views of Lake Champlain and Mount Mansfield. Hutcheson's mother bought Fern Hill shortly

after Pomeroy's death in 1881. Martha began working in her own garden there at about the same time.[6] As with Reef Point on Beatrix Jones Farrand, Fern Hill was a profound influence on Martha's childhood and, ultimately, on her choice of profession.

Not long after these first gardening experiences at Fern Hill, broader landscape vistas beckoned. When still in her teens, Martha visited Europe with her family: "Incidentally I had traveled to Italy, France and England, seeing in a personal way many gardens before ever realizing that I would know them later in a much more analytical way—for as years passed, more trips were made to Europe with very definite study the objective."[7]

In the 1890s, Hutcheson first took courses at the New York School of Applied Design for Women and subsequently studied watercolor painting of flower subjects with the English-born artist Rhoda Holmes Nicholls.[8] She redirected her career goals to landscape architecture after discovering a lost opportunity for what today is called a therapeutic garden: "About 1898, one day, I saw the grounds of Bellevue Hospital in New York, on which nothing was planted, and was overcome with the terrible waste of opportunity for beauty which was not being given to the hundreds of patients who could see it or go to it, in convalescence."[9] As Frederick Law Olmsted had been decades earlier, Hutcheson was convinced that a well-designed landscape could have a healing effect on body, mind, and spirit. She tried to find authorities at the hospital to allow her to plant the ground but was told that this would be

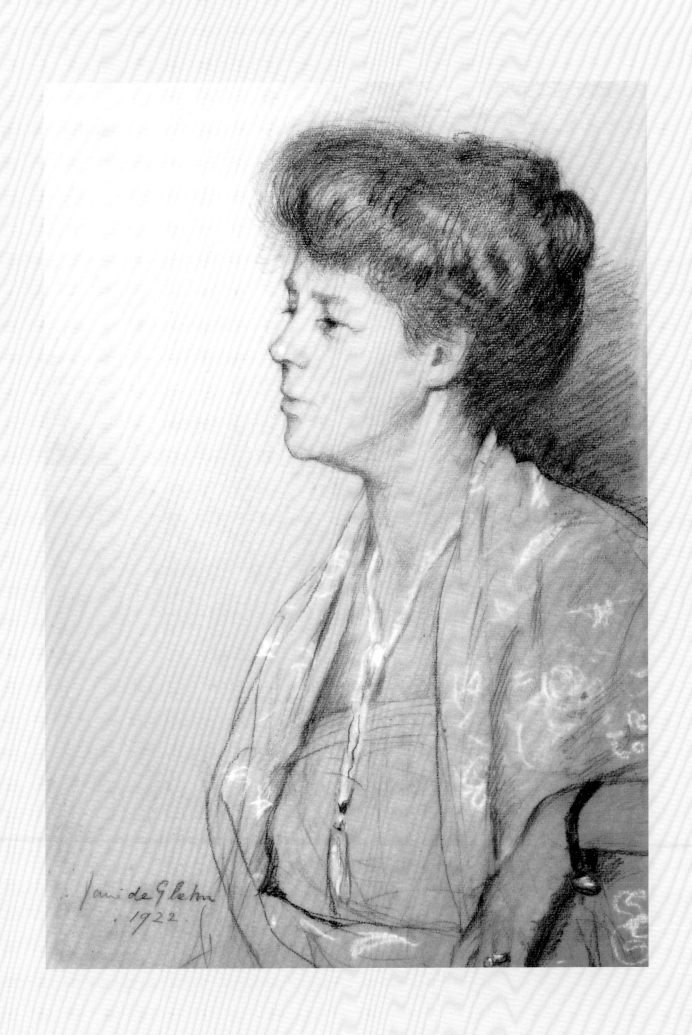

Jane de Glehn
1922.

"politically impossible." In the course of these inquiries, she learned about the landscape architecture program in formation at Massachusetts Institute of Technology, which would be open to women.[10]

Hutcheson later told Henry Atherton Frost, director of the Cambridge School of Architecture and Landscape Architecture, that when she broached the subject of attending MIT to her family, they were scandalized: "Such a thing was unheard of and unthinkable. A bleak future was painted. She would be socially ostracized. And when arguments did not prevail she was promised a trip to Europe."[11] Her mother was even ready to sacrifice her beloved Fern Hill: "she could tear the family country place to shreds and redesign it. Anything to save her honor—which meant the honor of the family. Think of trying to explain to one's friends such an abnormality. But the child won her point, although her morale was sadly shaken."[12]

Martha stood firm. She immediately began to study the mathematics needed for admission and to "try to put my private-school-tutored mind into as good shape as I could on the various subjects before entering the second year of the course in 1899–1900."[13] In the face of such fierce opposition, it is unlikely that she was able to persuade her family to pay her tuition. According to one source, Martha financed her education herself using a small bequest.[14] Nevertheless, as she told Frost: "On the opening day of the fall term, when she was to enter MIT, she walked around the block three times before she could screw up her courage sufficiently to climb the imposing flight of stone steps which led to her chosen prison."[15] She was admitted as a special student, although, during her relatively brief time at MIT, she took some (but by no means all) of the courses required of students in full standing.

Hutcheson's qualms about MIT were not unfounded. As we have seen in chapter 1, the program was rigorous in the extreme. Hutcheson had some difficulty with freehand and mechanical drawing, in spite of her earlier design preparation.[16]

While the courses Hutcheson took over a period of a year and a half included "architecture, plant knowledge, planting plans, grading plans, surveying in the field, geology, biology, mathematics, etc.," she felt that the curriculum did not give nearly enough time to the "plant world." She addressed this lack by studying on her own at the Arnold Arboretum and making exhaustive notes on the plants there, which she incorporated into her plant card catalog. In addition, she made frequent trips to local commercial nurseries to note "periods of bloom, combinations in color, variety of species in flowers and the effects of perennials after blooming."[17]

After completing her studies at MIT in 1902, Hutcheson opened an office in Boston, where she practiced for two or three years before leaving for a year-long study trip in Europe.[18] Edna D. Stoddard, an MIT classmate, served as her principal assistant for several years, apparently both in Boston and New York City. When Stoddard died in 1958, Hutcheson wrote of her: "A-1 is what I would say of her in everything that counts—not only for what she did but for what she was."[19]

During the years of her Boston practice, Hutcheson designed numerous gardens and entire estates on the North Shore of Massachusetts. Many of these clients continued to retain her after she moved to New York in 1906. One of her first commissions was Undercliff, designed for Charles Head in Manchester-by-the-Sea, which survives in private hands.[20]

Another outstanding design was Maudesleigh, the F. M. Moseley property in Newburyport, which she worked on for a number of years. By 1907 she had completed a large flower garden, the hillside setting for the property, a long approach walk, installation of grille gates that she had found in Italy, along with designs for a fountain dial, pergolas, and so forth. At the end of her brief account of this job in her professional record, she noted she had "changed entrance & induced client to rebuild house."[21] A persuasive practitioner indeed! Maudesleigh (renamed Maudsley State Park) is now owned by the Commonwealth of Massachusetts. Although all buildings on the site have been demolished, the outlines of Hutcheson's work remain. In 1997, the walls of the Italian and rose gardens were restored by the state and work on the main entrance gate was in the planning stage in 2001. Further restoration is projected.[22]

In 1904, Alice Longfellow, a daughter of the poet Henry Wadsworth Longfellow, asked Hutcheson to work on a formal garden designed by her father. Hutcheson retained some of Longfellow's design but made significant changes in layout and materials. More than thirty years later, she described the work for the Historic American Buildings Survey (HABS): "The Longfellow Garden at Cambridge I overhauled entirely. It had gone to rack and ruin. I reset box in the Persian pattern which the poet had originally planned, for sentiment, which pleased Miss Alice Longfellow very much. Then I added arbors, gates, fence, etc."[23] In 1925, Ellen Shipman prepared a plan for renovating the Longfellow garden.[24]

On her return from Europe, Hutcheson opened an office in New York, where, in a period of only five years, she developed an extensive clientele based largely in New Jersey, upstate New York, and Long Island. In 1911, she and her husband purchased a property in Gladstone, New Jersey, which they called Merchiston Farm. Much of her time from this point on was directed toward developing the farmhouse and the landscape around it.[25] In 1912, the Hutchesons' daughter, also named Martha, was born. Hutcheson had ongoing projects in her office in 1911, but, because of a pregnancy-related illness, was not able to oversee them. After the birth of her daughter, she closed her office but continued to consult on a number of landscape projects. She probably maintained studios in her New York town house and at Merchiston Farm.

Hutcheson by no means retired from the field. Instead, she channeled her considerable energies into promoting its values, which she did with an almost missionary zeal. In 1914, Hutcheson became a member of the newly formed Garden Club of Somerset Hills in New Jersey. She also participated actively in the Garden Club of America, which had been established in 1913, lecturing, contributing articles to the *Bulletin*, and judging flower shows. During World War I, Hutcheson was a founding member of the Woman's Land Army (formed to offset the diminishing availability of male farm workers) and gave lectures to raise war funds.[26]

Throughout this period, Hutcheson tried to redirect the role of the Garden Club of America, some of whose affiliates still functioned largely as social groups, and to infuse it with a broader social purpose. In 1919, Mrs. Willis Martin, then president, asked Hutcheson to draw up suggestions for the further development of the club. Hutcheson's proposal, "A Wider Program for Garden Clubs," included several "Aims," such as establishing a center in each village for garden club purposes, raising the quality of plantings around public buildings and churches, developing a more inclusive membership that would admit men and younger women, instituting educational programs for children, and collecting photographs and lantern slides of good and bad plantings. Additionally, she suggested that the influence of the members of garden clubs, who were assumed still to be mostly women, would extend to their husbands, who committed most of the "devastation" on roadsides.[27]

Hutcheson was appointed chairman of a Program Committee to achieve some of these "Aims," but the program was voted down later the same year.[28] In 1925, Hutcheson took up the cause again, when she delivered a statement to the President's Council of the Garden Club of America at its annual meeting in Detroit. The no-nonsense title of her address was "Are Our Garden Clubs to Progress in Unison or Die of the Inertia of the Commonplace?"[29] Although defeated on the national level, the "Aims" were eventually adopted by several local garden clubs and, by 1938, when Hutcheson wrote an account of the first twenty-five years of the club in the *Bulletin*, most of her goals had been achieved.[30]

After 1912, Hutcheson lectured widely, but never about her own work. Instead she focused on the same issues that she was championing for the Garden Club of America. Some representative titles were "Possible Inspiration through Garden Clubs Toward Wiser and More Beautiful Planting," "Better Front Dooryard Treatment for Rural Towns," and "Plants for City Use, —for Street and Yards." She lectured at least once in London on "Phases of American Gardens" to the Garden Club Ltd., at the invitation of Ellen Wilmott, a contemporary of Gertrude Jeykll; Wilmott had a famous garden in Essex. Hutcheson also lectured on "The Fine Art of Landscape Architecture" at the Metropolitan Museum of Art in New York City.[31]

She illustrated each of her lectures with about 150 large-format glass slides. In addition to lecturing, Hutcheson also occasionally served as a visiting critic at the Lowthorpe School.[32] Hutcheson joined ASLA in 1919 and was elected a Fellow in 1934.[33]

Hutcheson frequently contributed articles to national magazines, including "Garden Spirit," published in *The Cosmopolitan* in April 1901, "Landscape Gardening: A Conversation," in *The Outlook*, July 1909, and "New England Gardens," in *New England Gardens*, May 1914. After 1916, she wrote regularly for the *Bulletin of the Garden Club of America*. She continued writing articles at least through the 1930s.

In 1923, Hutcheson published her book, *The Spirit of the Garden*. She was prompted to do this by the fact that the majority of garden books on the market emphasized rare plants and "picturesque" effects rather than basic planning principles.[34] *The Spirit of the Garden* is organized into six chapters, the first a general commentary on the flower garden, and the rest devoted to specific garden elements or features such as the importance of axis, the hedge, arbors and gateways, greenhouses, and water in the garden. Each chapter is illustrated with a variety of European landscapes, the majority of them Italian Renaissance or Baroque gardens such as the Boboli Gardens, the Villa Medici, and the Villa d'Este. With a few exceptions, the American gardens in the book were designed by Hutcheson. These include Undercliff and Maudesleigh[35] as well as five Long Island gardens, which are plentifully illustrated with photographs but no plans. It is fair to conclude that Italian gardens were the most important European influence on Hutcheson, but it was the three-dimensional planning of these gardens that impressed her rather than specific details.[36] Hutcheson's gardens never looked Italian. She did not try to use native Italian plants, which in most cases would not thrive in the northeastern United States, nor did she simulate the steep slopes and elaborate terracing of many Italian gardens.

Several of Hutcheson's later consulting projects are of considerable interest. Although minimal information is available for most of them, further research in college archives might uncover more documentation for two. In 1919–20, Hutcheson designed the Katrina E. Tiffany Memorial at Bryn Mawr College in Bryn Mawr, Pennsylvania. This was a flower garden on the Wyndham estate, which was owned by the college. According to Hutcheson, the plan was carried out by an associate of Beatrix Farrand, who apparently also had a consultancy at Bryn Mawr, although there is no record of a Bryn Mawr project in lists of Farrand's work or in the list of plans for her projects at Berkeley.[37]

Between 1932 and 1934, Hutcheson made planting plans for drives at Bennington College in Vermont that had been laid out by the college architects Dodge and Ames. In addition, she made plans for future drives. This work was done pro bono.[38] Bennington College was founded in 1932 after almost a decade of planning and fundraising. The initial schemes were Beaux-Arts in plan and Georgian Revival in detail, but, by the time the college was ready to break ground, the realities of the Depression had struck. The architectural plans were scaled down to an assemblage of modest white clapboard buildings in a New England village green configuration.[39] It is entirely in character that Hutcheson would have wanted to help a new progressive women's college with an emphasis on the arts, especially one in Vermont.

A vivid sense of Martha Brookes Hutcheson as a person is evident not only in her own writings but also in the words

3.2 *Main garden.
Mrs. Robert Bacon
Residence, Westbury.
Photograph.* From *Hicks
Nurseries,* "Home Land-
scapes," Spring and Summer
1923. Courtesy Hicks
Nurseries

of those who knew her. Buell Hueston, a reporter who interviewed Hutcheson but whose article was never published,
described her as "this dynamic personality—this low-voiced
woman of positive manner. . . ." He went on to say, "Mrs.
Hutcheson dislikes or rather, refuses, to talk about herself,
her work or even her own home. This is not shy reticence
on her part, for Mrs. Hutcheson is not at all shy, but rather
militant modesty perhaps prompted by an absorption in her
field of activity. To her, landscape architecture is vastly
important, but Mrs. Hutcheson is not."[40]

The author of Hutcheson's Biographical Minute recalled
her encouraging young landscape architects at a time when
the country was in economic crisis: "In the early 1930s, she
gave a tea at her home in New York for young women then
starting in the profession of landscape architecture. These
were depression days and there seemed little future in what,
at the moment, seemed like a luxury profession. However,
she exhorted us to keep the true faith." Later, Hutcheson
invited some of the women to Merchiston Farm to observe
"at the source" how this fine landscape had been made.[41]

William Anderson Hutcheson died in 1942, and Martha
Brookes Hutcheson died on July 23, 1959. In 1972, their
daughter, Martha, and her husband, Charles McKim Norton, an architect and urban planner, gave Merchiston Farm
to the Morris County Park Commission along with some
of Hutcheson's personal and professional papers.[42] Her
vast collection of lantern slides, including views of a number of Garden City communities in England and the
United States, is also preserved there. Unfortunately, the
only plans in this collection are for Merchiston Farm. The

grounds of Merchiston Farm are being restored (2001–8)
by Heritage Landscapes, a landscape architecture and
preservation firm based in Charlotte, Vermont, and Norwalk, Connecticut.

HUTCHESON DESIGNED nine landscapes on Long Island, all of
them private gardens. Some were consultancies only, completed after she withdrew from active practice, and mea-
gerly documented. Portions of two of Hutcheson's Long
Island landscapes may survive, but in the absence of plans,
it is difficult, even for an experienced person, to determine
what portions of a designed landscape may remain. Great
vigilance is also necessary to avoid confusing later work by
other landscape architects on the same site or by the owners themselves with Hutcheson's designs.

An early project and one of the most important was Old
Acres (referred to as Oldfields in *The Spirit of the Garden*),
which she initially designed for Mr. and Mrs. Robert Bacon
in Westbury between about 1904 and 1910.[43] Hutcheson
apparently began consulting with Mrs. Bacon even before
construction on the house, which was designed by John
Russell Pope, was under way.[44]

When the house was nearing completion in October
1908, Mrs. Bacon asked Hutcheson to make plans for a
large garden adjacent to the building on a site that had a
naturally level grade and good soil. At the end of a broad
turf path, on axis with the main garden, was a small classical temple. In 1934, when Hutcheson submitted her fellowship application to the ASLA, several plans,
photographs, and a planting list for the Bacon property

remained in her files. Unfortunately, these are no longer among her records at the Morris County Park Commission. No survey was required for this project, and no construction drawings were prepared, since the work was all done by the Bacons' gardener. The Bacons also supervised the construction of a pool and steps, following Hutcheson's plans exactly, including her choice of brick. All of the plants were ordered through Hutcheson's office from a variety of nurseries. The cedars that framed the garden and outlined some of its paths were transplanted from a neighboring hillside by Hicks Nurseries and placed according to Hutcheson's plan.[45] A page from a 1923 Hicks catalog (fig. 3.2) shows the garden, pool, a row of cedars, what appear to be espaliered roses, a display of tall bearded iris, and low box edging. Overhanging the edge of the pool were hardy azaleas (fig. 3.3), which were also used elsewhere in the garden.

Another, smaller garden connected the library with the main garden. The small garden was a shady spot, on a slightly higher level than the main garden, with a central fountain (fig. 3.4).[46] In addition, there was a "spring garden" (fig. 3.5).[47] After the gardens were established, Hutcheson designed a semicircular entrance to the property. After 1912, Hutcheson advised Mrs. Bacon about an approach to the tennis court and about plantings along the paths that connected the main house with those of other family members, including her son, Congressman Robert L. Bacon, and her daughter and son-in-law, Mr. and Mrs. George Whitney.[48] One of these paths, which passed between groves of tall shrubs and trees, is lined with Japanese iris. All of the garden ornaments were brought from France by Mrs. Bacon, with the exception of the bronze fountain figure by Janet Scudder, which was installed in the small garden off the library at Hutcheson's suggestion.[49] In the 1920s, Ellen Shipman did further landscaping at the Bacon property, but the exact nature of her work there has not been determined.[50] The Bacon house and garden are no longer extant.

In 1907, Hutcheson worked on the grounds of the Payne Whitney residence in Manhasset. This seems to have been a minor project, which Hutcheson described as a "long path, connecting parts of place" with flowering trees and herbaceous plantings.[51]

From 1910 to 1922, Hutcheson undertook her first project for the Pratt family. This was Poplar Hill, the Frederic B. Pratt residence in Glen Cove.[52] Frederic, his five brothers, and his sister were the children of Charles Pratt, who had been instrumental, with John D. Rockefeller, in organizing the Standard Oil Company. Charles Pratt also founded the Pratt Institute, and Frederic served on the Institute's board all of his adult life.[53] Babb, Cook and Willard designed the house at Poplar Hill around 1898, but an architect named Trowbridge (probably the firm of Trowbridge & Ackerman) was doing additions or alterations at the time that Hutcheson was called in.[54] Poplar Hill was a challenging project that required an effective treatment for an extremely steep slope below what seems to have been an addition to the house. Hutcheson designed an impressive balustrade for the terrace overlooking the

slope and created a monumental stairway. Vines were carefully maintained so that they clothed the steps but did not conceal any important architectural features (figs. 3.6–3.8).[55] In 1929, Charles Platt designed a new house for the site but did not change any of Hutcheson's plantings.[56] In 1931, the Garden Club of America credited Hutcheson as the landscape architect of Poplar Hill, noting that "her use of trees on the long slopes, —years ago, — is what ties the whole place together."[57]

In 1911 and again in 1913, Hutcheson landscaped the grounds of Welwyn, the property of Harold I. Pratt, which was also located in Glen Cove and, like Poplar Hill, seems to have been initially laid out by Olmsted Brothers.[58] Harold I. Pratt, the youngest sibling, managed the Pratt family funds.[59] Welwyn seems to have been a major project, perhaps one of Hutcheson's most important on Long Island, and it is frustrating that there are no plans to clarify the precise extent and nature of her work. Another complication is that she was absent from the job during her pregnancy in 1911. In her own professional account, Hutcheson stated

3.3 *Hardy azaleas overhanging the pool, main garden. Mrs. Robert Bacon Residence. Photograph, by 1923.* Hutcheson, *The Spirit of the Garden*

3.4 *Small garden adjacent to the library. Mrs. Robert Bacon Residence. Photograph, by 1923.* Hutcheson, *The Spirit of the Garden*

3.5 *The spring garden.*
Mrs. Robert Bacon
Residence. Photograph,
Frances Benjamin Johnston,
by 1928. Shelton, *Beautiful*
Gardens in America

3.6 *Poplar Hill, The Frederick B. Pratt Residence, Glen Cove. Construction view, showing work on steep grade below house. Photograph, by 1923.* Hutcheson, *The Spirit of the Garden*

3.7 *Poplar Hill. Approach to garden. Photograph, by 1923.* Hutcheson, *The Spirit of the Garden*

3.8 *Poplar Hill. Garden
steps, showing appropriate
vine maintenance. Photo-
graph, by 1923. Hutcheson,
The Spirit of the Garden*

that she had "furnished plan and planting plan for terraced garden, pool, steps, arbor, etc."[60] She went on to say that, in her absence, her plans were executed without her knowledge by James Greenleaf and that Greenleaf later claimed Welwyn as his own work. Further, she contended that Greenleaf had then made a plan for the property of John T. Pratt, which he derived from her own plan for Welwyn, while making some modifications of his own.[61]

Hutcheson did not indicate that she had prepared any tree planting plans for either the front or rear lawns at Welwyn, and this may have been something that Greenleaf initiated. Hutcheson had reached the point of preparing planting plans for the garden but does not seem to have ordered the plants. Both of Long Island's two major nurseries, Hicks Nurseries and Lewis and Valentine, specialized in transplanting full-grown trees to newly established landscapes. Greenleaf was a loyal patron of Lewis and Valentine. The firm frequently featured his work, including Welwyn, in their catalogs, thus inadvertently perpetuating the misattribution of Hutcheson's work at Welwyn to Greenleaf.[62] The lawn in front of the house was planted with numerous fine, mature specimens of American elm, all decades older than the house (fig. 3.9).

Hutcheson's terraced garden, the pierced brick wall around it, the pool, and the arbor at Welwyn are well represented in photographs in *The Spirit of the Garden* and in some especially fine views by Mattie Edwards Hewitt. For

The Spirit of the Garden, Hutcheson chose the photograph in fig. 3.10 in order to "illustrate the interest gained by going down into a garden," a principle of her designs.[63] The Hewitt series (figs. 3.11–3.14) begins with the garden and its central pool, with the grape arbor at the rear. Among the plantings are a few good-sized American elms asymmetrically placed, as well as a number of mature box shrubs. Transplanting fully grown box was another Lewis and Valentine specialty. Outlining the planting beds is a continuous line of low box hedging. As Hutcheson wrote, she intended a "lavish use of green" in this garden.[64] Another view shows a variety of herbaceous plants offsetting the predominant green of the box. Another section featured a sundial supported by a sculpted figure by Edward McCartan, the sundial marking an important axis, as well as more herbaceous plantings.[65] It is difficult to identify specific plants in this photograph, but lupines seem to be among them. The final Hewitt photograph (fig. 3.14) shows a detail of the garden, with an elegantly sinuous line of low box hedging. To create this effect and sustain it would have required the most meticulous maintenance imaginable, of a sort prohibitively expensive today.

The grounds at Welwyn survive as part of the Welwyn Preserve in Glen Cove, and the house is now a Holocaust Museum. The west garden survives only as a space. The plantings are not Hutcheson's, although the structure of her landscape remains.[66]

3.10 *Garden, Welwyn.*
Photograph, by 1923.
Hutcheson, *The Spirit*
of the Garden

3.11 *Garden, Welwyn.*
Photograph, Mattie Edwards
Hewitt, by 1928. Shelton,
Beautiful Gardens in America

3.12 *Garden, Welwyn.*
Photograph, Mattie Edwards
Hewitt, by 1928. Shelton,
Beautiful Gardens in America

3.13 *Garden, Welwyn. Photograph, Mattie Edwards Hewitt, by 1928.* Shelton, *Beautiful Gardens in America*

Beginning about 1910, Hutcheson designed a flower garden for Mrs. Daniel Lord at Sosiego, her property in Lawrence.[67] This appears to have been a very interesting project, although it is poorly documented. By the time Hutcheson arrived, the site had already been at least partially developed; an artificial pond had been constructed at some point in the early 1880s. Hutcheson, however, might have been responsible for planting weeping willows around it.[68] The central feature at Sosiego was a large enclosed herbaceous garden (fig. 3.15). Nearby was an arbor of rough locust-wood construction that supported grapevines and roses. As of 1981, the house still stood, although the neighborhood around it had been heavily subdivided, probably destroying any remnants of Hutcheson's landscaping.[69]

Martha Brookes Hutcheson's active design career was brief but distinguished. Today, she is remembered chiefly as the author of *The Spirit of the Garden*, a fine and still timely book that was reissued in 2001. Her actual design work, however, deserves more attention, despite the challenge to scholars posed by scarcity of plans. Her lecturing and work

with the Garden Club of America, her chief activity after the birth of her daughter, are also highly significant. From her youth through her maturity, she was tireless in promoting landscape architecture as a vehicle for effecting social progress. Hutcheson was a "New Woman" every bit as much as Farrand and other women landscape architects discussed here, who practiced for decades rather than years.

Nowhere is Hutcheson's crusading spirit more evident than in her reply to Clarence Fowler's request for an account of her entry into her profession. Realizing that Fowler's article would be read by many women landscape architects in the early stages of their careers, she addressed them directly:

> We who first lit the way for women in the profession, would beg of those who are following, on a far easier path, to hold the torch higher and higher until the world in general learns that Landscape Architects are to be reckoned with and that the profession ranks in importance with those of the other Fine Arts.[70]

3.14 *A detail of the garden, Welwyn. Photograph, Mattie Edwards Hewitt, by 1923.* Hutcheson, *The Spirit of the Garden*

3.15 *Flower garden, Sosiego. Photograph, by 1923.* Hutcheson, *The Spirit of the Garden*

CHAPTER 4

Marian Cruger Coffin

1876–1957

MARIAN CRUGER COFFIN was born on September 27, 1876 in Scarborough, New York, the only child of Alice Church Coffin and Julian Ravenel Coffin. A few years after their marriage, Coffin's parents separated, and in 1883, her father died from complications of malaria.[1]

Marian Coffin's lineage was distinguished. Her father was a descendant of early settlers of Nantucket Island, Massachusetts. This branch of the Coffin family relocated to South Carolina, where they acquired a town house on the Battery in Charleston and plantations on St. Helena Island, all of which were lost during the Civil War when Julian Coffin was a student in Germany.[2]

The Churches were prominent in Allegheny County, New York, where they had a country place, Belvidere, on the Genesee River. Coffin's ancestors on this side included the Colonial artist John Trumbull, as well as Benjamin Silliman Sr., a nineteenth-century professor of science at Yale University. Mrs. Coffin's brother Benjamin Church was one of the engineers who laid out the Olmsted and Vaux plan for Central Park.[3]

Not long after Julian Coffin's death, Alice Church Coffin and her daughter moved to Geneva, New York, living first with her sister Harriet and then with her brother John Barker Church and his wife Maria. Like Beatrix Jones and Martha Brookes Brown, Marian Coffin was tutored at home. Unlike them, she had no early formative gardening experiences, although she always loved the country and the "great outdoor world."[4] Coffin, like Farrand, became an accomplished horsewoman and a skilled golfer.

While Alice Coffin's income appears to have been greatly reduced after the death of her husband, she and her daughter retained their privileged social connections. One of Mrs. Coffin's closest friends was Mary Pauline Foster, who married Colonel Henry Algernon du Pont. Growing up, Marian was close to the couple's two children, Louisa and Henry Francis, known as Harry. He would later become Marian's client at Winterthur, the du Pont family estate in Delaware.[5]

As we have seen in chapter 1, Marian Coffin as a girl had dreamed of becoming a great artist, but exceptional ability in the musical, literary, or pictorial arts were not among her gifts. Unmarried and approaching her mid-twenties, she was aware that her mother's family could not support her indefinitely and that, at some point, her mother would become her responsibility. As she wrote to Clarence Fowler,

> So my artistic yearnings lay fallow until I realized it was necessary to earn my living, when talking over the problem with some friends, one of them, an architect, said he thought some courses in "Landscape Gardening" for women were to be started in this country and that it would be an interesting thing for a woman to go in for. At the same time I had been hearing of Beatrix Jones' novel profession and the success she was making of it, so on further investigation I found by far the most worthwhile course being offered, was at the Massachusetts Institute of Technology, and off I went gaily expecting to be welcomed with open arms.[6]

When Coffin presented herself for an interview at MIT, the reception was not what she had hoped:

You can imagine how terrifying such an institution as "Tech" appeared to a young woman who had never gone more than a few months to a regular school, and when it was reluctantly dragged from me that I had had only a smattering [of] algebra and hardly knew the meaning of the word 'geometry,' the authorities turned from me in calm contempt. Only Professor Chandler, head of the architectural school, seemed to have some realization of my disappointment when I was told that I was totally unprepared to take the course and refused admittance. It was owing to his kindness and also to Professor Sargent's and Mr. Lowell's encouragement that I persevered and was able by intensive tutoring in mathematics to be admitted as a 'special' student in Landscape Architecture, taking all the technical studies and combining the first two years in one so that I finished in three years.[7]

Marian and her mother moved to Boston in 1901 for the duration of Marian's studies. It is probable that Mrs. Coffin's siblings paid Marian's tuition and the living expenses of both women. In Marian's MIT class, there were three other women, two of whom were studying "straight" architecture. The other landscape architecture student was Frances Ropes, a native of Salem, with whom Coffin stayed in touch after they completed their studies.[8]

Coffin later looked back on her MIT years as "one long grind," although broken by a summer studying landscape design in Italy and France. Contrary to the widely held anxiety that mixed gender classes would lower morale among the male students, Coffin enjoyed a lively congeniality with her colleagues of both sexes:

In the drafting rooms and in our classes the four women students . . . were thrown in all our work in competition with the men, and the invasion of their province as well as our specialty (which was a new and untried architectural development) put us on our mettle to prove that we, too, were serious students and competitors. This association of boys and men I found very helpful as we had a fine spirit of comraderie in the drafting room, and many a helping hand was given me at a critical moment.

Even harsh criticism was welcome: "one had to steel oneself to hear many a severe criticism, which was perhaps even more valuable!"[9]

Marian Coffin entered MIT as a special student in January 1901 and completed her studies in 1904. During nearly every warm-weather term, she took courses in horticulture with John G. Jack at the Arnold Arboretum, for which she received credit at MIT. Other courses that she took regularly were freehand drawing with Charles L. Adams, mechanical drawing and descriptive geometry with Linus Faunce, shades and shadows with Harry W. Gardner, and watercolor with Ross Turner. During her last three terms, she studied landscape design with Guy Lowell. Although she completed all her courses with good grades (Cs—Credit, or Ps—Pass), Coffin did not prepare a thesis and thus could not receive a degree.[10]

During her years at MIT, Coffin remained in close touch with Harry du Pont, who was an undergraduate at Har-

vard for much of this time, studying horticulture and related fields at the Bussey Institute adjacent to the Arboretum. A particularly cherished Christmas gift from du Pont in 1902 was a set of Liberty Hyde Bailey's four-volume *Cyclopedia of American Horticulture*. Probably at Sargent's suggestion, if not in his actual company, Marian and Harry toured Boston-area landscape landmarks, such as Sargent's own Holm Lea, Isabella Stewart Gardner's Green Hill, and Faulkner Farm, all in Brookline, as well as the H. H. Hunnewell property in West Needham (now Wellesley).[11] Beatrix Jones and other Sargent protegées visited the same famed country places both before and after Coffin's time at MIT.

After finishing her studies and spending the summer abroad in 1904, Coffin looked without success for a position in the offices of male landscape architects. Her interviewers all questioned her ability to supervise construction crews, although Beatrix Jones had been doing this successfully for some years. Finally, Coffin decided to "hang out her shingle" and seek out a clientele on her own. Since she could not afford to rent commercial space, Coffin and her mother moved into the National Arts Club at 15 Gramercy Park, where Coffin set up her first office. In 1906, she became a member of the American Society of Landscape Architects and received her first commission, a garden for Mr. and Mrs. Edward Sprague in Flushing, New York.[12]

In 1918, Coffin was made a Fellow of the ASLA and served the organization in many ways. She attended chapter and annual meetings regularly and was active on standing committees dedicated to exhibitions. Coffin also exhibited at the Architectural League of New York and received its Gold Medal in 1930.[13]

In 1920, Coffin became a member-at-large of the Garden Club of America and, in May of the same year, published an open letter to the membership in the *Bulletin*. Like Hutcheson, Coffin looked well beyond the still somewhat superficial aspects of this organization and, in the aftermath of World War I, emphasized the "opportunity for cooperation between the Garden Clubs, the Landscape Architects and the Local Village Improvement Societies which should open up all sorts of possibilities in the future for achievements of real value and real beauty."[14]

There is no record of the genesis of the Sprague project, but a second commission, the grounds of the William Bullitt residence in Oxmoor, Kentucky (1909–10) came to Coffin through Harry du Pont. Coffin had an exceptionally long career. From the Sprague commission in 1906 to a final visit to Winterthur in 1955, she was active for nearly fifty years. Coffin preferred to design the entire acreage of a property rather than discrete elements within it, a goal that she frequently, although not always, achieved.[15] In addition to her Long Island projects, some of the high points of Coffin's work were the Dr. J. Clifton Edgar property, Greenwich, Connecticut (1920); The Pavilion, Fort Ticonderoga, New York (1920–26); the Philip Marshall Brown residence in Princeton, New Jersey (1925); the Edgar W. Bassick property in Bridgeport, Connecticut (1927–45); and the New York Botanical Garden,

New York City (1948–53). Two major commissions for the du Pont family, either directly or indirectly, were the men's and women's campuses of Delaware College (1918–53), now the University of Delaware, and Winterthur (1911–13; 1928–55), a landscape that evolved over decades as the house itself evolved; it may be considered Coffin's masterpiece.[16]

Coffin's office expanded slowly. Her first professional employee seems to have been Elizabeth F. Colwell, who worked on the redesign of the formal garden at Winterthur between 1911 and 1913. A few years later, Coffin engaged James M. Scheiner, an architect and engineer, who worked for her briefly before serving in World War I. He returned in 1919 and continued to be associated with her for the rest of her career. This was a rare case, indeed quite extraordinary at the time, of a woman landscape architect employing a man directly rather than as a consultant. Like most other landscape architects, Coffin appears to have had little work until some time after the Armistice on November 11, 1918. Approximately a year later, she opened a "real little office" at 830 Lexington Avenue, where she welcomed back Scheiner and a new employee, Ethel D. Nevins, who was to become her chief planting supervisor until the late 1940s. By this time, Coffin and her mother were living at 73 East Ninety-second Street. In 1921, she bought a modest summer house, Wendover, in Watch Hill, Rhode Island, which she turned into a garden showplace and a frequent stop on Garden Club of America tours. The years leading up to the Depression were extremely successful for Coffin.[17]

In the late 1920s, Coffin suffered a serious hip infection, which was largely healed by 1927, although from that time on she used a cane. In the same year, she and her mother received a legacy that allowed them to purchase a house at 165 Bishop Street in New Haven, Connecticut, a city where they had numerous relatives. Every day, Coffin went into her New York office, which was now at One East Fifty-third Street. Her chauffeur, Jack Lambert, often drove her to site visits with clients, sometimes lifting her in and out of an open touring car when residual problems with her hip made this necessary. At 165 Bishop Street, Coffin transformed a small back yard into a charming outdoor space, where she held an annual spring garden party. She also held innumerable teas, cocktail parties, musicales, and buffet suppers. For the first time in her life, Coffin had both the physical space and the financial means to entertain elegantly.[18]

The relocation to New Haven was a fortunate move. The Depression soon required Coffin to retrench. She moved her part of the firm to New Haven, while Scheiner and Clara Stimson Coffey, a recent employee, remained in New York. Coffin also began to take in roomers, chief among them, starting in 1929, Warren Hunting Smith, who became her close friend, a virtual surrogate son, and the eventual savior of her archives.[19] In 1932, Coffin's mother died. An additional source of sadness to Coffin during these years was the fact that many of her clients could no longer afford to maintain the landscapes she had designed during the 1920s.[20]

During the Depression, Coffin proved to be a canny investor, buying common stocks at low prices, rather than investing only in conservative bonds. In addition to Smith and other regular boarders, groups of scholars rented the entire house at Bishop Street during the summer, bringing in further funds.[21]

Hip surgery in 1941 allowed Coffin to move more freely. She was also enjoying success with her second love, still life and botanical paintings, which were exhibited by the Studio Guild Gallery in New York City in 1942.[22] This creative work seems to have sustained her emotionally during the professionally dry years of World War II, although some landscape work continued to come into her office.[23]

Although Marian Coffin was close to seventy years old at the end of World War II, her postwar period was productive. Among her late works were the Foxcroft School in Middleburg, Virginia (1947–48), which again came her way through Harry du Pont; a tree-peony garden for Mrs. Daniel Ross in Wilmington, Delaware (1952); Mount Cuba for Mr. and Mrs. Lammot du Pont Copeland in Greenville, Delaware (1950); late projects at Winterthur and the New York Botanical Garden. In 1946, Coffin received the honorary degree of Doctor of Letters from Hobart and William Smith Colleges in Geneva, New York.[24]

Over the course of her career, Coffin published more than twenty articles in such periodicals as *House and Garden*, *House Beautiful*, and *Country Life in America*. A fortunate product of the Depression years was her first book, *Trees and Shrubs for Landscape Effects*, published in 1940.[25] Coffin did not want to add yet another flower gardening book to the many already on the market but instead wished to focus on the role of trees and shrubs: "Trees are to gardens what architectural features, such as spires, towers, and accented façades, are to buildings. A garden without trees is apt to be without interest, and a lawn without them to lack shadows which make so infinitely for variety. Too much emphasis has been laid by gardening books on the ephemeral value of color and color schemes, and too little on the enduring importance of sculptural form, which is given by trees and trees alone."[26]

Coffin discussed in detail the use of trees and shrubs in a variety of residential settings: in the approach to the house, surrounding the house, on lawns and terraces, along formal and informal walks, and in designed woodlands. As always, she emphasized the necessity of proper soil preparation. Extensive lists of appropriate plants were also provided. Today, when electric shears are almost universally used for pruning shrubs, Marian Coffin's words on the subject are telling:

> The shears in the hands of the average jobbing gardener are, indeed, a dangerous implement. As much devastation can be done in a few moments as will take an equal number of years to repair. This I have learned to my sorrow in having some gardens absolutely ruined whose main feature was the display of graceful free-growing shrubs—the idea of the unconscious devastator being apparently that any growth other than the regularity of a clipped hedge is untidy.[27]

In spite of the fact that she had a weak voice and was not a natural public speaker, Marian Coffin lectured frequently, especially to garden club audiences. In 1920, she offered five different lantern slide lectures on various aspects of gardening, for which she charged a fee of fifty dollars. (At the same time, Beatrix Farrand commanded seventy-five dollars for her talks.)[28] Although the maxim does not appear in any of her writings, Coffin liked to tell her audiences that a successful garden demanded "money, manure, and maintenance."[29]

Coffin was also an inveterate traveler who sometimes ventured to exotic locales. Shortly after completing her studies at MIT, she made one or possibly more trips to Europe and England with her mother and Harry du Pont. On one such trip, she may have met Edith Wharton through Walter Berry, a close friend of Wharton and a connection of the Coffin family.[30] In August 1907, the trio went to the Dalmatian coast of the Adriatic Sea, where they traveled under rough conditions but were rewarded by breathtaking views and drifts of native wildflowers. Coffin wrote an article about this trip for *National Geographic*, illustrated with her own photographs.[31] In 1931, despite the Depression, she took a group of friends to visit Italian gardens. In 1939, she went to Guatemala.[32] These were almost certainly not her only foreign trips.

In February 1954, Coffin wrote to Harry du Pont about her doctor's orders: "I must space jobs and take time between to rest up, but *not* think of retiring."[33] In fact, she seems never to have retired but to have stayed closely in touch with the New York Botanical Garden as well as remodeling a games court at Winterthur into a sundial garden.[34]

Coffin died in New Haven on February 2, 1957. An Episcopal service was held at 165 Bishop Street, after which she was buried at Island Cemetery, Newport, Rhode Island, where many of her relatives were also buried.[35]

Warren Hunting Smith bought 165 Bishop Street from Coffin's estate and lived there for the next thirty-two years, continuing the traditional mid-May garden parties.[36] Smith donated the papers, photographs, and plans that he found in the house to the Henry Francis du Pont Winterthur Museum. The manuscript of Coffin's second book, *Seeing Eye*, which she wrote in her late seventies, may have been lost when her cousin, Maria Trumball Dana, and her long-time secretary, Selina Appleyard, cleaned out 165 Bishop Street shortly after her death. About 1990, Smith gave the house to Yale University. More than thirty years after Coffin's death, an auctioneer for the university found an old Bergdorf Goodman box tucked away in a corner of the attic that Smith had apparently never penetrated. Filled not with dresses but with many additional photographs and plans of Coffin's work, the box was purchased by Mr. and Mrs. Richard C. Ballard, rare book collectors, who donated its contents to the Winterthur Library in 1992.[37]

We owe much to Smith and the Ballards. That said, there are some puzzling voids in the two collections at Winterthur, chiefly the almost total lack of plans and professional correspondence for all but the du Pont commissions.

There is ample photographic coverage of all of her work, much of it in the Ballard Collection. It is possible that Coffin herself did some "weeding," perhaps as early as her 1927 move to New Haven.

COFFIN DESIGNED seventeen projects on Long Island, and they are among her most interesting and ambitious works. Many of these projects are no longer extant, but there are some fortunate survivals. The formal garden at Clayton, the Childs Frick residence in Roslyn, now occupied by the Nassau County Museum of Art, was rehabilitated in 2000–2003. Restoration is also planned for the series of gardens at Hillwood, the Edward F. Hutton and Marjorie Merriweather Post residence in Wheatley Hills, now the property of C. W. Post University. Although, with the exception of Harry du Pont's Chesterton House in Southampton, there are no original plans or blueprints at Winterthur for Coffin's Long Island work, much of it was published. In addition, there are blueprints for Clayton in the archives of the Nassau County Museum of Art.

Marian Coffin's debut as a landscape architect was the Edward E. Sprague garden in Flushing, Long Island. The house was an existing structure on slightly more than an acre and a third of land. In 1912, Coffin wrote an article on this project for *Country Life in America*, which she illustrated with a plan and numerous photographs.[38] On her plan (fig. 4.2), Coffin drew arrows indicating the angles from which the photographs were taken, a technique pioneered in 1902 by her teacher Guy Lowell, which was regrettably adopted by few later landscape writers.[39]

Except for the frontage on Sanford Avenue, already endowed with a good lawn and specimen trees such as *Cornus florida rubra* (pink flowering dogwood) and *Halesia tetraptera* (silverbell), and a stable and chicken run at the rear of the lot, which Coffin screened, the entire landscape was reworked. Since the Spragues had a summer place elsewhere, the plantings were chosen for color in spring and fall. The main lawn was planned as a play area for the Sprague children as well as a gathering place for the entire family. In addition to the trees in front of the house, there were a few good specimen trees to the rear.

Coffin's general layout was quite simple, but it was sufficiently varied that the garden appeared larger than it actually was.[40] Coffin created a cruciform plan: a gravel path planted with peonies ran directly from the rear porch on the east side of the house to a cross path, where she concentrated some of the most effective displays of bloom. On each side of the cross path were wide, irregularly shaped flower beds varying from 10 to 15 feet in depth. On one side (fig. 4.3) were irises and tulips, with fillers of spring-blooming perennials, and on the other side was a blue border planted with dwarf iris, lilac phlox (*Phlox divaricata*), and, later, blue lupines and larkspur. The iris display lasted six weeks. At the intersection of the two paths, Coffin positioned white lilacs and tree peonies because she felt that it was very important that there be variety in the height of plants in a small garden. By 1918, a rustic arbor covered with climbing roses had been built at the intersecting

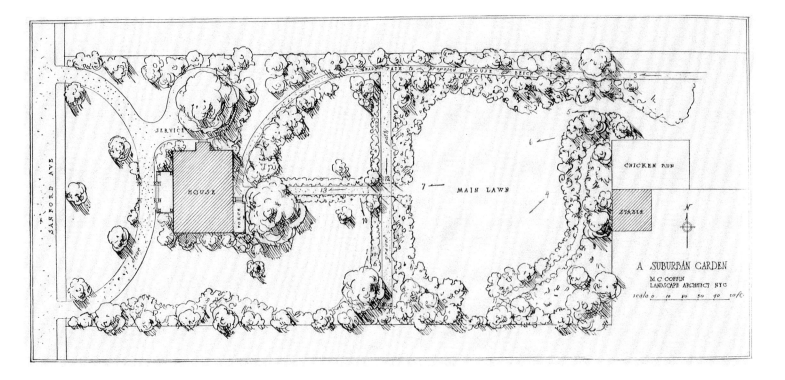

4.2 *Plan of the Sprague residence, Flushing, New York, ca. 1906.* From *Country Life in America,* February 15, 1912

paths. In a pink border north and west of the main lawn, she planted the salmon-rose tulip Clara Butt and the Japanese flowering crab (*Pyrus floribunda*). In early summer, pink lupines, sweet william, canterbury bells, poppies, and hollyhocks bloomed in this bed. Also featured was the popular white phlox Miss Lingard. There was also a "red" bed containing Ghent and Mollis azaleas, red tulips, and Oriental poppies. In early spring, drifts of narcissus and other bulbs naturalized in the grass bloomed underneath the trees bordering the main lawn (fig. 4.4).[41]

The Spragues recognized that Coffin needed to make regular field visits to their garden to make sure that the intended effects of color and massing were maintained.[42] All landscape architects, including Olmsted, recommended repeat visits to private properties, although clients did not always understand the necessity of such visits—a perpetual problem for landscape architects.

At some point after 1916, Coffin designed the grounds of the William H. Woodin house on Lily Pond Lane in East Hampton. The house, which is extant, and double gardener's cottage, are attributed to Grosvenor Atterbury. Unfortunately, this project was never published, and there is no landscape plan. The one photograph located to date (fig. 4.5), while stunning, leaves many questions unanswered. Within the angle of the wings is a garden enclosed by a hedge, probably of privet. Although it seems to contain some topiary, no other plantings are visible. Roses tumble over a wall to the right. An opening in the hedge leads to a large garden decorated with a birdbath. To the lower left and taking up most of the space in the photograph are masses of flowers growing in meadow-like profusion. Whether these are a continuation of the birdbath garden or are perhaps a cutting garden cannot be determined.[43]

In 1919, Coffin laid out the grounds of Bayberryland, the Charles H. Sabin property on Peconic Bay next to the National Golf Links in the Shinnecock Hills. Sabin was the chairman of the Guaranty Trust Company of New York. Cross and Cross designed the English-style manor house, and Coffin collaborated closely with the firm.[44] By carefully adjusting the roof lines, Coffin and the architects kept the house as low as possible to avoid breaking up the horizontal line of the surrounding land. They also set it a little below the edge of the slope of the area where the landscape treatment would be concentrated.[45]

Coffin's design for Bayberryland (fig. 4.6) was a tour de force of spatial and environmental planning. Although the overall property totalled 314 acres, the landscaped area took up a relatively small part of it. Flat, windswept, and sandy, the site was bleak. To approach the house, visitors passed under an arch in the garage, which doubled as a gate lodge. On the side facing Peconic Bay, there were three major landscape units: a flat grass terrace on axis with the principal façade, and a flower garden on axis with the angled living room wing. Both of these areas were walled, although the far end of the flower garden was enclosed only by a hedge (fig. 4.7). Nestled into the irregular piece of land between them was the third major element—"The Tritoma Path," or "The Path to the Sea"—a curving flagstone walk lined with red and orange tritoma (poker plant or "red hot" pokers) set off by wide swathes of gray-foliaged plants (fig. 4.8).

In addition, there were also smaller garden areas on the grounds, including a rose garden, a sundial garden, and a playing field. The Sabins had not one but two sundials, one in the form of a crowing cock and the other an armillary sphere.[46] Coffin's greatest triumph at Bayberryland was perhaps the formal flower garden with its circular and rectan-

4.3 *Cross path at the Sprague Residence, Flushing. Photograph, W. H. Wallace.* From *Country Life in America*, February 15, 1912

4.4 *Spring bulbs naturalized in the grass, Sprague Residence, Flushing. Photograph.* From Ruth Dean, *The Livable House: Its Garden*, 1917

4.5 *Garden, William H.
Woodin Residence, East
Hampton. Photograph,
Samuel Gottscho, ca. 1928.*
From *East Hampton's
Heritage*

gular pools. Two medium-sized American elms were brought in to mark the middle distance, and the central part of the more distant Peconic Bay view was framed by an arched gate that acted as an "eye-catcher" (fig. 4.9). She also reconfigured the sand dunes just beyond the gardens and stabilized them with beach grass and other salt-water-resistant plantings. In order for Coffin to create these magical gardens by the sea, the Sabins had to buy a nearby farm and strip it of all its topsoil.[47]

After Charles Sabin died, his widow, Pauline, married Dwight F. Davis, founder of the Davis Cup.[48] In 1949, she sold Bayberryland to the Joint Industry Board of the Electrical Industry, to be used as a convalescent home for members of Local 3 International Brotherhood of Electrical Workers. A few years later, the house was expanded to serve additionally as an educational center and summer camp. In 1969, 120 motel-style units were constructed to augment the convalescent facilities. As of 1983, the house and at least the outlines of some of the landscaped areas survived.[49] In 2002, the property was purchased by a developer. By 2005, the house and surrounding landscape had been demolished. The developer has turned the site into an "organic" golf course.[50]

In the late teens, Coffin also designed a garden for Mr. and Mrs. J. Harry Alexandre in Glen Head. The site, or at least the part of it that Coffin landscaped, was not large, probably no more than half an acre at most. The design in fig. 4.10 is described as Coffin's "first" plan, indicating that changes were almost certainly made. As with the Sprague garden, existing trees on the street frontage were retained.[51] The main feature of the Alexandre garden was a long path through rose and perennial borders, each border backed by an arborvitae hedge. The path terminated in a white bench in front of a decorative trellis (fig. 4.11). Running parallel to the main path to its east was another grass path. Off to the west of the main path was a "little bird lawn," with a central fountain and oval pool, along with a single bench, all enclosed within a picket fence.[52]

The plantings along the main path (fig. 4.12) are of exceptional interest. After a circular space just beyond the rear of the house is a rose garden, containing a mixture of old fashioned varieties in each of its four quadrants. In the borders beyond, Coffin planted drifts of summer-blooming perennials: hollyhocks, delphiniums, hibiscus, salvia, daylilies, lupines, lilies, and so on. In the front section of the borders, spilling over onto the path, were low growing flowers like veronica. The overall color scheme was predominantly blue, yellow, orange, and white.

In 1920, Coffin began landscaping the Winter Cottage at Caumsett, the property of Marshall Field III on Lloyd Neck. The Caumsett commission, on which she worked for the next three years, helped initiate a major expansion of her practice. Scheiner, who before joining Coffin had been a draftsman for John Russell Pope, architect of both the Winter Cottage and the main house at Caumsett, may have been instrumental in bringing this job into the office.[53] The Fields lived in the Winter Cottage until the main house was completed; it presumably housed their guests after that point.

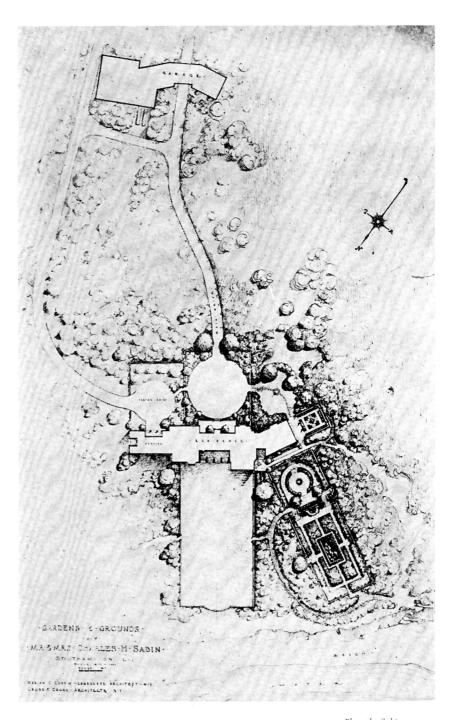

4.6 *Plan, the Sabin Residence, Southampton, New York. Photograph, ca. 1919.* From P. H. Elwood, *American Landscape Architecture*, 1924

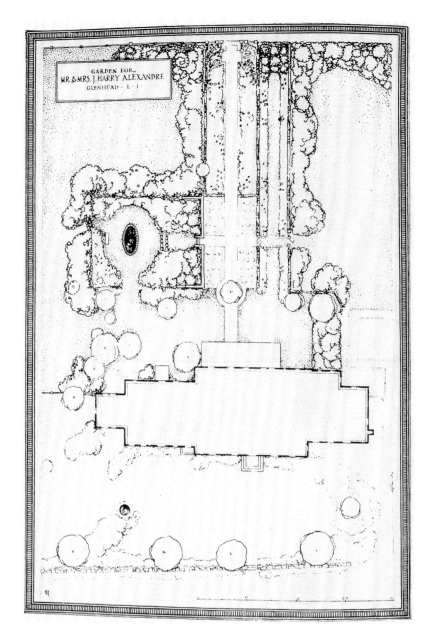

4.10 *Plan for the J. Harry Alexandre Residence, Glen Head.* From *House and Garden,* October 1920.

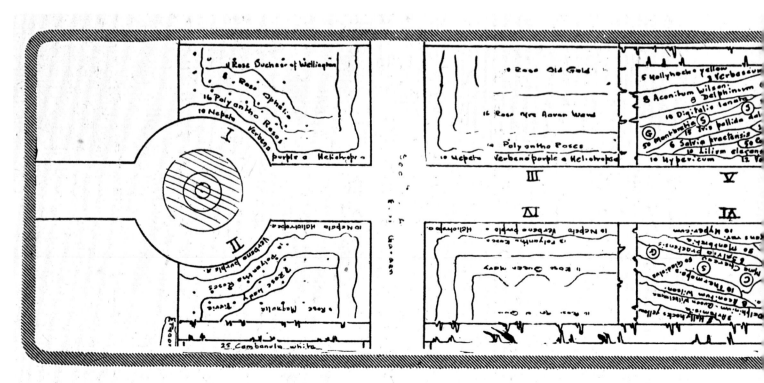

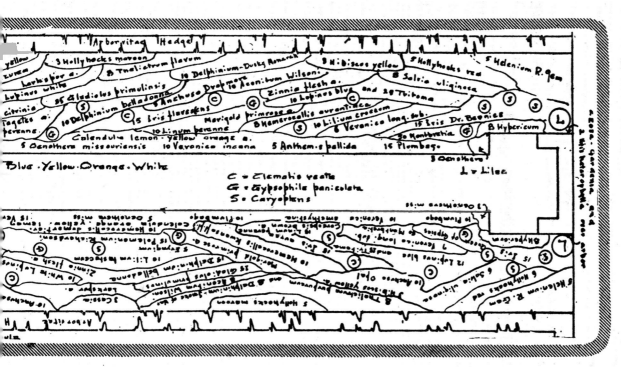

4.13 *Evergreen garden, Winter Cottage, Marshall Field Residence, Lloyd Neck. Photograph, Mattie Edwards Hewitt, ca. 1928.* Courtesy, Henry Francis du Pont Winterthur Museum, Winterthur, Wilmington, Delaware.

The overall layout of the 2,000-acre grounds of Caumsett was a brilliant scheme that must be credited to Pope, along with his associated architects Warren and Wetmore.[54] The design and construction of this huge property (more than twice as large as Central Park) was so complex that it required an organizational chart headed by a business office and divided between design and engineering, each with its own field office. In Pope's view, landscaping, gardening, and fine grading seemed to be fairly low in the pecking order, since these activities were relegated to the bottom tiers of the chart.[55]

No Coffin plans seem to have survived for the Winter Cottage garden, but there are numerous photographs at Winterthur and elsewhere. The stone cottage was in a secluded spot, shaded by oaks and other old trees, just off the main approach road. Although she apparently planted drifts of spring bulbs at Winter Cottage, the shady conditions and acid soil at the site probably were a major factor in Coffin's decision to make this predom-

inantly an evergreen garden. A carriage sweep led to the front of the house, which was landscaped only with foundation plants and some (probably existing) trees. At the rear, stone steps led down to a circular garden planted primarily with mountain laurel and overhung by the mature trees. A flagstone path enclosed the perimeter of the garden, and in its center was a small circle of English ivy with a figure of Pan set in the middle (figs. 4.13 and 4.14).

In 1924, John Russell Pope asked Olmsted Brothers to collaborate on tree planting at Caumsett. The Olmsted firm, concerned that there might be an impediment because of Coffin's prior involvement, at first demurred.[56] Coffin would surely have welcomed this opportunity, but she either bowed out or, more likely, was never approached by Pope. In addition to the tree planting, for which Hicks Nurseries moved fully grown trees to the site by barge, the Olmsted firm eventually designed a flower garden, a rock garden, and the surroundings of the indoor tennis court for the

4.14 *Evergreen garden, Winter
Cottage, Marshall Field Residence,
Lloyd Neck. Photograph, Mattie
Edwards Hewitt, ca. 1931.* From
American Society of Landscape
Architects, *Work of Members*, 1932

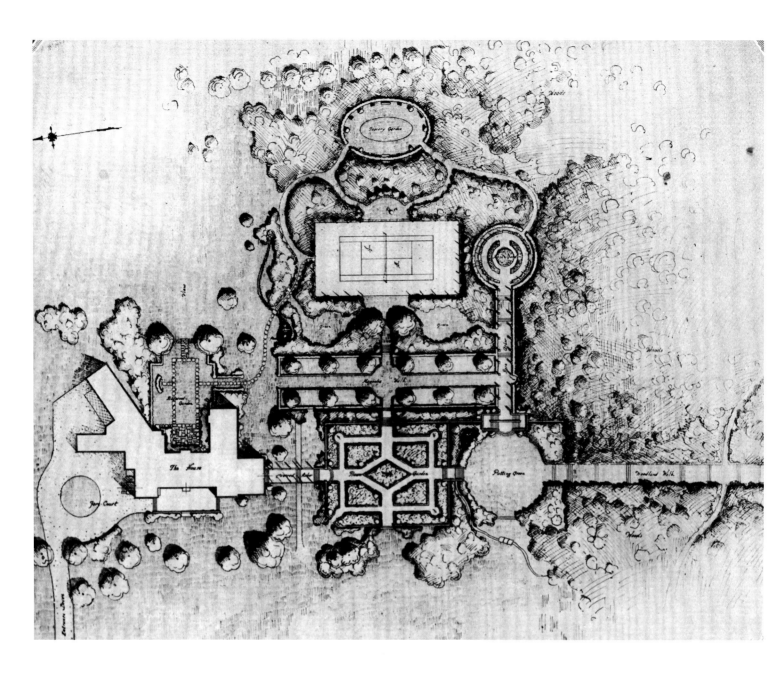

Fields. Caumsett is now a state park. The Winter Cottage still stands, but Coffin's plantings have not survived.

In 1921 and 1922, Coffin designed one of her most remarkable projects on Long Island: the grounds of Hillwood, the home of Mr. and Mrs. Edward F. Hutton in Brookville. Mrs. Hutton, the former Marjorie Merriweather Post, was the daughter of Charles W. Post, founder of the Postum Cereal Company, which eventually became the General Foods Corporation. After the death of her father in 1914, Marjorie, at the age of twenty-seven, inherited the firm. In 1920, she married Edward F. Hutton, a New York stockbroker who founded E. F. Hutton and Company. The Huttons divorced in 1935, and, after three subsequent marriages and divorces, Marjorie took back her maiden name and was known thereafter as Mrs. Marjorie Merriweather Post.[57]

Shortly after their marriage, the Huttons began making plans for a summer place in Brookville, commissioning Charles M. Hart of Hart & Shape, a New York firm, to design a rambling, half-timbered, Tudor-style house. Eventually, a second house for one of Mrs. Post's daughters and numerous outbuildings were built on the property.[58]

Coffin began her landscape plans while the house was being designed. She envisioned not a single garden but a series of interlocking landscape units that either related closely to the principal living spaces of the house or that led away from it up a steep rise to the east (fig. 4.15).[59] Wedged between two wings on the east side of the house was a "boxwood court." Meandering away from this formal area was a diminutive, stone-edged stream built over an existing small road that was eliminated in Coffin's scheme (fig. 4.16). Water for the stream came from the overflow of the ice box. When the photograph in fig. 4.16 was taken, irises were in season and blooming abundantly. As in other parts of the Hutton property, all of the trees were moved in by Lewis and Valentine at the size shown in the early photographs. Large box bushes were similarly transplanted for instant effect.[60]

A covered arbor at the south end of the house led

directly into what Coffin called the "English Brick Garden." Figure 4.17 shows this garden at "tulip time," although only the tulip part of the scheme had been completed; the yews clipped into topiary shapes that appear in later photographs had not yet been installed. Beyond the English garden was a putting green, golf being a sport that the Huttons enjoyed. Beyond that was a woodland vista, its terminus indistinct, which was framed by laurels, rhododendrons, and "other woodloving [sic] plants." Coffin felt that "landscapes should suggest the mystery of unseen areas . . . much as life itself presents the constant suspense of leading on to an unpredictable future."[61]

One of the simplest and most charming elements in the Hutton grounds was the magnolia walk, consisting only of two rows of *Magnolia soulangeana* (saucer magnolias), low box hedging, and grass, backed on each side by a high arborvitae hedge (fig. 4.18).[62] At the south end of the walk was a brick rose arbor (fig. 4.19), which led up to a circular rose garden surrounded by brick posts connected to

each other by chains and by brick benches pierced with oval openings. To the north of the rose garden was a tennis court.[63] To the east of this, at the highest elevation, an oval topiary garden was planned. There are no photographs of this garden, and it may not have been built.[64]

Coffin's series of interwoven garden spaces at Hillwood is one of her most impressive achievements. In contrast to her experience at Caumsett, she achieved her ideal of designing an entire property, or at least all of the land in the immediate vicinity of the house. In the 1950s, Hillwood was acquired by Long Island University, and the house is now an administrative center on the C. W. Post campus. Much of the hardscape of Coffin's design remains, although the plantings are no longer those that she specified.[65] Virtually the entire area could be successfully restored, and such work is planned by the university. As of December 2007, work on the house has been completed, and restoration of the landscape will commence in 2008.[66]

4.16 *Edward F. Hutton Residence, Brookville. Photograph, Mattie Edwards Hewitt, undated.* Courtesy, Ballard Collection, Henry Francis du Pont Winterthur Museum, Winterthur, Wilmington, Delaware

4.17 *English Brick Garden, Edward F. Hutton Residence, Brookville. Photograph, Mattie Edwards Hewitt, undated.* Courtesy, Ballard Collection, Henry Francis du Pont Winterthur Museum, Winterthur, Wilmington, Delaware

4.18 *Looking down magnolia walk, Edward F. Hutton Residence, Brookville. Photograph, Mattie Edwards Hewitt, undated.* Courtesy, Ballard Collection, Henry Francis du Pont Winterthur Museum, Winterthur, Wilmington, Delaware.

4.19 *Rose arbor, Edward F. Hutton Residence, Brookville. Photograph, undated.* Courtesy, Ballard Collection, Henry Francis du Pont Winterthur Museum, Winterthur, Wilmington, Delaware

In 1923, Coffin designed a garden at Wind Swept, the Albert B. Boardman residence, in Southampton. This was the Boardmans' second house and garden in the town; they had previously built Villa Mille Fiore, modeled on the sixteenth-century Villa Medici in Rome. Wind Swept was designed by Polhemus and Coffin on another site in Southampton after the sale of Villa Mille Fiore.[67] Like many gardens on this part of Long Island, Wind Swept was enclosed within a brick wall to protect it from brisk ocean breezes. This garden consisted of at least eight flowerbeds planted for summer bloom and separated by grass paths (fig. 4.20). While there is no planting plan for Wind Swept or specific written information about the individual flowers that Coffin used, the photographs show a considerable quantity of white phlox.

Between 1924 and 1928, Coffin landscaped the grounds of Chesterton House in Southampton for Harry du Pont and his wife, Ruth. In December 1925, Coffin asked du Pont to clarify her position with the architects, Cross and Cross, and to confirm in writing "that I am to take entire charge of the landscape grading, dune building, soil preparation, planting, as well as any paths not already shown under the contract for the roads."[68] This stipulation suggests that Coffin's earlier collaboration with the firm at Bayberryland may not have been entirely free of problems. Of the approximately twenty-seven plans for this property at Winterthur, most are strictly architectural plans or are signed jointly by Cross and Cross and Coffin. Oddly, no photographs seem to exist. Chesterton House was located right on the sand dunes, which were individually numbered by Coffin. Chesterton House is extant; the status of the grounds is unknown.

Beginning in 1925, Coffin designed portions of the grounds of Clayton, the Childs Frick residence, in Roslyn, including the formal (sometimes called the Colonial or Georgian) garden, one of Coffin's most acclaimed works. In addition, she designed a spring garden, an azalea garden, and a Zodiac Garden on the property. The Georgian Revival brick house, designed by Ogden Codman, on two hundred acres of land was a wedding present from Frick's father, Henry Clay Frick, a cofounder of U. S. Steel. Childs Frick was a paleontologist who served many years as a trustee of the American Museum of Natural History and the renowned Frick Collection. At Clayton, Frick added two new tennis courts, one clay and one grass, as well as a new practice polo field on the site of a former vegetable garden. Next to the polo field was a large rectangular flower garden, a legacy from the previous owners, the Lloyd Bryces.[69]

This garden, measuring 450 feet long, was enclosed within high privet hedges and subdivided into four sections by yew hedges. Grass paths crossed the garden on each of its major axes and met at a high circular bed of roses.[70] In 1922, Clarence Fowler prepared a conceptual sketch for redesigning the garden, which the Fricks did not accept.[71]

Three years later, the Fricks contacted Coffin, who proposed a greatly strengthened scheme for the garden without radically reconfiguring its major spaces. The basic

4.20 *Boardman walled garden from above, Southampton, New York. Photograph, Mattie Edwards Hewitt, undated.* Courtesy, Ballard Collection, Henry Francis du Pont Winterthur Museum, Winterthur, Wilmington, Delaware

system of two cross paths and four quadrants containing garden rooms was retained. The greatest change was in the center where the mounded roses were removed and replaced with a still, circular pool, which caught pristine reflections of the trees and shrubs encircling it and of the new pleached privet bower that Coffin designed for one of the principal entrances (fig. 4.21). Within the quadrants were scrolls and hedges of low, trimmed box and parterres of roses and other flowers (fig. 4.22). In 1931, the Fricks invited three firms, including Coffin, to submit plans for a garden pavilion. The Fricks did not select Coffin's design but instead chose an airy treillage structure by the New York firm Milliken and Bevin. At the opposite end of the garden, near its main entrance to the north, Coffin designed an ante-garden consisting of flowering trees and shrubs arranged naturalistically.[72]

The extent to which Coffin's plan was carried out, in particular her specific planting recommendations, is difficult to determine. After 1935, Mrs. Frick depended increasingly on Dorothy Nicholas, an amateur gardener who at some point made the transition into professional design, and did not continue to retain Coffin.[73] Nicholas apparently made many planting changes.[74] Samuel Gottscho photographed the formal garden at Clayton in July 1931 (figs. 4.21 and 4.22). He returned in 1939 and 1949, and in these later photographs it is difficult to identify which

plantings are Coffin's, which are Dorothy Nicholas's, and which may have been added by Mrs. Frick.

A particularly striking design by Coffin was the Zodiac Garden (fig. 4.23), which is extant, although the materials and the pattern of the stone were changed in the 1990s. The formal garden retains the basic outline of Coffin's design, while taking into consideration the needs of the Nassau County Museum of Art.

Coffin's design for Crossways, the W. W. Benjamin residence in East Hampton, was apparently completed by 1928. Crossways included a perennial garden with a privet arch, a small pool, and a long grass allée (fig. 4.24). Another relatively late project was the Irving Brokaw residence in Mill Neck, completed about 1930. This landscape, designed in association with Scheiner, included a box terrace next to the house. A long vista, framed by more box shrubs, terminated in a pool and views of distant hills

FACING PAGE
4.23 *The Zodiac Garden at Clayton, the Childs Frick Residence, Roslyn. Photograph, ca. 1931.* From American Society of Landscape Architects, New York Chapter, *Ninth Annual Exhibition,* 1932

4.24 *Perennial garden, Crossways, the Mrs. W. W. Benjamin Residence, East Hampton. Photograph, Mattie Edwards Hewitt, September 1928.* LISI, 5687.242

AMENYA

4.25 *View from upper terrace, Mr. and Mrs. Irving Brokaw Residence, Mill Neck. Photograph, Yosei Amemya, ca. 1930.* Courtesy, Henry Francis du Pont Winterthur Museum, Winterthur, Wilmington, Delaware

framed in the middle distance by existing oaks (to the left) and an American elm (right), the latter moved in to balance the oaks (fig. 4.25). Olmsted Brothers appears to have had some involvement with the Brokaw property (job number 6297), although the date and extent of the firm's work there is unknown, and they appear to have drawn no plans for the Brokaws.[75]

At an unknown date, Coffin designed a very interesting garden consisting of a series of concentric ovals for James Blackstone Taylor in Oyster Bay (fig. 4.26). Probably in the late 1920s, she designed a large perennial garden for Mr. and Mrs. Eric MacDonald in Southampton (fig. 4.27), with an adjacent grass terrace.[76] At about the same time, she laid out a distinctive flowering shrub garden with a large central pool for Mr. and Mrs. W. Allston Flagg in Westbury (fig. 4.28).[77]

4.26 *Garden, James Blackstone Taylor Residence, Oyster Bay. Photograph, George H. Van Anda, undated.* Courtesy, Henry Francis du Pont Winterthur Museum, Winterthur, Wilmington, Delaware

4.27 *Perennial garden, Mr. and Mrs. Eric MacDonald Residence, Southampton. Photograph, ca. late 1920s.* Courtesy, Henry Francis du Pont Winterthur Museum, Winterthur, Wilmington, Delaware

4.28 *Flowering shrub garden with large pool, Mr. and Mrs. W. Allston Flagg Residence, Westbury. Photograph, ca. 1930.* From American Society of Landscape Architects, New York Chapter, *Yearbook*, 1931

Within the strict context of early twentieth-century American landscape architecture, Marian Coffin may be said to have fulfilled her youthful aspiration to become a great artist. The consistently high quality of her work, her profound knowledge of trees and shrubs, and her mastery of three-dimensional design make her one of the most distinguished landscape architects of her era. Such achievement was earned by constant application and meticulous attention to detail throughout her long career. Looking back in 1932, she wrote to Clarence Fowler:

We were pioneers, and moreover pioneer women in a new–old profession and one in which all one's ability to see and interpret beauty out of doors taxed all our resources, and we were determined to show what enthusiasm and hard work could accomplish.[78]

CHAPTER 5

Ellen Biddle Shipman

1869–1950

ELLEN MCGOWAN BIDDLE was born on November 5, 1869 in Philadelphia, the first daughter and third child of Ellen Fish McGowan Biddle and Colonel (later General) James Biddle, a career soldier. Her mother's family came from Elizabeth, New Jersey, while her father was a member of the illustrious Philadelphia Biddle clan.[1] Ellen married Louis Shipman in 1893; she continued to use the Shipman name after their divorce in 1900.

Unlike Farrand, Hutcheson, and Coffin, whose childhood summers were spent in the pastoral surroundings of New England and upstate New York, the young Ellen Biddle's first memories were of frontier outposts in Nevada, Colorado, and the Arizona Territory, where her father was stationed. The family enjoyed exploring nearby deserts and canyons, where Ellen saw what an easterner would consider exotic vegetation, including mesquite and acacia trees and many varieties of cactus.[2] Fine gardening was not an option in this environment, but Colonel Biddle arranged for water to be brought in from a great distance to nourish the young trees that he had planted along the drives of their Nevada post—the only trees in the vicinity. On their first trip east to visit their grandparents, Captain and Mrs. John McGowan, in New Jersey, Ellen and her brothers were excited to see gardens and cultivated fruit trees for the first time.[3]

When Ellen was six years old, her brothers were sent to school in Connecticut, but she remained at Fort Whipple in the Arizona Territory with her parents. When she was ten, Ellen was sent to school in New Jersey and, for the first time, enjoyed extended exposure to gardens and garden-

ing.[4] She was overjoyed to find a "real garden" at her grandparents' house and, as an adult, credited them and her father with implanting in her "a deep love of growing things."[5] To a young girl who had spent her formative years in the rugged surroundings of the Far West, the highly cultivated landscapes of the northeastern United States must have seemed immensely appealing but also totally artificial.

When Ellen reached adolescence, she was sent to finishing school at Miss Sarah Randolph's in Baltimore, Maryland. As noted in chapter 1, her artistic talents were recognized by the headmistress, who awarded her an architectural dictionary as a history prize. As she later wrote, "It is such seeds that blossom into plants."[6]

Between 1887 and 1889, Ellen's father was posted to the War Department in Washington, D.C., where, as her mother observed, the young woman "tasted to the full . . . all that a society life could give her."[7] During the academic year 1892–93, she attended "The Society for the Collegiate Instruction of Women" of Harvard University, informally known as the "Annex," which, a year later, was officially named Radcliffe College.[8] While in Cambridge, Ellen shared a rented house with several other young women. She took only an introductory philosophy course, in which she performed poorly.[9] Her interest in philosophy seems to have arisen unexpectedly. Indeed, the fact that she went to a "finishing" school suggests that she and her parents had not anticipated college-level education.

Ellen certainly had the ability to do well at Radcliffe, but she may have been distracted by meeting her future

husband, Louis Evans Shipman, who was at Harvard College. Louis, the son of a New York City contractor, had previously attended Brooklyn Polytechnic Institute. The two were married in October 1893 and shortly thereafter moved to Connecticut. Their first child, also named Ellen Biddle Shipman, was born in August 1894.[10]

The following August, Ellen and Louis Shipman made their first visit to the quiet village of Cornish, New Hampshire. After 1885, when the sculptor Augustus Saint-Gaudens, his wife Augusta, and son Homer settled there, Cornish had become a much sought after summer colony for artists including Charles A. Platt, Stephen Parrish, and Thomas and Maria Dewing. These artists were in turn succeeded by writers and those who, like Louis Shipman, had literary aspirations. Rose Standish Nichols, niece of Augusta Saint-Gaudens, became a distinguished landscape designer and garden writer (see chapter 8). Beginning with Saint-Gaudens, who created his own landscaped environment at Aspet, the Cornish colonists developed gardens that were widely published and much admired.[11]

Initially, the Shipmans shared a farmhouse with the writer and editor Herbert Croly and his wife. They then rented an old brick tavern, which they renamed Poins House, where Ellen planted her first garden, and Louis wrote stories and plays that won critical acclaim but did not bring in much money. The Shipman family grew: a son, Evan, was born in 1904, followed four years later by a second daughter, Mary. The educational opportunities offered in Cornish at the time were located some distance from Poins House, so Shipman homeschooled all of her children.[12]

In 1903, the Shipmans purchased the John Gilkey farm in Plainfield, a town adjacent to Cornish. Ellen finally put her talents in architectural and garden design to a specific use. Brook Place, as the Shipmans renamed their new property, was a late-eighteenth-century homestead, which included a cottage and a barn; it was bordered by a brook. The couple's first plans were for a modest remodeling of the cottage to be followed by the construction of an entirely new house. Following the Panic of 1907, the Shipmans decided instead on an expansion of the existing cottage that nearly doubled its size. Although Ellen's architectural plans were developed by Charles Platt's office, there seems to have been no personal involvement by Platt in the landscape at Brook Place. Shipman's design of the grounds, which included an extensive lawn, a tennis court, and a large flower garden, followed on the heels of the architectural plans. The garden reached its peak around 1923, when it was photographed in a series of remarkable views by Mattie Edwards Hewitt. Shipman's Cornish garden was her laboratory. As she wrote much later: "Working daily in my garden for fifteen years . . . taught me to know plants, their habits and their needs."[13]

It was Platt who recognized Shipman's innate design ability. Platt also came to appreciate the depth of her horticultural knowledge, an expertise that he himself lacked. Near the end of her life, Shipman described how he became her mentor:

After going to Cornish to live and after planning innumerable houses for desirable and unprocurable sites, I was working on still another plan when we spent the winter of 1899 in Charles and Eleanor Platt's house . . . and Mr. Platt was good enough to say that I might use his studio, which was at that time in his house. . . . I had forgotten and left my drawings on his board. For Christmas I received a drawing board, T square and all necessary drafting implements and fastened to the board was Charles Platt's card and written on it: 'If you can do as well as I saw, you better keep on.'. . . The tools have been worked hard for over forty years.[14]

Subsequently one of Platt's assistants taught her to use the tools more expertly. Before long, Shipman was preparing planting plans for many of Platt's numerous residential commissions. During this period, the Shipmans' marriage, which had been faltering for some time, failed irretrievably.[15]

As a young woman, Shipman does not seem initially to have been propelled by the same single-minded drive for artistic expression that fired Farrand, Hutcheson, and Coffin. Instead, the career that she more or less "fell into" ultimately proved her economic, emotional, and creative salvation.

Clarence Fowler might well have asked Shipman for an account of her early years in her profession, but, for reasons unknown, he did not. Beyond Platt's well-timed encouragement and tutelage, there is no explicit record of what motivated her to seek out this particular vocation. It would be nice to know—but we probably never shall—whether Shipman would have become a landscape architect if her marriage had not failed or whether she would instead have continued to confine her energies and talents to Brook Place. In the early 1940s, she wrote a friend, "Each year—each day you spend alone only makes you see the future—I know—I have found work to be the only help—except for my children and grandchildren."[16]

Before establishing her own practice, Shipman collaborated extensively with Platt, an "apprenticeship" that probably began around 1910. Her work for Platt was not confined to horticulture; she also prepared construction drawings for walls, pools, and garden structures. With Platt's advice, she also began to build a garden library. Platt and Shipman's first documented collaboration was at Fynmere, the summer property of James Fenimore Cooper II in Cooperstown, New York, where Shipman had primary responsibility for the garden design. This garden also featured a sculpture by Herbert Adams, a Cornish summer resident. Another joint project was The Causeway, the James Parmalee residence in Washington, D.C. (1914), where portions of Shipman's walled garden can still be discerned. Yet another was the Fahnestock property in Katonah, New York, where around 1912 Shipman succeeded Olmsted Brothers. In 1915, Shipman made plans for the Merrill property in Seattle, Washington, which Platt had initially laid out six years earlier. In 1919, Shipman began working on a Platt project in Grosse Pointe, Michigan, the first of forty-four commissions that Shipman would ultimately carry out in this wealthy cluster of Detroit suburbs. Shipman's documented collaborations with Platt number at least ten, with many more likely. By the time Shipman undertook an independent practice, nineteen of her clients were also clients of Platt and were undoubtedly referred to her by him. She continued to work with Platt through the 1920s.[17]

After about two years working with Platt, Shipman began accepting projects on her own. The first phase of her independent career extended roughly from 1912 through 1919. In contrast to Platt's architectural approach, which frequently involved radically reshaping the ground, Shipman preferred to "design as nearly as possible to the existing grades."[18] She also advised designers to "remember that the design of your place is its skeleton upon which you later plant your picture. Keep that skeleton as simple as possible."[19] Throughout her career, she consistently adhered to the axial approach to design that she had learned from Platt, although she generally departed from his tendency to recontour the land. Shipman's planting plans were exceptionally detailed, and she consistently included complete horticultural instructions, often written directly on the plan.[20]

One of Shipman's most remarkable projects was Grahampton, the Henry Croft residence in Greenwich, Connecticut (1917). The existing grounds, which had been designed by James L. Greenleaf, were left in place, while Shipman designed three new landscape areas, all diminutive in scale. All three were enclosed, and none was visible from the Greenleaf spaces or from each other. It is evident from this project and others that Shipman's mastery of planting design continued to develop and strengthen during her first decade of independent practice.[21]

During the years of her collaborations with Platt and for some time thereafter, Shipman ran her office out of Brook Place, where she then lived year round. As her practice grew and made increasing demands on her time, she was fortunate to have an able and willing mother's helper in her elder daughter Ellen, who, while still a teenager, took on considerable responsibility for her younger brother and sister and for running the household.[22] By 1920, Brook Place was no longer the most convenient location for Shipman's practice. By this time, her youngest child, Mary, aged twelve, was attending boarding school. Shipman purchased a corner-lot town house on Beekman Place in New York City that overlooked the East River. Architects Butler and Corse remodelled the building for Shipman's varied needs: an office, a private residence, and two other apartments (probably income-generating), all of them functionally separate. Clients who entered at Beekman Place had no contact with comings and goings at the private quarters on East Fiftieth Street.[23]

Like Farrand, Hutcheson, and Coffin, Shipman developed geographical nodes of patronage, with clusters of clients in Greenwich, Connecticut; Grosse Pointe, Michigan; Mount Kisco, New York, and a total of fifty-nine projects on Long Island (not all of them executed).[24] She also designed numerous projects in the affluent suburbs of Pittsburgh.[25]

Shipman's office staff also expanded. Like Farrand and Hutcheson, she employed women exclusively, several of whom later went on to start on their own firms. (Prejudices were still sufficiently entrenched that male applicants were unlikely to approach women practitioners.) Some of Shipman's employees started out in Cornish and then accompanied her to New York. Toward the end of her life, Shipman paid tribute to these women:

> I must express my gratitude to the group of young women, nearly all Lowthorpe graduates, who made my work possible. Elizabeth Leonard, now Mrs. Robert Strang, who was not only my first assistant, but who taught me every day she was with me,—a graduate of Cornell, later instructor at Lowthorpe. She was loved and admired by all who knew her. Louise Jocelyn, now Mrs. Julian Clark. Our profession lost a great talent when she married, and I the daily companionship of a beloved friend. Then Louise Payson came fresh from Lowthorpe, so young and full of ability, and after twelve years with me, started out brilliantly for herself. Also Florence Stroh, the most competent head of an office one could imagine, and finally, Frances McCormic, without whom work during old age would have been impossible. There have been many more. . . ."[26]

In addition to those Shipman mentioned here, her assistants included Eleanor Hills Christie, Dorothy May Anderson, Edith Schryver, Mary P. Cunningham, and Agnes Selkirk Clark.[27]

As explained in chapter 1, educational methods at Lowthorpe stressed the design of English-style perennial borders, a form and style that Shipman found sympathetic. She also felt that the overall training at the school was "unsurpassed."

Shipman ran her office in much the same way as did Farrand, Hutcheson, Coffin, and most male landscape architects of the period.[28] As did most of the other landscape architects, Shipman generally subcontracted out engineering aspects of her practice to consultants. Her horticultural surveillance, however, was more intensive than that of almost any other of her contemporaries with the exception of Farrand.

Every summer until World War II, Shipman's entire office, draftswomen included, moved to New Hampshire. The pace of work was somewhat more relaxed in the country, but Shipman entertained elaborately and participated fully in the busy life of the Cornish summer community.[29]

Many of Shipman's major projects date from the halcyon years of the 1920s. While a number of her commissions in this period were large in scale, she produced equally distinguished plans for small projects, including a geometric walled garden for the Windsor T. Whites in Chagrin Falls, Ohio (1919), which she worked on in association with Warren Manning. Among the others were the Robert S. Brewster Jr. residence in Mount Kisco, New York (early 1920s); the Mrs. Holden McGinley residence in Milton, Massachusetts, a suburb of Boston (1925), which was still partially extant in the early 1990s; and the Edward Lowe residence, Grand Rapids, Michigan (1922).[30]

Among the most impressive larger projects of this era was the walled English garden at Stan Hywet Hall in Akron, Ohio, begun in 1928 for Mr. and Mrs. Frank Seiberling as a spatially independent component of a landscape initially laid out by Warren Manning.[31] It was Manning himself who

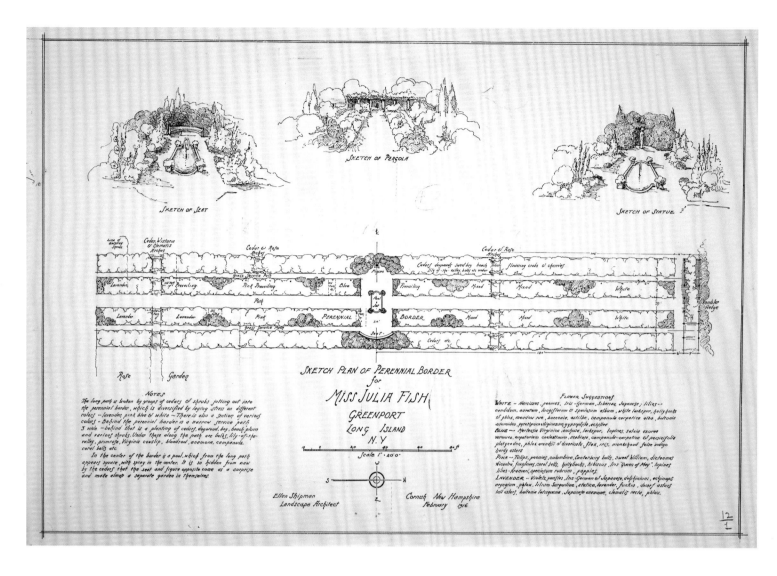

5.2 *Sketch plan of perennial border, Residence of Miss Julia Fish, Greenport, February 1916.* Rare and Manuscript Collections, Carl A. Kroch Library, Cornell University, hereafter Cornell

recommended Shipman to the Seiberlings, describing her as "one of the best, if not the very best, Flower Garden Maker in America."[32]

Another major commission was Longue Vue in New Orleans, Louisiana, begun in 1931 for Mr. and Mrs. Edgar B. Stern. The Sterns were extraordinarily receptive to Shipman's advice, even acceding to her recommendation that they replace their old house with a new one. After a false start with Chicago architect David Adler, the Sterns' new house was designed by William and Geoffrey Platt (sons of Charles A. Platt), with heavy involvement by Shipman herself. Longue Vue is extant and under ongoing restoration. Yet another Shipman landscape, now the property of the National Park Service, that is partially extant is Chatham in Fredericksburg, Virginia, a 1721 house for which Shipman designed a large garden in 1924, with Colonel and Mrs. Daniel B. Devore as clients.[33]

Like all American landscape architects, Shipman was hard hit by the stock market crash of October 1929. Nevertheless, a few large commissions from exceptionally wealthy clients like the Sterns kept her afloat. New business did, of course, slack off, enabling Shipman, presumably with the help of savings from her more prosperous years, to travel abroad for the first time. In 1929, she visited Italy and then made two trips to England in the early 1930s.[34]

Unlike Farrand, Hutcheson, and Coffin, Shipman never

joined the American Society of Landscape Architects, and she never sought any other professional affiliation. In 1946, she turned down an invitation from architect Aymar Embury II to become a member of the Institute of Arts and Letters, advising him to look for a younger person to whom the honor would mean more. Shipman never volunteered an explanation for her lack of interest in the ASLA. After Shipman's death, Frances McCormic was pressed on the matter and came up with some rather lame reasons: Shipman was "too busy" to join the ASLA; she "didn't approve of it;" and she found the members "dull."[35]

In fact, Shipman did not need the ASLA, and the ASLA did not need her. Her most satisfying contacts and the majority of her commissions came to her through the Garden Club of America. While Hutcheson, Coffin and others found it valuable to belong to both organizations, the ASLA seems to have been irrelevant to Shipman. Unlike Hutcheson and Coffin, Shipman seems to have felt no need to urge the Garden Club and its affiliates to embrace a higher social purpose.

During the 1930s, Shipman expanded her repertoire of lectures, drawing on her recent travels in England and Italy. A tall woman of regal bearing, Shipman was a charismatic speaker, and audiences found her lectures riveting. In 1932, she gave a talk in Winston-Salem, North Carolina entitled "The Evolution of a Garden," illustrated with one hundred slides of her own work taken by noted photographer Harry G. Healy.[36] Shipman's audiences were not limited to garden clubs; she also lectured to the Cosmopolitan Club of New York City, the Junior League of Boston, and the Lowthorpe School. While Hutcheson's slides have fortunately survived, Shipman's have not.[37]

During World War II, Shipman became a fervent proponent of victory gardens. In 1945, with the help of Anne Bruce Haldeman, she started to put together a book that would serve as a compendium of practical advice, along with statements of her own philosophy of garden design, as well as some autobiographical information. The *Garden Note Book* was never finished, although partial manuscripts remain at Cornell and in two other locations.[38] Even if Shipman had been able to complete this work in a form suitable for publication, it would probably have met the same fate as the manuscript of Coffin's second book. The 1940s were simply not a propitious time for garden books that still assumed the affluence of the 1920s. Shipman's practice, already hard hit by the Depression, shrank further, and, in October 1946, she sold her New York City residence, office, and furnishings to the Sterns, who seem to have allowed her to remain there for a few months.[39]

Beset not only by financial difficulties but also by declining health, Shipman closed her office early in 1947. At seventy-eight, she found this major life transition extremely painful. She relocated to Brook Place and found solace in her family. In the winter months, she lived in Bermuda, where she had built a house, well situated with stunning views over the island. Almost until the end, Shipman happily looked forward to further travels, but, on March 27, 1950, she succumbed to pneumonia.[40]

When she closed her office, Shipman had to decide which of her thousands of plans to keep and which to destroy. In her will, she directed that her books, plans, and photographs be given to one of four designated institutions: Vassar College, Cornell University, the Cambridge School of Architecture and Landscape Architecture, and the New York Public Library. Cornell accepted the bequest. She left her slide collection to the Garden Club of America, although it is not now among the Club's archives at the Smithsonian Institution in Washington, D.C.[41] When Shipman winnowed through her office records in 1947, she must have decided to destroy her client correspondence, since this is not at Cornell or anywhere else, except in the few cases where the client's own archives have survived.

SHIPMAN'S NAME is associated with fifty-nine Long Island projects. While there are plans and photographs at Cornell for a substantial number of these, many appear only on a client list drawn up in 1945 by Frances McCormic. That list itemizes more than six hundred clients, about half of whom are also represented by plans or photographs at Cornell. However, it should not be assumed that the three hundred or so projects without documentation were not carried out. In some cases, sets of blueprints belonging to Shipman's clients have survived in archives outside of Cornell, but, sadly, not for any Long Island clients.[42] Remnants of a few Long Island projects may survive.

5.3 *The fish garden, Greenport, under construction. Photograph, ca. 1916.* Cornell

5.4 *Perennial borders, Fish Garden, Greenport. Photograph, 1916.* Cornell

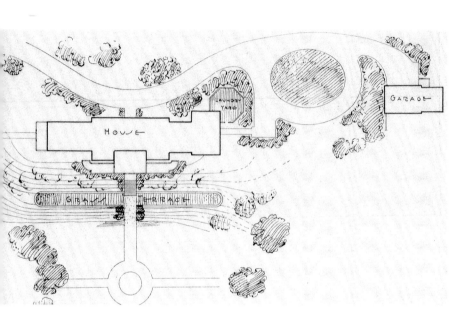

5.5 *Plan of grounds,*
Pidgeon Hill, Residence
of Mrs. Meredith Hare,
Huntington. From
Architectural Record, 1920

5.6 *Garden elevation,*
Pidgeon Hill, Residence
of Mrs. Meredith Hare,
Huntington. Photograph,
undated. Courtesy Lewis
& Valentine

Shipman's first project on Long Island appears to have
been at Longfields, the residence of William P. T. Preston in
Jericho. She started this in 1913, the same year that
Peabody, Wilson & Brown designed the house. Since the
holdings at Cornell consist only of four photographs of a
garden wall, it is likely that Shipman's role was quite limited.[43] At an unknown date but probably quite early in her
career, Shipman had an apparently minor involvement at
The Braes, the Herbert L. Pratt residence in Glen Cove.
James Greenleaf had done the overall layout of this property in 1912. The only item in the Shipman collection for
this project is an undated drawing of construction details
for a wooden door in the drying yard.[44]

Another early commission (1916) was a double perennial border for Julia Fish in Greenport (fig. 5.2). The borders, which were 240 feet long, were separated by a wide
turf path. As Shipman wrote on the plan, "The long path is
broken by groups of cedars and shrubs jutting out into the
perennial border . . . ." A construction photograph (fig. 5.3)
illustrates the bleakness of the site before improvement and
also the fact that the cedars were moved in fully grown.
Each perennial bed was approximately 6 feet, 9 inches
deep. Between each bed and its heavy backing of flowering

trees and cedars was a narrow service path that gave the gardener access to both sides. Under the backing trees and shrubs were spring bulbs, lily of the valley, etc. At various points, the backing plants were punctuated by arches with roses, clematis, and wisteria. At the north end of the garden was a pergola that carried additional vines. Again, as Shipman wrote on the plan: "In the center of the border is a pool. . . . It is so hidden from view by the cedars that the seat and figure opposite come as a surprise and make almost a separate garden in themselves." A path from the southeastern end of the border led into a rose garden.

Shipman used a palette of perennials that ranged from lavender to pink to blue on the south and from blue to white on the north. Shipman was perhaps influenced by Gertrude Jekyll's 1908 book *Colour Schemes for the Flower Garden*, which she owned in its third (1914) edition. Here she used impressionistic drifts of color, à la Jekyll, rather than the jewel-like contrasting colors that characterized her later borders.[45] Quite un-Jekyll-like, however, were the four large groups of mixed-color flowers about three-quarters of the way down the border between the blue and white groups. Shipman did not specify individual plants but instead left the choice to her client, offering suggestions for each color group on the plan. While most of these bloomed in the summer, there were also tulips and some autumn-blooming perennials in the lists. The Fish garden bloomed luxuriantly only months after construction and planting (fig. 5.4), its appearance of well-established maturity greatly enhanced by the tall cedars.

In the same year, Shipman began landscaping the grounds of Pidgeon Hill, the Mrs. Meredith Hare residence in Huntington. The house was designed by Charles A. Platt in a Long Island variant of the Colonial Revival. On the entrance side, Shipman planned a curving, tree-lined drive, with informally grouped trees, that skirted an octagonal, fenced drying yard. On the rear, steps led down to a grass terrace about the same length as the house (fig. 5.5). Beyond this was a circular pool surrounded by turf paths and flower beds (fig. 5.6).[46] Lewis and Valentine provided the plants, or at least the trees, but there is no further information about what Shipman specified.

In 1917, Shipman did some work at the property of Lewis Cass Ledyard Jr. in Syosset. Platt had designed Ledyard's house three years earlier, and Annette Hoyt Flanders did further landscaping there at some time prior to 1931 (see chapter 7).[47] The same year, Shipman prepared plans for Wolver Hollow, the C. Oliver Iselin residence in Brookville. So many landscape architects, including Olmsted Brothers and Beatrix Farrand, were involved at Wolver Hollow at one time or another that it is very difficult to sort out their individual contributions.[48]

The garden that Shipman designed for Mary and Neltje Pruyn in East Hampton ranks as one of her finest early works, not only on Long Island but nationally. House and garden alike were on a modest scale. Platt had recently remodeled the cottage for the Pruyn sisters, who were artists and volunteer social workers. The garden was only 50 feet square but within it was great variety. In the plant-

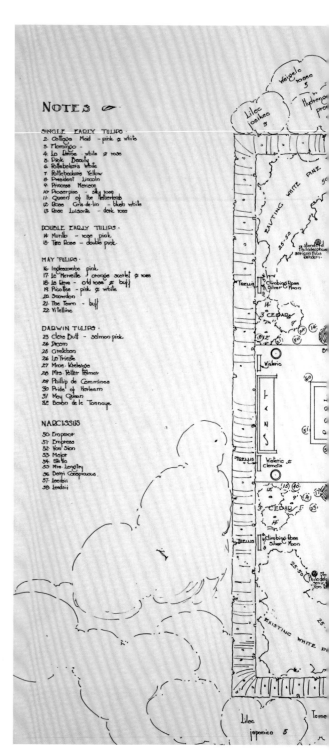

5.7 *Shrub and bulb planting plan, Misses Pruyn Residence, East Hampton, February 1920. Cornell*

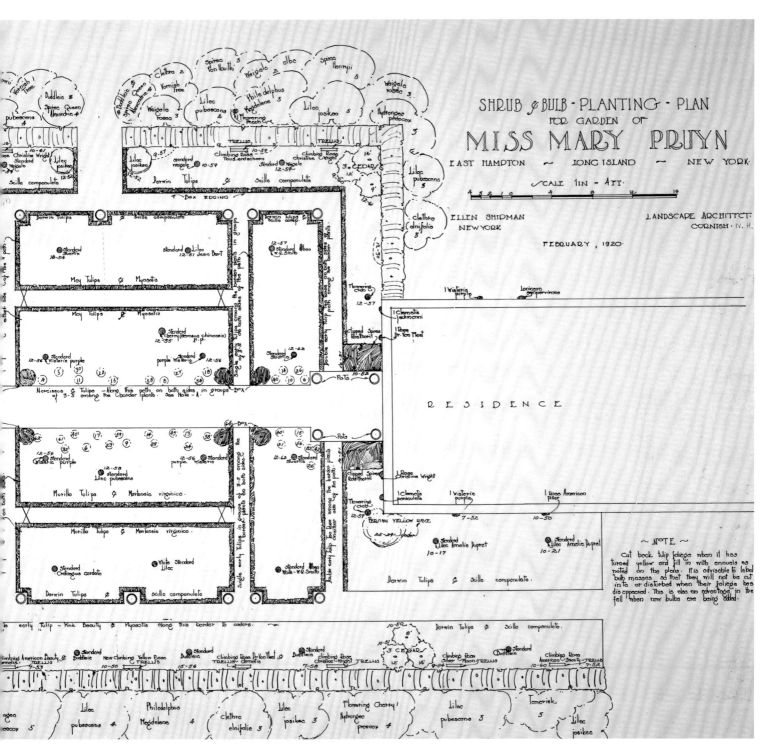

FOLLOWING PAGES
5.8 *Perennial planting
plan, Misses Pruyn
Residence, East Hampton,
February 1920.* Cornell

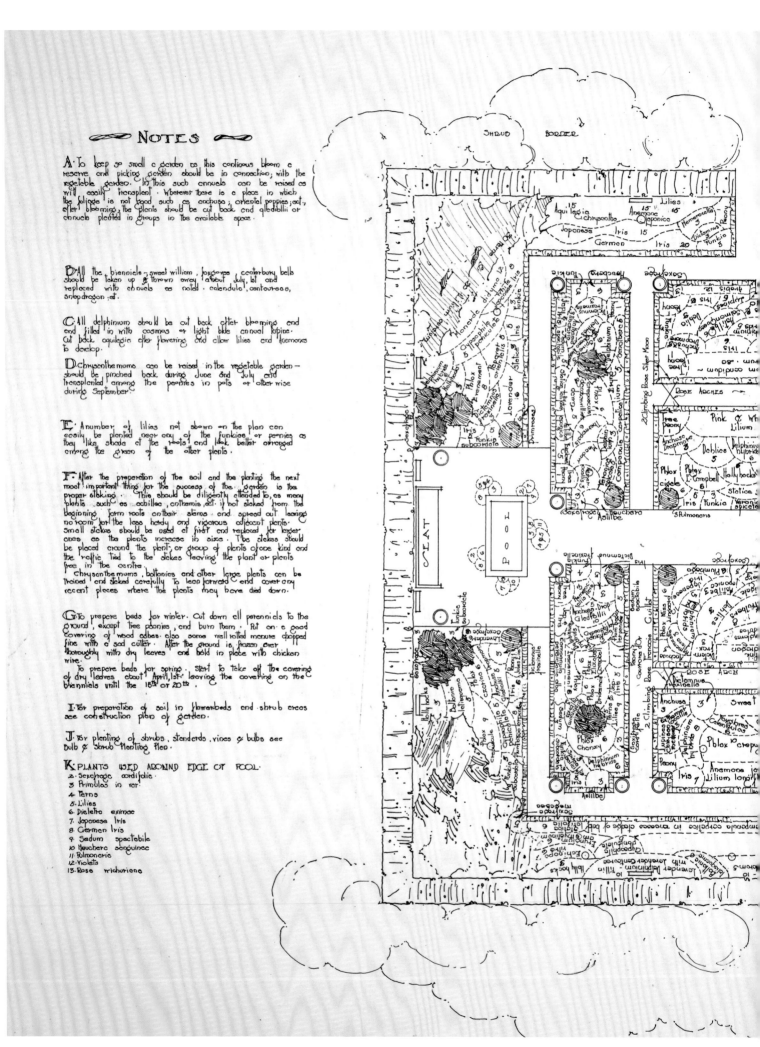

⌘ NOTES ⌘

A. To keep so small a garden as this continuous bloom a reserve and picking garden should be in connection with the vegetable garden. In this such annuals can be raised as will easily transplant. Wherever there is a place in which the foliage is not good such as anchusa, oriental poppies, et., after blooming, the plants should be cut back and annuals planted in groups in the available space.

B. All the biennials, sweet william, foxgloves, canterbury bells should be taken up & thrown away about July, 1st and replaced with annuals as noted, calendula, centaureas, snapdragon, et.

C. All delphinium should be cut back after blooming and and filled in with cosmos or light blue annual lupine. Cut back aquilegia after flowering and allow lilies and anemones to develop.

D. Chrysanthemums can be raised in the vegetable garden — should be pinched back during June and July and transplanted among the peonies in pots or otherwise during September.

E. A number of lilies not shown on the plan can easily be planted near any of the funkias or peonies as they like shade of the roots and look better arranged among the green of the other plants.

F. After the preparation of the soil and the planting the next most important thing for the success of the garden is the proper staking. This should be diligently attended to, as many plants such as achillea, anthemis, et. if not staked from the beginning form roots on their stems and spread out leaving no room for the less hardy and vigorous adjacent plants. Small stakes should be used at first and replaced for longer ones as the plants increase in size. The stakes should be placed around the plant, or group of plants of one kind and the raffia tied to the stakes leaving the plant or plants free in the centre.

Chrysanthemums, boltonias and other large plants can be trained and staked carefully to lean forward and cover any recent places where the plants may have died down.

G. To prepare beds for winter. Cut down all perennials to the ground, except tree peonies, and burn them. Put on a good covering of wood ashes, also some well rotted manure chopped fine with a sod cutter. After the ground is frozen over thoroughly with dry leaves and hold in place with chicken wire. To prepare beds for spring, start to take off the covering of dry leaves about April, 1st leaving the covering on the biennials until the 15th or 20th.

I. For preparation of soil in flowerbeds and shrub areas see construction plan of garden.

J. For planting of shrubs, standards, vines & bulbs see bulb & shrub planting plan.

K. PLANTS USED AROUND EDGE OF POOL.
2. Saxifraga cordifolia.
3. Primulas in var.
4. Ferns
5. Lilies
6. Dieletra eximea
7. Japanese Iris
8. German Iris
9. Sedum spectabile
10. Heuchera sanguinea
11. Pulmonaria
12. Violets
13. Rosa wichuriana

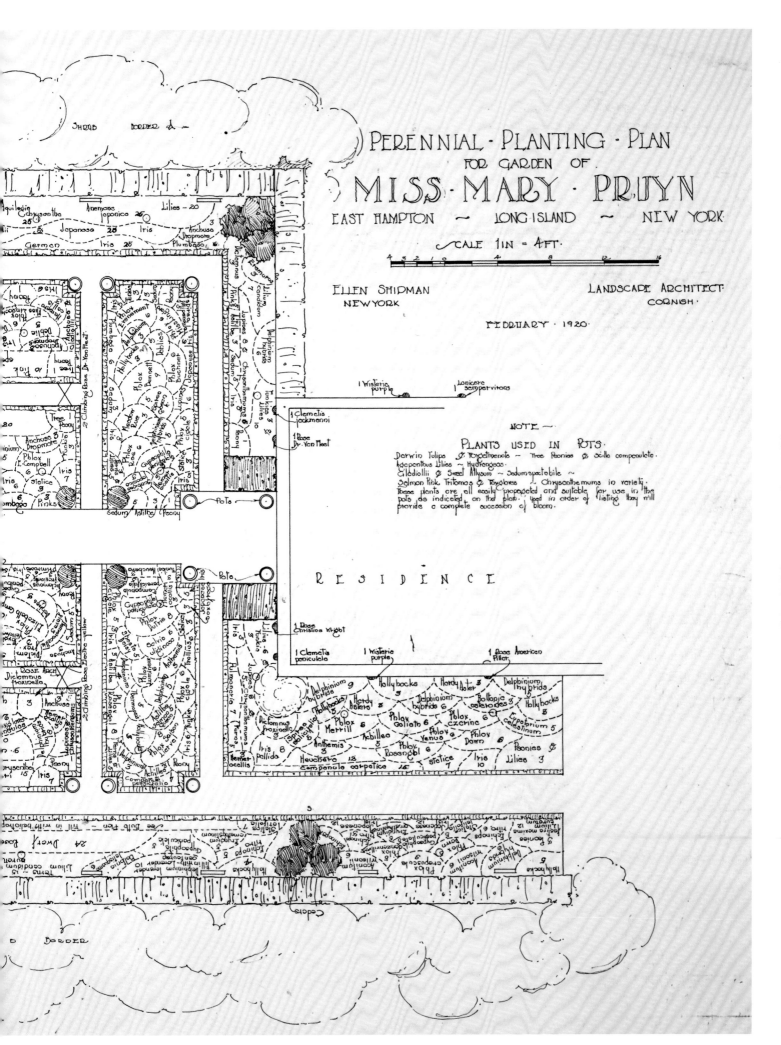

PERENNIAL · PLANTING · PLAN
FOR GARDEN OF
MISS · MARY · PRUYN
EAST HAMPTON ～ LONG ISLAND ～ NEW YORK

SCALE 1 IN = 4 FT.

ELLEN SHIPMAN
NEW YORK

LANDSCAPE ARCHITECT
CORNISH ·

FEBRUARY · 1920.

NOTE ～

PLANTS USED IN POTS.

Darwin Tulips & Forgetmenots ~ Tree Peonies & Scilla companulate.
Agapanthus Lilies ~ Hydrangeas.
Gladiollii & Sweet Allysum ~ Sedum spectabile ~
Salmon Pink Tritomas & Foxgloves ~ Chrysanthemums in variety.
These plants are all easily propagated and suitable for use in the
pots as indicated on the plan. Used in order of listing they will
provide a complete succession of bloom.

RESIDENCE

ing plans, Shipman provided for a succession of bloom from early spring through the summer. Evidently, the Pruyns were tulip fanciers, for, in addition to narcissus, the shrub and bulb planting plan (fig. 5.7) called for an extended display of tulips from the early single varieties to the early double types, then May tulips, followed by Darwin tulips. Surrounding the garden itself were groups of white pines and other trees and, on the far side of the trellis enclosure, were numerous shrubs, including many varieties of lilacs. After the bulbs were spent, the perennials (fig. 5.8) took over, with unusual juxtapositions of foliage and flower, among them iris, peonies, baby's breath, delphinium, and astilbe (fig. 5.9).[49]

The subtle but studied lack of symmetry (which, as we have seen, Farrand also favored) extended into other aspects of the Pruyn garden. As Fletcher Steele, then emerging as one of the finest American landscape architects of his generation, observed, "Part of the unusually successful Colonial feeling here is due to the fact that stiff accuracy has been avoided. Note even that one side of the path is edged with brick—the other with a board."[50]

In 1920, Shipman laid out the grounds of Picket Farm, the A. Ludlow Kramer residence in Westbury. The house had been designed a few years earlier by Peabody, Wilson & Brown. Unfortunately, Cornell has no plans for this property, but there are numerous photographs in the Shipman Collection, and the garden was widely published.[51] Perennial borders were a major feature of the Kramer landscape. Planted with Shipman's characteristic profusion, flowers spilled out onto the flagstone walk (fig. 5.10). As in the Pruyn garden, there were contrasting types of foliage and blossom. Cedars were used as accents. Surrounded by a low brick wall, the garden also featured birdbaths, apple trees, and a swimming pool (fig. 5.11). The house was severely damaged by a fire in the late 1970s and later demolished.[52]

In 1925, Shipman received a second commission from Philip Gossler, chairman of the board and president of Columbia Gas and Electricity Company and a director of the Guaranty Trust Company of New York. Having previously laid out the grounds of his house in New Canaan, Shipman began to work on his residence in Wheatley Hills.[53] John Russell Pope had designed the house about eight years earlier for J. Randolph Robinson in a Colonial Revival style modeled closely on Mount Vernon. Gossler commissioned Pope to make additions and alterations to the house, including a semicircular porch off the living room and a new stable and garage complex.[54]

At the same time, Gossler asked Shipman to design an elaborate series of gardens on the west side of the house, as well as a large cutting garden, completely screened by trees, to the southeast (fig. 5.12). Shipman prepared a wide range of plans, including several studies for driveway changes. From the house, the land sloped steeply to the north, and the contiguous flower gardens in this direction were connected by several series of short steps, ending in an overlook with a table and four seats. As in the Pruyn garden—although on a much larger scale—spring bulbs and flowering shrubs were succeeded by perennial borders (figs. 5.13–5.15).

The Gosslers enjoyed this garden for about a decade. The property was then purchased by Edward F. Hutton after his divorce from Marjorie Merriweather Post. Hutton made additional architectural alterations, but there seems to be no record of further landscape changes. The Robinson/Gossler/Hutton house is now the fine arts center at C. W. Post College, Long Island University. Shipman's terraces remain at this property, and the university plans to restore the landscape using Shipman's planting plans at Cornell.[55]

Shipman seems to have learned much from her work on the Gossler property, for in the following year she designed a magnificent series of gardens and outdoor spaces for Rynwood, the property of Sir Samuel A. Salvage, in Glen Head. The rambling Tudoresque house, designed by Roger H. Bullard and constructed of limestone, was completed in 1928. Salvage, founder of the American rayon industry, was an elite figure even among Bullard's glittering clientele, and the design of Rynwood won architect and landscape architect alike much recognition.[56]

Bullard and Shipman collaborated on the site plan (fig. 5.16). A rare photograph of a model of the house and nearby grounds survives in the Shipman collection. The site plan was a remarkable accomplishment: a highly articulated, precisely defined scheme that organized a varied collection of spaces and structures into an ensemble that, in lesser hands, might have become cluttered. The library, sun room, and living room all looked out onto a rose garden and a large flower garden, which were linked by a picturesque dovecote modeled after a similar structure at Snowshill Manor in the English Cotswolds. A flagstone path connected the dovecote with a teahouse on the far

5.10 *Perennial borders,*
A. L. Kramer Residence,
Westbury. Photograph,
Mattie Edwards Hewitt,
undated. Cornell

side of the large flower garden. On the east side of the house, beyond grass terraces, were a paved court planned around an existing oak tree, as well as a service court and a fountain garden.[57] All of these formal areas were surrounded by a wall.

The plantings were similarly varied. Near the dovecote were box shrubs, hydrangeas (kept surprisingly low), phlox, and small fruit trees (fig. 5.17). Some of the beds near the house were mass-planted with petunias.[58] In the center of the teahouse garden was a pool edged with *Bergenia* over which hung an old apple tree.[59] The Salvages must have spent part of the spring at Rynwood, since there were also mass plantings of tulips (fig. 5.18).

Beyond the two formal gardens on the west side of the house was a swimming pool within its own garden enclosure and a tennis court and, beyond these, a large meadow. The approach road entered the property at a gatehouse at the northwestern corner (inset in fig. 5.16), curved around part of the northern perimeter, skirted thick woods, crossed a bridge over a ravine, and ended at a circular turnaround in front of the house. To the east of the house and well out of view was a large farm group.

5.11 *Garden, A. L. Kramer*
Residence, Westbury.
Photograph, Mattie Edwards
Hewitt, undated. From *House*
Beautiful, March 1924

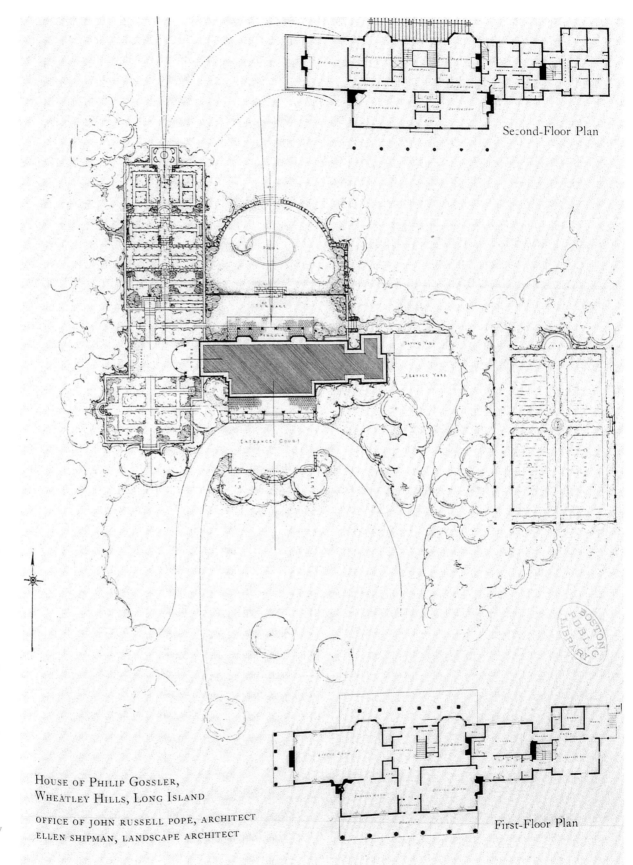

Second-Floor Plan

5.12 *Ellen Shipman and John Russell Pope. Site plan for house. Philip Gossler Residence, Wheatley Hills. undated.* From *Architecture,* December 1926

FACING PAGE
5.13 *Perennial planting plan, upper garden. Gossler Residence, Wheatley Hills. undated.* Cornell

5.14 *Perennial planting plan, lower garden. Gossler Residence, Wheatley Hills. undated.* Cornell

PAGES 126–27
5.15 *Flower garden, Gossler Residence, Wheatley Hills. Photograph, undated.* From *Architecture,* December 1926

HOUSE OF PHILIP GOSSLER,
WHEATLEY HILLS, LONG ISLAND

OFFICE OF JOHN RUSSELL POPE, ARCHITECT
ELLEN SHIPMAN, LANDSCAPE ARCHITECT

First-Floor Plan

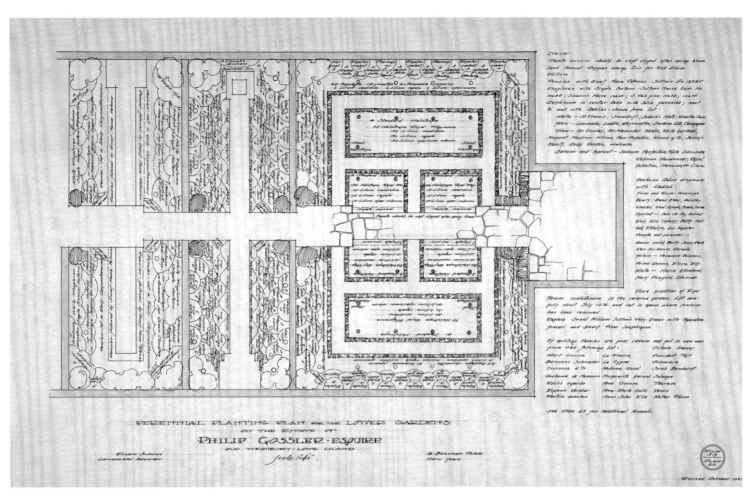

PERENNIAL PLANTING PLAN for the LOWER GARDENS
ON THE ESTATE OF
PHILIP GOSSLER · ESQUIRE
OLD WESTBURY · LONG ISLAND
scale 1:40'

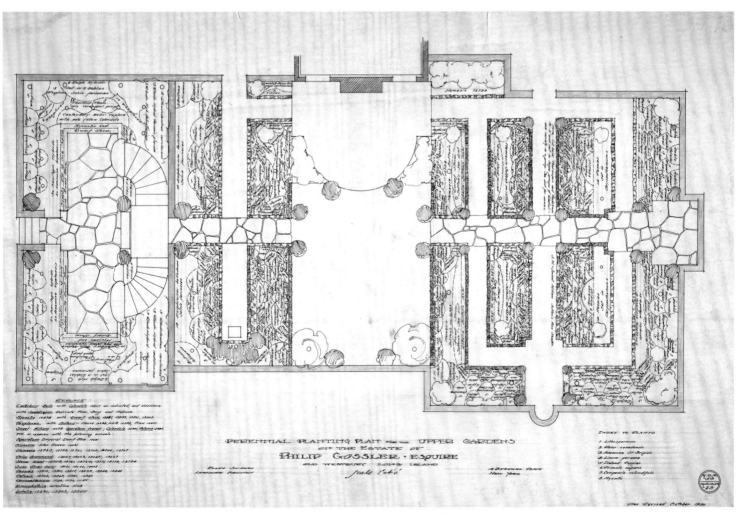

PERENNIAL PLANTING PLAN for the UPPER GARDENS
ON THE ESTATE OF
PHILIP GOSSLER · ESQUIRE
OLD WESTBURY · LONG ISLAND
scale 1:40'

5.16 *Roger H. Bullard and Ellen Shipman. House and gardens for Samuel A. Salvage, Glen Head, 1926.* From *Architectural Forum,* July 1930

5.17 *Garden, Samuel A. Salvage Residence, Glen Head. Photograph, Mattie Edwards Hewitt, undated.* Cornell

Rynwood is now the corporate headquarters of Banfi Vintners, a wine importing concern, and is known as Villa Banfi. Around 1980, the grounds around the house were redesigned by Innocenti and Webel.[60] Shipman's plantings had probably disappeared much earlier, but Innocenti and Webel did preserve her garden spaces, which remain, as do the dovecote and teahouse.[61]

In 1926–27, Shipman designed gardens for Windy Hill, the property of Lansing P. Reed on Snake Hill Road in Lloyd Harbor, at the same time that Charles A. Platt was designing the house. Windy Hill was Platt's last residential commission on Long Island. Reed, a successful attorney who, like Platt, was a member of the Century Association, was also a trustee of Phillips Academy in Andover, Massachusetts, where Platt was carrying out a number of projects during the same years.[62]

The entrance drive, which was undoubtedly designed by Platt, was L-shaped, ending in an impressive straight allée that, in turn, terminated in a circular carriage sweep. Shipman laid out an elaborate formal rose garden with beds in the shapes of diamonds and segments of circles, each bed

framed by low box hedges and brick edging. She also designed shrub plantings and extensive flower gardens (fig. 5.19).[63] Windy Hill still stands, but it is unclear whether anything remains of Shipman's gardens.[64]

The Ellery S. James residence in East Hampton may have been Shipman's second, or possibly even third, collaboration with Roger H. Bullard. Although there are no drawings at Cornell, Bullard wrote an article about the project.[65] The site of the James house was extremely exposed, the structure poised on sand dunes overlooking the Atlantic Ocean. As an extension of the first-floor plan (fig. 5.20), Bullard indicated a walled garden and, in an accompanying photograph, showed interesting plantings near the front entrance. Since he did not credit Shipman in the article, it is unclear whether the garden and entrance plantings were her work.

In 1928 and 1929, Shipman designed the grounds of the Syosset houses of Franklin B. Lord and George deForest Lord, two brothers who were also law partners. Both houses were designed by the New York firm of Beers and Farley. The garden at Cottsleigh, the Franklin Lord resi-

5.18 *Detail of garden,*
Samuel A. Salvage
Residence, Glen Head.
Photograph, Mattie Edwards
Hewitt, 1934. LISI, 5687.374

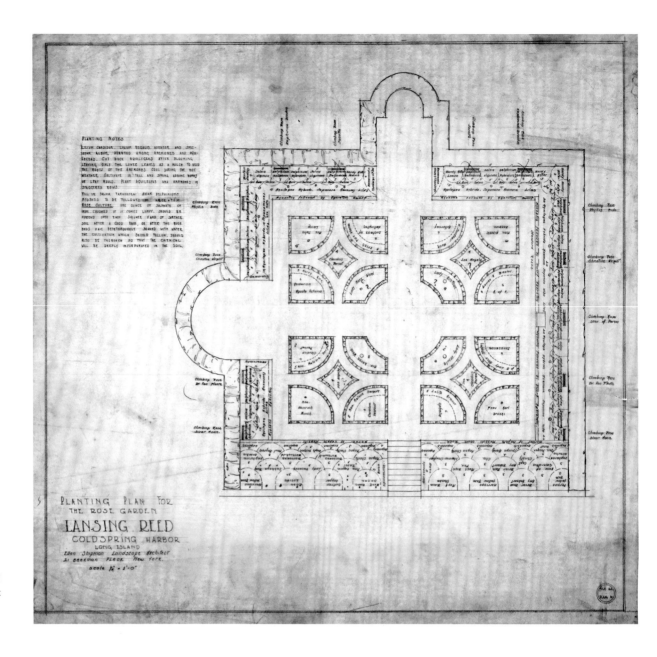

dence, consisted primarily of shrubs and perennial beds surrounded by low box edging (fig. 5.21). Cottsleigh is extant but the status of the grounds is unknown. Shipman also emphasized perennial plantings in beds with brick edgings at Overfields (fig. 5.22). Overfields is extant, and the gardens are said to be well maintained.[66]

An intriguing project, unfortunately undated, was the Red House, the residence of Eleanor Swayne, in Shinnecock Hills in Southampton. Grosvenor Atterbury was Miss Swayne's architect. Among the plans that Shipman prepared were numerous schemes for the entrance drive, terraces, and for flowering shrubs plantings, and so on. Several plans were also made for an annual garden (also called a cutting garden and a picking garden) and for a sweet pea planting.[67]

In the summer of 1895, on her very first evening in Cornish, Shipman was invited to a party of charades at High Court, home of art patron Annie Lazarus. The house at High Court, located on a spectacular site facing Mount Ascutney, and its grounds had both been designed by Charles Platt.[68] Several years would pass before Shipman and her husband purchased Brook Place and before Platt discovered the young woman's design gifts. But, Ellen, then a young mother, undoubtedly anticipating what she thought would be a long and happy marriage, had a nocturnal epiphany that eerily prefigured her professional future:

The valley was still filled with rolling clouds . . . as the moon was full and had risen above them. In the distance was Ascutney Mountain, . . . and just a few feet below, where we stood upon a terrace, was a Sunken Garden with rows bathed in moonlight of white lilies standing as an altar for Ascutney.

As I look back I realize it was at that moment that a garden became for me the most essential part of a home. But years of work had to intervene before I could put this belief, born that glorious night, into actual practice.[69]

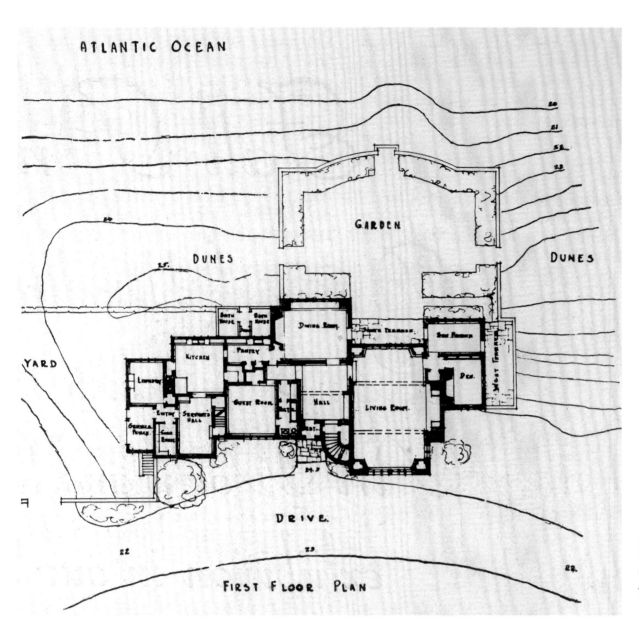

ATLANTIC OCEAN

GARDEN

DUNES

DUNES

YARD

BATH HOUSE · BATH HOUSE

DINING ROOM.

KITCHEN

PANTRY

GUEST ROOM

HALL

LIVING ROOM.

DEN.

SERVANTS HALL

ENTRY

LIBRARY

DRIVE.

FIRST FLOOR PLAN

5.20 *Roger H. Bullard. First-floor plan and plan of walled garden, Ellery S. James Residence, East Hampton, 1929. Art and Decoration, October 1929*

5.21 *Franklin B. Lord garden, Syosset. Photograph, Mattie Edwards Hewitt, September 1930.* LISI 4500.225

5.22 *George deForest Lord garden, Syosset. Photograph, Mattie Edwards Hewitt, 1937.* LISI 5687.332

CHAPTER 6

Ruth Bramley Dean

1889–1932

RUTH BRAMLEY DEAN was born in November 1889 in Wilkes-Barre, Pennsylvania, the daughter of Alexander S. Dean, a bookkeeper, and Emma Dean. One of five children, she had three older sisters and a brother.[1] She married the architect Aymar Embury II in 1923 but continued to be known professionally as Ruth Dean.

As one of her sisters wrote after her death, Dean was born into a gardening tradition: "the two generations next preceding her own were thorough exponents of amateur gardening. Ruth Dean's maternal grandfather was among those New Englanders early interested in horticultural experiments, and in the next generation, Ruth Dean's mother was a devotée of flowers. Her gardens both indoors and out flourished under her loving personal care."[2] Dean's mother encouraged each of her children who wanted one to have a private garden.[3] In 1929, Dean told Frances D. McMullen, a reporter for *The Woman's Journal*, about the time when she first considered landscape architecture as a career: "I got the notion from my mother, who was always digging around the flowers. This seemed to me to be a very nice thing to do; and so when I knew I had to make my own living, I decided I'd like to go in for gardens. I thought it would mean an outdoors life, which offered great appeal."[4]

Dean attended Wilkes-Barre public schools. When she was in high school, botany, drawing, chemistry, and geometry were her favorite subjects. In her spare time, she practiced the piano, gaining facility, although not taking on the

most challenging repertoire.[5] She graduated from the Wilkes-Barre High School in 1907.[6]

In 1908, over strong opposition from her father, which was eventually smoothed over by "maternal tact and encouragement," Dean entered the University of Chicago, enrolling in the College of Literature.[7] During the next two years, she took numerous courses in math and science, as well as English, French, political science, and literature. Her "major," if she had one, is unclear. She did not study drawing, drafting, or design but, within the botany department, took two courses in ecology. Dean left the University of Chicago without receiving a degree, but, in December 1916, she was granted a certificate.[8]

After leaving the university, Dean worked in the office of the Chicago landscape architect Jens Jensen, at first as his unpaid apprentice and then on a small salary. Aside from the courses in math and science that she took in college, her only preparation would seem to have been her study of drawing in high school. Jensen or his assistants must have taught Dean to design landscapes. It also seems reasonable to assume that she must have drawn very well to be accepted into the office. Jensen may have been the first male landscape architect to hire a woman. A proponent of native plant materials, he was a lasting influence on Dean's career.[9] Dean then drafted maps for a cartographer, presumably in Chicago, until she had enough money to relocate to New York City. Once there, she worked for various

New York architects, including Aymar Embury II, whom she later married. As McMullen wrote,

> This period . . . was invaluable, for in the circles where houses and their grounds are brought into being one of Ruth Dean's leading assets is considered her ability to develop gardens that tie in with the houses instead of standing apart as separate entities, as not infrequently happens. She catches the architect's point of view and understands where his work leaves off and hers commences, and how both can be welded together to turn out a harmonious whole.[10]

Finally, in 1915, Dean borrowed two hundred fifty dollars to open her own small office at 38 East Fifty-seventh Street, where she hired an office boy primarily for show. As work came in, she replaced him with an assistant who could type, and her career was underway.[11] Dean's earliest project appears to have been the Frank P. Smith residence in Dwight, Illinois (1915). In 1917, there were several commissions, including the James C. Brady residence, Gladstone, New Jersey; the Gretchen Patch Rose residence, Pittsburgh, Pennsylvania; and the grounds of the Knickerbocker Country Club, Tenafly, New Jersey (probably begun before 1917).[12] The same year she began her first projects on Long Island: the Fannie Mulford residence in Hempstead and the Arthur G. Schieren residence in Great Neck. The Knickerbocker Country Club and the Schieren residence were both designed by Embury, suggesting that his referrals were critical to Dean's early success.

During her seventeen-year career, Dean wrote regularly for periodicals and architectural magazines such as *House and Garden* and *Architectural Forum*.[13] In 1915 alone, the first year of her practice, she published three articles in *Country Life in America* and *The Garden Magazine*.[14] Dean's articles tended to be practical, stressing general landscape problems that applied to relatively small residential sites. Only rarely did they feature her own work. It is hardly surprising that, in 1917, Embury selected her to write *The Livable House, Its Garden*, the companion volume to his own book, *The Livable House*. In his introduction to Dean's work, Embury wrote,

> Miss Dean was chosen because of her very wide familiarity with the problem of planting with regard to its ultimate effect and her great success in the treatment of the house garden, both in informal and formal ways, and the admirable manner in which she has used native shrubs in combination has tended to give her work a more quiet and less exotic character . . . her training has been under men who represented rather extreme differences of opinion in regard to landscape work . . . is able to apply to any particular problem the solution which best fits it.[15]

Embury may have been referring to the differences between himself and Jensen or between himself or Jensen and the other as yet unidentified New York architects with whom Dean had worked.

Ruth Dean's book may be the first written by an American woman landscape architect, preceding Martha Brookes Hutcheson's *The Spirit of the Garden* (1923) and Marian Cruger Coffin's *Trees and Shrubs for Landscape Effects* (1940). (There are several earlier books by women garden writers who were not practitioners.) *The Livable House, Its Garden* is divided into five chapters: The Grounds as a Whole, General Planting, The Flower Garden, Times and Seasons, and Garden Architecture. Like her articles, Dean's book is practical rather than theoretical, seemingly intended for the home gardener, although illustrated with the work of professional landscape architects and architects. Among the landscape architects featured are Jens Jensen, Lay and Wheelwright, Charles W. Leavitt, Ferrucio Vitale, Sears and Wendell, Marian Coffin, Pray, Hubbard, and White, and Olmsted Brothers. Frequently a garden or landscaped area is not attributed to a landscape architect but to the architect alone. These architects include McKim, Mead & White, Aymar Embury II, Delano and Aldrich, Kilham and Hopkins, Peabody, Wilson and Brown, Ralph Adams Cram, and Charles A. Platt. Dean gave much attention to Forest Hills Gardens in Queens, New York City, an exemplary collaboration between architect Grosvenor Atterbury and Olmsted Brothers.[16] There is substantial text in the body of the book, but the captions to the illustrations Dean selected convey her messages in capsule form.

The first chapter deals with the "position of the house with respect to exposure, drainage, accessibility from street, and possible garden site. Forms and kinds of drives. Grading on approximately level ground and on irregular ground. Terraces, retaining walls and steps." It is illustrated with a variety of forecourts, turn-arounds, footpaths, and drives.

Chapter 2 considers "foundation planting; purpose of, appropriate and inappropriate sorts. Border planting; woodland and gardenesque. Planting along drives and walks. Screen planting. Specimen planting. Miscellaneous flower planting." In vivid language, Dean castigated badly planned foundation plantings; her warning, like Coffin's on the mechanical shearing of shrubs, is as applicable today as it was in the early years of the twentieth century:

> Probably the most common of the inappropriate sorts of foundation planting is that which appears to consist of one each of all the different kinds of evergreens contained in the nursery-man's catalogue. Every suburb and real-estate development abounds in houses whose foundations are surrounded with a lot of little yellow and green and blue balls, cones, and pyramids, which present a bristling, unnatural look and contribute nothing of repose or dignity to the house. What could be less appropriate, less calculated to make the house look as if it belonged to its particular bit of country, than this collection of "specimen" evergreens?[17]

Chapter 3 is especially interesting. Reflecting on her experience working with architects, Dean strongly advocated that a flower garden should be planned with the house and should also be "'tied up' to it in some fashion. . . —perhaps the entrance to the garden may be through a sun porch, perhaps the first flower beds border a paved terrace intimately. . . ."[18] The Fannie Mulford garden in Hempstead is illustrated in this chapter, as is that of Aymar Embury II in Englewood, New Jersey; the house and presumably the garden of the latter, which was not attributed to Dean, were designed by Embury. Much attention is given to the property of Charles W. Hubbard in Weston, Massachusetts, designed by Olmsted Brothers in 1916.[19]

Financial and time constraints had almost certainly prevented Dean from taking the European study trips that were part of the professional preparation of Farrand, Hutcheson, and Coffin, but she was conversant with publications on European and especially English gardens. In chapter 2 of her book, she used a photograph by Thomas Sears of William Robinson's Gravetye in Sussex, England to make the point that a pond should be planted "with those trees and shrubs that grow naturally near water."[20] She had carefully read Gertrude Jekyll's *Colour Schemes in the Flower Garden* and, in chapter 3, discussed Jekyll's principle of graduation of color in a border:

> Miss Jekyll says that it is possible to plant, beginning with yellow through orange and red to pink, purple, violet, and blue—and this is undoubtedly true of one of those illimitable English borders which seem to stretch away to infinity. Unfortunately, American gardens are sadly lacking in borders fourteen or fifteen feet wide and three hundred feet long. For the most part our gardens are small, and it has been my sad experience that some of the vivid zinnias have been just as blighting separated from the pink phlox by a patch of white as they would have been next door to it."[21]

Consequently, Dean advised limiting flowers in a garden to varieties that harmonized.[22] She also warned that "the general rule that tall things should be kept to the back of the border with lower growing plants in front, ought not to be enforced to the point of giving the plants an appearance of tier arrangement."[23]

Chapter 4 deals with "Times and Seasons," referring less to seasons of bloom than to the proper times for moving, planting, and pruning trees and shrubs, as well as seasonal care for other plants. Her last chapter is about "Garden Architecture," in which she examines the design of gates, trellises, fences, pergolas, garden houses, statuary, gazebos, and fountains. There are numerous photographs of the walled garden at Gray Gardens in East Hampton, the property of Mrs. Robert C. Hill, which was designed by the owner, although its distinctive enclosure was the work of local carpenters and masons.[24]

The publication of *The Livable House, Its Garden* coincided with the entry of the United States into World War I in April 1917. For a period of months, Dean put her piano training to good use entertaining troops in France.[25] Given the condition of France at the time, it is highly unlikely that she visited any gardens.[26]

Within a few years after the conclusion of World War I, Ruth Dean's career was back in full gear. As early as 1915, possibly at the suggestion of Embury, she had exhibited at the Architectural League of New York. In 1921, she was

elected to membership in the American Society of Landscape Architects.[27] By the same year, she had accumulated a number of new commissions, including the David E. Pomeroy and Mrs. Seward Prosser residences in Englewood, New Jersey, and the Gates W. McGarrah residence in Woods Hole, Massachusetts.[28] In general, Dean's projects were modest in scale. As a rule, her clients were well off but not extraordinarily wealthy, with the exception of Vincent Astor, for whom she designed a subdivision on Long Island discussed below, as well as possibly a city garden in New York.[29] Dean adhered to the principles laid out in *The Livable House, Its Garden* throughout her career. She consistently advocated that gardens be laid out along rational lines and that they should nearly always be closely related to the house. In addition to country and suburban residences, Dean was known as a talented designer of city rooftop gardens.[30]

Dean and Embury married in 1923, after the death of his first wife. Their daughter, Judith Dean Embury, was born four years later. A Princeton graduate, Embury designed many residential projects, including some town houses in Manhattan in the early years of his career. In addition to *The Livable House*, he published several other books.[31] Embury is best known as the architect of many Works Progress Administration (WPA) projects in New York, including the Bronx-Whitestone and Triborough Bridges (1939 and 1936, respectively), both collaborations with O. H. Ammann. Embury also designed a number of imaginative swimming pools in Play Centers throughout the city as well as the original buildings of the Central Park Zoo and the bathhouses at Orchard Beach.[32]

In the late 1920s, Ruth Dean's career rode the crest of national prosperity, and numerous commissions came into her office. In 1929, she was awarded the Gold Medal for Landscape Architecture of the Architectural League of New York for a group of gardens in Grosse Pointe, Michigan, for Mrs. Howard Bonbright, Mrs. Robert Derrick, Hiram Walker, and Ledyard Mitchell, all probably completed just before 1929. The Bonbright garden was only one acre in size, a fact that Dean disguised, along with the rectangular dimensions of the lot, by arranging an oval-shaped stretch of turf, a small pool, an arbor, a flower garden, and a vegetable garden, defined by radial paths spreading out from behind the house. All of the Bonbright landscaped areas were screened from adjoining properties by carefully planned boundary plantings.[33]

Ruth Dean was the first woman to receive the Gold Medal for Landscape Architecture, her award preceding Marian Coffin's by one year. It was undoubtedly because of this distinction that *The Woman's Journal* dispatched Frances McMullen to interview her.[34] *The Woman's Journal* was published by the Woman Citizen Corporation, which seems to have been either sponsored by or affiliated with the League of Women Voters.[35] Just prior to interviewing Dean, the magazine had either interviewed or published articles on singer Geraldine Ferrar, actress Eva La Gallienne, mystery novelist Mary Roberts Rinehart, and tennis star Helen Wills.

Upon meeting Dean, McMullen was charmed: "Small,

youthful, almost girlish in appearance, she is really one of the simplest, friendliest, most unpretentious persons imaginable."[36] Although McMullen asked Dean about the circumstances of her initial choice of career, she focused on her current, hectic situation, providing a rare firsthand account of a landscape architect at work. She began by describing the workplace: "There are two brass nameplates on the door of Miss Dean's office suite—cosy offices they are, too, with gracefully patterned old woodwork and precious Hepplewhite pieces looking out on a tiny courtyard, embellished with lattice work and a fountain, where azaleas and tulips bloom. One of these plates bears the inscription, Aymar Embury, architect; the other, Ruth Dean, who is Mrs. Embury."[37]

At the time of the interview (presumably May 1929), Dean had fifteen active projects in her office, at least one of them a city rooftop garden that had to be installed via service elevator. She had five women on her staff, some of whom had taken professional courses and others whom she was training herself. As McMullen explained, the assistants "handle most of the detail day-to-day supervision on the various jobs; while she confers with clients, supplies ideas, evolves plans, and administers the work."[38] The identity of at least three of these women is known: Mary Lois Deputy Lamson (see chapter 8), who took over Dean's practice after her death; Vera Poggi Breed, an alumna of the University of Massachusetts; and Dean's niece Marianne Dean McMasters, who was educated at the University of

Chicago and Carnegie Tech. Later, Lamson and Breed both established independent practices, Breed's based in Connecticut, where she frequently collaborated with her husband, architect Nelson Breed.[39] McMasters joined Dean's office in 1928 and left after Dean's death. Later, she worked for the New York City Department of Parks.

The Woman's Journal article also offers a glimpse into Dean's private and domestic life. When McMullen asked if she had time to do anything but work, Dean replied, "Only now and then to look in on the baby."[40] The Emburys, including "curly haired Judith, aged twenty months," lived in a four-story brownstone at 280 East Sixty-second Street, around the corner from their joint office. Dean took care of her husband and daughter, and ran the home, which had a backyard garden that she had designed, in addition to the office, except, she added, during planting season, "when they just have to get along the best they can."[41]

At this time, Aymar Embury and Ruth Dean still frequently, although not always, collaborated.[42] When McMullen inquired whether her career might appear to some to be a man's job, Dean replied that the uninitiated client has such hazy ideas of the landscape architect's duties that the woman practitioner is little handicapped![43]

In 1932, Ruth Dean died suddenly in her New York City home.[44] Although her practice must have been affected by the stock market crash of October 1929 there was enough work in hand at the time of her death that Mary Deputy Lamson continued the firm for two years, with the assis-

6.3 *Garden, Miss Fannie Mulford Residence, Hempstead. Photograph, Mattie Edwards Hewitt, ca. 1921.* LISI 4500.161

tance of at least some of her colleagues. In July 1934, Lamson and the others "disbanded Ruth Dean Associates."[45] The absence of office archives makes it impossible to gauge the full extent of Dean's work. At present, about forty-five projects by Dean have been identified.[46] There must have been many more, although it is highly unlikely that fifteen projects per year was her average workload throughout her career.

OF DEAN'S KNOWN PROJECTS, ten, or possibly eleven, were located on Long Island. Original plans have been located for only the Embury residence in East Hampton; a limited number of photographs and a few plans of other Long Island gardens were published in garden periodicals or annuals like the yearbooks of the Architectural League of New York.

Dean's first project on Long Island was the Fannie Mulford residence on Fulton Avenue in Hempstead.[47] The exact acreage of this garden is unknown; it appears to have been relatively small and densely planted with flowers. Near the entrance was a shaded flagstone path with box-edged flower beds on either side, leading to a stone bench (fig. 6.2). Among the identifiable plants in this spring photograph are tall bearded iris and foxgloves. A vine-covered pergola is also visible. The focal point of the Mulford garden was a curved wooden trellis with a central arbor adorned with two benches and a sundial (figs. 6.3 and 6.4). On the right in fig. 6.4 are iris (probably Siberian or tall bearded vari-

eties), and the path appears to be lined with candytuft. The arbor probably supported roses, although these were not fully in bloom when this photograph was taken. The Mulford garden contained other ornamental furnishings.

Also begun in 1917, although further work seems to have been done in 1921, was the garden for Beachleigh, the G. Arthur Schieren property in Great Neck. Designed by Embury, the large brick Federal Revival house is typical of the architect's residential design.[48] Dean's garden was located at the foot of a flight of steps leading from a two-story piazza at the side of the house. In plan (fig. 6.5), the garden was composed of paths, lined on each side with flower beds, which fanned out from the piazza steps to a colonnaded pergola that connected three pavilions, bathhouses at either end and a central teahouse (see fig. C.5). Over the pergola were Lady Gay roses, climbing hydrangea, clematis, and wisteria. In front was a perennial border with hollyhocks and delphiniums at the back, Shasta daisies, peonies, white phlox, anchusa, and iris in the middle, and grass pinks for edging at the front. Spiraeas and lilacs were placed at the corners as accents. The middle beds contained roses interplanted with pink tulips, followed in summer by pink and white snapdragons, with edgings of ageratum and heliotrope. At the crossing of the paths was a sundial with English ivy growing on it and standard borders in the beds at its base. The entire garden was surrounded by a wall. The concept for the Schieren grounds was somewhat similar to that of the Bonbright garden in

6.4 *"Arbor in the Centre of a Curved Trellis." Garden, Miss Fannie Mulford Residence, Hempstead. Photograph, ca. 1916.* From Dean, *The Livable House, Its Garden*, 1917

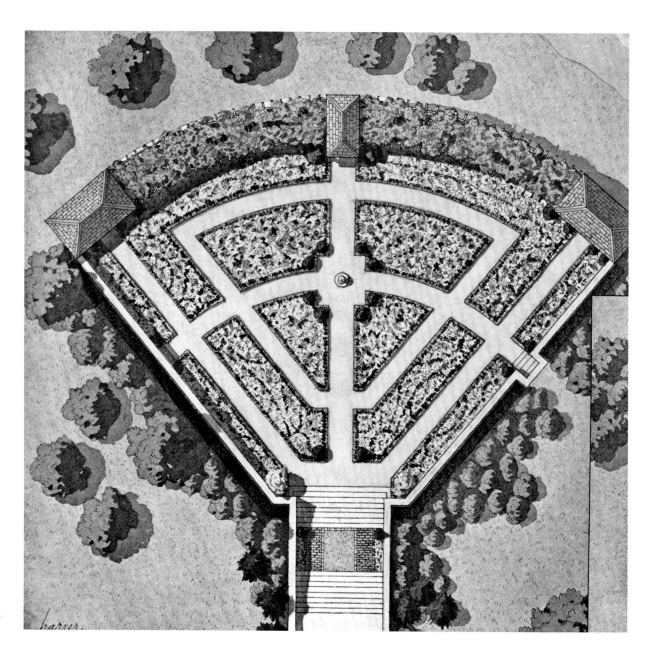

6.5 *Garden, G. Arthur Schieren Residence, Great Neck. Plan, ca. 1917*. From *House and Garden*, May 1932

Grosse Pointe, although the site was much larger. Glimpses of Manhasset Bay could be seen through the doors of the teahouse (figs. 6.6 and 6.7). The Schieren house still stands, but the status of Dean's garden is not known.[49]

In 1922, Dean designed a garden for Mrs. George N. Gales in Great Neck, whose house had been designed by Embury at an earlier date.[50] For this project, she used another variant of the basic scheme of some of her other gardens.[51] The Gales garden, nicely framed by potted geraniums on a rear terrace, was laid out along an axis that extended from the terrace through an oval greensward with a centrally placed sundial to an arbor at the rear. Curving around on either side of the greensward were closely planted perennial beds (fig. 6.8), which, in early summer, overflowed with delphiniums and lupines. As she had with the Schieren garden, Dean used strategically placed clumps of *Phlox paniculata*, in this case the highly popular white "Miss Lingard" phlox.

Around 1924, Dean designed a spring garden for Mrs. Monroe Douglas Robinson in Syosset.[52] The house was designed by James W. O'Connor. Dean's plan (fig. 6.9) consisted of flower borders on a terrace to the rear of the house, separated by a grass walk and adjacent to a rose garden. There was also an arbor on the other side of the house. The flower borders were "arranged for sustained all-season bloom; in the foreground chiefly tulips, peonies and irises, backed by larkspur, Madonna and Henry lilies . . . sweet William, phlox, canterbury bells, hollyhocks," etc.[53] Behind the flowers were flowering shrubs and trees such as pear and hawthorn. The rose garden featured a variety of tea roses as well as standard roses at accent points and a carpet of hyacinths followed by verbenas. Below the gardens was a lawn with "bright bays of color" (fig. 6.10), created in the spring primarily by tulips.[54]

In 1926, Dean collaborated with her husband on a spacious and imaginative subdivision plan in Port Washington for Vincent Astor. Harbor Acres, as it was called, was to be laid out on 300 acres of Astor's property, Cloverley Manor. His house had been built only four years earlier from designs by Delano and Aldrich on a site that may have

6.6 *Garden, G. Arthur
Schieren Residence, Great
Neck. Photograph, John
Wallace Gillies, ca. 1917.*
From *Country Life in America,*
December 1917

6.7 *Teahouse, G. Arthur Schieren Residence, Great Neck. Photograph, ca. 1921.* From Architectural League of New York, *Yearbook and Thirty-sixth Annual Exhibition,* 1921

6.8 *Garden, Mrs. George Gales Residence, Great Neck. Photograph, ca. 1921.* From Architectural League of New York, *Yearbook of Thirty-seventh Annual Exhibition,* 1922

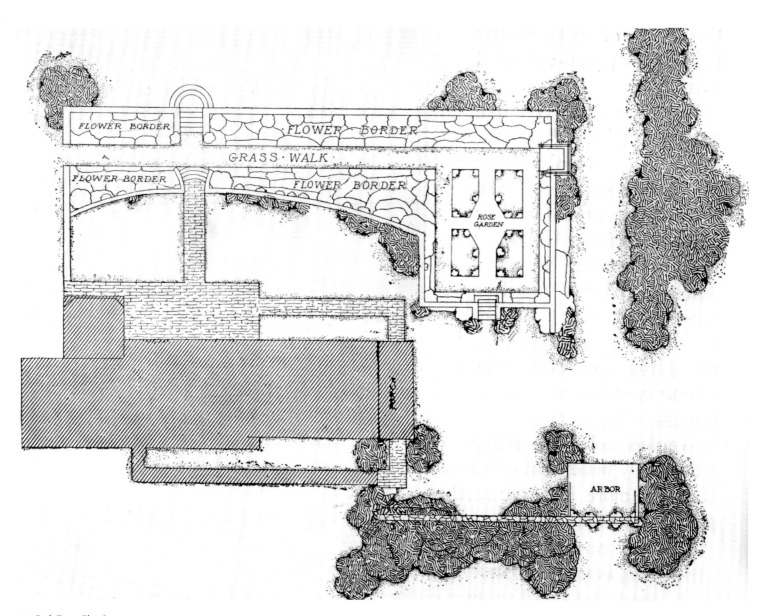

6.9 *Ruth Dean, Plan for the garden of Mrs. Monroe Douglas Robinson, Syosset. Ca. 1924.* From *Garden Magazine and Home Builder*, March 1925

Labels within plan: FLOWER BORDER · FLOWER BORDER · GRASS·WALK · FLOWER BORDER · FLOWER BORDER · ROSE GARDEN · ARBOR

6.10 *Garden, Mrs. Monroe*
Douglas Robinson, Syosset.
Photograph, Yosei Amemya,
ca. 1924. From *Garden*
Magazine and Home Builder,
March 1925

6.11 *A wooded walk in*
Harbor Acres, Hempstead.
Photograph, ca. 1927.
From *Harbor Acres,*
The Unusual Country Life
Community. Brochure,
ca. 1927 SPLIA

exceeded 1,000 acres.[55]

Astor probably intended to subdivide the northern part of his property from the beginning, but his motives are unclear. Since he sold the houses for the cost of construction, he could not have made any money on the project.[56] Astor was a noted philanthropist, but Harbor Acres was a private, gated community obviously intended for an upper-middle-class clientele, so philanthropy was not his goal here.[57]

There is no record as to why Astor chose the Embury/Dean team to design the subdivision, although both were by then quite well known. Located on Hempstead Harbor, Harbor Acres had its own private beach club, modern tennis courts, and several miles of bridle paths. Each house had between two and five acres of private land, so that, taking into consideration the generous amount of common land, there would have been fewer than a hundred houses altogether on the property. Sites were available for "the most elaborate establishment" or for more modest ones, for summer or for year-round use.[58] While there was no common stable at Harbor Acres, residents were permitted to erect their own stables, gardener's cottages, and other outbuildings (only one of each).[59]

The perspectives of the two houses in the folder "At Harbor Acres" have both Embury's and Dean's names on them. The site already had hills, vistas, and other attractive natural features. There were also well-established woods through which the designers threaded walks, drives, and bridle paths (fig. 6.11). Ruth Dean planted many varieties of new trees along the roads and, in some cases, elsewhere, frequently to define areas within the subdivision. On the house perspectives, she indicated trees and shrubs but in such a general way that it is hard to identify species with any certainty. In figure 6.12, two small American elms seem to be shown, and the shrubs are probably yews.

This distinguished project was conceived on the cusp of the Great Depression and ultimately fell victim to it. An aerial photograph of Harbor Acres, probably taken in 1927, shows only a few buildings, one of which, although buried in trees, may be Cloverley Manor (fig. 6.13). Only four of Aymar Embury's buildings were executed—the gate house (now a private residence), the Beach and Tennis Club, and two houses. Most of the houses on the site today date from the late 1940s and early 1950s.[60] The macadam roads were constructed early in the project and seem to be still there, although, without a subdivision plan, it is hard to be certain.[61] Dean's tree plantings are now lush and full grown. Unfortunately, they sometimes block her carefully planned views.

In 1928, Dean designed the grounds of the Henry J. S. Hall residence in Smithtown.[62] This garden was also framed by potted plants on the rear terrace, beyond which was a

6.12 *Aymar Embury II and Ruth Dean. Perspective, 1927, of a completed house, Harbor Acres.* From "At Harbor Acres," foldout plans and perspectives SPLIA

6.13 *Aerial photograph of Harbor Acres, ca. 1927.* From *Harbor Acres, the Unusual Country Life Community*. Brochure, ca. 1927 SPLIA

6.14 *Garden, Mrs. Henry J. S. Hall Residence, Smithtown. Photograph, ca. 1927.* From Architectural League of New York, *Yearbook and Forty-third Annual Exhibition*, 1928

6.15 *Garden, Mrs. Henry J. S.
Hall Residence, Smithtown. Photo-
graph, ca. 1927.* From American
Society of Landscape Architects,
New York Chapter, *Yearbook*, 1928

6.16 *Garden at Further-field, the George Roberts Residence, East Hampton. Photograph, Richard Averill Smith, ca. 1935.* From *House and Garden*, July 1936

broad greensward with thickly planted perennial beds on each side. At the far end of the perspective were large evergreen shrubs, probably yew, a small pool, and a diminutive garden house, with trees beyond (fig. 6.14). The Hall property was more extensive than it appears in this photograph. In a contemporary article, it was described as a "great Long Island estate" with "inviting formal stretches amid informal woods and flower plantings."[63] In one part of the garden there was another pool, surrounded by more perennial beds, all backed by a large deciduous tree, probably oak (fig. 6.15).

In 1930, Dean and Embury collaborated on two projects in East Hampton: Furtherfield, the George Roberts residence located between Middle and Further Lanes, and their own house on Main Street. Furtherfield, which still survives, was one of Embury's exercises in the Colonial Revival. The grounds consisted of a lawn the full width of the central part of the building and an ornamental garden

enclosed by planting beds placed at a diagonal to the house (fig. 6.16). At the far end of the garden was an unusual stone-edged pool in the shape of a lyre. Water lilies were planted in the pool, and the flowers in the beds included hosta. On the other side of the lawn, near the service court, was a cutting garden arranged in patterned beds.[64] The landscaping, which was completed by Mary Deputy Lamson after Dean's death, appears to have been at least partially extant as of 1989; the grounds contained a large grove of *Pieris japonica* dating from Dean's design, as well as a beech hedge around the service area, and the lily pond.[65]

In 1929, the Emburys purchased an early-eighteenth-century house (fig. 6.17), which Embury called "Third House." It was the third house he had owned, and he believed it to be the third oldest house in the town, although his date of 1685 was almost certainly too early. Once the interior renovations were completed, Dean began laying out

6.17 *Third House, the*
Embury Residence, East
Hampton. Photograph,
Harvey A. Weber, ca. 1980.
From Lancaster and Stern,
East Hampton's Legacy

the grounds.[66] Between February 15 and 20, 1930, she prepared an outline plan, a dimension plan, and a planting plan for the property, all of which exist in the form of faded prints. On the two more finished plans, she identified herself as Ruth Dean, Landscape Architect, and the client as Mrs. Aymar Embury II, as if these were two different people. In order to place their garden where they wanted it, the Emburys had to relocate a hundred-year-old entrance drive from the south side to the north side of their house.[67]

The garden to the side of the house and facing the living room consisted of scalloped beds of flowers outlined by low box shrubs. It was separated from the house by a thirty-foot lawn. A porch off the living room had views of the entire landscaped area at the side and to the rear of the house (fig. 6.18), including not only the side garden, but also an eighteenth-century terra cotta figure installed in a perspective trellis (fig. 6.19). The trellis, similar to others that Dean designed for New York City gardens, was a clever device for making a small space appear somewhat larger. To the side and extending to the rear of the plot was another clearly defined garden area framed at either end by box hedges and containing a small octagonal pool. Near the

pool was a bed of roses, and in the distance was a large honey-locust tree, which probably predated the garden. Rather than relying on Hicks Nurseries' or Lewis and Valentine's homegrown mature box, Dean imported hers from Virginia.[68]

Dean's planting plan of February 20, 1930 (fig. 6.20) shows how carefully she framed her landscape composition, using not only box but also fully grown hollies at the front of the property. In spite of her heavy schedule during the spring planting season, she and Embury must have spent some weekends in East Hampton, for there were liberal plantings of spring bulbs (narcissus, grape hyacinths, and tulips) near the front of the house. Late spring and summer flowers included peonies, delphiniums, a variety of lilies, daylilies, rudbeckia, and hostas. For fall bloom, there were asters. Third House is extant, but Dean's plantings are not.

Between 1930 and 1931, Embury designed the Guild Hall in East Hampton, an art and cultural center given by Mrs. Lorenzo E. Woodhouse, a prominent resident of the town. In 1931, Dean designed a sculpture garden, which now bears her name. This is a fenced and gated enclosure,

6.19 *Sculpture and perspective trellis, Garden, Mr. and Mrs. Aymar Embury II Residence, East Hampton. Photograph, Richard Averill Smith, ca. 1931.* From *Country Life in America,* March 1932

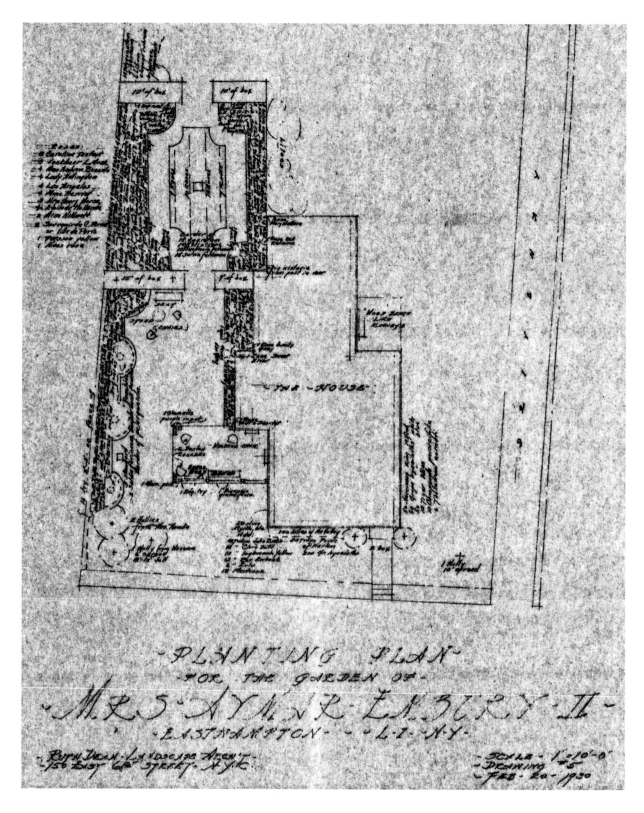

abutting the building, with a central open space for sculpture, framed by box borders and other small evergreen plants (fig. 6.21).[69]

The following year, Dean laid out the grounds of Lauriemore, the residence of Ellis L. Phillips on Bayview Road in Plandome Manor. The house was built around 1926; the architect has not been identified.[70] Phillips was the founder and first president of the Long Island Lighting Company, which had been established in June 1911. He and his wife were also philanthropists, giving generously to Ohio-Wesleyan and Cornell Universities. The Phillips property orig-

inally totalled forty acres.[71] The garden was approached by a gravel walk between an allée of lindens, with a ground-cover of English ivy below, a shady and somewhat mysterious entrance to a brilliant garden (fig. 6.22). Inside an ornamental wall, the gravel path continued, flanked on either side by box-edged perennial beds set in the lawn (fig. 6.23).[72] A feature that is not shown in the photographs was a kidney-shaped water trough.

Shortly after Phillips's death, the land was subdivided. Although the house and fragments of the wall survive, no trace of the garden or the allée is visible today.[73]

6.21 *The Ruth Dean Sculpture Garden, Guild Hall, East Hampton. Photograph, Richard Averill Smith, ca. 1931.* From *House and Garden*, May 1932

A garden at the East Hampton Free Library is sometimes attributed to Ruth Dean, but documentation is lacking. Embury designed the building in 1911, while Dean was still in Chicago. It is most unlikely that he could have known her at that date. However, it is possible that, at some point after the construction of the building, he might have suggested to the library that Dean design the garden space that he had proposed between the main part of the building and the stack wing.[74] The trellised arbor and sculpture that occupy this spot today resemble Dean's treatment of city gardens in constrained spaces.

Shortly after Ruth Dean's untimely death, her sister wrote:

Her work reflected her spirit. A straightforward mind . . . taking a positive stand always. This was the starting point and crux of her psychology. Modern in her attitude toward progress, yet all of this progressivism based on true classic tradition carefully studied and assimilated, and the result was a mind free of sententiousness, devoid of sentimentality, without fear or cowardice, she went ever forward.[75]

6.22 *Grounds, Ellis L. Phillips Residence, Plandome. Photograph, Richard Averill Smith, ca. 1931.* Visual Services Department, Frances Loeb Library, Graduate School of Design, Harvard University

6.23 *Garden, Ellis L. Phillips Residence, Plandome. Photograph, ca. 1931.* From *American Landscape Architect*, May 1932

CHAPTER 7

Annette Hoyt Flanders

1887–1946

ANNETTE LADD HOYT FLANDERS was born in Milwaukee, Wisconsin on September 16, 1887, the younger daughter of Hettie Pamelia Jones and Frank Mason Hoyt. On her father's side, Annette was descended from an early American family of pioneer stock. Her father was a well-known Milwaukee attorney, and her mother was a painter of floral subjects and a short-story writer.[1] Annette married Roger Yale Flanders in 1913. The couple began to live apart around 1916; after their divorce in 1920, Annette continued to use the Flanders name.[2]

Frank Hoyt was the most important early horticultural influence in Annette's life, sharing his interest in plants and taking her on trips within the United States and later to Europe and South America.[3] Her mother's artistic and literary interests must have been an influence as well.

Like Farrand, Hutcheson, and Coffin, Annette was educated by tutors as a child. She also attended two private preparatory schools, the Downer School in Milwaukee and the Balliol School in Utica, New York. In 1906, she entered Smith College in Northampton, Massachusetts, and received an A.B. in 1910. In her senior year, she was a member of the basketball team and was active in dramatics, playing the part of Florizel in Shakespeare's *A Winter's Tale.* As was usual at that time at Smith, Annette studied a very wide range of subjects, including botany, foreign languages, English, history, music, philosophy, and other liberal arts courses, as well as practically every course offered by the elocution department. Her two courses in botany included horticulture taught by Professor William Ganong,

director of the Botanic Garden, and Edward J. Canning, the head gardener. Within the music department, she took a course each semester (actually lessons) in piano and voice in her senior year. Surprisingly, given her eventual career, she took no art courses.[4] (Smith then did not have traditional majors as we know them today.)

In 1914, before receiving any formal education in the field, other than the course in horticulture at Smith, she began to practice landscape architecture, designing gardens primarily on a pro-bono basis.[5] In 1916, Flanders entered the University of Illinois at Urbana-Champaign, a land-grant institution, to study landscape design, which was then, as at Cornell, taught within the College of Agriculture. At the university, she studied some of what are still considered standard courses in landscape architecture, such as landscape design, planting design, landscape construction, and surveying, as well as several courses in trees, shrubs, flowers, and exotics. She also took courses in civic design and rural improvements. She wrote a thesis as well, although its subject is not indicated on her transcript, as was customary at MIT. Flanders was excused from most first- and second-year courses at the University, some of which were the same as those she had taken at Smith. She seems not to have studied drawing or drafting anywhere but might have learned how to draw as a child from her mother.

After receiving credit for nearly all her work at Smith and at Lake Forest College in Lake Forest, Illinois, where she seems to have taken a special program, she received a B.S in landscape gardening in February 1918. Flanders then

took special courses in civil engineering at Marquette University in Milwaukee. In 1918, she worked with the Telephone Operators' Unit, Signal Corps, and in the Canteen Service of the American Red Cross in France. The following year, she studied design, architecture, and the history of architecture at the Sorbonne in Paris.[6]

As an active practitioner, Flanders continued the plant-related pursuits to which her father had introduced her, using the winters (a "down" period for landscape architects) to study tropical plant material in the West Indies, Central America, the north coast of South America, Bermuda, and Hawaii over a period of twelve years.[7]

In 1919 or 1920, Flanders moved to New York City and joined the newly formed partnership of Vitale, Brincker-hoff & Geiffert.[8] She was already acquainted with the Florentine-born Ferruccio Vitale, since, in 1908, he had designed the grounds of Red Maples, the Southampton residence of her great-aunt, Mrs. Alfred Hoyt. When Mrs. Hoyt's daughter-in-law Rosina Hoyt inherited the property in 1913, Vitale was again engaged to continue the development of the gardens.[9] It has been suggested that Vitale was Flanders's mentor.[10] Certainly, he was her initial stylistic exemplar, and her work reflected his design philosophy even late in her career.[11] At Vitale, Brinckerhoff & Geiffert, Flanders was in charge of design and supervision of planting. Towards the end of her tenure, she had an unusual relationship with the firm. For some projects, such as the Myron C. Taylor property in Locust Valley, her name appears on plans as an "Associated" Landscape Architect, indicating that she was an independent practitioner associated with the firm and not an associate within it, as the term is customarily used today.[12] In 1922, Vitale offered her a partnership, which she declined, preferring to open her own office in New York City.[13] Like Beatrix Farrand at Reef Point, she maintained a secondary office at The Shelter, her family's summer place in Oconomowoc, Wisconsin.[14] In 1942, when, increasingly, her work was centered in the Midwest, she moved her practice to Milwaukee.[15]

In 1923, Flanders joined the American Society of Landscape Architects and was elected a Fellow in 1942. During her New York practice, she was an active member of that chapter, and, after relocating to Milwaukee, she joined the Chicago Chapter. She also exhibited regularly at the ASLA, New York Chapter, and the Architectural League of New York. In 1933, Flanders chaired an ASLA committee to relieve unemployment among landscape contractors.[16] Although she published one article in the *Bulletin of the Garden Club of America*, there is no evidence that she was particularly active in that organization or in any local garden clubs.[17] Flanders, along with other women landscape architects, was featured twice as a prominent professional by *House and Garden*.[18] In 1932, she was awarded the Gold Medal of the Architectural League of New York for the Charles McCann property in Oyster Bay.[19] In the same year, a major exhibition of her work was held at the Milwaukee Art Institute with an accompanying publication that appears to be a comprehensive record of at least her most important work to that time.[20]

Many women landscape architects got their start in Flanders's office, including her Smith College classmate Helen Swift Jones. In 1929, Flanders also took on Helen Elise Bullard, a Cornell graduate who had previously worked for Warren Manning.[21] (Jones and Bullard are both discussed in chapter 9.) Flanders's employees also included Iris Ashwell, Alice Bauhan, Mary Elizabeth Sprout, and Nelva Weber.[22] Also in her office for a time were two graduates of the Lowthorpe School: Margaret Eaglesfield Bell and Dolores Hoyle Richardson.[23] Around 1932, when the biggest job in her New York City office was the McCann property in Oyster Bay, she also hired a man—Herbert H. Cutler.[24] During World War II, Alice Upham Smith was an associate in the Milwaukee office.[25]

Like Beatrix Farrand, Flanders was convinced that a "cast-iron physique" was required for success in landscape architecture. The fatigue of traveling to nurseries and estates, the intense pressure of the planting season, and problems of shifting schedules caused by changeable weather were often particularly hard on women.[26] As noted in chapter 1, Frederick Law Olmsted, particularly in his later years, also found traveling and its associated pressures difficult, and other male practitioners undoubtedly did as well.[27]

Although, like her work in general, most of Flanders's Long Island landscapes were located on ample acreage, she also designed more modest projects. One of the smallest was a backyard garden for a teacher in Forest Hills Gardens, Queens. At the other end of the spectrum were both the McCann landscape and the forty-acre property of Mr. and Mrs. Charles W. Wright near Milwaukee in Ozaukee County, Wisconsin (1931–33), which included a lake, lawns, and terraced gardens.[28] In addition to residential projects, Flanders designed real estate subdivisions (including one in Philadelphia), the grounds of industrial plants, and recreational facilities. She also designed exhibition grounds, such as the Classic Modern Garden in the Century of Progress World's Fair in Chicago in 1933–34.[29]

Throughout her career, Flanders wrote articles for such periodicals as *House and Garden*, *Country Life in America*, and *Arts and Decoration*. In 1933–34, she was consultant garden editor for *Good Housekeeping*.[30] During the Depression, Flanders had to lay off some of her staff and also found it necessary to invest some of her inherited capital in her practice.[31] The four articles that she wrote in 1934 for *Good Housekeeping* reflect a new interest in gardens of a less luxurious sort than most of those she had designed in the past.[32] During the same year, she ruefully commented to a longstanding client, "People are afraid of me. I don't get small jobs."[33] One Hawaiian vacation also bore fruit in the form of three articles on the islands, all published in 1935.[34] With the exception of the 1932 exhibition catalogue, which illustrated Flanders's work but had no extended text by her, she wrote no books.

That exhibition was a large one with 151 items on display. In addition to the plans, photographs, and even models that one might expect, she included "pastel portraits" drawn by artists J. Floyd Yewell and Lizbeth C. Hunter from photographs. The colors, according to Flanders, were not "idealized" but were used as they actually appeared in the gardens. Several Long Island gardens were in this group, including the properties of Mr. and Mrs. Vincent Astor, Port Washington; Mrs. Patrick A. Valentine, Southampton; Mr. and Mrs. Charles E. F. McCann, Oyster Bay, and others. Although some of the original display materials have recently been located, others seem to have been given to friends and are dispersed. Even more unusually, Flanders devoted a section of the show to miniature models of gardens made of Staffordshire pottery, which were the work of an English artist. Flanders wrote that these were "accurate in scale and color," adding that "any house or garden can be reproduced in this manner from suitable plans and photographs." Included were models of the Astor property, a garden by Flanders in White Plains, New York, and several historic English gardens. The next sections in the exhibition focused on her naturalistic and informal work, her flower gardens, and her work on large estates. In the last group, there were many photographs of the McCann, Astor, Van Vleck, and Kiser properties, with special attention given to the French gardens at the McCann place. There were also New York City roof gardens, including one for Mr. and Mrs. Walter Hochschild on Fifth Avenue.[35]

Putting her college elocution studies to practical use, Flanders lectured extensively both in New York and in Milwaukee. In 1932 and again in 1941, she lectured at the Milwaukee Art Institute, the first a talk on "The Character of the Garden" and the second a series on plant material appropriate for the Midwest. She also gave courses, frequently in her own office, where she drew upon her collections of photographs, plans, reports, and books. In addition, she gave radio talks for garden clubs and charities.[36] By all accounts, Flanders was a formidable lecturer. A woman who attended a six-session practical course in landscape architecture wrote, "I feel Mrs. Flanders has a rare gift for teaching. She imparts an enormous amount of usable information in an incredibly brief space of time by the clear, simple manner in which she presents a subject she has at her finger tips. There is never a dull or lagging moment. The logical orderly sequence in which she presents one phase of landscape work after another stresses their relationship, and by this association of ideas she fixes them indelibly in one's memory. It is like taking hold of the end of a thread and unwinding it without a break."[37]

The student had expected to see "lovely colored lantern slides." These were eventually shown, but, first, Flanders laid out the basic principles of landscape design, giving her students "a foundation of practical knowledge." She sought to demystify the process, comparing it to making a sweater or a cake, a somewhat flawed analogy, since a cake is always a cake, and the most artful cook cannot vary cakes greatly, except in decoration.[38] Then she got to the heart of her argument, using charts to illustrate basic design principles and asserting, "All design is developed from a single straight line, all the gardens of Versailles can be reduced to one line."[39] Flanders explained how these simple elements

of lines, forms, and masses could combine and recombine to produce eventually finished landscape pictures.[40] This seems an unusually abstract approach to take to landscape design, but it was persuasive to her students. Using a three-dimensional cardboard model, she applied paper patterns cut to scale to place the house, outbuildings, and drives. Only then did she discuss choice of flowers and other plants.[41]

Flanders, who had always intended to teach, was not trying to make her students into landscape architects. Instead, she wanted to enable them to work better in their own gardens. If they worked with landscape architects, they would be more intelligent and actively involved clients. It is unfortunate that, at that time, none of the many educational institutions in New York City had a landscape architecture department where Flanders might have taught future professionals. In 1944, she wrote to a client indicating an interest in a faculty position at the University of Wisconsin-Madison, but this never materialized.[42]

Flanders's design principles are even more clearly explicated in "Landscape Design," an article published in the *Bulletin of the Garden Club of America* in 1938. Though brief, the text is densely packed with information and analysis. Like most landscape architects before her, including Olmsted, she stressed that good landscape design begins with a survey made by a civil engineer. She also urged that the architect and landscape architect choose the site of the house together and that the landscape architect should lay out the drives, even if the owner doesn't wish landscape services after this point. She recommended that the entire property be designed at the outset, even when implementation would have to proceed in phases. She also emphasized the importance of simplicity and lack of ostentation, a consistent principle throughout her career.[43]

It can be inferred from these recommendations that Flanders, like Olmsted, Coffin, and most other landscape architects, preferred to prepare comprehensive plans for entire properties and to be part of the design process from the beginning. However, as the discussion of her Long Island projects will show, she was often brought in after a house had been built or to design gardens for existing properties.

The most fascinating part of the article is the discussion of composition, which Flanders describes as "a group of related objects put together to form a landscape picture."[44] She also advised changing the existing topography of a place as little as possible, then determining the owners' preferences and mode of life, and, finally, considering how much upkeep the developed landscape can be given. Proceeding directly with the process of composition, she showed how lines combined to become forms, then forms combined into patterns and given three-dimensionality with mass, then compositions that can be arranged in different ways. These abstractions only become a landscape, however, when light, shade, and color are added.[45] The process is the same as when a composer writes a symphony, starting with the notes of the scale, "bending" them to create melodies, developing the main theme and subsidiary themes, adding harmonies, modulating from one key into another and back to the original, and, only then, orchestrating the piece. Indeed, Flanders often compared landscape architecture with music (fig. 7.2).[46] While Flanders may have learned some of this process at the University of Illinois, it is also possible that she had thoroughly absorbed the principles of design that formed the basis of Vitale's brand of rationalism.[47]

People who knew Flanders described her as determined, diligent, strong, opinionated, and forceful, qualities that also come through in her "Landscape Design" article.[48] Like the designers already discussed in this book, she was a perfectionist. While Vitale was clearly a dominant influence, she also admired Gertrude Jekyll's color schemes and gradations of color and her technique of planting in drifts, which she emulated in many of her own designs.[49]

Over time, Flanders's career became increasingly national and even international in scope. Among her later works were Morven, the Charles A. Stone property near Charlottesville, Virginia, a garden in Honolulu for Mr. and Mrs. Vernon Tenney, and one for an unidentified client in the south of France. Her last project was the design of the grounds of the mountain-top home in New Mexico belonging to Mrs. David Van Acken Smith.[50]

Although she was ill for the last several years of her life, Flanders continued to work. She died June 7, 1946 at her home in Milwaukee.[51]

Until recently, there was no central, publicly accessible archive for Annette Hoyt Flanders. After her death, her office staff or her sister thoughtfully returned many complete sets of plans to her clients, and these have been retained by some of their descendants, chiefly those in the Midwest.[52] In the late 1980s, the glass slides that Flanders used in lecturing, some of her plans, photographs, posters, and even the pottery models from her 1932 exhibition were discovered by Patricia Filzen, then a graduate student in landscape architecture, in a private collection in Wisconsin. The holding included glass slides of several Flanders-designed properties on Long Island. Filzen photographed all of the Flanders material, as well as that relating to three other women landscape architects from Wisconsin who were part of her thesis. These, and Filzen's own oral history tapes and transcripts, are now in the Sophia Smith Collection, Smith College, Northampton, Massachusetts.[53] In 2004, a dealer in South Carolina approached me with news of yet another Flanders cache, consisting of photographs of some of her projects by noted landscape photographers, photographs of plans, and one original plan. These are also now in the Sophia Smith Collection.[54]

To date, a total of about seventy-five Flanders projects have been identified.[55] Of these, twenty-one, including the unidentified garden in Forest Hills, Queens, are on Long Island. No original drawings seem to survive for the Long Island projects, and only a few plans (although many photographs) were published. As outstanding examples of her work, Flanders' Long Island designs are rivaled only by some of her midwestern landscapes.

The first documented Long Island project by Flanders was designed in 1921, when she was still associated with the firm of Vitale, Brinckerhoff & Geiffert. This was Underhill Farm, the 79-acre property of Myron C. Taylor, on Factory Pond Road in Locust Valley. Taylor was the chairman of U.S. Steel, who became America's envoy to the Vatican. The house was a pre–Civil War structure that had been renovated by Harrie T. Lindeberg to accommodate twentieth-century needs.[56]

Flanders discussed Underhill Farm in two articles, making this debut project one of her best documented. The articles have substantial text, and the design principles and ideas expressed in them can probably be extrapolated to apply to her later work as well, as she wrote of Underhill Farm:

> To be successful a garden must never seem complex. It must not tire us by presenting a bewildering mass of beauty which, like a three-ringed circus, leaves us exhausted by our effort to take it all in. At first glance it must be simply lovely and inviting. Its beauties must unfold gradually so that we take them in without effort. Simplicity without obviousness is the secret of charm, for the obvious is never charming. It has no mystery. It holds nothing in reserve. That is why so many gardens fail. They spread before us like nicely patterned rugs, are seen at a glance, and leave nothing to explore.[57]

For Flanders, the opposite of such charm and simplicity was the "showplace," whether large or small. Although she was writing in 1922, she felt that the social and economic

A BRIEF AND PRACTICAL COURSE
IN
LANDSCAPE ARCHITECTURE
BY
ANNETTE HOYT FLANDERS

THESE NOTES

CAN BE DEVELOPED TO CREATE
A GREAT SYMPHONY

THIS LINE

CAN BE DEVELOPED TO CREATE
THE GARDENS OF VERSAILLES

7.2 *"A Brief and Practical Course in Landscape Architecture by Annette Hoyt Flanders." Title page from a promotional flier.* Flanders Collection, Sophia Smith Collection, Smith College

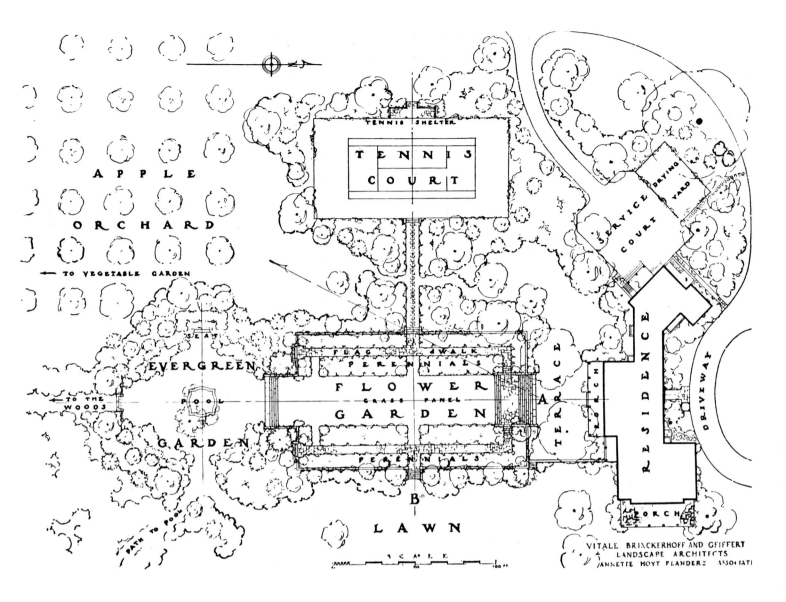

Within the plan image: APPLE ORCHARD · TO VEGETABLE GARDEN · TENNIS SHELTER · TENNIS COURT · SERVICE DRYING COURT YARD · RESIDENCE · DRIVEWAY · SEAT · EVERGREEN GARDEN · POOL · TO THE WOODS · PATH TO POOL · FLAG WALK · PERENNIALS · FLOWER GARDEN · GRASS PANEL · PERENNIALS · TERRACE · PORCH · LAWN · SCALE · VITALE BRINCKERHOFF AND GEIFFERT LANDSCAPE ARCHITECTS · ANNETTE HOYT FLANDERS ASSOCIATE

trend of the times was moving away from opulent display. Instead, she forecast "an increasing number of gardens of real charm; livable, lovable gardens planned to meet the needs of their owners and to be as inviting and much used as the rooms of their houses." To meet this goal, gardens, she felt, should be designed for "minimum upkeep . . . and have permanency of construction and planting . . . ."[58]

To Flanders, Underhill Farm exemplified this concept. The property, although large, was not ostentatious. The gardens, designed by Vitale, Brinckerhoff & Geiffert with Flanders, were grouped around the house (fig. 7.3). A curving drive about a quarter of a mile long passed by woodland, a cornfield, an apple orchard, and, as it neared the house, offered glimpses of a rhododendron path. The drive terminated in an oval forecourt before the front door, which was "festooned with wisteria and shaded by spreading elms and old locusts."[59] To the south of the house along its main axis was a walled and sunken garden. Still further to the south was an oval evergreen garden, where "we may sit in meditation looking at the pool shadowed by its picturesque guardian cedar, or read a favorite book without fear of interruption."[60] Also on the property was a tennis court close to the house but out of earshot, a lawn with a view of a pond, and several carefully planted paths.

Flanders's subtle design sense and her eye for color can be best appreciated in her discussion of the flower garden at Underhill Farm (fig. 7.4). She wrote that this garden, "with its wealth of bloom and color . . . was the heart of the design and leads to every other part of the grounds. It is a large garden, but such is its arrangement and planting that it loses nothing of the intimacy usually found only in smaller and more secluded plans." The colors varied with the season:

In spring pinks predominate, of every shade from flesh to deep cérise. The shaded rose of apple blossoms and the trembling billows of pink and white flowering shrubs spill over the walls and trail downward in graceful uneven sprays. They tie in with the dogwoods which bloom above them, their fairy blossoms in relief against the pines, and with the flowers in the beds below where early peonies, poppies, tiaralla, lupins, and a host of lovely little edging plants carry the color to our very feet. Everywhere . . . hundreds of Darwin tulips in every shade of pink rise on their slender stems from the green carpet formed by the growing foliage of later blooming perennials. . . . In June the pink all vanishes and blue and gold and white, the larkspur, coreopsis, lemon lilies, and Japanese irises, with clumps of Madonna lilies like altar candles, rise to take their place.[61]

7.3 *Vitale, Brinckerhof and Geiffert with Annette Hoyt Flanders, Associated. Layout of the home grounds, Underhill Farm, Myron C. Taylor Residence, Locust Valley.* From *Country Life in America*, May 1922

167

In July, the pinks were succeeded by multicolored phlox, followed in turn in August by lavenders and pastel shades. In the fall, golds and purples predominated.[62]

In her second article on Underhill Farm, Flanders expanded on her tulip planting scheme.[63] She also repeated her dictum about simplicity: "A restless garden has no beauty—gives no joy. Therefore use only what you must have to create your garden picture. I can give you no more valuable advice than to keep to one simple theme for your main effect, and satisfy your collector's instinct in your cutting garden."[64] In addition, she included two plans: one for the tulips (fig. 7.5) and another for the herbaceous plants that would fill the beds after the tulips were spent (fig. 7.6). For background plantings behind the garden wall, she used white pines, dogwood, and crabapples.

In the beds, she placed twelve kinds of tulips, in shades of pink, with lavender and purple. She explained her tulip planting technique as follows:

> In every way their colors must reinforce and bring out the design. The corners must not be blurred with weaker shades but should gain an added strength of form from color. There should be no pale shades planted up against the wall except as accidental notes. The colors must not blend in even runs nor be grouped in masses like a patch work quilt, but should be kept intermingled in a joyous mass of irridescent [sic], blending, glowing color.
>
> To gain this end I worked out this bulb planting plan as a guide by which to scatter out my bulbs, every one of which must be placed before you start to plant, and as you scatter the groupings overlap or you will get that patch work quilt effect.[65]

These words, although written years earlier, illustrate the precepts of Flanders's 1938 "Landscape Design" article put into practice. The herbaceous plants that grew in after the tulips faded included tall bearded iris, Siberian and Japanese iris, delphiniums, peonies (among them *Festiva Maxima*, still popular today), hollyhocks, veronica, and several kinds of phlox.

In 1924, Taylor terminated Vitale's involvement on the project and instead hired Olmsted Brothers.[66] The house at Underhill Farm is now owned by the Episcopal Diocese of Long Island, and the status of Flanders' landscape is not known.[67]

In the early 1920s, Flanders designed a garden for Mrs. Benson Flagg at Apple House in Brookville. The garden was planned around an old apple tree that gave the house its name (fig. 7.7). It included a small terrace, slightly elevated, and a wide double perennial border planted with lupines, iris, and peonies, which were followed by early phlox and monkshood. To soften the effect of the bricks in the narrow path between the beds, Flanders used tufted sandwort (*Arenaria verna*) in the crevices. The path ended in a diminutive gate.[68]

Flanders designed the landscape of Mañana, the E. Mortimer Barnes residence on Cedar Swamp Road in Glen Head, in 1924. The house had been designed ten years ear-

7.4 *Garden, Myron C. Taylor Residence, Locust Valley. Photograph, Mattie Edwards Hewitt, ca. 1922.* LISI 13232

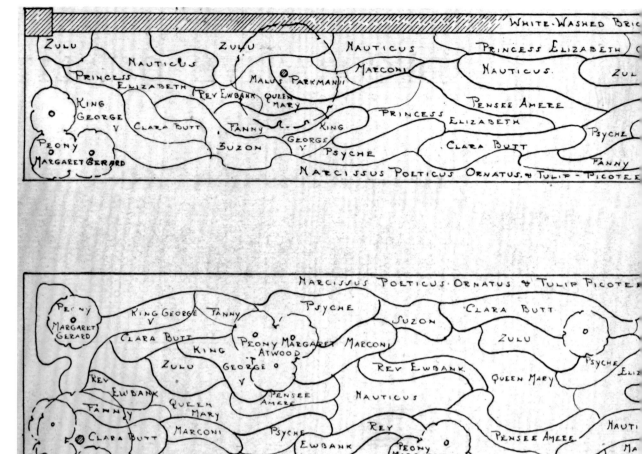

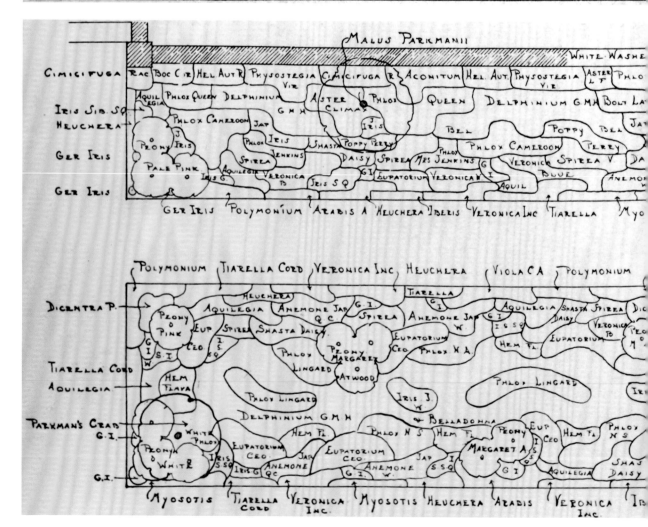

7.5 *Vitale, Brinckerhoff and Geiffert with Annette Hoyt Flanders, Associated. Tulip planting plan for the Myron C. Taylor Residence, Locust Valley, ca. 1921.* From *House and Garden,* September 1923

7.6 *Vitale, Brinckerhoff and Geiffert with Annette Hoyt Flanders, Associated. Perennial planting plan for the Myron C. Taylor Residence, Locust Valley, ca. 1921.* From *House and Garden,* September 1923

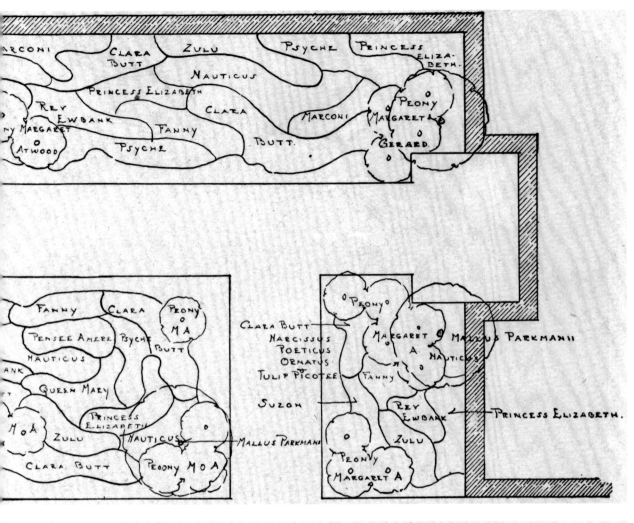

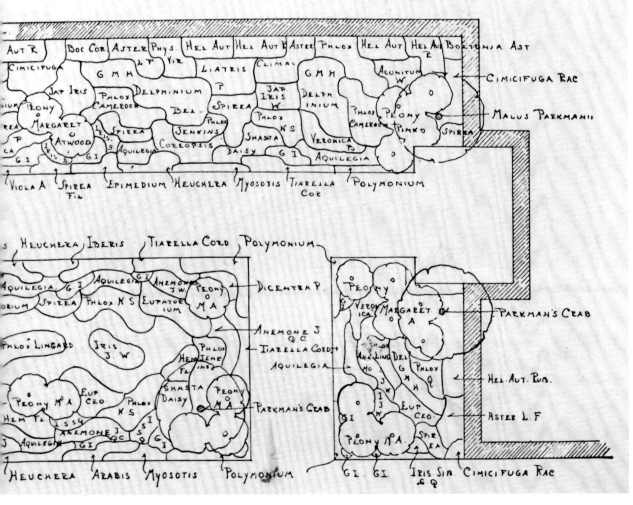

171

lier for Barnes, a stockbroker, by Thomas H. Ellett. For this landscape, Flanders used plant materials supplied by Lewis and Valentine. Flanders's work included a terrace and a walled garden adjacent to the house, which contained a pergola and a dovecote. The garden (figs. 7.8 and 7.9) was exquisitely proportioned and designed with Flanders's characteristic understated elegance. In the center was a round pool whose curb was practically flush with the ground. Around the edges were fully grown box shrubs. A

spring photograph (fig. 7.8) shows tulips, certainly one of Flanders's favorite flowers, growing in the spaces between the box plants and a luxuriant display of wisteria over the pergola. Behind these is the dovecote.[69] She also designed a "wilderness garden" with rough-cut, naturalistically placed stone steps, located presumably at some distance from the house.[70]

Around 1925, Flanders designed a garden for the F. C Demarest residence, a relatively modest house in Rockville

7.8 *Garden, E. Mortimer Barnes Residence, Great Neck. Photograph, ca. 1928.* SPLIA

7.9 *Garden, E. Mortimer Barnes Residence, Great Neck. Photograph, ca. 1930.* From American Society of Landscape Architects, New York Chapter, *Eighth Annual Exhibition*, 1931

7.10 *Terrace, F. C. Demarest Residence, Rockville Center. Photograph, Mattie Edwards Hewitt, ca. 1925.* From *House and Garden*, June 1926

Center. There were two parts to the landscape: a brick terrace under existing large trees (fig. 7.10), at least two of which appear to be Tree of Heaven (*Ailanthus altissima*), now considered a weed tree, and a small formal garden of perennials.[71] The Demarest landscape demonstrates that Flanders was proficient at designing small gardens well before the Depression forced her to seek out such projects.

During the same period, Flanders designed a garden on the grounds of Cloverley Manor, the residence of Mr. and Mrs. Vincent Astor on West Shore Road in Port Washington, discussed in passing in the previous chapter. The house, designed in 1922 by Delano and Aldrich, was approached through a gate lodge and a drive lined with densely massed shrubs, among them rhododendrons (fig. 7.11).[72] The rear elevation of the house featured a large terrace with two towering elms that faced an expansive lawn. In contrast was Flanders's intimate side garden, which centered on French doors on the second level of the house. The 1932 exhibition catalog included a photograph of the Staffordshire pottery model (fig. 7.12). A pair of curved stairs descended to the garden, which featured twin pools surrounded with flowers. Between the stairs there was a

door at ground level. Photographs of this garden, which include a color reproduction of one of the "pastel portraits" in the exhibition (see fig. C.6), show large box shrubs defining the far end, a flowering tree, a vine trailing over the stairs, tall bearded iris, and edging flowers.[73] Oddly, the whole composition is framed by two monumental brick stairways flanking the house, which seem disconnected and out of scale with the building. The Astor house, as noted in chapter 6, still stands.[74] The status of Flanders's garden is unknown, but a garden of this delicacy is unlikely to have survived.

About 1927, Flanders began to design her masterpiece, the grounds of the Mr. and Mrs. Charles E. F. McCann residence in Oyster Bay. Construction of all elements of the landscape probably took place over a period of at least three years. The house was designed around 1914 by George B. de Gersdorff for Mr. and Mrs. Fay Ingalls, who called their property Sunken Orchard, a name the McCanns retained. The original landscaping was by Innocenti and Webel, although the Ingallses do not appear on the client list in a recent book about that firm.[75] At the time the McCanns purchased the property, probably around 1927, James W.

175

O'Connor made minor alterations to the house and designed the playhouse and indoor tennis court around which a good deal of Flanders's work was clustered.[76]

Mrs. McCann, the former Helena Woolworth, was an heiress to the five- and ten-cent store fortune. She reportedly spent $3.5 million for the house and land at Sunken Orchard, subsequent architectural improvements, and the twelve gardens designed by Flanders. A connoisseur of Chinese export porcelain, her collection is now in the Metropolitan Museum of Art. Mr. McCann, a former Tammany lawyer, was a partner in the brokerage firm of Douglas, Armitage & McCann.[77] In 1934, the McCanns bought Beauport, the Henry Davis Sleeper property in Gloucester, Massachusetts, a treasure trove of American decorative arts. They fell in love with the house, which they had first seen from their yacht, and made almost no changes to its rich but somewhat eccentric interior. In 1942, after the death of the McCanns, their children saw that Beauport entered the collections of the Society for the Preservation of New England Antiquities (now Historic New England), thus preserving it for posterity.[78]

At the time of the McCann ownership, Sunken Orchard totaled more than 195 acres. It seems that Flanders received the Gold Medal of the Architectural League of New York only for the formal French gardens near the play-house rather than for the overall landscape design. While we do not know whether she prepared a comprehensive plan for the entire acreage, she did extensive landscaping beyond the French gardens. She probably began with the areas near the house and the informal parts of the landscape, since these were the first parts of the grounds to be published. The naturalistic work included a woodland carpeted with wild flowers, a pond bordered with iris and azaleas, the existing sunken orchard that Flanders planted with a carpet of violets, a bridle path, a pond made in the woodland, and a dogwood allée surrounding an outdoor tennis court (figs. 7.13 and C.7). Outside the French gardens, she also designed a path flanked by perennial beds, another large perennial garden, a house terrace, a swimming pool (see fig. C.8) next to the outdoor tennis court, and a boxwood garden. In early summer views (figs. 7.14 and C.9) of the perennial beds along the path, delphiniums, phlox, Japanese iris, and Oriental poppies are blooming. In spring, a brilliant display of Darwin tulips, edged with tiarella, creeping white and lavender phlox, viola, candytuft, and forget-me-nots filled the same beds.

The French gardens were an astonishing tour de force, superimposing a formal French baroque plan in the style of André Le Nôtre (albeit on a diminutive scale) onto a complex designed for twentieth-century recreation and enter-

FACING PAGE

7.13 *Dogwood Allée, Mrs. Charles McCann Residence, Oyster Bay. Photograph, ca. 1928. From American Society of Landscape Architects*, Sixth Annual Exhibition, *1929 (see also fig. C.7)*

ABOVE

7.14 *Perennial-bordered pathway, Mrs. Charles McCann Residence, Oyster Bay. Photograph, ca. 1927.* From Country Life in America, June 1928

177

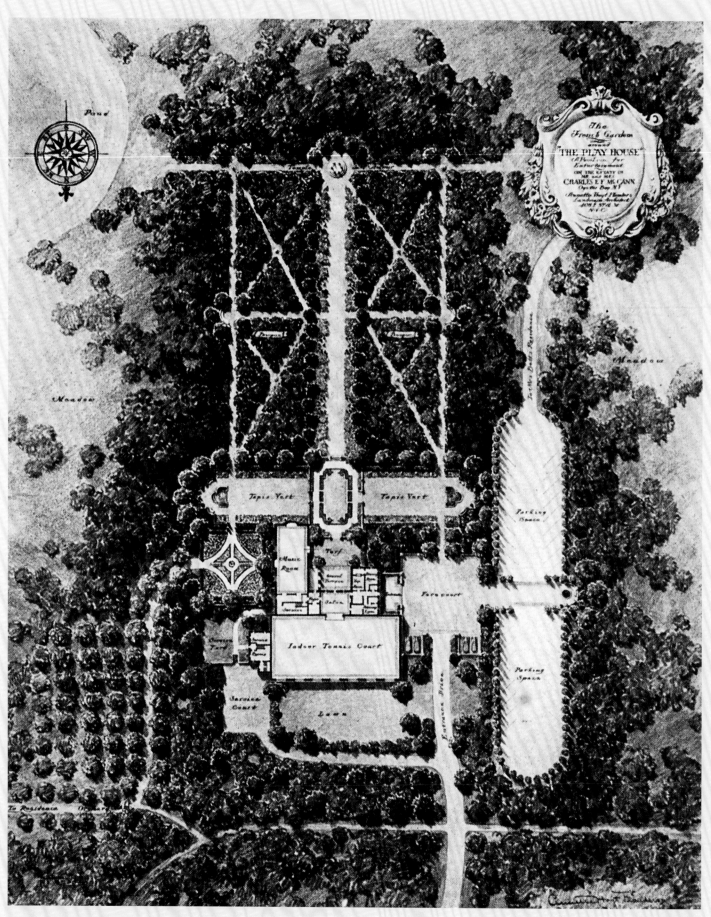

7.15 *Plan of the French
Gardens, Mrs. Charles
McCann Residence, Oyster
Bay, ca. 1930.* From Flanders,
*An Exhibition of Landscape
Architecture*

tainment. As Flanders wrote, the playhouse and its gardens were "used for informal entertainment as well as for large formal affairs. Gardens designed in the manner of the formal French gardens best met the client's requirements for these two types of entertainment, as they afford spaces for large numbers of people and more intimate places for small gatherings."[79] The playhouse contained the indoor tennis court, a music room, a ballroom, and other smaller rooms for more casual gatherings. The landscape plan for the French gardens (fig. 7.15) shows a long vista that originates at the front of the building (best seen from the balcony over the south door), extends over a grass panel edged with ivy or other groundcover, then down a grass allée terminating in a classical temple (fig. 7.16). The reverse view of the long axis terminates in a treillage composition (see fig. C.12). The sculpture here and elsewhere in the garden was by Milton Horn. The grass panel and the allée formed the main axis of the composition, while a *tapis vert* on either side of the turf panel, each terminating in a fountain, formed the cross axis (fig. 7.17). On either side of the allée were axial and radiating paths running through the woods in the typical French baroque fashion. Next to the music room, there was also a knot garden planted with

white flowers and designed to be viewed from above (fig. 7.18).[80] For the McCanns and their guests, this miniature Versailles must have been a magical place.

The McCann house is still a private residence, although the west wing was removed in the 1960s and much of the land between the house and playhouse has been subdivided. Portions of the landscape near the house are also extant. The playhouse complex survives in separate ownership, although only the forecourt, turf panel, and *tapis vert* sections of the French gardens remain. The allée, temple, and woods have disappeared beneath the tennis court of an adjacent property. The sunken orchard is also extant, although most of the trees are gone.[81]

By 1929 (the date of the earliest photographs of the property), Flanders had designed extensive grounds for Ballyshear, the residence of Mr. and Mrs. Charles E. Van Vleck Jr. in Southampton, apparently the first of her many projects in this town. The property had previously been owned by Mr. and Mrs. Charles B. MacDonald, for whom Rose Standish Nichols had designed two gardens (see chapter 8). For the Van Vlecks, Flanders designed a blue garden, a rose garden, an east lawn, and a magnolia terrace. Playground and swimming pool developments were

7.16 *Vista from playhouse to temple, Mrs. Charles McCann Residence, Oyster Bay. Photograph, Samuel Gottscho, ca. 1930.* From Flanders, *An Exhibition of Landscape Architecture*

7.17 *Axial view to
fountain, Mrs. Charles
McCann Residence, Oyster
Bay. Photograph, ca. 1930.*
From Flanders, *An Exhibition
of Landscape Architecture*

7.18 *Samuel Gottscho,*
Knot garden, Mrs. Charles
McCann Residence, Oyster
Bay. Photograph, ca. 1932.
Avery Library, Columbia
University

7.19 *The terrace garden,
Ballyshear, the Mr. and Mrs.
Charles E. Van Vleck, Jr.
Residence, Southampton.
Pastel drawing, ca. 1931.*
From Flanders, *An Exhibition
of Landscape Architecture*

7.20 Perennial walk to woods, Ballyshear, the Mr. and Mrs. Charles E. Van Vleck, Jr. Residence, Southampton. Photograph, ca. 1929. From American Society of Landscape Architects, New York Chapter, Seventh Annual Exhibition, 1930

7.21 *Blue garden.*
Ballyshear, Mr. and Mrs.
Charles E. Van Vleck Resi-
dence, Southampton.
Photography, ca. 1929, by
Maltie Edwards Hewitt.
From *American Landscape*
Architect, August 1930

7.22 *Rose Garden, Ballyshear, The Charles E. Van Vleck Residence, Southampton. Photograph, ca. 1929, by Mattie Edwards Hewitt.* From American Landscape Architect, August 1930

7.23 *An early development of the playground area, Ballyshear, Mr. and Mrs. Charles E. Van Vleck, Jr. Residence, Southampton. Photograph, ca. 1929, by Mattie Edwards Hewitt.* From American Landscape Architect, August 1930

planned, but it is unclear to what extent they were implemented. The "pastel portrait" in the 1932 exhibition, reproduced in black and white in figure 7.19, shows irregularly set paving stones with grass in the interstices on the terrace, along with a magnolia tree, and an ivy-covered stone railing with large potted hydrangeas perched at intervals along it, all backed by high evergreens dating from Nichols's "winter" garden. In another part of the grounds, a grass path flanked by perennial borders led to woodlands. Iris foliage and hollyhocks at the rear of the borders are about the only identifiable flowers in a midsummer photograph (fig. 7.20).[82]

Probably the most important element in Flanders's reworking of the Ballyshear landscape was the blue garden (fig. 7.21), which featured a central, stone-edged pool bordered with English ivy and with jars of blue agapanthus at each corner. Around the entire panel was a low brick wall with a base planting of blue annuals and perennials. The rose garden, on the site of Nichols's flower garden, was planted with hybrid tea roses and heliotrope with four corner beds of pink zinnias (fig. 7.22). Flanders retained Nichols's grape arbor, which surrounded the entire rose

garden. Pairs of tree lilacs, 10 to 12 feet in height, marking each of the three entrances to the rose garden probably also dated from the Nichols design. Figure 7.23 shows an early development of the playground area. Flanders wrote of Ballyshear:

> While it may be said that the treatment of Ballyshear is English in character, or at least English in feeling, no deliberate effort was made with the view of making it so. Rather, it was the purpose to design gardens, lawns and other areas that would harmonize with the dignity and beauty of the Georgian character of the residence, and yet attain a degree of livableness that would reflect the informality and outdoor life of an American summer colony. . . .
>
> One of the charms of 'Ballyshear,' we believe, is the ready access from any part of the estate to another. On the walks one may go, seemingly without effort, from one type of development to another; and there is ever some new, yet unobtrusive, interest that invites appreciation afresh.[83]

The house at Ballyshear and some of the landscaping are said to be extant.[84]

7.25 *West garden as seen
from house terrace, Mr. and
Mrs. John W. Kiser,
Southampton. Photograph,
September 1930, by Mattie
Edwards Hewitt* LISI, 28405

7.26 Woodland garden of Mr. and Mrs. Cass Ledyard, Jr., Syosset. Photograph by Samuel Gottscho, ca. 1933. From American Society of Landscape Architects, New York Chapter, *Seventh Arrival Exhibition,* 1934

In 1929, Flanders laid out the eastern part of the property of Mr. and Mrs. Thompson Ross in Great Neck. (See plan in fig. C.14.) Her design featured a rock garden and a flat, flower-bordered terrace with box scrollwork directly overlooking Long Island Sound (see fig. C.15).

In 1929–30, Flanders designed a garden for Mr. and Mrs. William R. Simonds (formerly the Russell property) in Southampton. A paved terrace similar to the one at the Van Vlecks was enclosed by a lightweight metal railing and accented by clipped, potted shrubs. The garden itself was rectangular with a central circular bed of ivy surrounded by four segmental flowerbeds and long perennial beds along the walls (fig. 7.24). All of the paths were grass. At the far end were a pool and a vine-covered trellis with three arched openings.[85] Flanders also designed a cutting garden, "pictorially arranged."[86]

About the same time, Flanders designed a sunken garden for Mr. and Mrs. John W. Kiser on Ox Pasture Road in Southampton. The house had been built about three years previously, but the architect is unknown. This garden (fig.

7.25) featured a central ornamental pool with lead swans at each corner and flower beds on two levels at the perimeter. The flowers around the pool included light-blue ageratum, heliotrope, and purple petunias planted in the swans.[87] The borders featured gladioli, among other flowers. From the garden, steps led up to the level of the lawn, with a view of water. A detail of this garden is shown in figure C.15. There was also a large cutting garden to one side of the house. The fully grown trees came from the Frankenbach Nursery in Water Mill. In a 1987 interview with Mac Griswold, Charles Smith, retired foreman of the nursery, described Flanders's fussiness about the exact positioning of trees and the way in which his men would resort to a bit of playacting to placate her: "Sometimes when we'd moved that tree about halfway around in the hole and it looked fine to me, I'd tell the men that the next time she asked for a little more this way or that, they should just shake that tree hard, and groan a little bit. Always seemed to suit her just fine.[88]

The Kiser house is extant.[89]

7.27 *Pathway from garden. Mr. and Mrs. Warren S. Crane Residence, Cedarhurst. Photograph, ca. 1929.* From American Society of Landscape Architects, New York Chapter, Yearbook, 1930

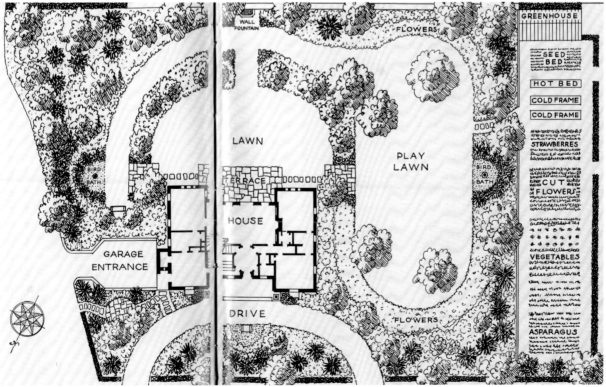

GREENHOUSE

SEED BED

HOT BED

COLD FRAME

COLD FRAME

STRAWBERRES

CUT FLOWERS

VEGETABLES

ASPARAGUS

WALL FOUNTAIN

FLOWERS

LAWN

PLAY LAWN

BIRD BATH

TERRACE

BIRD BATH

HOUSE

GARAGE ENTRANCE

DRIVE

FLOWERS

7.28 *Detail of Garden, Mr. and Mrs. Thompson Ross Residence, Great Neck. 1980s slide from a 1930s slide.* Filzen Collection

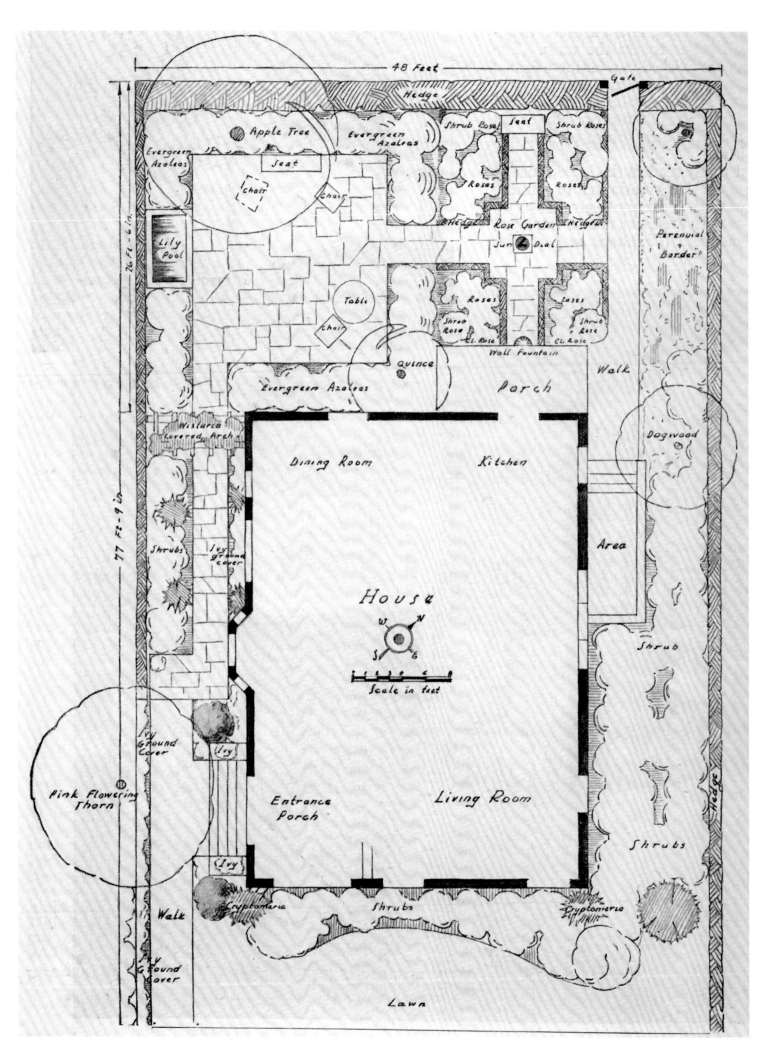

48 Feet

Gate

Hedge

Shrub Roses | Seat | Shrub Roses

Apple Tree

Evergreen
Azaleas

Evergreen
Azaleas

Seat

Chair

Chair

Roses | Roses

Hedge | Hedge

Rose Garden

Sun Dial

Perennial
Border

Lily
Pool

Table

Chair

Roses | Roses

Shrub
Rose | Shrub
Rose

Cl. Rose | Cl. Rose

Evergreen Azaleas

Quince

Wall Fountain

Porch

Walk

26 Ft. 6 in.

Wisteria
Covered Arch

Dining Room | Kitchen

Dogwood

Shrubs

Ivy
ground
cover

77 Ft. 9 in.

House

W N
S E

Scale in feet

Area

Shrub

Ivy
Ground
Cover

Ivy

Pink Flowering
Thorn

Entrance
Porch

Living Room

Shrubs

Ivy

Cryptomeria

Shrubs

Cryptomeria

Walk

Ivy
Ground
Cover

Hedge

Lawn

In 1931, Flanders designed a terraced garden, woodland garden, cutting garden, and pool for Mr. and Mrs. Lewis Cass Ledyard in Syosset. These consisted of changes made to a garden originally designed by Charles Platt and built in 1914 with a planting design by Ellen Shipman. Among the elements that Flanders designed was a woodland garden (fig. 7.26) with a central pool overhung by trees. The house is extant.[90]

A number of interesting gardens were included in the 1932 exhibition but not illustrated in the book. Fortunately, a few were published elsewhere. For Mrs. Patrick Valentine of Southampton, Flanders designed a formal rose and heliotrope garden (see fig. C.17), a particularly striking color combination.[91] She also designed a *jardin potager* for Mr. and Mrs. DeLancey Kountze in Roslyn.[92] Flanders laid out what she described as a "small estate" for Mr. and Mrs. Warren S. Crane Jr. on Polo Lane in Cedarhurst. East View, which still stands, was designed around 1932 by Bradley Delehanty as a wedding present for the Cranes from Walter S. Crane Sr. The walled garden (fig. 7.27) featured perennial borders and flowering trees and shrubs.[93] Flanders laid out two other small estates, one for Mr. and Mrs. George S. Olds in Great Neck and another for Dr. and Mrs. T. Lawrence Saunders in Westbury.[94]

Around 1934, Flanders designed a landscape for Mrs. Arthur Peck in Cedarhurst. The house was modeled after one "reminiscent of French Louisiana" designed by Bradley Delehanty and published in the June 1932 issue of *House and Garden*.[95] The garden (see fig. 7.28; see also fig. C.18) was divided into several rooms separated by massed shrubbery. There was a flagstone terrace at the rear of the house facing a small lawn. There was also a large play lawn (although apparently no play equipment) for Mrs. Peck's children, or perhaps her grandchildren. Connecting the lawns was a wide grass path. At one side was a large fruit, vegetable, and cutting garden, and a small greenhouse.[96]

By 1934, Flanders had also designed a diminutive garden for a schoolteacher in Forest Hills Gardens, Queens. Within the confined space (26 by 48 feet), she was able to satisfy her client's wishes for a goldfish pool, a bird bath, lilac bushes, an apple tree, a terrace, a rose garden, perennial borders, and a honeysuckle-covered arbor.[97] The plan (fig. 7.29) also shows quince, dogwood, a pink flowering hawthorn, and wild pink azaleas. Although Flanders described the rose garden as "tiny," it held thirty hybrid tea roses, a significant maintenance task for someone who probably did not have a gardener.[98] This commission from an unidentified client during the Depression years reflected Flanders's interest in recasting herself as a designer of small gardens.[99]

An undated Long Island project by Flanders was a cottage garden at Applewood, the residence of Mr. and Mrs. Montague Flagg on Wolver Hollow Road in Upper Brookville. Flagg, an architect like his better-known, younger half-brother Ernest Flagg, designed the house himself around 1915. The house is extant.[100] The relationship, if any, between Flanders's early client Mrs. Benson Flagg and Ernest and Montague Flagg is unknown.

Flanders's Long Island career ended with a curious coda: a plan and perspectives for a "*Jardin Potager* in the Period Manner," designed for Henry Leuthardt (see fig. C.19) and a sketch plan for a "House of Jewels."[101] The first drawing was made for the Henry Leuthardt Nurseries, still in business in East Moriches, which specializes in dwarf and espaliered fruit trees.[102]

Perhaps thinking about the Mortimer Barnes garden, the critic Royal Cortissoz wrote about a Flanders design that the garden was

an epitome of the present temper of the art in this country. One looks from between low hedges across a lawn with a pool in the center. The curb of this pool is practically on a level with the turf and is absolutely unobtrusive. . . . The garden by Mrs. Flanders . . . is positively endearing in its simplicity and in the adjustment of its balanced design to the sentiment of place. Flowers are used, but they are used sparingly. The note of color is not forced. The broad effect of turf and hedge contributes enormously to the prevailing atmosphere of peace and charm.[103]

7.29 FACING PAGE
Garden for a schoolteacher in Forest Hills Gardens, Queens. Plan, ca. 1934. From *Good Housekeeping,* March 1934

The Second Generation, I

THE "PIONEERS" of landscape design were succeeded by a second generation of women who benefited from their success in establishing independent practices and achieving national recognition. For the most part, these women started their careers somewhat later than the first six, although three were contemporaries of Beatrix Farrand and Ellen Shipman. Some also had the advantage of formal training, not only at the architecture program at MIT and its short-lived landscape architecture option, but also at two Boston-area schools set up exclusively for women: the Lowthorpe School of Landscape Architecture for Women in Groton, established in 1901, and the Cambridge School of Architecture and Landscape Architecture in Cambridge, begun in 1916. Two women studied landscape architecture at Cornell University, a program begun in 1904 that was always open to women, at least in theory. A number of the "second-generation" women joined the offices of the "pioneers" before establishing their own practices. Those in the second generation discussed here are: Mary Rutherfurd Jay, Rose Standish Nichols, Louise Payson, Marjorie Sewell Cautley, Isabella Pendleton, and Eleanor Roche. Mary Deputy Lamson Cattell, Nellie Beatrice Allen, Helen Elise Bullard, Helen Swift Jones, Janet Darling Webel, and Alice Recknagel Ireys are the subject of chapter 9.[1]

Mary Rutherfurd Jay

1872–1953

MARY RUTHERFURD JAY was born on August 16, 1872 in Fair Haven, Connecticut, the daughter of the Reverend Peter Augustus Jay and Julia Post Jay and a descendant of John Jay, the first Chief Justice of the United States. In 1906, she either took courses in architecture at MIT or was tutored in that program; she also studied plant-related subjects at the Bussey Institute.[2] In other words, she followed the same educational path as Martha Brookes Hutcheson and Marian Cruger Coffin, although she spent less time at MIT than they did.

In 1924, a reporter asked Jay what the impelling circumstances were that led her into her profession. She answered that she had studied painting, drawing, and design, had traveled in Europe, and lived for a time in Florence. Most importantly, she noted: "I have always believed that everyone is under obligation to be a producer of one kind or another, and not a mere consumer. To profit by the activities of others but do nothing oneself to make the world better and more beautiful is wrong."[3] Once she made her decision to be a garden architect (her title of choice), she immediately took steps to get the proper training, observ-

ing that it was very difficult then for a woman. She mentioned the Bussey Institute and the Arnold Arboretum but not MIT, although she stated that she needed to study engineering. Like Farrand, Flanders, and others, she remarked that the profession was strenuous.[4] Her first project was apparently planting a *plaisance* on the grounds of a friend in Connecticut. This may have been the F. D. Wells property in Greenwich, a job undertaken in 1907.[5]

Jay opened her practice in New York City in 1908. Her work was primarily residential, and her projects were concentrated in New York, Connecticut, and Rhode Island, with others in New Jersey and Massachusetts and a few in Pennsylvania, Virginia, California, and Florida. Nonresidential New York City projects included the grounds of Grace Church (1910), John Jay Park (undated), and a roof garden for the *New York Times* (undated). In 1912, she spent an extended period traveling around the world and toured in England in 1929. Throughout her career, she used the slides from these and other trips to illustrate lectures on international gardens.[6]

Like Hutcheson, Dean, and Flanders, Jay was active in the war effort during World War I. She worked for the American Committee for Devastated France, was in the charge unit of the "farmerettes" working with the United States Army Garden Service in Versailles, France (June 1918), and volunteered with the American Red Cross (1918–19). For these services, she was decorated with the Cross of Mercy (Serbia) and the Silver Medal of the American Committee for Devastated France.[7] Jay was a Fellow of the Royal Horticultural Society in London and belonged to the New York Horticultural Society, the Garden Club of America, and the Garden Club of Orange and Dutchess Counties, New York. She seems not to have been a member of the American Society of Landscape Architects, but her work was exhibited at least once by the Architectural League of New York.[8]

Most of Jay's commissions were clustered between 1907 and 1928; she seems to have been almost totally inactive during the Depression and throughout most of World War II. Her two last projects were apparently the John William Morgan property (1944) and the Bernatschke residence (1945), both in New York City. Two particularly fine projects outside of Long Island were the property of John W. Chapman in Greenwich, Connecticut (1910–12) and the W. Willis Reese residence in New Hamburgh, New York (1921–28).[9]

In 1931, Jay published *The Garden Handbook*, which was produced in a small format so that readers could bring it into the garden.[10] This seems a puzzling choice since nearly half of the book was devoted to a discussion of garden types and details drawn from all over the world. Only the two appendices offer the practical information that might be used while in the garden. The book demonstrates a truly astonishing grasp of gardens not only in Europe but also in the Middle East, South America, and Asia. Jay gained this insight primarily through her own reading and travels, although some of the photographs in the book were given to her by others, including the French landscape architects

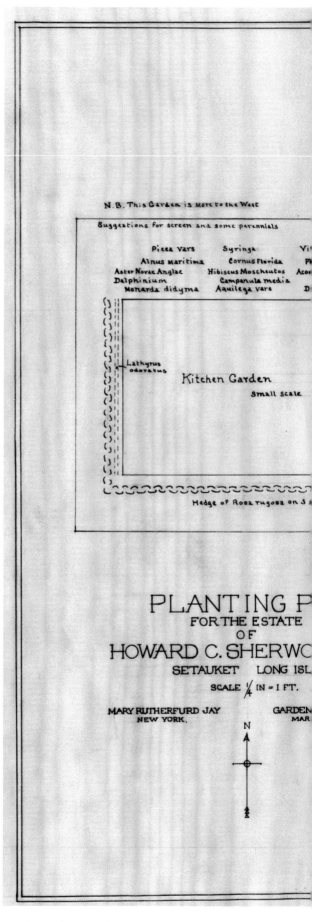

8.2 *Planting plan, Howard C. Sherwood Residence, Setauket. Ink on linen, March 1909.* CED

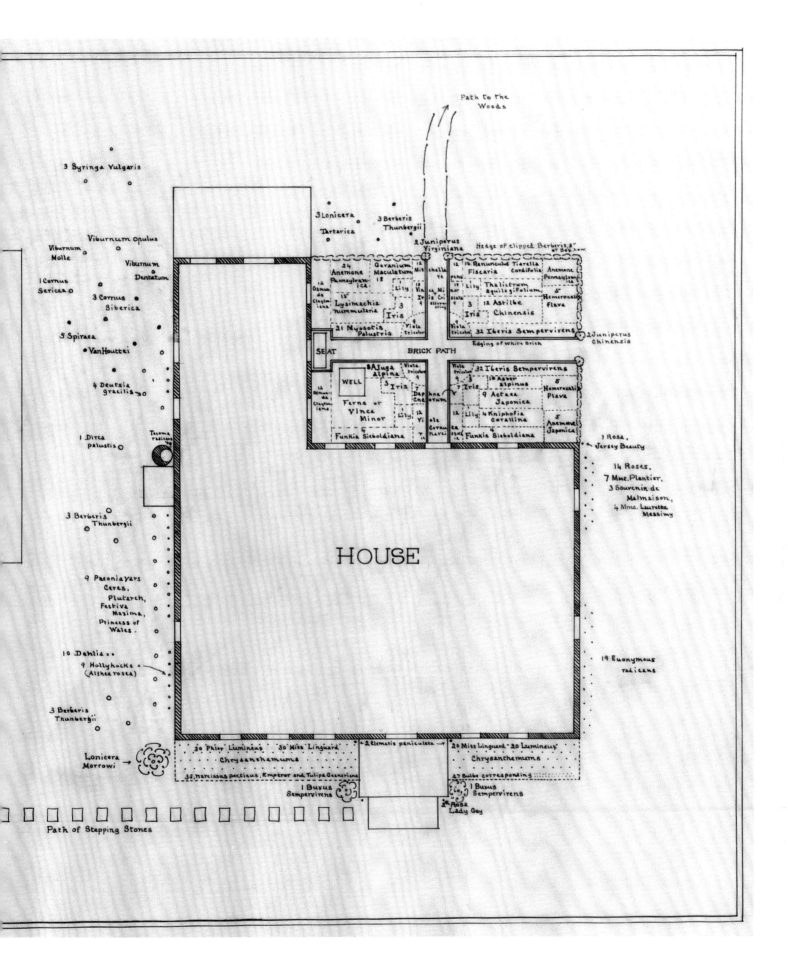

3 Syringa Vulgaris

Viburnum Opulus
Viburnum Molle
Viburnum Dentatum
1 Cornus Sericea
3 Cornus Siberica
5 Spiraea
Van Houttei
4 Deutzia gracilis
1 Dirca palustris
Tecoma radicans
3 Berberis Thunbergii
9 Paeonia vars
Ceres,
Plutarch,
Festiva Maxima,
Princess of Wales.
10 Dahlia
9 Hollyhocks (Althea rosea)
3 Berberis Thunbergii
Lonicera Morrowi

3 Lonicera Tartarica
3 Berberis Thunbergii
2 Juniperus Virginiana

Hedge of clipped Berberis 3" or Box Low

24 Anemone Pennsylvanica
Geranium Maculatum 18
Mitchella
12 Osmunda Claytoniana
Lysimachia Nummularia
3 Iris
21 Myosotis Palustris
Lily
Iris Cri
Viola tricolor

SEAT
12 Osmunda Claytoniana
WELL
Ferns or Vinca Minor
4 Funkia Sieboldiana

8 Ajuga Alpina
Viola tricolor
3 Iris
Daphne Cneorum
Lily
Viola
Iris Cornuta
Narci

BRICK PATH

14 Ranunculus Tiarella
Ficaria Cordifolia
Anemone Pennsylva
Lily Thalictrum aquilegifolium
3 12 Astilbe Chinensis
Iris
32 Iberis Sempervirens
Edging of white brick
5 Hemerocallis Flava

32 Iberis Sempervirens
15 Aster alpinus
9 Actaea Japonica
4 Kniphofia coralina
Funkia Sieboldiana
5 Hemerocallis Flava
5 Anemone Japonica

2 Juniperus Chinensis

1 Rosa Jersey Beauty
14 Roses,
7 Mme. Plantier,
3 Souvenir de Malmaison,
4 Mme. Laurette Messimy

HOUSE

19 Euonymus radicans

30 Philip Lumineux   30 Miss Linguard
Chrysanthemums
35 Narcissus poeticus, Emperor and Tulipa Generviera
1 Buxus Sempervirens

2 Clematis paniculata

20 Miss Linguard   20 Lumineux
Chrysanthemums
27 Bulbs corresponding
1 Buxus Sempervirens
1 Rosa Lady Gay

Path of Stepping Stones

195

Achille Duchêsne and Jacques Gréber and the American architect Bertram Grosvenor Goodhue. There are lovely photographs of, for example, Argentine *estancias* (estates), French chateaus, and the famous garden of the Generalife in Spain. In the final section, entitled "American Adaptations," Jay showed several examples of gardens in this country, some of which she described as estate-sized but others that were smaller. A number were her own designs, while some were the work of other landscape architects or of the owners. In the introduction, Jay pointed out that the United States has a vast range of climate, topography, and vegetation, which is certainly true. For nearly all of the American gardens she illustrated, she listed a European or other style prototype, asserting that there was no one type that could be called an "American garden," a statement that is debatable.[11] In the Northeast at that time, most gardens, to the extent that a single label can be put on them at all, tended to be in the American Colonial Revival or the English Arts-and-Crafts style, with others reflecting Italian influence. Jay's clients undoubtedly digested this information and took her advice. Still, the average American homeowner who purchased the book might have been a bit overwhelmed by such erudition and uncertain as to how to apply it.

Toward the end of her life, Jay gave her office archives, including drawings and photographs of her own work, as well as the two thousand lantern slides she used in lecturing, to Beatrix Farrand to add to the Reef Point Gardens Collection (see chapter 2). When the plan to turn Reef Point into a landscape education center fell through, Jay's materials, along with Farrand's and the plans of English garden designer Gertrude Jekyll, were given to the University of California, Berkeley, where they are now in the Documents Collection of the College of Environmental Design. Jay died at her country home, Rutherfurd Lodge, Drum Hill, Wilton, Connecticut, on October 4, 1953.[12]

Berkeley has plans for forty-six projects by Jay, five of which are on Long Island.[13] It is likely that plans for a number of other projects have been lost and are not included in the Berkeley collection. In the Preface to *The Garden Handbook*, Jay thanked six clients who are not on the Berkeley list for allowing her to photograph their gardens.[14] At least two of these had properties on Long Island, but Jay did not identify clients by name in her text on American gardens.

Nothing is known about how Mary Rutherfurd Jay ran her office. Given the limited number of documented projects, it seems likely that it was a modest operation. The fact that she was able to leave for an extended period to travel around the world would seem to support this assumption. Jay must have employed draftswomen and assistants, but none have been identified.

JAY'S FIRST LONG ISLAND commission was a garden for Howard C. Sherwood, who founded the Society for the Preservation of Long Island Antiquities in 1948. Sherwood, a native of California and a Harvard graduate, briefly practiced law in New York City. In 1908, he purchased what is now the Sherwood-Jayne House, a SPLIA property in

Setauket, and added a wing to the structure. The following year, he contacted Jay. For the next several decades, he devoted most of his time to collecting Americana and used the house primarily as a weekend retreat.[15] Jay's planting plan (fig. 8.2) shows numerous proposed flowering shrubs, perennial, and bulb plantings, as well as a clematis vine on either side of the front door. The main feature is a Colonial Revival–style garden located between the main mass of the house and the new wing; it is divided into four quadrants by brick paths. Most of the plants are spring or summer blooming perennials. Jay also planned a kitchen garden on the west side of the house, where the vegetables were to be surrounded by a hedge of *Rosa rugosa* on three sides and by trees, shrubs, and perennials on the fourth. Since there are no photographs of this project in the Jay collection, it is uncertain whether the plan was carried out. In any case, nothing remains of this planting today.

Jay's project for Mrs. George W. Wickersham in Cedarhurst, designed in 1914, is more fully documented and definitely was executed. A large pond on the site (fig. 8.3) inspired Jay to propose a Japanese garden. As she had observed on her travels, quiet still water was often a central feature of gardens in Japan. Jay drained the existing pond and laid cement as a foundation for the islands, which were traditionally four in number (fig. 8.4). The existing island, designated as the Master's Island, was built up, and a large stone lantern was placed on it. The Master's Island also contained a Stone of Easy Rest. A curved bridge painted dark red led to a smaller Guest's Island with an Interviewing Stone, where the Master would greet his guests (fig. 8.5). On the same island, there was also another large stone decorated with two bronze cranes. A large isolated rock represented the traditional Windswept Island, while to one side was the Elysian Island, which could be reached only by boat. Jay planted the shores of the pond with evergreen trees, rhododendrons, and bamboo, with clumps of Japanese iris at the water's edge. The dominant plant around the upper (northern) part of the pond was *Azalea mollis*. Following Japanese custom, the banks were held in place with driven piles of wood.[16]

In 1915, Jay prepared alternate plans for a flower garden for the H. W. Cannon property in Huntington. Since both of these plans were labeled as "suggestions," it is unclear whether they were carried out. In 1916, she designed a rose and perennial garden and possibly another garden for Mrs. John T. Livingston in Woodmere. Between 1916 and 1920, she designed a rose garden, a formal garden, and a wild garden for Mrs. H. T. S. Green in Hewlett. Since the Green drawings included planting plans, it is quite likely that the gardens were carried out.[17]

At some point, probably in the 1920s, Jay supervised the installation of a garden designed by Mrs. C. Oliver Iselin at Wolver Hollow, the Iselin property in Mill Neck. Several other landscape architects had worked at this site, including Olmsted Brothers, Beatrix Farrand, and Ellen Shipman. By 1931, Mrs. Iselin's garden had been replanted by Isabella Pendleton (see below).[18] Jay probably never drew any plans for this garden, and there are none at Berkeley.

8.3 *George W. Wickersham Residence, Cedarhurst, before Construction of Japanese Garden. Photograph, 1914.* CED

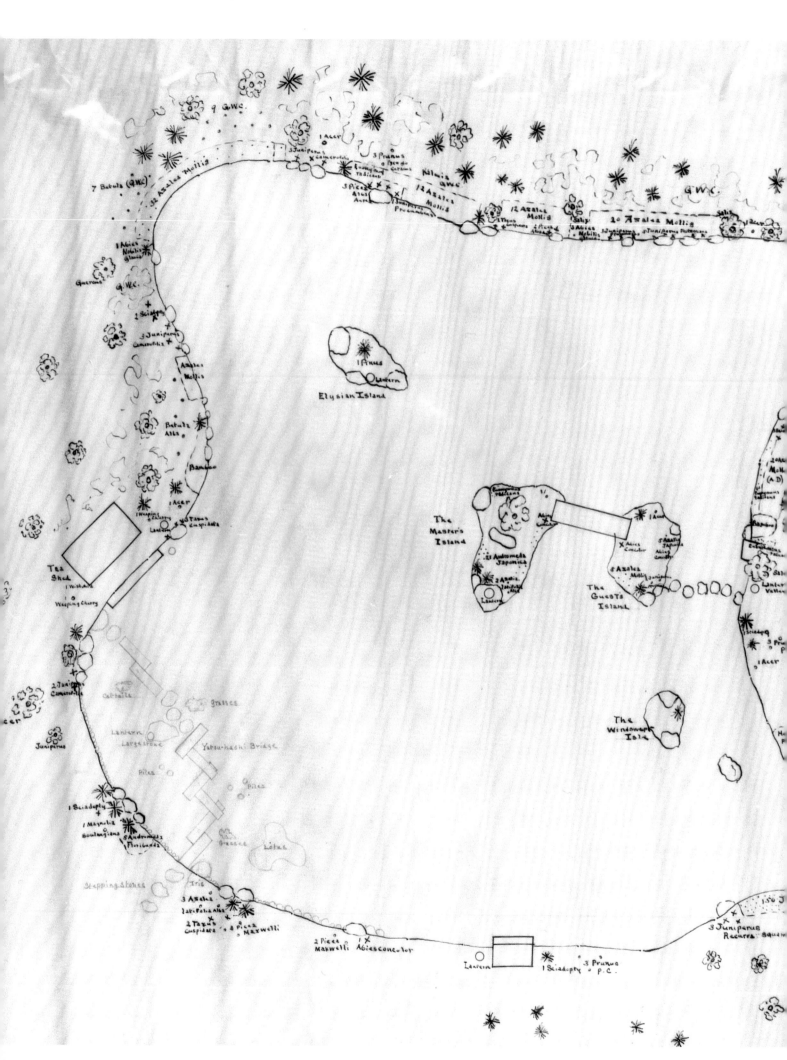

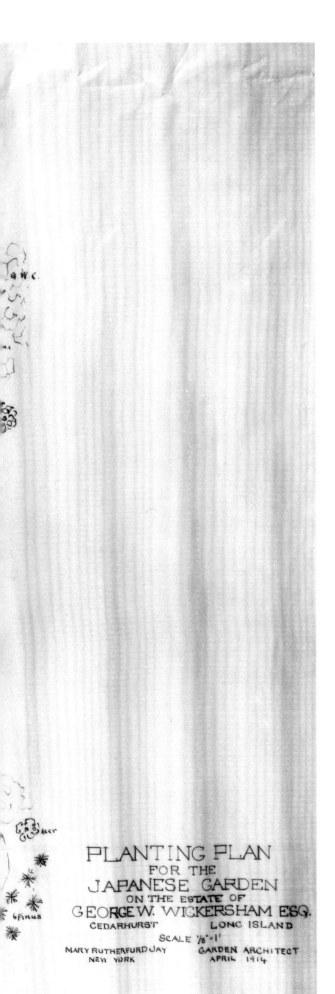

PLANTING PLAN
FOR THE
JAPANESE GARDEN
ON THE ESTATE OF
GEORGE W. WICKERSHAM ESQ.
CEDARHURST   LONG ISLAND
SCALE ⅛"=1'
MARY RUTHERFURD JAY   GARDEN ARCHITECT
NEW YORK   APRIL 1914

8.4 *Planting plan, George
W. Wickersham Residence,
Cedarhurst, April 1914.* CED

8.5 *Japanese Garden,
George W. Wickersham
Residence, Cedarhurst.
Photograph, Frances
Benjamin Johnston,
undated.* Library of Congress,
Prints and Photographs Divi-
sion

The Iselin house is extant, in corporate hands.[19] Whether
anything remains of the contributions of the five landscape
architects is unknown.

Jay's client list included Mrs. Arthur N. Peck, who lived,
initially at least, in Woodmere, but there are no plans for
this project at Berkeley.[20] Annette Hoyt Flanders designed
a garden in 1934 for Mrs. Peck at a new house in
Cedarhurst (see chapter 7). A small formal garden in Glen
Head is illustrated in Jay's book, but none of her documented clients lived in that town.[21]

Rose Standish Nichols

1872–1960

8.6 *Rose Standish Nichols. Drawing, Taylor Green, 1912.* Nichols House Museum, Boston

ROSE STANDISH NICHOLS was born in Boston on January 11, 1872, the eldest of three daughters of Dr. Arthur Nichols, a homeopathic physician, and Elizabeth Homer Nichols.[22] In an interview with a *Boston Globe* reporter when she was in her eighties, Nichols recalled, "My active interest in garden making began when, as a child, under the guidance of my grandfather, Thomas Johnston Homer, I cultivated a tiny posy bed on his Roxbury estate."[23] In 1889, her family bought a property known as Mastlands in Cornish, New Hampshire, where her aunt and uncle Augustus and Augusta Homer Saint-Gaudens already had a summer house with a garden of the sculptor's own design.[24] At some point, Nichols studied horticulture with Mrs. Benjamin Watson and "became interested in the so-called 'formal' style in gardens, revived in England and opposed to the sinuosities of the romantic school."[25] She decided to study garden layout from the point of view of an architect and found a willing tutor in her Cornish neighbor Charles Platt.[26] (This seems to have been before Platt similarly took Ellen Shipman under his wing.)

As her next step, Nichols studied architecture in the office of Thomas Hastings of Carrère and Hastings, while living with the Saint-Gaudenses in New York City.[27] She then returned to Boston and, in 1899, took two design courses at MIT with Professor Desiré Despradelle, focusing on how to apply architectural principles to the plans of gardens.[28] She also studied in Paris with Professor Despuis of the Ecole des Beaux-Arts, and in London with

F. Inigo Triggs, author of *The English Formal Garden*. Her visits to famous gardens in England became the source of her first book, *English Pleasure Gardens*, published in 1902.[29] This was a pioneering study, although the bulk of the text was devoted to early formal gardens in England and especially to their antecedents. One chapter, entitled "Eighteenth-Century Extremes," discussed the period that today is considered England's most innovative; the concluding chapter, "Modern Gardens," covered the entire nineteenth century.

In 1896, Nichols laid out a garden modeled on the Pond Garden at Hampton Court, England, at Mastlands.[30] Like Jay, Nichols preferred to call herself a garden architect, but in 1903, she became the first women to be listed under the heading "Landscape Architect" in the Boston City Directory; her offices were at 5 Park Street, not far from the family house at 55 Mount Vernon Street on Beacon Hill.[31]

Nichols's first project for a client seems to have been a large flower garden in Newport for Ellen Mason, a neighbor on Beacon Hill. The Mason property had previously been landscaped by the Boston civil engineer and landscape gardener Ernest W. Bowditch (1880) and then by the firm of Frederick Law Olmsted (1882). Olmsted's work coincided with the remodeling of the interior of the house by H. H. Richardson. (The architect and landscape architect were close friends.) The Mason house burned in 1899 or in 1902 (sources vary), and a new house, designed by the California architect Irving Gill, was built on the property. Ellen Mason brought in Olmsted Brothers in 1902 and

Nichols, probably shortly thereafter.[32] In concept, the Mason garden was similar to that at Mastlands, except that a round, central grass panel with a sundial replaced a round pool with a fountain, and the planting beds appear to be more densely packed with perennials.

Two Boston-area collections preserve some family papers, but neither is very useful in reconstructing Nichols's career.[33] Her projects appear to have been somewhat limited in number and rather widely dispersed across the country, with a significant cluster in Lake Forest, Illinois, and other examples in Santa Barbara, California, and Tucson, Arizona. She published two more books, one on Italian gardens and another on those of Spain and Portugal.[34] She apparently was not a member of the American Society of Landscape Architects, but she was active in garden clubs.[35] Nichols had many interests besides landscaping and gardens. While still in her twenties, she founded the Beacon Hill Reading Club. She was also a pacifist with broad interests in international affairs. She was an expert at embroidery and collected antique examples. Portraits of Nichols as a young woman show a penchant for elaborate dresses and complicated hats and hair styles. As an old woman, she was described as "tall, stately, regal in bearing," but "with an inquiring twinkle

in her eye."[36] Nichols died in Boston on January 27, 1960. Although she set aside the Mount Vernon Street house by legacy to become a private house museum and to preserve and display her collections of art, antiques, and historic needlework, her plans and office records have not survived.[37]

NICHOLS'S SOLE Long Island landscape was Ballyshear, the residence of Charles Blair McDonald in Southampton, completed by 1913. MacDonald was a Chicago businessman who moved to New York City in 1900 and eventually became a partner in the stock-brokerage firm of C. D. Barney & Company. As a student at St. Andrews University in Scotland, he had become enamored of golf, a passion that remained with him throughout his life. In 1892, he laid out a few holes for a group of friends in Lake Forest, Illinois, one of the first golf courses of any kind in the country. He was also involved in organizing the Chicago Golf Club and laying out its first courses. Around 1906, he and a group of seventy other people purchased two hundred acres at Sebonac Neck in Southampton and engaged Seth J. Raynor, a local civil engineer, to lay out the National Golf Links, although the course also included many holes of MacDonald's own design.[38] Nichols was an enthusiastic

8.7 *Plan of part of property, Charles B. MacDonald Residence, Ballyshear, Southampton, by 1915.* From Howe, *American Country Houses of Today*

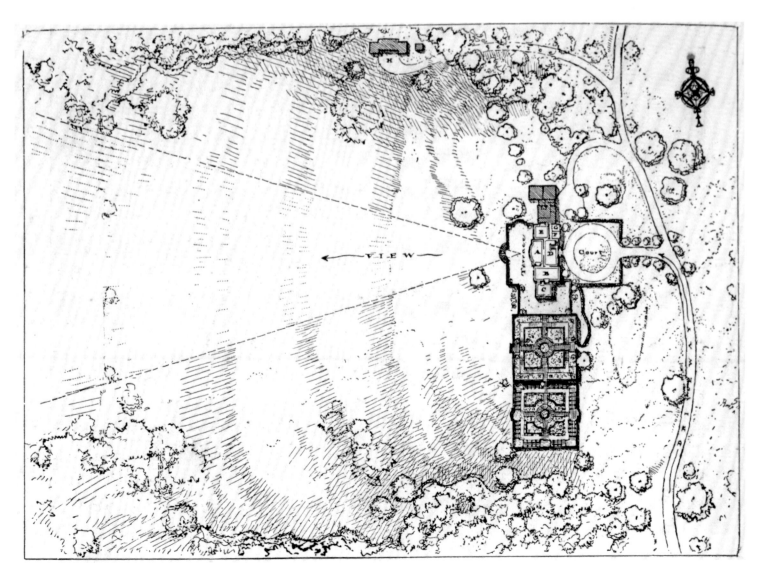

8.8 *Garden, Charles B.
MacDonald Residence,
Ballyshear, Southampton.
Photograph, Mattie Edwards
Hewitt, ca. 1915.* LISI

golfer, which was probably how she met MacDonald. Interestingly, the Saint-Gaudens property in Cornish also had a
small golf course.

To create Ballyshear, MacDonald purchased several hundred acres of adjacent land, which included over two miles
of waterfront and commissioned F. Burrrall Hoffman Jr. to
design a brick Georgian-revival house overlooking Peconic
Bay and the golf course.[39] In its complexity, Nichols's landscape design for Ballyshear represented a departure from
the relatively straightforward schemes of Mastlands and the
Ellen Mason garden. The site plan (fig. 8.7), architectural
design, and garden design were all superbly knit together.
The house was reached by an approach road more than a
half mile in length designed by Raynor and ended in a circular forecourt. To the west of the house was a broad

unbroken vista from the center of the terrace to the water.
Nichols designed two walled gardens on the south side of
the house. The first (the "Winter Garden") consisted almost
entirely of evergreen plantings, including cryptomeria,
except for a border of herbaceous plants next to the wall.
A few steps below this garden was the flower garden, with
old fashioned annuals and perennials accented by standard
roses and lilacs and by sculptures. The lower garden was
surrounded by a wooden arbor covered with grapes (figs.
8.8. and 8.9).[40]

By 1930, Annette Hoyt Flanders designed additional gardens for the Van Vlecks, subsequent owners of Ballyshear.
Flanders introduced many new elements, but she left intact
a good deal of the Nichols layout, including the drive and
forecourt and the grape arbor (see chapter 7).

8.9 *Detail of garden with grape arbor, Charles B. MacDonald Residence, Ballyshear, Southampton. Photograph, Mattie Edwards Hewitt, ca. 1915.* LISI, #3635

Ellen Louise Payson
1894–1977

LOUISE PAYSON was born in Portland, Maine, on November 12, 1894, the third child of Edgar Robinson Payson and Harriet Estabrook Payson. She was always known as Louise, not Ellen. Her father was a prominent businessman who, at one time, owned the Portland Water Company. Her mother, a teacher of deaf children, died of typhoid fever in 1898. For a few years thereafter, Louise's aunt, Jeannette Payson, lived with the family and helped raise the children. Even after Edgar Payson remarried in 1901, Louise remained close to her aunt and her aunt's friend, Annie Oakes Huntington.[41]

It was probably Annie Huntington who first stimulated Louise's interest in plants. Huntington had studied with Charles Sprague Sargent at the Arnold Arboretum and later was a tutor at the Arboretum herself. In 1902, she published an influential book called *Studies of Trees in Winter*. Louise Payson attended the Waynflete School in Portland and graduated from Walnut Hill, a prestigious preparatory school for girls in Natick, Massachusetts. She then entered the Lowthorpe School of Landscape Architecture for Women, from which she graduated in 1916.[42]

In the same year, she began work in the office of Ellen Shipman, along with fellow Lowthorpe graduates Eleanor Christie and Eleanor Roche.[43] Between 1922 and 1923, Payson continued her studies at Columbia University's School of Architecture.[44] In 1922, while still in Shipman's office, Payson won second prize for a design for a suburban backyard garden in a competition sponsored by the Society of Little Gardens in Philadelphia.[45] In the same year, she traveled to Provence with her family, and, in 1924, she spent the entire year abroad. In Europe, she collected photographs of historic buildings and gardens. She returned to Shipman's office in 1925, but she also independently designed landscapes for family members in Portland and in Falmouth Foreside, Maine.[46]

In 1927, Payson started her own firm in New York City. She was a trustee of the Lowthorpe School from 1926 through 1928 and contributed regularly to landscape periodicals. In 1931, she became a member of the American Society of Landscape Architects, an affiliation she maintained for eight years.[47] In 1933, she was honored, along with Shipman, Flanders, and three other women, in "*House and Garden's* Own Hall of Fame."[48]

In 1941, at the outset of World War II, Payson closed her New York office and moved back to Portland, where she continued to design gardens for friends while ostensibly semiretired. Royce O'Donal, a landscape contractor who installed many of these late projects, described Payson as "always in control and always a lady."[49] Payson was active in many organizations, including the Colonial Dames, the Victorian Society of Maine, the Longfellow Garden Club, the Maine Audubon Society, and the State Street Congregational Church, Portland. She died suddenly on June 8, 1977 at the age of eighty-two while on a cruise in the Mediterranean.[50]

During her fourteen-year independent practice, Payson designed at least seventy projects, all apparently residential but varying considerably in size. Drawings, photographs, and magazine articles relating to her work are now housed at the University of Maine, Orono.[51]

PAYSON APPEARS to have designed fourteen landscapes on Long Island. Unfortunately, detailed information is lacking for all but a few of them. At least two projects seem to date from her years with Ellen Shipman: the Edward Streeter residence in Great Neck (1923) and the Phillip Gossler residence, Westbury (undated).[52] The first well-documented project, and one of the finest of her career, was the property of her cousin Charles Shipman Payson and his wife, the former Joan Whitney, on Shelter Rock Road in Manhasset. Delano and Aldrich designed the house in 1927, and Payson did the landscaping the same year. Although the Paysons owned six houses, they seemed especially fond of their one-hundred-acre Manhasset property.[53]

Payson laid out a number of garden spaces, most of them tightly organized around or near the main axis of the house (fig. 8.11), giving nearly every room a view of one or more of these gardens. The house was approached by a long drive lined with rhododendrons and planted abundantly with daffodils for early spring bloom. In the central part of the forecourt, there was a long panel of grass edged with box shrubs. At the left of the forecourt was a stone wall with an arched doorway leading to a small garden with a lead sculpture (fig. 8.12). Another small garden with a central pool and fountain was tucked between the service wing and the main block. Beyond was a large grass terrace. To the west were two enclosed gardens, with two others projected for later construction. An unusual feature was a 'long walk' running parallel with the main axis of the house and continuing beyond the forecourt to another series of garden rooms on the east. Apparently, the Paysons liked to live casually at Manhasset, but there is little evidence of that on the plan, which has no provision for any form of active recreation.[54] To the south, however, Louise Payson laid out an informal lawn leading to a manmade pond (figs. 8.13 and 8.14). The Payson house is extant, in religious use.[55]

In 1929, Payson designed the gardens of the John P. Kane residence on Wellington Road, Matinecock (Locust Valley) (fig. 8.15). The approach road ended in a huge

8.11 *Suggested arrangement for the gardens on the estate of Mr. and Mrs. Charles S. Payson, Manhassett. Plan, December 25, 1927.* University of Maine, Orono

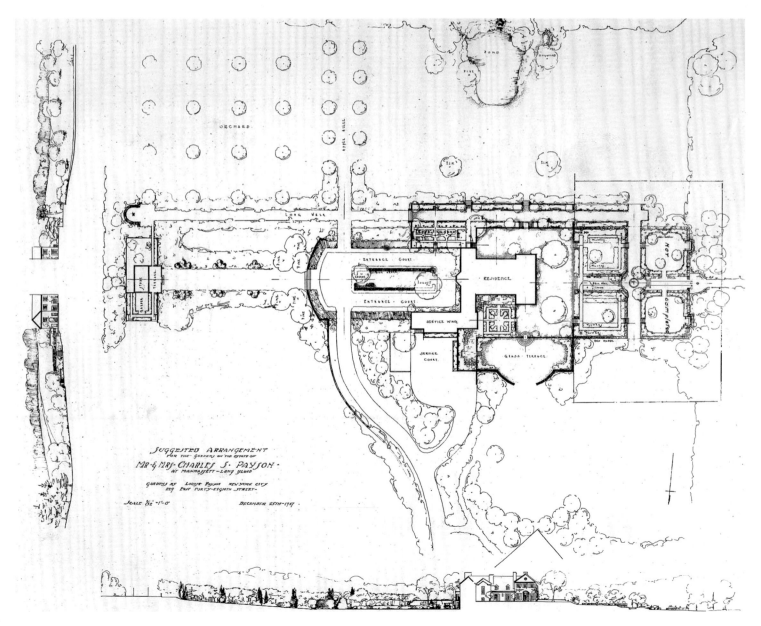

8.12 *Garden, Mr. and Mrs. Charles S. Payson Residence, Manhassett. Photograph, ca. 1930.*
University of Maine, Orono

8.13 *Pond under construction, Mr. and Mrs. Charles S. Payson Residence, Manhassett. Photograph, ca. 1928.* University of Maine, Orono

8.14 *Completed pond, Mr. and Mrs. Charles S. Payson Residence, Manhassett. Photograph, ca. 1930.* University of Maine, Orono

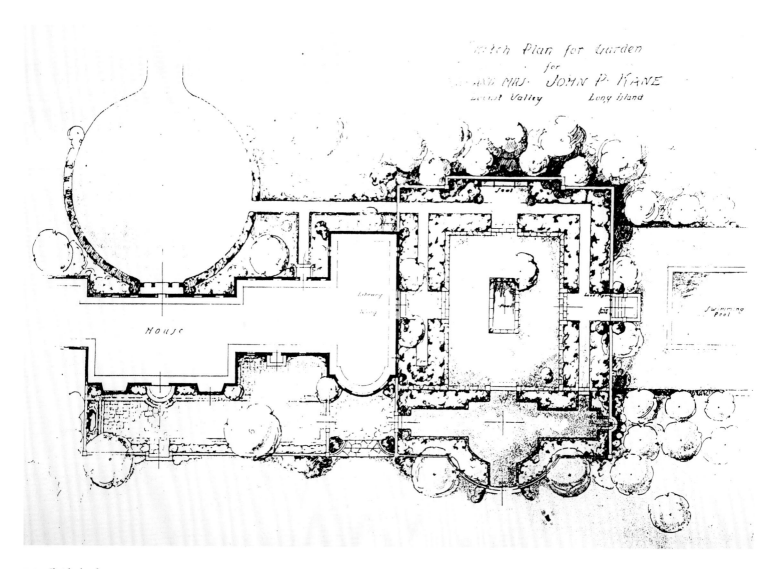

8.15 *Sketch plan for garden for Mr. and Mrs. John P. Kane, Locust Valley, 1929.* University of Maine, Orono

round forecourt. On the opposite side of the house, there was a flagstone terrace. Off the library wing was a large, walled garden planted with flowering trees and shrubs, spring bulbs, and perennials, all arranged around turf panels and a central pool (fig. 8.16). To one side of this garden, there was a terrace, apparently grass, and, to the rear, down some steps, was a swimming pool.[56] The Kane house is extant; the status of the landscaping is unknown.[57]

8.16 *Garden, Mr. and Mrs. John P. Kane Residence, Locust Valley. Photograph, Van Anda, ca. 1930.* From American Society of Landscape Architects, New York Chapter, *Work of Members*

Marjorie Sewell Cautley
1891–1954

MARJORIE LOUISA SEWELL was born on August 5, 1891 in the Mare Island Navy Yard, Vallejo, California, on the northern shore of San Francisco Bay. She was the daughter of Commander, United States Navy, William Elbridge Sewell and Minnie Moore Sewell, who was a fine watercolorist. Her maternal grandfather was Admiral John W. Moore. Marjorie was the oldest of three talented sisters. The youngest, Helen, became a noted and extremely prolific author and illustrator of children's books; the middle sister, Barbara, was a nurse. Some of Helen's books are still in print. The family lived in Japan and then in Guam, where Commander Sewell was Governor. After the death of their parents, Marjorie and her sisters returned to the United States where they were raised by relatives in New Jersey and in Brooklyn, New York. The Sewell sisters knew that they would not receive legacies from their parents or other relatives and so focused on preparing themselves for careers. Marjorie prepared for college at the Packer Institute for Collegiate Studies in Brooklyn. An important influence on Marjorie's career choice was undoubtedly the Boston architect William Emerson, later dean of the MIT School of Architecture and Planning, who had known her since she was a child. As we have seen in chapter 1, she studied landscape architecture at the Cornell University School of Agriculture, where she received a B.S. in 1917.[58]

After graduation, Sewell entered the office of Warren Manning, whose practice was then at its busiest. In 1918, she moved to Alton, Illinois, to work with the California

architect Julia Morgan on the design of a hotel for women war workers and then returned to New Jersey to start her own practice.[59] Early projects included Roosevelt Common, a thirty-acre park in Tenafly, New Jersey, with an arboretum of native plants (1921)[60] and a city garden on a restricted site, probably in New York City.[61] In 1922, she wrote a series of seven articles for *Country Life in America* on the design of gardens for modest homes.[62]

In November 1922, Marjorie Sewell married Randolph Cautley, a Cornell graduate with a degree in engineering.[63] In 1927–28, after the birth of their daughter, Ruth Patricia, she built a studio/home called Cricket's Hearth in Ridgewood, New Jersey.[64] After the birth of her daughter, Cautley had two miscarriages, then looked into adopting a child, which, fortunately, as it turned out, did not happen.[65]

In 1924, Cautley was asked to do the planting design for Sunnyside Gardens in Queens, New York City, which was being laid out by Clarence Stein, an architect and planner, and Henry Wright, an architect and landscape architect. She was probably a subconsultant to Wright and Stein. Both Wright and Stein were advocates of the English Garden City Movement and attempted to realize its goals in the United States.[66] Cautley was similarly employed on other Stein and Wright projects, including Radburn (1928–30) in Fairlawn, New Jersey, Phipps Garden Apartments in Queens, New York City (1930, 1935), and Hillside Homes in New York City (1935).[67] Cautley became a member of the American Society of Landscape Architects in 1925.[68] In 1929, she designed a private development in

Ridgewood that reflected Garden City and Stein and Wright ideals.[69]

Between 1935 and 1937, Cautley lectured on landscape design and site planning at the School of Architecture at Columbia University and in the Department of Architecture and Planning at MIT, where she was the only woman lecturer. She was also the landscape consultant to the State of New Hampshire to implement Civilian Conservation Corps (CCC) projects in ten of New Hampshire's state parks, as part of the New Deal program.[70] In the early part of 1935, she planned an extended Garden Club of America lecture tour, which had to be cut short because of the pressure of work on Hillside Homes.[71]

Initially, Cautley appears to have been a sole practitioner. Even after building Cricket's Hearth, which was intended to be both a family home and a studio, she used the "front

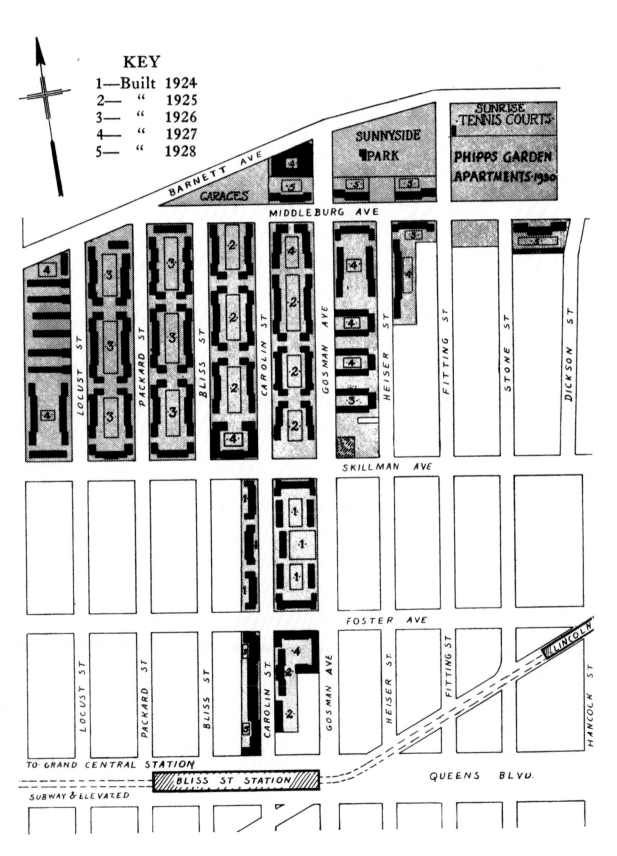

8.18 *Clarence Stein. General plan of Sunnyside Gardens, Queens, New York City, 1924.* From Stein, *Towards New Towns for America*

211

room" (presumably the living room) as her office and the dining room as a drafting room, making it unclear where the family actually "lived." Cricket's Hearth must have been in a fairly secluded area of Ridgewood, since Cautley liked to weed her vegetable garden bare-breasted![72] About 1930, she engaged Catherine Dodd Cole, a Vassar graduate, who combined drafting with clerical duties.[73] In 1935–36, Alice Recknagel Ireys (see chapter 9), a Cambridge School graduate, joined the staff and prepared planting plans for Hillside Homes.[74] In May 1935, Cautley wrote that she had had a "full office force" working on Hillside Homes for the past six months.[75] If she actually had a full office force, which would normally be considered more than two employees and a principal, it is uncertain who they were and where she put them.

In 1935, Cautley published *Garden Design: The Principles of Abstract Design as Applied to Landscape Composition.*[76] Her book preceded Annette Hoyt Flanders's article on landscape design (see chapter 7) by three years. As the subtitle of the book indicates, Cautley and Flanders both stressed the abstract "skeleton" of their design process. Otherwise their approaches were quite different. Cautley took as her basis a standard art text, Arthur W. Dow's *Composition*, which she had used in her art classes as a child, translating it from two dimensions into three.[77]

Cautley's career thrived in the Depression years, but her husband's did not. He lost his job in 1937, and Cautley became the sole support of the family. Perhaps because of the stress of this situation, Cautley began to show signs of emotional instability. In the same year, her husband committed her first to the Payne Whitney Psychiatric Clinic of New York Hospital (probably a brief stay) and then, presumably when funds ran out, to a public mental institution in New Jersey, where she was diagnosed with "neurasthenia," a term no longer in use.[78] She remained in the New Jersey hospital for four years until she was finally released through the efforts of highly placed friends, including Harold Ickes, Roosevelt's Secretary of the Interior, Robert D. Kohn, head of the Public Works Administration, and Clarence Stein himself.[79] Between 1941 and 1944, Cautley sought work in city planning, which she considered her strength, but was largely unsuccessful, in spite of letters of recommendation from people like William Emerson.[80] In 1942, she was an associate landscape architect to Russell Van Nest Black, landscape architect, for the development of Meuser Park, Wilson Borough, Pennsylvania.[81] In 1943, she earned a Master of Fine Arts in city planning from the University of Pennsylvania, which she had attended on a scholarship. Her thesis was on ways in which blighted areas of Philadelphia might be rehabilitated.[82] In 1944, she divorced her husband, resuming her maiden name, an unusual step at the time.[83]

Unfortunately, in the same year her illness recurred. Initially, a family friend, with great reluctance, committed her to Fairmount Farms, a hospital in Philadelphia.[84] Although this was a private facility with attractive grounds, Cautley objected strenuously and was transferred to the Norristown State Hospital in Norristown, Pennsylvania. From there,

she entered the private Alcluyd Hospital and Sanitarium in Berwyn, Pennsylvania, run by Dr. Joseph Lerner, a psychiatrist and neurologist, and his wife, Margaret.[85] Lerner gave Cautley considerably more freedom than she had had previously, and, when his sanitarium moved to Maryland, Cautley moved with it.[86] In spite of her illness, Cautley was able to write a considerable amount, not only on landscape architecture and planning, but fiction, poetry, and memoir as well, during her period of remission in the early 1940s.[87] (Her fiction was thinly disguised memoir.)

Only two years before her death, Cautley asked Cornell for a scholarship application to earn a degree in public health, with an emphasis on occupational therapy. She wanted to help wounded veterans.[88] She apparently never followed through with her application.

Cautley died on July 16, 1954 in Frederick, Maryland.[89] Her former husband donated her plans for Radburn and Phase I of Phipps Garden Apartments to the Avery Library at Columbia, but he seems to have destroyed the rest of her office archives. Few other original plans from her twenty-year practice are known to have survived.[90] Other archives, primarily personal in nature and including family photographs and correspondence, were given by her daughter to the Rare Book and Manuscript Collections at Cornell University. The donation apparently included a few plans.

SUNNYSIDE GARDENS in Queens was the first development of the City Housing Corporation, a limited dividend company organized in 1924 by Alexander M. Bing to build, ultimately, a full-scale American Garden City. Sunnyside was a "pilot project" toward this goal. Wright and Stein hoped to gain experience in large-scale planning, building, and community organization that could later be applied to a more ambitious development. As Stein wrote, "It was a laboratory, an experiment, a voyage of discovery, and an adventure."[91]

The City Housing Corporation purchased a flat 77-acre site near public transportation in Queens and planned a development of 1,202 family units. The site was already laid out in the standard grid of city blocks (fig. 8.18) in contrast to the streets in the English Garden Cities in England, which followed the natural contours of the land and were generally curvilinear. Nevertheless, Stein and Wright found ingenious solutions for breaking up the monotony of the blocks, dividing them into (generally) three groups of houses, each with an inner court and courts opening off the street. The brick buildings, designed by Frederick L. Ackerman, consisted of one-, two-, and three-family houses, and apartment houses. This mixture was possible only because the land was zoned industrial for its former owners the Long Island Railroad, rather than residential.[92]

No landscape plans by Cautley for Sunnyside have survived, although she did take construction films of the site.[93] However, she must have designed the planting in the large interior courts, which were intended for common use but not for active play or sports (fig. 8.19). A three-acre park for such uses was located at one end of the development. Residents also had private gardens that they could plant

8.19 *An inner court built in 1926. Sunnyside Gardens, Queens, New York City. Photograph, August 1949.* From Stein, *Towards New Towns for America*

and maintain themselves. All of the living rooms and most of the bedrooms at Sunnyside faced the interior courts. The trees included sycamores, maples, willows, and Lombardy poplars.[94]

In 1928, after the success of Sunnyside, the City Housing Corporation decided to launch a larger scale garden city called Radburn on a two square-mile tract in Fairlawn, New Jersey. Even if completed, Radburn would not have been a *complete* Garden City, since there was not enough land to surround it with the Green Belt of the English prototypes, Letchworth Garden City and Welwyn Garden City. However, Stein was still able to conceive and partially implement what he called the Radburn Idea. Essentially, by the use of what he termed "superblocks," he almost totally reversed the usual relationship between streets, interior living spaces, and green spaces that exist in a typical suburb.[95] Cautley was again the landscape architect. The Depression, in addition to ruining the City Housing Corporation, fatally stalled the full realization of Radburn, but the two completed superblocks with their spacious interior greens remain impressive today.[96]

Stein and Cautley designed Phipps Garden Apartments on a site adjacent to Sunnyside Gardens for the Society of Phipps Houses. Founded by steel magnate and Long Island resident Henry Phipps, Phipps Houses had been formed to provide housing for the working classes. Previously, the group had built compact tenements for manual laborers in the inner city. By contrast, Phipps Garden Apartments was planned for white-collar clerical workers. The buildings on the rectangular lot were brick, four-story walk-ups and six-story elevator apartments. Openness and luxuriant plant-ing were high priorities.[97] As Stein wrote: "The Phipps family were liberal clients. They wanted a sound job—and an attractive one. . . . The landscaping by Marjorie S. Cautley was rich, varied, and imaginative."[98]

Cautley's "Planting Plan No. 3 for the Northwest Court, Revised August 4, 1931" (fig. 8.20) does indeed show a rich plant palette. The trees were American elms, Lombardy poplars, sassafras, and flowering cherries, with hedging of Japanese barberry; the shrubs included privet, mockorange, butterfly bush, and common barberry. For vines, Cautley provided climbing roses and ivy. Flowers were used sparingly—only near the exits.[99] The Phipps family approved the expenditure of $2,900 for six 40-foot-tall American elms (a very high price at the time), which made "the great court a living green place from the beginning."[100] The planting plan for the Court Garden, October 15, 1931 (fig. 8.21), specifies tree of heaven (*Ailanthus altissima*) and oriental planes (*Platanus orientalis*) for shade, as well as rhododendrons, evergreen ilex, and 10-foot-high tree lilacs. The new lawns were protected by edgings of purple-leaf barberry on both sides of every walk (fig. 8.22). Cautley also made post-construction films of Phipps Garden Apartments. In April 1932, she wrote out detailed instructions for spring care of the grounds, making this one of her best documented landscapes.[101] Cautley also landscaped the grounds of the second phase of Phipps Garden Apartments. The courts there were imaginatively planted in a palette similar to the one she had used in Phipps, Phase I.[102] The grounds of Phipps Garden Apartments were restored beginning in 1985 by Schnadelbach Associates, R. Terry Schnadelbach, Principal, of Gainesville Florida.[103]

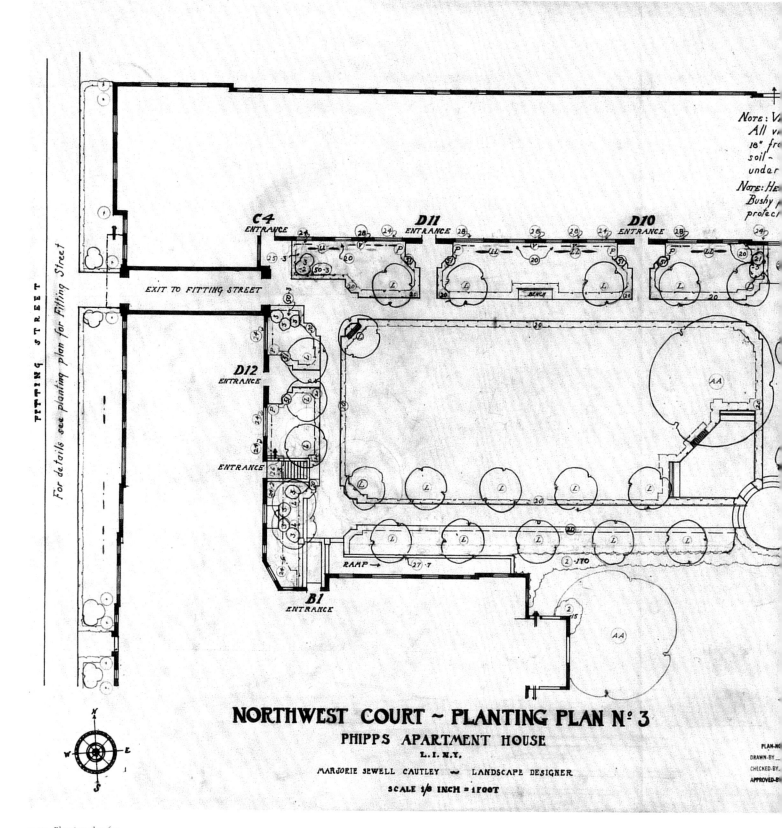

C4
ENTRANCE

D11
ENTRANCE

D10
ENTRANCE

EXIT TO FITTING STREET

D12
ENTRANCE

ENTRANCE

BENCH

AA

FITTING STREET

For details see planting plan for Fitting Street

ENTRANCE

RAMP →

B1
ENTRANCE

AA

NORTHWEST COURT ~ PLANTING PLAN Nº 3
PHIPPS APARTMENT HOUSE
L. I. N. Y.
MARJORIE SEWELL CAUTLEY ～ LANDSCAPE DESIGNER
SCALE 1/8 INCH = 1 FOOT

N
W E
S

PLAN-NO
DRAWN-BY
CHECKED-BY
APPROVED-BY

8.20 *Planting plan for Northeast Court, Phipps Garden Apartments, Queens, New York City. Ink on linen, Revised August 4, 1931. Drawings Collection, Avery Architectural and Fine Arts Library, Columbia University*

PLANT LIST ~ NORTHWEST COURT

KEY	NAME	QUANTITY	SIZE
TREES:			
AA	Ulmus americana American Elm	1	14' col
CC	Ailanthus glandulosa	1	typical
L	Tilia vulgaris European Small Leaf Linden spreading over path ~ 7 ft head room	24	12'
LL	Tilia vulgaris to be trained flat	4	15'
P	Populus nigra italica Lombardy Poplar	10	15'
HEDGING:			
20	Dautzia gracilis (white)	1000	1½
SHRUBS:			
2	Barberis vulgaris purpurea Purple European Barberry bushy	200	2½-3'
3	Ligustrum ovalifolium California Privet clipped specimens	8	5-6'
	~~Ligustrum ovalifolium~~ ~~clipped specimens~~	3	3-4'
21	Rosa rugosa (white)	10	3'
22	Syringa vulgaris Common Lilac	5	4-5'

— V — indicates vines

VINES:			
24	Forsythia suspensa trained as vine	7	2-3'
25	Lonicera heckrotti Everblooming Honaysuckle	10	2-3'
26	Lonicera halliana	25	2-3'
27	Lonicera samperrirans	10	2-3'
28	Roses - climbing to be salected	7	2-3'
FLOWERS:			
EXITS:	Crocus susianus (yallon) Spring Flowering Crocus	50	
	Crocus sativus (lilac) Autumn Flowering Crocus	50	
	Blue Iris		
ENTRANCES: 51	Yucca filamentosa	12	18"

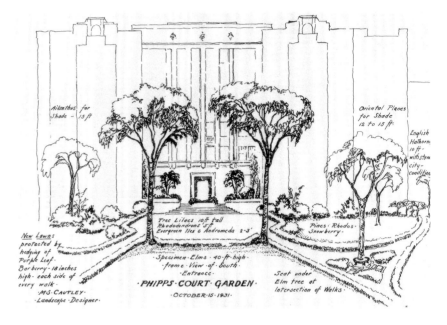

8.21 *Tree planting plan for Phipps Court Garden, Phipps Garden Apartments, Queens, New York City. Ink on linen, October 15, 1931.* Drawings Collection, Avery Architectural and Fine Arts Library, Columbia University

8.22 *Great Central Court, First Unit, Phipps Garden Apartments, Queens, New York City. Photograph, ca. 1945.* From Stein, *Towards New Towns for America*

Isabella Pendleton Bowen
1891–1965

8.23 *"Isabella Pendleton Studies a Flower."* *Photograph, Mosher Studios, 1954.* From *The Christian Science Monitor, August 26, 1954*

ISABELLA E. PENDLETON was born in Cincinnati, Ohio, on March 8, 1891, the daughter of Elliott Hunt Pendleton Jr., a lawyer, and Isabelle ("Belle") Gibson Eckstein.[104] She was a descendant of the Revolutionary War statesman Edmund Pendleton.[105]

Pendleton apparently showed an interest in gardening and landscape design from an early age, and her "forward-looking" parents encouraged her.[106] She was a founder of the Cincinnati Garden Club and, in 1915, when only twenty-four, became its president.[107] But it was an uncle, owner of a property in Nassau County, who jumpstarted her career:

> [He] gave her a boost with the insurance money from a yacht of his which had run aground en route from the Bahamas to Florida. He was through with boats and told her she could use the insurance money to come East, design his garden and establish herself on Long Island, but from then on, she must be on her own.[108]

Pendleton studied at the Lowthorpe School, graduating in 1917, the same year as Louise Payson. She returned to Cincinnati shortly thereafter.[109] With the exception of the garden for her uncle on Long Island, her earliest projects were probably all in Cincinnati, although these have not yet been identified. At some point, probably in 1922, she relocated to New York City.[110] With the "boost" of her uncle's gift, she may have opened an office on her own right away, since there is no indication that she ever worked for another landscape architect.

Like most Lowthorpe graduates, Pendleton was an expert plantswoman. In October 1920, her first article, "Striking Perennial Combinations," was published in *The Garden Magazine*.[111] The following year, the color chart for flowers that originally appeared in this article was published in a book by garden writer Mrs. Frances King.[112] Later in life, Pendleton described her "main stamping grounds" as Cincinnati; Nassau County, Long Island; and Princeton, New Jersey.[113] She also designed gardens in Connecticut. In 1925, she implemented a Gertrude Jekyll design for Mr. and Mrs. Stanley Resor, and, around 1932, designed a stunning iris garden for Mr. and Mrs. Z. G. Simonds, both in Greenwich.[114] In 1938, after studying old letters and other documents, Pendleton restored a Colonial-era garden for Trent House in Trenton, New Jersey, the early-eighteenth-century home of the founder of Trenton.[115]

Pendleton lectured frequently on garden subjects. On April 10, 1939, she spoke under the auspices of the Lowthorpe School at the home of Mrs. Henry V. Greenough in Brookline, Massachusetts, which had a garden designed by Ellen Shipman in 1926.[116] Pendleton published additional articles on landscape issues. At an unknown date, probably in the early 1930s, she wrote a one-page tract with Grace Tabor entitled "Suggestions for Roadside Planting," which was published by the Long Island Chamber of Congress.[117] Pendleton became a member of the American Society of Landscape Architects in 1933. In 1960, when she sent in her resignation, the Society refused to accept it and instead made her a lifetime member.[118]

In the mid-1930s, Pendleton's life changed profoundly when she married Ezra Bowen, an economist, artist, and ardent sailor, who retired as a professor of economics at Lafayette College in Easton, Pennsylvania in 1935 at the age of forty-four. After scouting southern England and the northeastern part of France, he settled on Martha's Vineyard as the perfect site for his new pursuit of painting.[119] Pendleton was Bowen's second wife. His first marriage, to biographer Catherine Drinker Bowen, ended in divorce in 1933.[120]

Ezra and Isabella Pendleton Bowen maintained a home in New York City as well as the cottage that Dr. Bowen had purchased in Chilmark on Martha's Vineyard. There Pendleton developed a wildflower garden that drew much comment.[121] In 1937, Pendleton had no clients other than herself, but this may have reflected the impact of the Depression rather than her newly married state.[122] Despite the cutback in her career activities, she retained her maiden name for professional purposes and, at some point, seems to have designed gardens for her neighbors on the Vineyard. Ezra Bowen died in 1945.[123] Three years later, Pendleton moved the Chilmark house to Starbuck Lane in Edgartown, remodeled it (acting as her own architect), and planned a small but varied garden to its rear.[124] Until 1963, she lived there regularly in the sum-

mer.[125] In 1964, one of her last professional activities was to sponsor, as one of a hundred members of the American Society of Landscape Architects, a traveling exhibition of the work of Frederick Law Olmsted.[126]

What were Pendleton's goals as a landscape architect? As was the case with Olmsted, suitability was her first concern. As she told a *Vineyard Gazette* reporter, "I cannot assert too strongly the need for building a country garden in the country, a suburban garden in the suburbs, and an urban garden in the city. The law of suitability!" She paused. And then she sighed deeply. "How frequently it has been violated."[127] She brought to all her designs "richness, through abundance in the planting; freshness through order; strength through pattern and design; gaiety through hospitality—many sitting places. . . . Light and height are to me the two basic requirements for every garden. So many people think you must have shrubbery for a background, but against shrubbery, one loses the iridescence of flower petals."[128] Oddly, Pendleton told her interviewer that "hers was not the creative spirit; she prefers not to control a garden, but to be controlled by it."[129] Like Farrand, she revisited her sites and saw things "better on the ground than on the drawing board."[130]

8.24 Spring garden, Mrs. Percy Chubb Residence, Glen Cove. Photograph, ca. 1923. Architectural League of New York, Year Book, 1924

For the last five years of her life, Pendleton was almost completely blind.[131] Still, in September 1963, when she decided to give up her Edgartown home, she wrote (or dictated), with her usual panache, a final letter to the *Vineyard Gazette*: "'Farewell' stirs the affectionate emotions more than the word 'good-bye' because, to me, it hopes for the well-being of those from whom we part—the grocer, the butcher, the fish man, neighbors, friends, children . . . to all I say 'farewell.'"[132]

Pendleton died on March 16, 1965 in Princeton, New Jersey, the college town where she had designed many gardens.[133] She was survived by a niece, Martha Hunt Nickerson, of Lyme, Connecticut.[134] No Pendleton archives have been located.

PENDLETON DESIGNED eight gardens on Long Island. These include the project for her uncle in Nassau County, which has not yet been identified. Unfortunately, no plans for her Long Island gardens were published, but photographs of five of them appeared in various landscape yearbooks and periodicals. (Only one photograph of each garden was published in the yearbooks, making it difficult to assess the full scope of Pendleton's work at these sites.) Two other

gardens were mentioned, but not illustrated, in the *Bulletin of the Garden Club of America* on the occasion of the club's 1931 tour of Long Island. In addition, some of the suggestions she and Grace Tabor made for roadside plantings on Long Island may have been implemented.

The first of the identified Pendleton projects on Long Island was a spring garden for Mrs. Percy Chubb at her property Rattling Spring in Glen Cove (fig. 8.24), which was published in 1924.[135] Beatrix Farrand had designed a terraced garden with a rose arbor for the Chubbs in 1900 (see chapter 2), but Pendleton's garden was located on flat terrain in what was apparently a different part of the grounds. It is possible that the recently graded rectangular area to the right of the house (fig. 2.3) was prepared for Pendleton's spring garden. This garden consisted of a double herbaceous border separated by a grass path, with the most abundant display of flowers in the sunny border to the left. The plantings included tulips and irises. The path led to a walled seating area, possibly overlooking Long Island Sound.[136]

Pendleton designed a formal garden for Mrs. Howard Whitney, also in Glen Cove, which was published in 1925 (fig. 8.25).[137] This was a terraced garden near the house and was also a double herbaceous border separated by a

8.26 *Formal garden,*
Mr. Henry Baltusan, Esq.
Residence, Mill Neck.
Photograph, ca. 1926.
Architectural League of
New York, Year Book, 1927

8.27 *Circular garden,*
Mr. Paul D. Cravath, Esq.
Residence, Locust Valley.
Photograph, ca. 1931.
Architectural League of
New York, Year Book, 1932

8.28 *Perennial garden,*
Mr. Paul D. Cravath, Esq.
Residence, Locust Valley.
Photograph, ca. 1930.
Country Life in America,
May 1931

grass path. The lower level was planted somewhat less formally than the upper terrace. Pendleton apparently collaborated on this project with the architect Howard Major.
The Whitney house and garden do not survive.[138]

By 1927, Pendleton had designed a small garden for
Henry Baltusan in Mill Neck (fig. 8.26).[139] Although she
labeled it as a formal garden, the Baltusan garden apparently
consisted only of a small seating area surrounded by somewhat informal plantings of flowers and shrubs. Probably in
the same year, Pendleton conferred with the architect Bradley
Delehanty on the site of a new house for Paul D. Cravath, a
corporation lawyer who was then president of the Metropolitan Opera Association. Still Place, as it was called, was the
last of four houses built in Locust Valley or Lattingtown for
Cravath.[140] One element in the landscape was a charming
circular garden with a pool overhung by dogwood and
weeping willows (fig. 8.27). Flowers, ferns, and low shrubs
grew between the trees. Just off the breakfast porch at Still
Place, Pendleton designed a double perennial border edged
with clipped box and enclosed by very low whitewashed
brick walls (fig. 8.28). She also designed a terrace off the

south elevation of the house.[141] The Cravath house still
stands on Duck Pond Road in Locust Valley, but the status
of Pendleton's landscaping is not known.[142]

Around 1930, Pendleton redesigned the formal terraced
gardens at The Braes in Glen Cove, the residence of Mr.
and Mrs. Herbert L. Pratt, which had been originally laid
out by James Greenleaf about thirty years earlier.[143] She also
designed a new iris garden for the Pratts (fig. 8.29), in
which the colors were restricted to blue, mauve, and purple.[144] The house at The Braes survives as the Webb Institute of Naval Architecture.[145]

There are no photographs or descriptions of the garden
Pendleton designed for Mrs. C. Oliver Iselin at Wolver Hollow in Mill Neck, which replaced the one designed by Mrs.
Iselin and installed by Jay.[146] By 1931, Pendleton had
designed a terraced hillside and pool at Eagles Beak, the
residence of Mrs. Walter James in Cold Spring Harbor.[147]
The house, which was designed by Grosvenor Atterbury,
does not survive.[148]

8.29 *Iris garden, Mr. and Mrs. Herbert Pratt Residence, Glen Cove. Photograph, Mattie Edwards Hewitt, ca. 1931.*
Country Life in America,
June–July, 1932

Eleanor Louise Roche
1892–1975

ELEANOR LOUISE ROCHE was born in East Orange, New Jersey on January 21, 1892, the daughter of Auguste and Sophie Agnes Glorieux Roche. Her father was an importer of religious objects. Her paternal grandfather was born in France, and her mother was of French and Belgian descent. Her mother was very interested in plants and, in a suburban location, had orchards, flower and vegetable gardens, a grape arbor, a lily bed in the front yard, and other plants. Wisteria grew over the front porch and garden phlox in front of it.[149]

After completing East Orange High School, Roche, who was known as "Rochie" to friends, studied at the Lowthorpe School, graduating in 1917 with Louise Payson and Isabella Pendleton. With Payson, Roche went to work in Ellen Shipman's New York City office. In 1926, she set up her independent practice in New York, concentrating on residential projects.[150] In the same year, she became a member of the American Society of Landscape Architects.[151] She traveled with the ASLA to Africa and other places.[152]

Anticipating continued prosperity, Roche hired several assistants when she opened her office, but three years later, when the Depression struck, she had to lay them off. From that point on, she intentionally limited her practice, taking on only those jobs that she could handle by herself.[153] She was also resourceful in finding other ways to contribute to her profession. In October 1933, she co-authored an article in *Landscape Architecture* on an important Spanish garden.[154] The following winter, Roche led a tour of Mediterranean gardens for ASLA members and others.[155]

Her few 1930s projects are small but charming. In 1932, she published a garden she had designed for Mrs. G. Peats in New Canaan, Connecticut, and another for an unidentified client in Princeton, New Jersey.[156] In 1934, a delightful city garden by Roche for a court at St. Luke's Hospital in New York City was published.[157] It can be assumed that Eleanor Roche's practice was impacted still further by World War II. About 1950, she relocated to Michigan, where she designed projects for the Ford family.[158]

Roche died on July 30, 1975 in Grosse Pointe, Michigan. Although no design archives have been located, the Roche-Leake family has extensive correspondence, memoirs, and genealogical information.

ONLY ONE LANDSCAPE on Long Island by Roche has been identified: a garden for Jackson A. Dykman in Glen Cove, laid out about 1929.[159] This was an interesting project in which Roche transformed a large vegetable garden, which the family felt was no longer necessary and which lay in full view of the house, into an informal flower garden (fig. 8.31). The background for the garden consisted of well-established trees, including one centrally located old oak. Beneath it, Roche placed a small pool in roughly a half-moon shape (fig. 8.32). Reflecting its former use, the site was rectangular, but, by including irregularly shaped flower beds and a winding flagstone path around its perimeter, Roche created an undulating oval. In many places, the path was lined by informally grouped perennials and wildflowers (fig. 8.33). Among the shrubs that

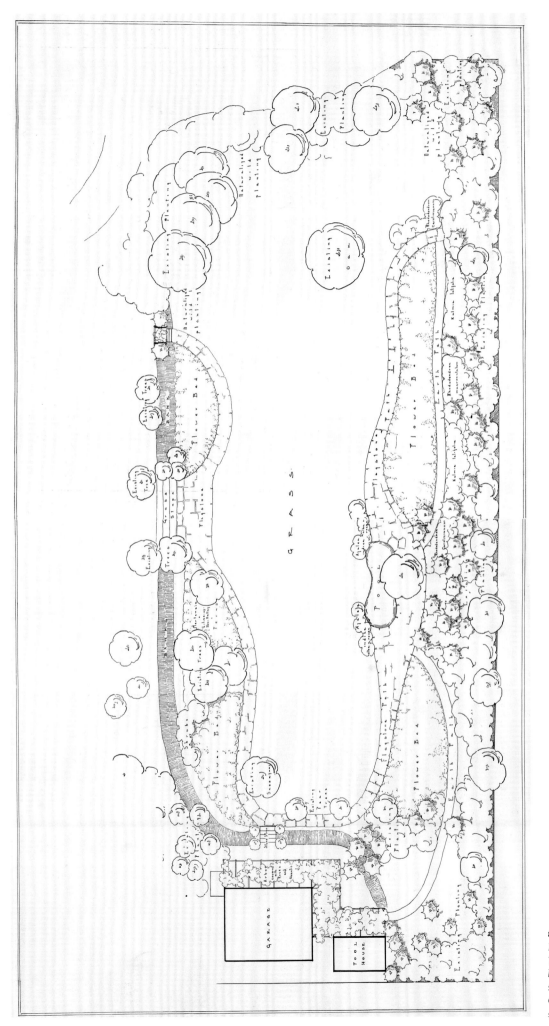

8.31 *"Sketch Plan of the Informal Flower Garden That Replaced the Vegetables," ca. 1929, for the Jackson A. Dykman Residence, Glen Cove. American Landscape Architect, March 1931*

8.32 *Pool in flower
garden, Jackson A. Dykman
Residence, Glen Cove.
Photograph, ca. 1929.*
American Landscape Architect,
March 1931

8.33 *Path in flower garden,*
Jackson A. Dykman
Residence, Glen Cove.
Photograph, ca. 1929.
American Landscape Architect,
March 1931

Roche added were numerous rhododendrons and mountain laurel. She also screened the rear of a garage and tool shed with an arbor covered with roses and clematis. Under it was a seating area where the owners and their guests could view the garden.[160]

Eleanor Roche's niece, Alice Leake, remembers her aunt Rochie driving her around Grosse Pointe and showing her gardens that she had designed.[161] She also remembers her as "a most capable, independent woman completely caught up in her chosen profession and at ease with those with whom and for whom she worked."[162]

The Second Generation, II

THIS CHAPTER EXAMINES the Long Island work of six women landscape architects who began their careers somewhat later than those in chapter 8. Four of the women (Lamson, Jones, Webel and Ireys) went to the Cambridge School of Architecture and Landscape Architecture. All of these but Ireys had a B.A. from a liberal arts institution. Bullard studied at Cornell when it was an undergraduate program. Allen began her studies at the Lowthorpe School when she was about 42, a more unusual step then than it would be today. Although all practiced well into the twentieth century, only Webel designed in what could be considered a "modernist" idiom.

Mary Lois Deputy Lamson Cattell
1897–1969

MARY LOIS DEPUTY was born on September 6, 1897 in Paris Crossing in southern Indiana, the only child of Manfred Wolfe Deputy, an educator, and Carrie G. Gault Deputy.[1] The future landscape architect was fortunate in her childhood surroundings at Indiana University in Bloomington, where her father was a graduate student. Years later she wrote, "Much of my own early knowledge of shrubs and trees was absorbed as a small girl in a college town where the superintendent of grounds was a fine horticulturist. He had brought in over a long period

of time many rare and valuable shrubs and trees and used them to excellent effect on the grounds of the college. Each one was carefully labeled, both with the Latin name and the common name."[2] The Deputy family offered a prize to anyone who could identify every tree on the campus.[3] During the time that Manfred Wolfe Deputy was a student, there were two long-term groundskeepers at the university and a very involved faculty, including an advisory committee on campus planning.[4] Today, the Indiana University campus is considered one of the most beautiful in the country.[5]

Mary Lois Deputy studied for two years at the State Normal School in Mankato, Minnesota, before transferring to Indiana, where she received an A.B. in June 1919 and an A.M. in October 1919, both in English. She also took several credits in fine arts and other subjects related to her future profession, including freehand drawing, trigonometry, surveying, botany, and nature study.[6] In 1919, she was granted the first James D. Maxwell Award presented by the Women's Athletic Association for "high scholarship, participation in university athletics," as well as for various personal qualities.[7]

After receiving her master's degree, Deputy apparently returned to Minnesota for about a year. She applied to the Cambridge School for the year 1920–21, where she hoped to gain advanced standing and earn a certificate in landscape architecture in two years, with a special emphasis on city planning (which the school did not offer).[8] This plan for an abbreviated course of study apparently worked out, since she spent only two years at the school. Henry Atherton Frost felt that this very well-educated woman needed to study

architectural as well as landscape design. She took these courses "unwillingly" but later wished she had taken more.[9] After completing her studies, Mary Deputy returned to Minnesota, where she was the director of physical education at Bemidji State Teachers College for about a year. She also began the practice of landscape architecture in Bemidji.[10]

Deputy moved to New York City in 1924, where she joined Ruth Dean's office. In November 1926, Deputy married Frank Vernon Lamson, a graduate of the School of Engineering of the University of Missouri.[11] They had no children. In 1933, the Lamsons bought a 30-acre farm, Briar Patch, in Milan near Rhinebeck in upstate New York, where they spent most of their free time.[12]

After Dean's death in 1932, Lamson and other members of the firm practiced as Ruth Dean Associates. In 1934, Lamson opened an office of her own at 108 East Fifty-sixth Street.[13] Half a year after opening her office, Lamson reported that the past six months had been "the most fun of any of these eleven years in New York—the nicest clients, interesting jobs and enough work to keep me comfortably busy."[14] At this point in her career, most of her jobs were small.[15] In 1935, Lamson, with four other Cambridge School graduates, received an M.L.A. degree from Smith College, with which the Cambridge School had by then merged.[16] In May 1942, she reported that her own office was engaged exclusively in private work, mostly in the New York City area, and that she lectured and wrote occasional articles.[17]

Other than these rather general statements, it is difficult to get a sense of the extent of Lamson's overall practice. She is said to have designed city backyards and penthouses, small suburban gardens, large estates, farms, and college campuses; her geographic range apparently extended from Maine to Florida and westward to Kansas City.[18] Among her farms was certainly her own, but no college campuses by Lamson have thus far been identified. Outstanding among her published designs was a garden and terraced hillside on the west bank of the Hudson River in Nyack, New York, for Mr. and Mrs. Charles MacArthur (Helen Hayes).[19] Other clients were Philip Barry, presumably the playwright (location unknown), and Mrs. Dwight Morrow, mother of writer Anne Morrow Lindbergh. This was probably Next Day Hill, the Morrow home in Englewood, New Jersey, where the Lindberghs were married in 1929.[20]

Lamson lectured "near and far" and wrote articles for *House and Garden*, *House Beautiful*, *Home Garden*, *McCall's Magazine*, *Today's Woman*, *Plants and Gardens*, the *New York Times*, and the *New York Herald Tribune*.[21] Lamson's articles tended to be short and extremely practical.[22] Oddly, she rarely published her own work. She seems not to have been a member of the American Society of Landscape Architects, meaning that she did not publish in *Landscape Architecture* or exhibit in the ASLA New York Chapter's annual shows.[23]

Although there were three assistants in the office in 1946, Lamson's practice must have felt the effect of World War II.[24] Like Marian Coffin, she responded to a reduced workload by writing a book. *Gardening with Shrubs and Small Flowering Trees* (1946) was apparently the first to discuss shrubs in detail.[25] Her audience was the small suburban homeowner with a yard of limited size, who, without guidance, would be likely to group shrubs without regard to color, who might have trouble gauging their ultimate size, and who was often also the target of "tailgate" salesmen marketing foundation plantings "by the yard."[26] A particularly valuable chapter is "How to Learn from an Arboretum, Park or Botanical Garden."[27] Of all the books discussed, Lamson's is probably the least dated and would still be of practical use today. Like Coffin, she hated energetic but misguided pruning:

There is probably no garden tool so dear to the hearts of the men of the family as the pruning shears. Nobody has ever satisfactorily explained whether it is atavistic instinct of chopping one's way through a jungle or just the small boy's love of destruction, but pruning shears, pruning knives and pruning saws arouse more energy than any other kind of garden weapon. Unfortunately, a great deal of this energy is misapplied and considerable damage results in the great burst of enthusiasm.[28]

9.2 *Cutting garden, George Roberts Residence, East Hampton. Plan, ca. 1945.* From *House and Garden*, April 1946

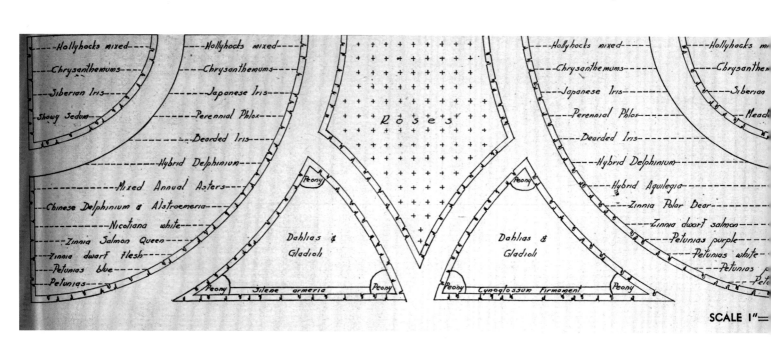

9.3 *Cutting garden, George Roberts Residence, East Hampton. Photograph, ca. 1945.* From *House and Garden*, April 1946

This book was reissued in 1949 under the title *Gardening with Shrubs*.

In 1951, Lamson published *Garden Housekeeping*. In the first chapter, she noted the profusion of books and articles on the postwar servantless house and explained that her book addressed the related problem of the gardenerless garden.[29] She offered a compact compendium of detailed advice on such matters as weeding, mulching, watering, labeling, pests, compost piles, and so on.

In the late 1940s, the Lamsons divorced. By 1954, Mary Lois had married William W. Cattell, who predeceased her.[30] Mary Deputy Cattell died in Red Hook, New York, on December 19, 1969.[31] Aside from the records in the archives of Indiana University in Bloomington and the few documents relating to her in the Cambridge School Archives, Sophia Smith Collection, Smith College, there are no known Lamson archives.[32]

LAMSON DESIGNED four landscapes on Long Island. Lamson's successful completion of the George Roberts garden in East Hampton, begun by Ruth Dean in 1930, led to the commission for the Robertses' city garden in 1939.[33] By 1946, Lamson added a cutting garden to the East Hampton prop-

erty, which appears to have been her own design, rather than part of the earlier Dean scheme.[34]

Lamson wrote about the Roberts cutting garden and another for Mr. and Mrs. Graham Douglas, also in East Hampton, in the same article.[35] Before describing the gardens, Lamson discussed some general issues about the design of cutting gardens. She stressed, in particular, that, although such gardens should not be too conspicuous in the overall arrangement of the grounds, they need not be tucked away in corners behind high fences and that the flowers should not be planted in straight rows like a vegetable garden. She then touched on such issues as the size of the house, the size and frequency of parties, and the color schemes of the rooms. The cutting garden, she felt, should include perennials as well as annuals. She also wrote about the special requirements of gladioli and dahlias, then the most popular mid- to late-summer flowers, noting the astonishing fact that, for adequate gladioli bloom, five hundred bulbs were needed.[36]

Lamson described the Roberts cutting garden (figs. 9.2 and 9.3) as "medium-size," although it was intended to supply all the flowers for a large house from June through September. This garden was designed in symmetrical

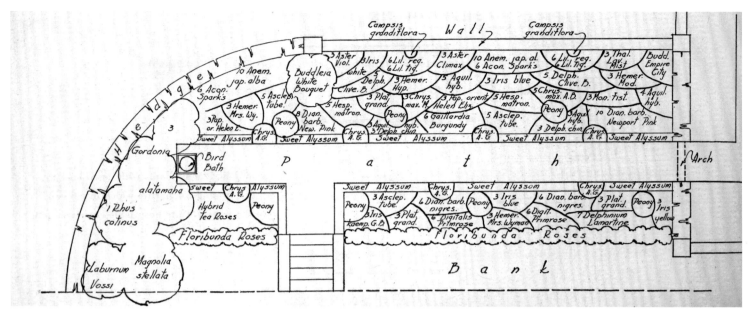

9.4 *Cutting garden,*
Graham Douglas Residence,
East Hampton. Plan,
ca. 1945. From *House*
and Garden, April 1946

9.5 *Cutting garden,*
Graham Douglas Residence,
East Hampton. Photograph,
Gottscho-Schleisner, 1945.
From *House and Garden,*
April 1946

"patterns." In the center was a bed of one hundred hybrid tea and floribunda roses with two beds containing both dahlias and gladioli below. On either side were curving beds of mixed perennials and annuals, such as hollyhocks, perennial phlox, delphiniums, bearded iris, Siberian iris, annual asters, and so on. Surprisingly, there were quite a few petunias, which are not useful as cut flowers. In order for the garden to be attractive when there was no bloom, the beds were surrounded by dwarf box edging.[37]

By contrast, the Douglas cutting garden (figs. 9.4 and 9.5) was located along a path between the house and a box garden a level below it. Since it was fairly visible, it was planted closely so that the profuse bloom would mask any holes where flowers had been cut. In addition, some rows in the vegetable garden were reserved for flowers. With the exception of irises and peonies planted to blend with a wisteria arbor behind them, there were no spring flowers for the Douglases, who were in residence in East Hampton from July through mid-October. Mrs. Douglas

decorated the house in white, yellow, copper, and various shades of lavender, which were the colors that Lamson emphasized in the cutting garden. The plants included white Japanese anemones, blue and violet asters, lemon daylilies, light and dark blue delphiniums, as well as gold and yellow zinnias and marigolds and snapdragons in autumn shades.[38]

In 1936, Lamson designed the grounds of the Van S. Merle-Smith property in Oyster Bay (fig. 9.6). Merle-Smith was a career Army officer who also wrote a history of seventeenth-century Oyster Bay.[39] Around 1940, Lamson also designed extensive gardens for Joseph Ramée in East Hampton. The rambling shingled house appears to have been built onto one end of a large windmill, or, at least, a structure that was intended to look like a windmill. Part of the garden consisted of beds of annuals and perennials divided by gravel paths (fig. 9.7). There was also a long herbaceous border, as well as plantings of vines and flowers along a stone wall near the house (fig. 9.8).[40]

9.7 *Garden, Joseph Ramée
Residence, East Hampton.
Photograph, Richard Averill
Smith, 1944.* LISI

9.8 *Grounds, Joseph Ramée Residence. Photograph, Richard Averill Smith, 1944.* LISI

Nellie Beatrice Osborn Allen
ca. 1874–1961

Nellie Beatrice Osborn was born in Cameron, Missouri, the daughter of Davis Osborn, a farmer, and Pauline Osborn. She was the fourth of five children and one of four girls. Her parents had both been born in Virginia. The federal census of 1880 says only that Nellie was six by June 8, 1880, the date of this particular census sheet.[41] We shall probably never know the exact date of her birth, since recordings of birth began sporadically in Missouri in 1883 but only became mandatory in 1910.[42] Her parents may well have relocated to Missouri in order to take advantage of the 1862 Homestead Act.[43] Details are lacking about what led to her ultimate decision to become a landscape architect. Similarly, the date of her marriage to Sidney P. Allen, who became the founder of the Louisiana Land and Exploration Company, is unknown.[44]

Whatever the motive for her career choice, Allen did not act on it until she had divorced her husband and her daughter had been "launched" into New York society. She entered the Lowthorpe School in Groton in 1916 and graduated in 1919 at the age of about 45 under the name of Beatrice Osborn Allen. Her first project was for Mrs. William D. Miller in Ashburnham, Massachusetts, a commission that may have come her way through the noted Boston landscape architect Fletcher Steele, who was then teaching at the Lowthorpe School. In 1921, she traveled to Italy and England, where she met Gertrude Jekyll at her home, Munstead Wood, in Surrey, and was profoundly influenced by her work. Allen traveled to Europe a number of other times between 1921 and 1949.[45]

Allen never became a member of the American Society of Landscape Architects. At the time of her death, she was a member-at-large of the Garden Club of America and was also a member of the English-Speaking Union in London and the committee on old roses. She did considerable lecturing on garden design and history in New England and also exhibited regularly with the Architectural League of New York. Although her work was well published, she wrote little about her own commissions.[46]

Not surprisingly, given her late start, Nellie B. Allen never developed a large-scale national practice. Her office was located in New York City between the 1920s and the 1940s, where she specialized in private work, especially those projects focusing on perennials and planting design. About sixteen of her commissions have been identified, most in the New York/New England area. At some point, she laid out the Bishop's Garden at the National Cathedral in Washington, D.C., although this design has gone through modifications and may have been altered since. Allen's particular interests were knot gardens and geometrically hedged green gardens.[47] A particularly fine example was the garden at Thornedale, the Oakleigh Thorne property in Millbrook, New York (1934).[48]

Nellie B. Allen died in New York City on Christmas Day 1961.[49] A limited number of her plans and drawings are located in the Rare and Manuscript Collection, Carl A. Kroch Library, Cornell University. These include some very interesting examples of her student work at Lowthorpe.[50]

THE FIRST OF ALLEN'S three Long Island commissions was a garden for Kipsveen, the property of Clifford H. McCall on Apoquoque Road in East Hampton, designed in 1927. This was a walled garden with an arched entrance, an oval lawn surrounded by trees, shrubs, and informal perennial beds. At the far end was a round pool with seats and a fountain crowned with a figure of the goddess Diana by Janet Scudder (fig. 9.10). The second story of the house was destroyed by fire, and the garden has been altered.[51]

Allen's second project was a garden at Brookmeade, the Isabel Dodge Sloane property in Locust Valley. Mrs. Sloane had a famous stable at Brookmeade and owned many championship horses.[52] The grounds had been laid out by Vitale and Geiffert in 1924.[53] Around 1936, Allen added two splendid herbaceous borders for Mrs. Sloane. In their style, spaciousness, and masterful disposition of perennial groups, they were very much in the spirit of Gertrude Jekyll (fig. 9.11). The borders were intended primarily for summer bloom with a color scheme of blue and white. The taller plants near the back were planted in diagonal strips,

allowing for profuse bloom throughout this area. These plants included lupine, delphinium, lilies, phlox, and veronicas. Tall asters planted behind the summer perennials extended the season into the fall, while *Campanula latifolia* growing in low drifts toward the front could be lifted and replaced with autumn flowers.[54] The Sloane property is now incorporated into the cemetery of St. John's Church, Lattingtown.[55]

In 1938, Allen collaborated with Constance Boardman, another Lowthorpe graduate, to design two parterre gardens at the 1939 World's Fair in Flushing honoring the Lowthorpe School and the Horticultural Society of New York.[56] The two landscape architects consulted with Mrs. Harold Irving Pratt, who also donated the plant material. The gardens consisted of swirls of box hedging mounting in an ascending scroll. Within the swirls was a planting in a color scheme of green (ivy) and gray (lamb's ear and dusty miller). White plantings in the spring consisted of tulips, followed by white petunias, and, in the fall, by white chrysanthemums (fig. 9.12).[57]

9.10 *Garden, Clifford H. McCall Residence, East Hampton. Photograph, Mattie Edwards Hewitt, 1927.* LISI

9.11 *Herbaceous borders, the Mrs. Isabel Dodge Sloane Residence, Lattingtown. Photograph, Richard Averill Smith, ca. 1935.* LISI #125-H-2.

9.12 *Two parterre gardens,
New York World's Fair,
Flushing, 1939.* From
Gardens on Parade, 1939

Helen Elise Bullard

1896–1987

9.13 *Helen Elise Bullard. Photograph, 1938.* Courtesy of the *New York Times/Redux*

HELEN ELISE BULLARD was born on June 28, 1896 in Schuylerville, New York, the daughter of Thomas Everett Bullard, a physician, and Elizabeth A. Huggins Bullard.[58] Her father, who maintained an apple orchard near the family home, encouraged her early interest in plants and trees.[59] After graduating from Schuylerville High School, where she received an exemplary secondary education, with emphasis on Latin, modern languages, mathematics, and science, Bullard entered Cornell University to study landscape architecture in the School of Agriculture.[60]

Immediately after receiving her B.S. degree from Cornell in December 1918, Bullard worked for two years as a residential designer for the Small Homes Grounds Department of the Wagner Park Nursery in Sydney, Ohio. Curiously, while working at the nursery, she used the pseudonym Janet Brown.[61] Between 1921 and 1927, she worked for Warren Manning in Cambridge, Massachusetts. She spent thirty-five weeks in Calumet, Michigan, implementing Manning's plans for the Calumet and Hecla Mining Company, an assignment that involved supervising miners who blasted holes in native rock. She also transplanted mountain ash trees. Among her other unusual responsibilities were supervising schoolchildren who transplanted ferns and wildflowers from nearby woods to the site of the park and directing a large-scale pageant on the history of copper mining activities in Michigan's Upper Peninsula.[62] In 1924, she heard that the University of Pennsylvania was establishing a department of landscape archi-

tecture and wrote asking to be considered as a graduate student and teaching assistant.[63] Information is lacking about whether or not she was accepted, but, in any case, she never followed this course. In 1927, she joined the firm of Annette Hoyt Flanders in New York City, where she worked on the Simonds and Kiser properties, both in Southampton (see chapter 7).[64]

Bullard never established an independent practice. After leaving Flanders's office in 1930 in the depths of the Depression, she spent the rest of her career as a civil servant, first for the Long Island State Park Commission and then for the New York City Parks Department, where she worked closely with then Parks Commissioner Robert Moses. Between 1937 and 1939, she worked as a landscape designer for the 1939 World's Fair. When this job came to a close and as the Depression was waning, she apparently considered returning to private practice and the design of residential properties. Instead, she accepted an offer from the New York State Department of Public Parks in Albany, where she remained until her retirement in 1964. During her career in the public sector, Bullard is estimated to have developed and supervised approximately fifty projects in New York City and State.[65] In all of her positions, her chief responsibility was the preparation of planting plans. Her professional activities included lecturing on garden design, city planning, housing, and Victory gardens. Some of her lecture notes have survived, but not her slides. She also attended National ASLA tours and meetings and participated in the New York Chapter of the Society.[66] In

1937–38, she seems to have taken some courses at the Washington Square College of New York University, possibly feeling that this was relevant in some way to her World's Fair work.[67]

Bullard traveled widely in the United States, often by Greyhound Bus. She went several times to the West but also visited New England and twice toured Virginia during Garden Week. She traveled to the Paris Exposition of 1937, which seems to have been her only trip outside the United States.[68] After she retired, Bullard devoted herself to community projects in Schuylerville. Bullard's longevity enabled her not only to be among the vanguard of American women landscape architects but also to observe the early stirrings of the women's liberation movement in the 1960s and 1970s on which she turned a skeptical eye and ear. After a fiery speech from a women's liberation leader, she was heard to remark that "I owe my success to the many fine men with whom I have been associated."[69]

Helen Elise Bullard died in Schuylerville on November 4, 1987.[70] Her nephew John Bullard transferred her papers to Professor Daniel Krall of Cornell University, who, in 2002, donated them to the Rare Books and Manuscripts Collection at the Carl Kroch Library, Cornell. There are few plans in this collection, which is not surprising since Bullard worked almost entirely in the public sector. There is considerable family data, including, as noted, her course notebooks from Cornell, church information, and numerous clippings from magazines of horticulture, and so forth.

BULLARD DESIGNED a number of projects on Long Island, mainly during her tenure with the Long Island State Park Commission. Among these were scented plantings at the Jones Beach Bath Houses (c. 1930), planting plans for the Brooklyn State Hospital, Queens (1930), planting plans for sections of the Northern State Parkway (early 1930s), planting plans for sections of the Southern State Parkway (1931), planting plans for the Montauk Parkway (undated), coordination of landscape and garden planting for the World's Fair (1937–39), and planting plans for the Infirmary Building, Central Islip State Hospital (1944).[71] There are specifications for many of these projects in the Bullard Collection at Cornell, but plans and photographs are almost entirely lacking. Her work at the Fair was briefly described in at least two newspaper accounts, but these were illustrated only with photographs of Bullard at her drafting table in the Fair headquarters.[72]

In March 1930, Bullard prepared planting plans and a specification for the Brooklyn State Hospital, Creedmoor Division, in Queens. This work was done under the aegis of the State of New York, Department of Public Works, Division of Architecture and Engineering, Department of Mental Hygiene. The hospital grounds included a farm that was cultivated by patients as part of their therapy, but Bullard's project seems to have been concentrated around the main hospital buildings and doctors' cottages.[73] The planting was intended to be phased, raising the possibility that only the work planned for spring 1930 (primarily the planting of large trees and other materials that would take

some time to mature) was completed. In any case, Bullard's plant palette for this project was rich and varied. Of the trees and shrubs that she specified, several, including maples, pines, spruces, evergreen trees, honeysuckle, mockorange, and lilacs were listed as being on hand; however, she directed that some of the "on-hand" plants be moved. The new trees and shrubs were largely native plants, and included Katsura trees, American beeches, tulip trees, sweet gums, weeping willows, azaleas of various kinds, Japanese barberry (used primarily to prevent trespassing and vandalism), hawthorns (used for the same reason), dogwood, mountain laurel, and others. Bullard also specified light use of Boston ivy to blur the demarcation of the red brick of the main building and the yellow brick of what was apparently an addition.[74] The Creedmoor project was an outstanding example of a therapeutic landscape, especially considering that it was a plan for a public hospital. Unfortunately, there seem to be no available photographs of the Creedmoor landscape during this period of its history.

The planting plans and specification for an infirmary building at Central Islip State Hospital, also for the New York State Department of Mental Hygiene, was somewhat similar to the Creedmoor project. As this was a planting for a single building, the plan was much smaller in scale, but it displayed considerable ornamental richness. Although there were a few large trees, such as American elms, maples, lindens, and hemlocks, Bullard also specified many flowering dogwoods and a few cherry trees. The greatest variety was in the shrub plantings, which included mountain laurel, rhododendron, privet, mockorange, and a number of different types of lilacs. The vines that Bullard specified were English ivy, English ivy *baltica* variety, Boston ivy, and Virginia creeper; for ground cover, she chose pachysandra and *Vinca minor*.[75]

While working on the Creedmoor hospital, Bullard met Robert Moses, who appointed her the landscape designer for the Long Island State Park Commission. The biographical minute written by David Bullard mentions her work at parks at Montauk, Hither Hills, Sunken Meadow, and Jones Beach, but there is no documentation for these projects at Cornell.[76] David Bullard also referred to her work on the Grand Central, Montauk, Wantagh, and Southern State Parkways, and the Jones Beach Causeway. For a time, she was even the official hostess at Jones Beach State Park and Supervisor of Women there.[77] The archive at Cornell includes specifications (two) for the Southern State Parkway (1931) and two blueprints for the Northern State Parkway (1941).

One of the specifications for the Southern State Parkway (dated March 1931) is for supplying nursery stock and collected plants for that part of the parkway near Wantagh. The work was to be completed only a month later. While the specifications for this project were probably supervised by Bullard, they were signed by a landscape designer named C. C. Combs. Among the plants specified were large quantities of *Rosa rugosa*, a rose that does well near salt water and is intensely fragrant (although not from inside a car).

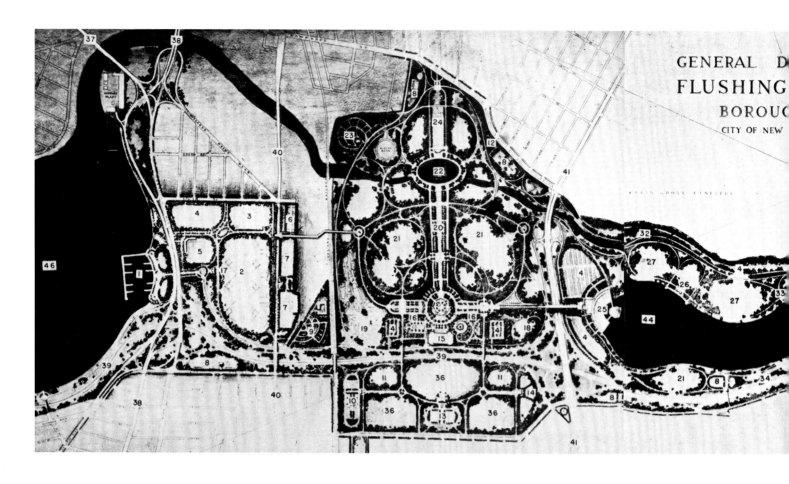

9.14 *New York City Department of Parks. Plan of the 1939 World's Fair, Flushing Meadows, New York, 1936.* From *Landscape Architecture,* July 1939

Large numbers of several other roses were also indicated, including the then-popular rambling variety "Dorothy Perkins." Also listed were junipers, flowering dogwood, amelanchier, honeysuckles, viburnum, hydrangeas, and so forth, in addition to American elm and numerous varieties of pines and other trees.[78] The other specification was for the actual planting of trees, vines, and shrubs and was also signed by C. C. Combs.[79] This document is mostly boilerplate and contains nothing unusual; the plant list corresponds fairly closely to the first specification.[80]

The 1939 World's Fair in Flushing Meadows was built on a most unpromising site: a dump described by F. Scott Fitzgerald in *The Great Gatsby* as "a fantastic farm where ashes grow like wheat into ridges and hills and grotesque gardens."[81] The 1,200-plus-acre site is adjacent to the Grand Central Parkway, which connects Queens directly to Manhattan via the Triborough Bridge. The initial "General Development Plan of Flushing Meadow Park" (fig. 9.14) was prepared by the New York City Department of Parks in February 1936.[82] This plan anticipated the site's conversion to a park after the Fair had closed; this was the identical approach that had been taken by Frederick Law Olmsted and his firm in their plan for Jackson Park and the Midway Plaisance in Chicago after the 1893 Columbian Exposition. There were three general types of buildings and structures in the Fair: those built by the Fair itself; those built by foreign nations; and those built by private exhibitors. The design of the two principal structures, the

Trylon and the Perisphere, was awarded to the architect Wallace K. Harrison and the engineer André Fouilhoux, who also designed other buildings on the grounds.

The detailed plan for the development of the site for the 1939 Fair was also generated by the New York Department of Parks, although one cannot rule out the possibility of some involvement by others, including Harrison and Fouilhoux and also Gilmore David Clarke, a landscape architect who had designed the Bronx River Parkway, and other early parkways, and who played a major role as a member of the Design Board of the Fair.[83] It was noted by a Paris magazine that the plan of the 1939 Fair had a strong resemblance to that of the 1937 Universal Exposition in Paris.[84]

As we have seen, a number of women landscape architects designed individual gardens in the "Gardens on Parade" section of the Fair. In contrast to these designers, Helen Elise Bullard was employed by the Fair.[85] Her role was central. She chose all of the trees and shrubs and designed the plantings for each new courtyard as the buildings went up. Initially, she made plans (which now appear to be lost), then supervised the digging and planting, working with "absolute precision."[86]

When interviewed by the *New York Times* in 1938, Bullard commented on the new challenge of modifying what had been traditional landscape treatments to harmonize with the modern lines of the Fair buildings: "Landscape design has for the most part to date utilized straight beds and pattern gardens, and modern principles for this

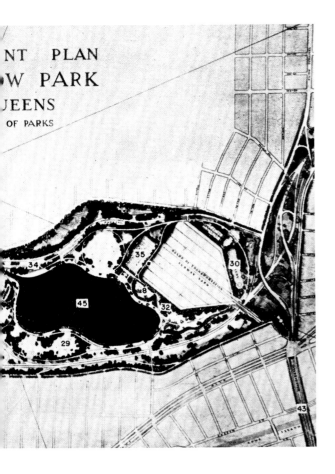

NT PLAN
W PARK
JEENS
OF PARKS

field are still undeveloped. But with modern buildings, we cannot depend on the classic forms. We have no precedents to follow, but, in general, the plantings will be designed in directional lines to give the feeling of motion."[87]

She went on to explain how the main color scheme of the buildings—a rainbow arrangement of yellow, red, and blue—would be set off by flowers in contrasting colors. Only the best and hardiest varieties of plants were to be used.[88]

In 1949, nine years after the Fair closed but while some of its buildings were still standing, Bullard gave a lecture/walking tour during which she recounted some of the history of the project. As she explained, at the start of the Fair project, about a quarter of the site was occupied by the ash dump, while the rest was a "salt marsh, formed by the meanderings of the so-called Flushing River, which wandered all over the map."[89] Before long, bulldozers, cranes, and trucks were at work, and "within six months, the ground took on a definite, useable form. The mountain of ashes was leveled down into the portions of the marsh to be filled."[90] Some of the meadow mat (the surface layer of the marsh) was excavated to form two lakes and a river. Much of the material excavated was used as a base for planting. These operations were followed by "pile drivers that drove large timbers . . . some of them as tall as a nine-story building deep into the ground to provide a firm foundation on which to erect Fair structures."[91]

Then came the planting of large trees, including maples weighing as much as twenty tons each, which were lifted by cranes attached to trucks. The trees came with large burlap-covered balls carefully graduated proportionally to the size of the tree stem and were placed in holes 13 feet in diameter and about 4 feet deep. Twelve hundred trees were planted in 1937 and the same number before June 1938, including American, English, and Asiatic elms, red and Norway maples, sycamores, several kinds of oaks, catalpas, ginkgos, and willows.[92] Once planted, the trees were carefully guyed so that they would hold steady until the roots became established.[93] This, of course, was standard procedure for transplanting large trees but it was done on a scale probably not seen since the nineteenth century and the tree plantings of Haussmann's Paris and Olmsted's Prospect Park in Brooklyn. At the 1939 World's Fair, there was practically no loss of trees.

By the time of Bullard's tour, the grounds had been largely transformed into Flushing Meadows Park yet the Fair's spaces, vistas, and trees remained. The east-west vista was a mile long. In formality and scale, Bullard thought this vista might be compared with the main axis at Versailles. Bullard reminded her audience that the Fair had been extraordinarily beautiful even in its first month, with a great display of spring flowering plants, including 250,000 pansies, 50,000 narcissus, 5,000 scilla, as well as 250,000 tulips. Framing all the bulbs and early annuals were masses of white flowering dogwood and crabapple blossoms.[94]

In the Bullard collection at Cornell there are several specifications for the 1939 World's Fair. Although most are for the planting of large trees, a few include bedding plants. One specification, for trees exclusively, will serve as an example. In contrast to the specifications for the Southern State Parkway, which awarded one contract for the supplying of trees and other plants and another for actually planting them, the 1939 World's Fair contract documents and specifications were for both supplying and planting. In 1937, the New York World's Fair 1939 Incorporated gave notice to prequalified contractors for tree planting in the fall of that year on the site of Section I of the Fair. There were twenty complete items of trees requested, for a total of 376 trees of various types and sizes. These included: twenty-two large Norway maples (*Acer platinoides*), a non-native maple that has now become invasive and is almost never planted; numerous red maples (*Acer rubrum*, a native species); eighty *Crataegus crusgalli*, a small tree with very large thorns, possibly used as a barrier plant; numerous honey locusts (*Gleditsia triacanthos*); oriental plane trees (*Platanus orientalis*), more commonly referred to as sycamores; large quantities of pin oak (*Quercus palustris*); lindens (*Tilia sp.*); as well as ten American elms (*Ulmus americana*). As these trees were needed for immediate effect, not as part of a landscape that would mature over time, all were extremely large, although not of uniform height, as that would have been monotonous. As can already have been deduced from Bullard's 1949 tour, instructions for preparations of the holes and planting the trees were extremely specific and detailed.[95]

Helen Swift Jones
1887–1982

HELEN SWIFT JONES was born on July 13, 1887, in Brooklyn, New York, the daughter of Wallace T. Jones, a manufacturer of chocolate, and Helen J. Swift Jones.[96]

Jones attended the Packer Collegiate Institute in Brooklyn and Smith College, where she was a classmate of Annette Hoyt Flanders.[97] After her graduation in 1910, Jones assisted in the biology department at Adelphi College, although this employment is not clearly documented. During World War I, she worked for the war effort, although the details of this service are also not known.[98] Between 1921 and 1924, Jones completed the course work at the Cambridge School but did not write a thesis. After leaving the Cambridge School, she worked in Flanders's office as an associate and then established her own New York firm. She was active in professional organizations, becoming secretary-treasurer of the New York Chapter of the American Society of Landscape Architects in the early 1930s. In 1935, she was awarded an M.L.A. by Smith College; these degrees were awarded to five women who had finished course work at the Cambridge School and had practiced for at least ten years but had not produced a thesis.[99] In 1936, she married Winthrop Merton Rice, said to have been an architect, although his career has not been traced, but retained her maiden name for professional purposes.[100] In 1953, she was elected a Fellow of the ASLA. She was also a member of the Architectural League of New York.[101] In the 1950s, she closed her Brooklyn office and relocated it to Stamford, Connecticut.[102] Jones wrote three slim books on practical landscape gardening, which are now very difficult to locate.[103]

During the Depression, Helen Swift Jones was one of the forty landscape architects set up by Robert Moses in a loft in the Madison Square Garden Building and put to work rehabilitating the city's park system.[104] By 1938, her practice seems to have revived, and, among other projects, she had designed two therapeutic landscapes: the roof garden for the children's ward of Bellevue Hospital, donated by the members of the Fruit and Flower Guild, and the gardens of the Mary Ogden Avery Convalescent Hospital in Hartford, Connecticut.[105] She and her husband lived in Stamford, Connecticut, where she designed the grounds of the Stamford Museum.[106] Among Jones's many residential projects were a garden for Mrs. Sargent Eaton in Fairfield, Connecticut (1955), her own garden in Stamford, a garden for the Misses Righter in Bedford Hills, New York (by 1932), a garden for Miss Elizabeth Lenox in Westport, Connecticut (by 1933), and a small lake for Mr. and Mrs. Edgar E. Ryan, also in Westport (by 1934).[107]

Helen Swift Jones was an indefatigable traveler, journeying not only to Europe but to more exotic locales such as Africa, Asia, Australia, New Zealand, Burma, Afghanistan, Nepal, Sri Lanka, India, and Iran. She continued to travel even after she had to use a wheelchair.[108] At some point, Jones acquired a "Red Book" by Humphry Repton for Mosely Hall near Birmingham, England, which Repton designed for John Taylor in 1792. Like all of Repton's Red Books, this is a unique manuscript and is now located in the Special Collections of Loeb Library at the Harvard Graduate School of Design.

Jones died on September 1, 1982, leaving a substantial bequest to the Landscape Architecture Foundation.[109] The Smith College Archives and the Sophia Smith Collection contain materials on her college and Cambridge School activities, and the Fairfield Historical Society has photographs and a plan of the Eaton garden. As recently as 1984, photographs of at least some of her work were in the possession of her brother, Carter F. Jones, along with copies of two of her three small gardening books. These were displayed in a small exhibition on the Cambridge School landscape architects held at the Smith College Museum of Art,[110] but they can no longer be traced. Carter F. Jones died in 1992.[111] Other than the Smith College Archives, the Sophia Smith Collection, and the Fairfield Historical Society, there is no Helen Swift Jones archive.

As far as is known, Helen Swift Jones designed no residential landscapes on Long Island. However, every account of her life and work mentions that she designed the "Mall and Garden" at Adelphi College, a reference that remained elusive until late 2004. It then emerged that in 1930–31, she planned and supervised an important tree planting on that campus (now Adelphi University) in Garden City. Adelphi College was founded in 1896, and its first location was in Brooklyn. It moved to Garden City in September 1929.[112]

In 1930, McKim, Mead & White prepared a campus plan for Adelphi, which was only partially executed.[113] The firm had maintained a professional relationship with the college since 1919, when the architects prepared a new plan for the Brooklyn campus; this plan was abandoned because it would have been much too dense. In 1927, Adelphi bought property in Garden City, and three buildings designed by McKim, Mead & White (the administration building, the classroom building, and the gymnasium) were in place before the official opening of the campus. The plan projected some elements of the tree planting plan that was realized by Helen Swift Jones: wrapping around the western half of the site, on its western and southern sides, the architects indicated a double row of trees (species not shown). On the northern side, a single row appears, undoubtedly because the Long Island Railroad line precluded a double row here. Widely spaced double rows demarcated the main axis and cross axis.[114]

In 1930, plans were also made to honor Adelphi's founder and first president, Charles H. Levermore, with a memorial planting of elms. A committee was formed, headed by Mrs. Harold M. Baily of Brooklyn, to raise funds from alumnae. (Adelphi was then a women's college.) Mrs. Baily appears to have contacted Helen Swift Jones in the fall of that year. While no plan for this planting signed by Jones or definitely issuing from her office has survived, a rough plan drawn up in 1931 for organizing the dedication ceremony clearly shows her arrangement. She adhered quite closely to the McKim, Mead & White campus scheme, wrapping a double row of American elms around the perimeter and another double row leading in the direction of the classroom building and the administration building. Initially, twenty-six elm trees were purchased from the Amawalk Nursery for $1,900 and planted by the North Shore Landscape Company for $312[115] (see fig. 9.16). However, other elms must have been added before the dedication on June 6, 1931, since sixty trees are shown on that plan.

In December 1930, Jones was asked to look into the feasibility of adding two rows of hedging on the outer side of the elms, but the idea was abandoned because of the expense of maintenance. Jones wrote that this hedging was called for on the architects' plans, but there is no hedging on the 1930 McKim, Mead & White plan.[116]

Jones was also commissioned to design the Levermore Gardens. There was much correspondence with Mrs. Baily about a "corner" planting, presumably the corners of the Levermore Gardens. These corners measured 40 by 60 feet, a considerable size, and Jones planned to use a pine and a hardy crabapple in each, as well as hardy shrubs, such as forsythia and currant.[117] Four white pines were reserved for Jones by the Oak Park Nurseries in East Patchogue and were apparently planted.[118] A bronze tablet was also made by the Forman Co.[119] A planting of spring bulbs and peonies was also supervised by Jones.[120] Over time, many of the Levermore elms had to come down to accommodate new buildings; the rest have succumbed to Dutch elm disease. There are no photographs specifically of either the elms or the gardens.

9.16 *The Adelphi College campus, showing the Levermore elms at an early stage of their growth. Photograph, ca. 1935.* Adelphi University Archives

Janet Darling Webel
1913–1966

9.17 *Janet Darling at the Cambridge School, 53 Church Street, Cambridge. Photograph, ca. 1935.* Cambridge School Archives, Sophia Smith Collection, Smith College

JANET DARLING was born on February 20, 1913. Her mother was Bella Crawford Darling. She graduated from the Horace Mann High School, a prestigious private school in the Riverdale section of New York City, in 1930, from Smith College in 1934 and, in 1937, received an M.L.A. from Smith College for her work at the Cambridge School of Architecture and Landscape Architecture.[121] She wrote a perceptive thesis on a proposed subdivision in Mount Kisco, New York.[122] To write such a thesis, she must have studied subdivision design, a departure from the school's generally strict emphasis on "domestic" design. In 1941, she was married to Percival Dixon.[123] After their divorce, she married Richard K. Webel, a landscape architect. The couple had one son, Richard C. Webel.

Information is currently lacking about Janet Darling's employment or other activities immediately after her graduate work at the Cambridge School. Since she used her maiden name throughout her professional career, it is likely that she practiced independently at least briefly and became known under that name. After her marriage to Richard K. Webel, she became a member of the firm Innocenti & Webel, a firm that continues under the direction of their son. However, Darling found that her design ideas did not always coincide with those of her husband, so she founded her own firm under the name Darling & Webel. In addition to residential work, this firm designed the grounds of public schools and other institutions in the New York City area. In 1964, Darling designed Damrosch Park at Lincoln Center adjacent to an earlier design by Dan Kiley.[124] She wrote at least one article, "Good Architecture Makes Good Planting Look Better."[125] Janet Darling Webel died April 11, 1966.[126] Shortly thereafter, Richard K. Webel set up the Janet Darling Webel Memorial Scholarship Fund at Harvard's Graduate School of Design.[127]

On Long Island, in 1956, Janet Darling designed the Jennings residence (location unknown), which included a swimming pool partially curvilinear in shape.[128] Between 1960 and 1963, the Webels collaborated on the Mr. and Mrs. Richard F. Coons residence in Oyster Bay. Richard K. Webel laid out the front gardens, and Darling designed an extraordinary pool in the rear. While so-called kidney-shaped pools were popular in this era, the spatial inventiveness of the Coons pool (fig. 9.18) exceeded that of Darling's contemporaries, including her husband.[129]

9.18 *Swimming pool,*
Mr. and Mrs. Coons
Residence, Oyster Bay.
Photograph, Samuel
Gottscho, ca. 1960–63.
Gottscho Schleisner
Collection, Library
of Congress

Alice Recknagel Ireys
1911–2000

ALICE RECKNAGEL was born on April 24, 1911, in Brooklyn, New York, the daughter of Harold S. Recknagel, an attorney who worked in the insurance industry, and Rea Estes Recknagel. For most of her life, she lived in a Brooklyn Heights town house that had been owned by her family since 1835. The house also became the headquarters of her independent landscape architectural practice. In 1943, Recknagel married Henry Tillinghast Ireys III, a graduate of the Virginia Military Institute, who was then working for a New York City construction company. They had a son and two daughters.[130]

Ireys's early horticultural and landscape interests were stimulated by her grandfather at the family farm at Green Harbor, Massachusetts, where she helped in the vegetable garden and had a small flower garden of her own. They were further nurtured by a youth program at the Brooklyn Botanical Garden.[131] Between 1920 and 1931, she studied at the Packer Collegiate Institute in Brooklyn and then spent four years at the Cambridge School of Architecture and Landscape Architecture.[132] The Cambridge School generally accepted only women with B.A.s but Ireys evidently persuaded Henry Atherton Frost that a diploma from Packer Collegiate was the equivalent of a junior college degree.[133] Nevertheless, Henry Atherton Frost took a rather hard line on academic credentials, which may explain why Ireys took four years to complete what was normally a three-year course. Since she lacked a B.A., she never received an M.L.A. from Smith College, but she received a certificate from the Cambridge School in 1935. The fol-

lowing year she became an assistant in the office of Marjorie Sewell Cautley in Ridgefield, New Jersey, where she prepared planting plans for the Hillside Housing project in the Bronx. This prestigious and important project was significantly underfunded. Alice told her parents that she received $3.00 a day, to which her mother responded, "But we pay the laundress $3.50 a day!"[134] Between 1936 and 1939, Ireys was the head draftsman for landscape architect Charles N. Lowrie in New York City. While working for him, she prepared a planting plan for one of the lakes at the 1939 World's Fair. The plan has not survived, and there seem to be no good photographs of this lake.[135] After Lowrie died in September 1939, Ireys took over his practice, although only five clients were willing to stay on with her.[136] Among other things, Ireys completed landscape plans for the Red Hook housing project in Brooklyn, the first of many housing projects for which she designed plantings. Between 1941 and 1945, she was associated with landscape architect Cynthia Wiley and designed more housing projects. From 1947 through the end of her career, she was an independent landscape architect.[137]

At the time of her marriage, she had been practicing for eight years and was reasonably well established. When her children were born, she reduced her practice somewhat but was also aided substantially by her mother, who lived with the family after Ireys's father's death and helped with the children.[138] About her profession, Ireys told an interviewer in 1998, "It was something I had to do. It was as important a part of my life as anything else."[139]

Between 1942 and 1945, Ireys taught landscape gardening at Connecticut College for Women in New London, Connecticut. She also lectured widely at such places as Longwood Gardens, the Brooklyn Botanic Garden, the New York Botanical Garden, Old Westbury Gardens, and various garden clubs on the east coast. She wrote articles for the *New York Sun*, the *New York Times*, *Plants and Gardens* (a publication of the Brooklyn Botanic Garden), and provided sketches of trees for *Architectural Graphic Standards*. After her husband died in 1963, she dealt with her loneliness by taking on book-length projects, eventually publishing four books: *How to Plan and Plant Your Own Property* (1967), *Small Gardens for City and Country* (1978), *Garden Designs* (1991), and *Designs for American Gardens* (1991).[140] Her books were all highly practical and oriented toward the homeowner rather than the landscape professional. *How to Plan and Plant Your Own Property* is especially detailed and deals with such subjects as suitable planting designs for different architectural styles and for a variety of sites and climatic conditions.

Ireys was a Fellow of the American Society of Landscape Architects and a registered landscape architect in New York State and West Virginia.[141] In 1991, the American Horticultural Society presented her with the Liberty Hyde Bailey Award, their highest honor.[142]

Ireys was described as being a "modest but confident woman," but some regarded her as "outspoken and opinionated."[143] She was a member of the Brooklyn Junior League, on the board of the Graham Home for Old Ladies, a member of the Brooklyn Brownstone Conference, and the Brooklyn Heights Garden Club, as well as undertaking many volunteer projects for the Brooklyn Botanic Garden. She was also active in Grace Episcopal Church in Brooklyn, although she had earlier affiliations with other churches in Brooklyn.[144] Alice Ireys practiced up to the day before she entered the hospital in her final illness. Just as Beatrix Farrand in her later years often swaddled herself in rugs and directed plantings from a camp stool and Marian Coffin's chauffeur sometimes had to lift her out of her car, Ireys dealt with the infirmities of old age by inspecting her projects from a golf cart, using her cane as a pointer.[145] In 1996, Ireys donated the bulk of her professional papers, including drawings, photographs, correspondence, and financial records, to the Sophia Smith Collection at Smith College. More documents were received in early 2001, after Ireys's death on December 12, 2000.

It is estimated that there are documents for over a thousand projects in the Ireys Papers at Smith. The actual number of her projects may be even greater. Many of her documented projects date from relatively late in

9.20 *Perennial garden, Mrs. Henry Sturgis Residence, Cedarhurst. Photograph, undated, ca. 1945–50.* Ireys Papers

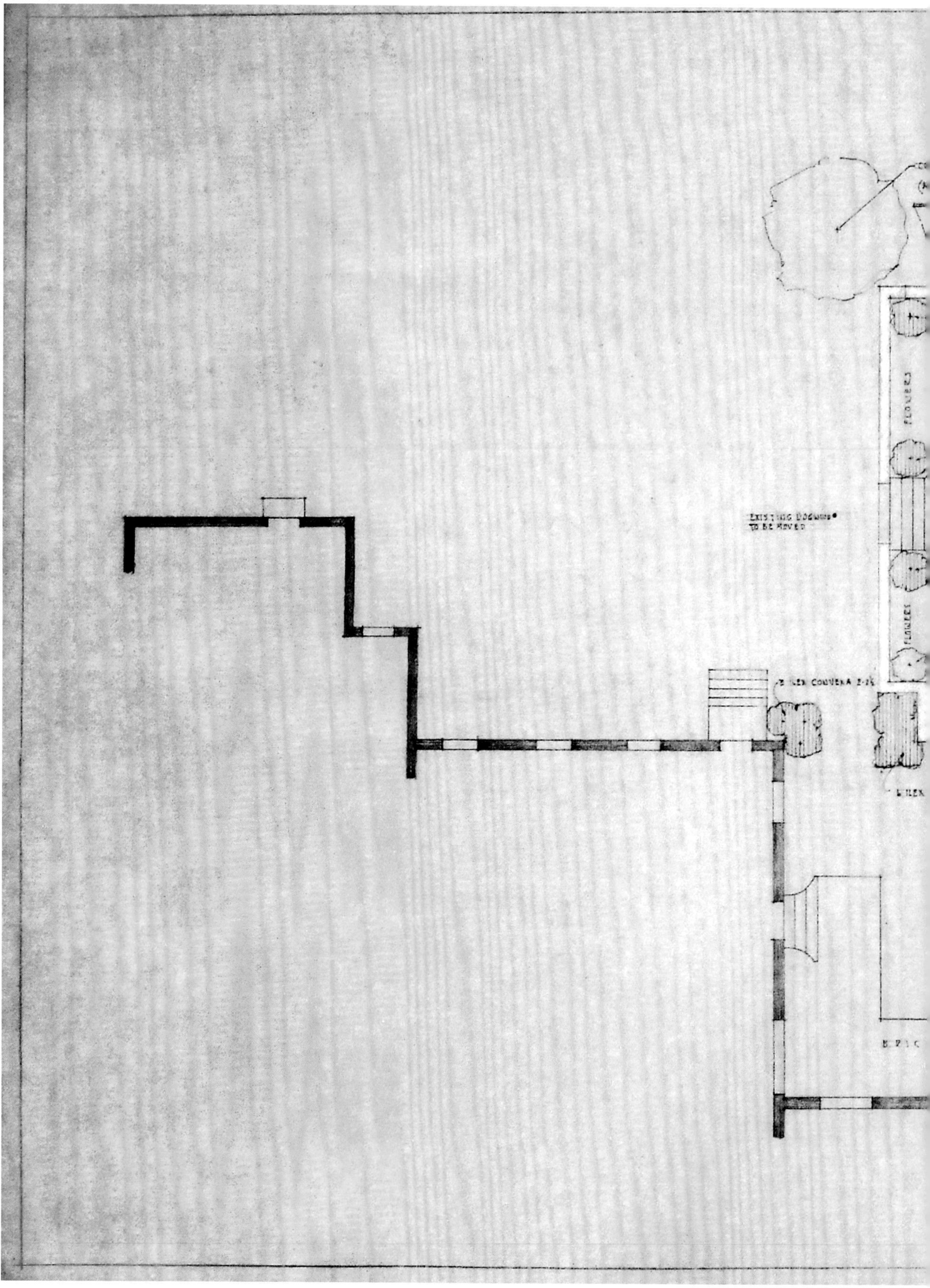
EXISTING DOGWOOD
TO BE MOVED
FLOWERS
FLOWERS

9.21 *Planting plan, azalea garden, Winter Harbor, the Mr. and Mrs. Robert Blum Residence, New Hyde Park. Pencil on tracing paper, January 1954.* Ireys Papers

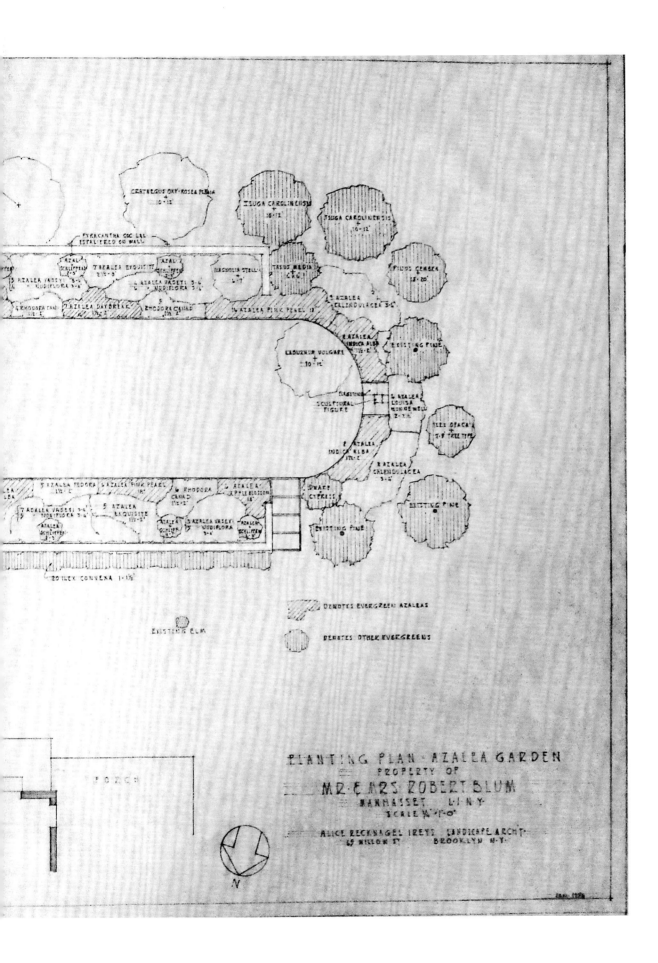

CRATAEGUS OXY·ROSEA PLENA
10·12'

PYRACANTHA COC·LAL
ESPALIERED ON WALL

TSUGA CAROLINENSIS
10·12'

TSUGA CAROLINENSIS
10·12'

AZAL.
SCHLIPPEN
2·3'

7 AZALEA EXQUISITE
2½·3'

AZAL.
SCHLIPPEN

MAGNOLIA STELL
5·7'

TAXUS MEDIA
6·7'

PINUS CEMBRA
15·20'

5 AZALEA VASEYI 3·4'
NUDIFLORA 3·4'

4 AZALEA VASEYI 3·4
NUDIFLORA 3·4'

5 AZALEA
CALENDULACEA 3·4'

4 RHODORA CAN
10·12'

7 AZALEA DAYBREAK
1½·2'

RHODORA CANAD
1½·2'

4 AZALEA PINK PEARL 15'

AZALEA
INDICA ALBA
1½·2'

EXISTING PINE

LABURNUM VULGARE
10·12'

EXISTING
SCULPTURAL
FIGURE

5 AZALEA
LOUISA
HONEYWELL
2·2½'

ILEX OPACA
7·8' TREE TYPE

2 AZALEA
INDICA ALBA
1½·2'

2 AZALEA
CALENDULACEA
3·4'

DWARF
CYPRESS

EXISTING PINE

5 AZALEA FEDORA 4 AZALEA PINK PEARL
1½·2'   15'

4 RHODORA
CANAD
1½·2'

2 AZALEA
APPLEBLOSSOM
15'

EXISTING PINE

7 AZALEA VASEYI 3·4'
NUDIFLORA 3·4'

5 AZALEA
EXQUISITE
1½·2'

AZALEA
SCHLIPPEN

5 AZALEA VASEYI
3·4'

AZALEA
SCHLIPPEN

AZALEA
SCHLIPPEN

20 ILEX CONVEXA 1·1½'

EXISTING ELM

DENOTES EVERGREEN AZALEAS

DENOTES OTHER EVERGREENS

PORCH

PLANTING PLAN · AZALEA GARDEN
PROPERTY OF
MR·E·MRS ROBERT BLUM
MANHASSET   L·I·N·Y·
SCALE ⅛"·1'·0"
ALICE RECKNAGEL IREYS LANDSCAPE ARCHT·
65 WILLOW ST·   BROOKLYN N·Y·

N

9.22 *Garden and wisteria pergola, Mr. and Mrs. Robert Blum Residence, New Hyde Park. Photograph, ca. late 1960s.* Ireys Papers

her independent career. It is very likely that space constraints in her Brooklyn home/office may have led her to discard some of the paperwork for her earlier projects. Some of her projects for which there are client files (correspondence and sometimes folded plans) and photographs have no other plans, suggesting that some of these too may have been discarded. It is probable that Ireys "weeded" some of the project files that she kept, as the Olmsted firm and many other landscape architects also did. Unlike the Olmsted firm, she did not number her plans, so it is difficult to tell what may be missing.

Significant projects included Allegheny College, Allegheny, Pennsylvania; the Clark Gardens in Albertson, New York, a ten-acre site with waterfalls and ponds; a planting plan and supervision of work for the Abigail Adams Smith Museum (now the Mount Vernon Hotel) in Manhattan; Crane Park in Cranford, New Jersey; a plan for the town center of Bridgewater, Massachusetts; a garden for the John Jay Homestead, Rye, Westchester County, New York; and a planting plan for Twin Lights, New Jersey. She also prepared design, construction, and planting plans for Davis Park, Charleston, West Virginia, an inner-city park.[146]

OF IREYS'S ONE THOUSAND PROJECTS, more than 25 percent were on Long Island. In contrast to the Olmsted firm, which generally designed most of the acreage of a site, Ireys's projects tended to be small and limited to specific areas. Clients often sought out women landscape architects for specific problems, and they sometimes returned to that designer for additional work in other parts of the grounds. This happened frequently with Ireys.

Ireys's projects on Long Island included a planting plan for the Garden City Library, a planting plan for the Shelter Island Library, a planting plan for the Garden City School, the design, construction, and planting for a Japanese demonstration garden at Old Westbury Gardens, and a planting plan for a perennial garden at Planting Fields Arboretum, Oyster Bay, which was not implemented.[147]

Thirty-seven are especially well documented. Five of these are discussed here: Kate and Henry Sturgis, Cedarhurst, 1945–57; Robert and Ethel Blum, Winter Harbor, New Hyde Park, 1951–63; the Garden of Fragrance for the Blind at the Brooklyn Botanic Garden, 1954–55; William S. and Barbara Paley, Kiluna Farm, Manhasset, 1962–72; Howard and Mary Phipps, Old Westbury, 1971–81 and 1992–97.

9.23 *Garden of Fragrance for the Blind, Brooklyn Botanic Garden, Brooklyn, New York. Photograph, Samuel Gottscho, undated, ca. 1955*

Ireys began to work with Kate and Henry Sturgis when she was still associated with Cynthia Wiley. Ireys designed a large perennial garden (fig. 9.20) with plants in shades of predominantly white, yellow, soft pink, terracotta, and blue. The flowers included monkshood, columbine hybrids, white and pink asters, artemisia, two kinds of campanula, several kinds of chrysanthemums, delphiniums, pinks, day lilies, candytuft, tall bearded iris, Japanese iris, selected varieties of lilies, peonies, and phlox, violas, and veronicas. This list accompanied a revised plan for the layout of the garden, and Ireys noted that the planting plan was underway.[148] This list was followed a few weeks later by another plant list that included trees and shrubs, mostly flowering ones such as dogwood, shrub roses, lilacs, and viburnums. Five climbing roses were also specified for the fence and house. Also attached was another perennial list, where particular peonies, delphiniums, phlox, etc. were specified by name, rather than just "in variety."[149] In April, Ireys ordered more roses from Jackson and Perkins.[150] Ireys continued consulting with Mrs. Sturgis, and a large bulb planting was put in during the early 1950s. There are photographs and colored slides of the Sturgis property in the Ireys papers but no reproducible plans.

In May 1951, Robert and Ethel Blum asked Ireys to design plantings to the south of their house, consisting of flowering trees and shrubs, a flower garden, and an azalea garden. The azaleas were to be in shades of pink and white, using most of the deciduous varieties and a few of the evergreen types.[151] In February 1954, Mrs. Blum decided that the construction costs for the azalea garden were too high. Ireys prepared an alternative sketch for a more informal scheme that would require less in the way of construction (fig. 9.21).[152] By November of that year, however, Mrs. Blum had decided to go ahead with the azalea planting and purchased the plants from Hicks Nurseries. The azaleas included two *Azalea schlippenbachi*, three *Azalea vaseyi*, two *Azalea arborescens*, and eight *Azalea indica alba*. Mrs. Blum purchased some other plants, including potted abelias, a spreading yew, holly, and cotoneaster.[153] Perennials and small flowering trees and shrubs were planted beside a pool on the opposite side of the lawn from the azalea garden, backed by a long terrace topped by a wisteria-covered pergola (fig. 9.22). There are no plans or client correspondence for the pergola, but this photograph and two details of the pergola are in the Ireys Papers, making it a virtual certainty that she designed it.[154] In 1962, the Blums bought

a new house in Old Westbury and had numerous trees and shrubs moved there, but none of the azaleas.[155] Ireys also worked on a property that the Blums owned in Lakeville, Connecticut.

Probably Ireys's most famous project, although one of her smallest, was the Garden of Fragrance for the Blind at the Brooklyn Botanic Garden. Modeled after a similar garden in Brighton, England, it was sponsored by the Women's Auxiliary of the Garden, of which Ireys was a member, and funded by the Auxiliary and other friends of the Garden. She undoubtedly got this commission through the Blums; Robert E. Blum was then president of the Brooklyn Institute of Arts and Sciences, and his wife was the honorary chairman of the Fragrance Garden.

In January 1955, Ireys produced a general plan of the Garden of Fragrance, which was designed to be accessible not only to the blind but also to people in wheelchairs. The oval space measured only 60 by 100 feet and was meant to bring visitors into close contact with plants. It could be reached both by steps and by a wheelchair ramp (fig. 9.23).[156] The two- and one-half-acre site was divided into quadrants, with fragrant flowers and/or foliage. Visitors were encouraged to touch, smell, and even taste the plants. Plants with light fragrance included several types of pinks, nicotiana, and verbena. Other plants were primarily for texture, others to taste, and still others, including lavender, rosemary, and thyme, to "pinch" for fragrance.[157] Braille labels, as well as labels for sighted visitors, identified the plants, and guide rails helped visitors through the site. It was estimated that 90 percent of all blind persons lose their sight after the age of twenty but retain memories of their sighted days. Thus, a rose could "smell" red.[158]

Alice Ireys remained committed to the Fragrance Garden in her native borough. On its fiftieth anniversary in 1994, she gave a retrospective account, and, in the summer of 2001, it was dedicated to her memory.[159] For those who could see and those who could not see, the garden was and is memorable.

One of the most elegant of Ireys's private commissions was a project for a part of the grounds of Kiluna Farm, the Manhasset home of William S. and Barbara Cushing Paley. The story is complicated by the fact that a number of other landscape architects were involved at Kiluna Farm. Columbia Broadcasting System President William S. Paley and Barbara Cushing were married on July 28, 1947. For each it was a second marriage, and each had two children by a previous marriage. They then had two children together. Barbara, always known as Babe, was the youngest of the three glamorous Cushing sisters.[160]

During his first marriage, Paley purchased Kiluna Farm from Ralph Pulitzer, son of publisher Joseph Pulitzer. Pulitzer had built the house, which was designed by New York architects Walker and Gillette, around 1910, and he gave the property its name.[161] Around 1913, Charles A. Platt designed a swimming pool and bathhouse in the woods and a formal garden with a circular lily pond and a rustic pergola south of the main house. Portions of the Platt landscaping may have been extant as recently as the 1980s.[162]

Babe Paley had a deep interest in plants and gardening. Unlike many other clients, she not only directed gardeners but did considerable work with her own hands. Kiluna Farm was located next door to Greentree, the property of her sister Betsey, who was married to John Hay ("Jock") Whitney. At eighty acres, Kiluna Farm was large but still less than a fifth the size of Greentree. There is little information about the overall layout of Kiluna Farm, although it is known that there were numerous guest cottages, a cottage for the children and their nanny, stables, a swimming pool (possibly Platt's), and a glassed-in, all-weather tennis court. There were flower and vegetable gardens, but their location and layout is not documented. Mrs. Paley is also said to have laid out the paths that ran through the property.[163]

The most striking landscape feature at Kiluna Farm was an oval pool set in a wooded hollow, close to the house but out of sight. In 1960, British landscape designer Russell Page visited Kiluna Farm and recommended that a pool be placed in the hollow, which was then occupied by a greenhouse.[164] At the time, Page was living abroad and was unable to oversee prompt implementation of the pool, which Mrs. Paley wanted immediately. Curiously, what was apparently an early rough sketch by Page shows the pool as an only slightly elongated circle, not the pure oval that was eventually constructed.[165] This is probably why, in the Ireys papers, it is generally referred to as "the punch bowl pool." In 1961, Mrs. Paley approached New York landscape architects Zion and Breen (who later in the 1960s would design Paley Park in New York City, the first "vest-pocket" park in the country) to expedite the Kiluna Farm project, which they brought to the level of construction details while accentuating the oval shape of the pool.[166]

Exactly what went wrong between Zion and Breen and Mrs. Paley is unclear. Possibly, they were busy and unable to proceed as rapidly as Mrs. Paley wanted. In 1962, Mrs. Paley asked Ireys to consult about the pool. Ireys prepared construction drawings and supervised the planting, much of which was apparently chosen by Mrs. Paley. As Ireys clarified some time later, the concept of the pool was Page's, but the details and implementation were hers. Both landscape architects liked the idea of having waterlilies in the pool, which was only 3 feet deep, but the lilies do not appear in any of the photographs and may never have been planted.[167]

As constructed, the pool (fig. 9.24) was both intimate and impressive. Immediately surrounding the pool, there were no trees, shrubs, or flowers, only a generous width of green grass. Beyond, there were white flowering dogwoods and azaleas, some white and others in shades of pink or red, including Knap Hill azaleas. The approach to the pool (fig. 9.25) was all Ireys's work. The pool was not only exquisite in itself but formed a perfect frame for Barbara Paley's classic profile when she worked at her pool garden.[168]

Ireys also designed a rose garden for Kiluna Farm, which was carried out.[169] In 1972, she also made a plan for a sculpture terrace at the other end of the grass steps.[170] This does not seem to have been realized; it is never mentioned and appears in no photographs.

After his wife's death in 1978, William S. Paley sold Kiluna Farm to Ed Klar, a developer. The house and children's cottage were destroyed by arson in February 1990. Around 1996, the property was resold to developers Bernard Janowitz and Jeffrey Kaplan of Westbrook Partners. The developers bought it with approval to restore part of the landscape, including the pool. The gardens, private roads, and tennis courts were to be maintained and supervised. Eighty-two houses were planned for the site, and Michael A. Michel of Glen Cove was to be in charge of the landscape restoration.[171] By 2004, the gated community had been completed. The Page/Ireys pool remains, although there have been a few significant alterations. The rim of a concrete liner is visible around the edge of the pool, changing the clean line of grass and water. While some very old trees remain, possibly dating from the Pulitzer ownership, new planting has been done, and there is a small bubbler fountain in the center of the pool, which, as a reflecting pool, was intended to have a still surface. Nevertheless, it is remarkable that it has survived. Ireys's steps down to the pool and her related plantings in that area have been significantly changed.[172]

Ireys's project for Howard and Mary Phipps in Old Westbury was designed in two stages. Their property was located across Post Road from Old Westbury Gardens, built by John Phipps and now a house and garden open to the public. In 1932–36, Innocenti and Webel did extensive design work here, probably the general landscaping of the entire property.[173] The site is a large one and has two addresses reflecting two different entrances. In 1972, Ireys designed a charming Japanese garden for the Phippses' grandson (fig. 9.26). She did additional work here in 1992–93 for a new entrance.[174]

Toward the end of her life, Ireys remarked that "at night when I can't sleep, I think about my different jobs and what fun they all were."[175]

9.26 *Japanese garden,*
Howard Phipps Residence,
Old Westbury. Photograph,
ca. 1975. Ireys Papers

CHAPTER 10

A Look Backward
and Forward

NOW THAT WE HAVE EXAMINED the lives and careers of eighteen women landscape architects, we can establish their position in the broader trends of which they were a part. By the end of the nineteenth century, women had made rapid progress in many of the arts. In 1844, the Philadelphia School for Design was founded to train women for employment in the industrial arts.[1] In what would seem to be the very masculine preserve of stained glass design, they also made a surprisingly early mark.[2] A group of women artists active in the Boston area between 1870 and 1940 has been well documented.[3]

A few influential women and men spoke out in favor of women in both architecture and landscape architecture long before Beatrix Farrand undertook her first project. The first champion of women in the building arts appears to have been Harriet Beecher Stowe, who wrote in 1863, "One of the greatest reforms that could be, in these reforming days. . . would be to have women architects . . . architecture and landscape gardening are arts in every way suited to the genius of woman, and there are enough who have the requisite mechanical skill and mathematical education."[4] Stowe's last statement about mechanical skill and education seems overly optimistic, although the writer designed her own house in Hartford, Connecticut.[5]

Calvert Vaux, later Frederick Law Olmsted's partner, was perhaps a more unexpected advocate of women designers. He wrote in 1864, "There can be no doubt but that the study of domestic architecture is well suited to a feminine taste, and it has, moreover, so many different ramifications

that it affords frequent opportunities for turning good abilities to profitable account . . . there is nothing in the world to prevent many of them from being thoroughly expert in architectural drawings, or from designing excellent furniture."[6]

In the 1860s, there were several impediments to women entering the architectural profession, of which the most significant was the lack of formal educational opportunities. In this period, aspiring male architects sometimes started out as builders or apprenticed to established architects. Neither was a route that a woman could readily take. In addition, the social conventions of the period tended to keep women confined to the domestic sphere.[7] Even Vaux suggested that they specialize in residential design. In 1869, Harriet Morrison Irwin, a mother of nine with no architectural training, patented a design for a spatially efficient hexagonal house. At least one was built, and it still stands in Irwin's hometown, Charlotte, North Carolina.[8]

During the Civil War, Olmsted served as executive secretary of the United States Sanitary Commission, an organization of volunteers, mostly women, that was formed to create better conditions for Union soldiers on the battlefields. This appears to have been one of the first times that significant numbers of women left the domestic realm for a more public sphere, helping, for example, to nurse soldiers in field hospitals.[9] Olmsted was much impressed by their administrative abilities. In 1890, he wrote to a friend regarding increasing opportunities for women, "I rejoice in it with you . . . I think that hardly another man has as high an estimate of the possible capacities of women as compared with men in respect to organization, method and discipline in the management of affairs as I have as the result of my Sanitary Commission experience."[10] He wrote about a former Sanitary Commission colleague, Mrs. Francis Bacon, the former Georgie Woolsey, that she would ". . . upon orders, take command of the channel fleet, aim, equip, man, provision, sail and engage the enemy, better than any other landsman know."[11]

As far as can be determined, Louise Blanchard Bethune was the first professional woman architect in the United States. She announced the opening of her architectural office at the Ninth Congress of the Association for the Advancement of Women held in Buffalo, New York, in 1881. She and her husband and architectural partner, Robert Armour Bethune, had both worked in the office of Richard A. Waite, an established Buffalo architect. Blanchard learned technical drafting, construction detailing, architectural design, and construction supervision and became Waite's assistant. The firm, R. A. and L. Bethune, designed numerous schools, industrial and commercial buildings, a women's prison, a hotel, an armory, and a transformer building. About ten of these projects can be attributed primarily or exclusively to Louise Blanchard Bethune. She was admitted to the Western Association of Architects in 1885. In 1888, she was elected to the American Institute of Architects and, in 1889, became its first woman Fellow.[12] In 1891, Blanchard Bethune wrote: "The great architectural societies of the country, the American Institute and its state and city Chapters, are all open to [women] upon proof of qualification. Thank, with me, the noble-hearted men whose far-seeing polity and kindly nature had laid this stepping-stone."[13] She remained active as an architect until her retirement in 1908.[14]

Minerva Parker Nichols, another early practiner, studied at the Philadelphia Normal Art School before joining the office of Philadelphia architect Frederick G. Thorn in 1882. When Thorn retired in 1888, she took over his practice for the next seven years. In 1896, she and her husband left the Philadelphia area, and thereafter she limited her practice to designs for friends and relatives. Among her projects during her independent career were women's clubs, the Brown and Nichols School in Cambridge, and, most impressively, two factories. She also entered the competition for the Woman's Building at the World's Columbian Exposition in 1893.[15]

The Woman's Building competition was won by Sophia B. Hayden, who in 1890 was the first woman to receive an architectural degree from MIT.[16] Hayden's design was damned with faint praise as being delicate and refined and betraying the gender of its architect. She also received a much lower premium than the male architects of the Exposition buildings. Hayden suffered a nervous collapse during the construction of the building and never designed another structure.[17] Rallying to Hayden's defense, Minerva Parker Nichols wrote, "It is time to put aside prejudice and sentimentalism, and judge women's work by their ability. Let the conditions and restrictions be exactly the same as those under which men work . . . so that the restriction shall be one of ability, and not sex. We do not need women as architects, we do not need men, but we do need brains enough to lift the architecture of this country beyond the grasp of unskilled and unqualified practitioners."[18] There was no question that Hayden's architectural education was the finest available, but, in Boston, no architect was willing to accept her as a draftswoman. Instead, she earned her living by teaching art in a high school. In Nichols's view, Hayden suffered from a lack of practical experience, which is hardly surprising since no male architect would hire her.[19]

Of the "pioneer" landscape designers who have been discussed in this book, the only one who took the path of apprenticing to or working as a draftswoman for an established landscape architect was Ruth Dean, who apprenticed with Jens Jensen. Most, including Beatrix Jones, did not even attempt to approach a male landscape architect for such in-office training. Why were Bethune, Nichols, and Dean successful in finding work in offices when this eluded most women, including Sophia Hayden?

There are probably a number of factors, perhaps most importantly the state of the market. In 1876, although there was a national depression, Buffalo was undergoing a building boom, and architects were desperate for draftsmen, which must have contributed to Bethune's success.[20] The 1880s were a prosperous decade across the country, which would have been in Nichols's favor. Obvious talent in freehand drawing and/or drafting would have encouraged "noble-hearted" male architects and landscape architects to hire women. Bethune and Nichols had both studied art for some years. Ruth Dean studied drawing in high school but not during her two years at the University of Chicago. Additionally, the pre–World War I years, when Dean worked for Jensen were also prosperous. Ecology was Jensen's great strength, and he was probably impressed that Dean had studied this discipline for two years at the university.

Then, there are indefinable matters of personality, which are difficult to assess in long-dead individuals. Bethune and Nichols seem to have both been very determined people, but more so than Hayden or Coffin? The interview quoted at length in chapter 6 makes it clear that Dean was both determined and charming.

From the portraits in the preceding chapters, it will have become apparent that the first female landscape practitioners in this country were a group of strikingly attractive women. This probably helped them. However, for those who were beautiful, including Marian Coffin, it may sometimes have been a disadvantage. Prospective employers may have perceived an incongruity between the way Coffin looked and the work she proposed to do. They may also have feared that she would marry and leave them stranded. Farrand was a beautiful young woman as well. In 1900, Calvert Vaux's son, Downing Vaux, wrote that "Miss Jones" came to an American Society of Landscape Architects dinner "in a most becoming getup and . . . carried the Fellows by storm."[21] She was rewarded with a position on the ASLA Executive Committee.[22] In her more mature years, Farrand favored a very tailored and somewhat severe mode of dress.

Changing dress styles undoubtedly aided the emergence of women in the professions. When the first women began practicing, it had been only a matter of decades since they had been liberated from hoop skirts, with their multiple petticoats and pantaloons, and even less time had passed since the bustle had fallen out of fashion.[23] On the other hand, the corset seems to have been required underdress until the flapper era of the 1920s. This very confining garment, which reduced a woman's lung capacity by half, was sometimes rejected earlier in the twentieth century by reform-minded women.[24] When Beatrix Farrand began practicing in 1896, she wore her "bicycle suit" for business, which she said was "conventional, quiet looking and . . . not in the way."[25] As late as 1917, when Helen Elise Bullard took an out-of-door surveying lab at Cornell, she wore "a gauze combination, a woolen combination, a paper jacket, a corset, a muslin combination, and a petticoat and corset covering, shirt waist, suit, winter coat, shoes & stockings, galoshes, gloves, muff, and hat."[26] Although Bullard's "layering" was motivated more by a desire to keep warm than by modesty or propriety, this is still an amazing array of garments.

The first woman to graduate from a land-grant college in a field related to landscape architecture appears to have been Kate (Katherine Olivia) Sessions. A native of San Francisco, she graduated from the University of California in Berkeley in 1881 with a degree in science; her senior thesis was entitled "The Natural Sciences as a Field for Women's Labor." In 1885, she launched her horticultural career by purchasing a nursery in San Diego, which was followed by others in various locations in the area, including, in 1892, Balboa Park (then City Park). As rent for this space, she planted one hundred trees a year in the park and supplied three hundred more for planting elsewhere in the city. She was also a leading figure in the introduction of foreign plant species into California. Today, some of the trees Sessions planted in Balboa Park and at the sites of other nurseries are still magnificent specimens. Was she a landscape architect? Yes, at least on a small scale. She designed plantings for some buildings by noted modernist architect Irving Gill.[27]

With the passage of the Morrill Act in 1862, it would seem that impediments to women's education in architecture and landscape architecture should have come to an end. Unfortunately, that was not the case. As late as 1914, when Bertha Yerex Whitman presented herself to the dean of architecture at the University of Michigan, she was told: "We don't want you, but, since the school is coeducational and state owned, we have to take you if you insist."[28] Whitman persevered. She graduated in 1920 and was still practicing in 1971.[29] One wonders if Annette Hoyt Flanders received a similar response when she applied to the University of Illinois at Urbana-Champaign in 1916, particularly as she was still a married woman.

Elizabeth Jane Bullard deserves the title of first American woman landscape architect, although not without some qualification, because, in her own words, her practice was always very "modest." She has been described as an artist, although no details about her education are known. She was the daughter of Oliver Crosby Bullard, who had served with Olmsted in the United States Sanitary Commission. One of his duties was establishing a field hospital in preparation for the Battle of Gettysburg. O. C. Bullard became an expert at moving large trees, although where he acquired this expertise is also unknown. As a young girl, Elizabeth Jane Bullard accompanied her father when he was transplanting trees in Prospect Park in Brooklyn. She later became his unofficial assistant when, as park superintendent, he was engaged in planting Beardsley Park in Bridgeport, Connecticut, another early Olmsted and Vaux design.[30] When O. C. Bullard died suddenly in 1890, Elizabeth Jane Bullard became responsible for the plantings in Beardsley Park as well as for a planting at Smith College, another Olmsted and Vaux project. She was not the landscape architect for these projects but simply implemented the planting plans prepared by the Olmsted firm. The president of the Bridgeport Park Commission thought that Elizabeth Jane Bullard would be the best person to succeed her father as superintendent. Olmsted enthusiastically supported her, praising her abilities, and stating, in addition, that she would "stimulate the Commission to higher manliness."[31] Bullard, however, withdrew from consideration, apparently because the Beardsley Park project was already controversial and she did not want to stir up more civic animosity by reason of her gender.[32]

After her father's death, Bullard needed to support herself, a situation, as we have already seen, that later spurred the careers of Farrand, Coffin, Shipman, and Dean. Her career, however, never approached theirs in scope or national reputation. After finishing her father's planting supervision work, Bullard acquired new clients among her circle of friends, but none of her projects has been identified. However, in 1899, Bullard became the first woman elected a Fellow of the American Society of Landscape Architects.[33] (Farrand was, as previously noted, a charter member and Fellow of the ASLA.) Bullard must have been proposed by Olmsted's sons and successors John Charles Olmsted and Frederick Law Olmsted Jr.[34]

As we have seen in chapter 2, Beatrix Jones Farrand never sought traditional classroom instruction, opting instead for private tutoring. While she was studying at the Arnold Arboretum, she and her mother, who was her constant companion, visited George W. Vanderbilt, whose enormous property, Biltmore, in Asheville, North Carolina, was then being developed by Olmsted. A comment made by Olmsted in a letter written at Biltmore has frequently been taken out of context and badly misinterpreted. In February 1894, at Biltmore, he met "Mrs. And Miss Jones who were at the Sargent's [sic] last week and who are supposed to be in some way inclined to dabble in Landscape Architecture"[35]

This comment is totally out of character with the other remarks by Olmsted about women quoted earlier in this chapter and in many other contexts. It is unlikely that

Olmsted talked to the women at any length, for, if he had, he would not have included Mary Jones, who could barely recognize a daisy, as an aspiring landscape architect. He would also have realized that Beatrix Jones's horticultural knowledge, even then, was far more advanced than his own.[36] Furthermore, Beatrix Jones's study year, 1893–94, was Olmsted's next to the last year as an active practitioner. His remark about her cannot be construed as an evaluation of her work, because he never knew her work.[37]

In 1900, there were 100 women architects in the United States and 10,500 male architects.[38] For the same year in landscape architecture, there were two women members in the American Society of Landscape Architects (Beatrix Jones and Elizabeth Jane Bullard), then in its second year, and at least ten men.[39] There were undoubtedly other women and many other men who were not interested in the ASLA. One was Annette McCrae, who began practicing in 1893 but who worked primarily in the southern and western parts of the country for railway companies.[40]

A brief but useful study on education and landscape architecture was published in 1924.[41] The author, Sarah Pattee, the librarian of the Landscape Gardening Library at the University of Illinois, gathered information from thirty-eight professional schools, state universities, and colleges. She broke these down into several categories. Twelve schools, all land-grant colleges, offered a full four-year course of instruction leading to a B.S. degree. Two universities, both also land-grant institutions, offered a five-year course leading to a special degree, B.L.A. in the case of Cornell and M.L.D. in the case of the University of Michigan. Only Harvard University had a program for graduate students only, leading either to an M.L.A. or an M.L.A. in City Planning. The Lowthorpe School, the Cambridge School, and the Missouri Botanical Garden all offered special courses leading to a certificate. One other school was a cooperative institution, and two trained people for special landscape positions, such as park superintendents. (All three of these were land-grant colleges.) Out of the total, several other institutions, most of them land-grant colleges, offered between one and four landscape subjects. However, Vassar College offered two courses under the botany department, and Wellesley College offered three such courses, also under botany. Wellesley's courses were all electives; one of these was a history of landscape gardening.[42]

Only Harvard was restricted to men, but five were restricted to women. The Cambridge School had an enrollment of thirty-five, a staff of eight, and nineteen graduates, 90 percent of whom were still in practice in 1924. The Lowthorpe School had an enrollment of eleven and a staff of eight, an incredibly high teacher-student ratio, but some of the faculty may have been visiting critics brought in only occasionally. Lowthorpe had eighty-three graduates of whom 75 percent were still practicing in 1924. Smith College had an enrollment of thirteen and staff of one; the other categories do not apply, since this program was within the botany department. Among graduates of all thirty-eight programs, only Cornell and Harvard had any significant number of ASLA members, most landscape architects apparently

feeling no special need of this affiliation.[43]

The Cambridge School had a remarkably informal beginning. Its history is outlined here, largely in the lively words of its founder and only director Henry Atherton Frost: "In the fall of 1915 there were two young and exceedingly unimportant instructors at Harvard, one of them, Bremer Pond, trained as a landscape architect and teaching in the Graduate School of Landscape Architecture, and the other, myself, holding a similar position in the School of Architecture."[44] James Sturgis Pray, head of the Landscape School, called Frost into his office in October and told him that a young woman who was a graduate of Radcliffe College and was to enter the Lowthorpe School the following year, wanted to study architectural drafting at Harvard. She had been told that this was impossible, but that a young instructor might able to tutor her in her home two or three afternoons a week. This was arranged, and, together, the young woman, Katherine Brooks, and Frost "attacked" the classic orders of Vignola.[45]

By December, Pray had received inquiries from three other women who wanted to study architecture or landscape architecture. In addition, two other women, who had studied at MIT, applied to Bremer Pond for help after the landscape option was discontinued:[46] "These student inquiries caused Mr. Pond and me some concern. I had already decided that tutoring the Tuscan orders on a teetering card table in a lady's parlor produced a certain sense of unreality and indifferent draughting, and I had told my student that if she wished to continue, it must be at a solid draughting table in my office where I could drop in every day, oversee her work, and perhaps accomplish something."[47]

Frost thought that these conditions might deter the young woman, but, instead, Miss Brooks

accepted with considerable alacrity, kept strict office hours from nine to five daily, and gave me no peace if I did not appear regularly at least once a day for criticism and instruction. And to my surprise I was discovering that she could draught, could discuss quite as intelligently as my students at the College, had no difficulty in understanding our architectural jargon, and showed surprising enthusiasm in her work. Teaching a woman what we had always considered strictly a man's job was not the painful ordeal it had promised to be.[48]

Frost and Pond leased an additional space adjacent to their offices in the Brattle Building in Harvard Square and accepted the five new women, assessing them a "stiff" charge of twenty-five dollars per month per student. The school as yet had no name. Students called it the Little School, and a wag referred to it as the Frost and Pond Day Nursery.[49]

Looking back from a vantage point of almost thirty years, Frost wrote, "We grew up in a period when women were more and more assuming responsibilities outside their homes. Their struggle for equal suffrage meant simply to us that they wanted to vote, and we who did not vote if to do so was inconvenient marveled at their tenacity."[50]

In Frost's opinion, women studying architecture, landscape architecture, engineering, and other "mechanical" subjects in state universities were often not successful in these subjects, because they grew up playing house rather than taking watches apart.[51] One wonders on what he based that opinion, since it appears that his students at both Harvard and the Cambridge School had all studied at liberal arts colleges, not at "state schools," as he termed them. If some of the women at state schools had trouble, it was more likely because that they had taken few mathematics and science courses in high school. Frost also felt that women in "mechanical" fields needed remedial education, and the fact that they were from six to a dozen among two or three hundred men made it difficult to do this. It is true that women entering MIT often had to take remedial math (generally much more math than landscape architects really need) before they could enter. Primarily for this reason, Frost thought that women were best taught separately from men, contradicting the positive experience that Marian Coffin had when studying at MIT.[52]

During the spring of 1916, there were many more inquiries about the "Little School," and Frost and Pond made an official announcement that the school would continue as a three-year program with new courses and a few new instructors. It was also given its first and probably its best name "The Cambridge School of Architectural and Landscape Design for Women."[53] In 1919, the official title became "The Cambridge School of Domestic Architecture and Landscape Architecture." In 1924, it was briefly "The Cambridge School, Inc." Frost regretted the official name, which implied that women could design only small houses and gardens. These were not then and never have been hard and fast specialties of architecture and landscape architecture for either men or women, although some practitioners of both genders in each profession sometimes emphasize residential over other work.[54]

The inability of the Cambridge School to grant degrees was a perennial problem, affecting architectural students in particular, since, in most states, degrees were required for registration and independent practice.[55]

In 1928, Frost and William R. Sears, a landscape architect and Cambridge School faculty member, wrote a report entitled *Women in Architecture and Landscape Architecture*. It was published by the Institute for Coordination of Women's Interests, itself funded by the Laura Spelman Rockefeller Memorial. The Institute, based at Smith College, was concerned about the numbers of women who studied for professional careers but dropped them after marriage. It tried to identify careers that could be interrupted and resumed without serious repercussions. The yardstick career, they felt, was freelance writing, which could be interrupted with a certain ease and no major problems (aside from loss of income).[56]

In assessing education in architecture and landscape architecture, Frost and Sears stressed that complete training was a necessity: first a college course, then three years of professional training, with some foreign travel, and, finally, an apprenticeship in a large office.[57] They also pointed out the difficulty of obtaining accurate statistics for the participation of women in either profession, a difficulty that persists today. In 1928, only four women were members of the American Institute of Architects, and fifteen were members of the American Society of Landscape Architects, figures that seem inordinately low. They investigated six of the many schools that then offered women instruction in these fields and found that 173 women had completed regular courses of study.[58] Sixty-seven were married and ninety-eight were single. There were thirty-eight married and seventy-eight single women still practicing. Fourteen married women and thirty-five single women ran their own offices, and eleven married women and thirty-seven single women were working in the offices of others. Thirteen married women worked "on the side," presumably part-time, and nine single women taught.[59]

Under "Requirements and Opportunities," there were cautionary but inspiring words:

> A person to whom wealth is the sole end of effort does not choose the professional life. A profession should not be attempted unless one feels that in it lies her greatest happiness. To be truly successful one must love the work she is doing . . . In such professions as architecture and landscape architecture so many types of ability are in demand that a person with a real love for the profession and with determination can usually find a nook into which she will fit.[60]

The authors resoundingly concluded: "The question of success in either architecture or landscape architecture does not necessarily involve sex."[61]

At the Cambridge School, enrollment grew during the 1920s, but so did the issue of granting degrees. Other institutions were approached as potential partners. Harvard would not even consider the possibility of this union. Radcliffe College declined because it was assumed that the partnership would have required a change in the college's charter. (This was not actually the case.) Even Columbia University, which had flirted with the idea of a school of landscape architecture, refused. A partnership with Smith College, with its long-standing interest in horticulture and landscape design, seemed far more promising and could even lead to the granting of professional degrees. In 1932, the Cambridge School became part of Smith College, but remained at the Dalby House at 53 Church Street in Cambridge. Between 1932 and 1938, all went well. A positive development was the elimination of the word "Domestic" from the title of the program.[62] In 1934, Smith awarded the degree of Master of Architecture to twenty women and the Master of Landscape Architecture to twenty-nine, including Katherine Brooks Norcross, Frost's first tutee.[63] Five other women, who had completed requirements for the Cambridge School certificate some years previously, received the M.L.A. degree in 1935. These included Helen Swift Jones and Mary Deputy Lamson.[64]

This victory was short-lived. In 1942, beset by financial difficulties resulting from the entry of the United States into World War II, Smith College decided to close the program.

At the same time, Harvard University announced that it would enroll women in its architecture and landscape architecture schools "for the duration of the War." Many women in the Cambridge School/Smith program expected that they would, as a group, be admitted into the Harvard schools, but this was not the case. About twenty-eight women in this program were eligible to apply, but only a few were admitted, despite the fact that they were receiving the same instruction from the same teachers as at Harvard. On the other hand, after the war, Harvard continued to accept women in these schools, although in rather small numbers.[65] The Lowthorpe School closed at about the same time, re-establishing itself as the Lowthorpe Department of Landscape Architecture at the Rhode Island School of Design in Providence.[66]

At the time of World War II, few private universities other than Harvard offered programs in landscape architecture. If Frost's figures were accurate, it can be safely assumed that many of the male students went to war. Their places would have been taken by women and the proportion between male and female students radically altered.

Writing in 1943, Frost recalled the intellectual excitement at the Cambridge School. The place of its students was not in the "home." Instead he maintained, "These students were of a different breed. They drove us. They, not we, proposed steps to make the training more effective, and having won their point, they were the ones who worked harder and came back with more demands for better training."[67] Frost was rewarded by overhearing a student remark, "It's not that he knows so much, because he doesn't. It's his enthusiasm that gets you."[68] Frost was at first incensed, then amused, and finally realized that this was perhaps the greatest compliment that could be given a teacher. He added, "We had no degrees to offer, and our certificates of accomplishment were signed by unknown names. We were pioneers, and probably attracted youth in whom the pioneering instinct was strong."[69]

Frost also recognized that the disciplines of architecture, landscape architecture, and even engineering, were not "three parallel grooves of learning" but were "component parts of a single problem."[70] Although now rather widely accepted, this was not at the time standard philosophy at Harvard, where the landscape and architecture schools both occupied Robinson Hall but otherwise had little to do with each other. Frost's realization led to the decision that the curriculum for the first year and the first half of the second year should be the same for all students. At the time, the Cambridge School was the only institution that offered such a collaboration between design disciplines.[71] Frost wrote of himself and Bremer Pond, "Perhaps the "little school" was our escape. Here we could rant and rave, plan and dream, try and discard, safe in the knowledge that there were no traditions to be broken, no toes to be stepped on other than our own—except our students'."[72]

Frost had great trouble placing graduates in offices, although, as he noted, landscape architects were more "cordial" to women than architects. There was widespread fear that introducing a woman into a large male drafting force would disrupt the morale of the office. The fear, as he observed, turned out to be groundless: "The women were not dangerous, nor were the men oversusceptible."[73]

The lack of "cordiality" among male practitioners forced women to accept commissions on their own before they were ready. Then, the instructors at the Cambridge School guided the new architects and landscape architects in a kind of informal postgraduate tutorial.[74]

Although membership in the American Society of Landscape Architects was not sought by all landscape architects, whether male or female, the membership lists, which were published in the early 1930s, offer some measure of involvement in the profession. In 1934, out of almost three hundred members in all membership categories, there were four female corresponding members (people in related professions, such as writers and librarians in landscape architecture programs). The corresponding members included Farrand's aunt, Edith Wharton, who was then living in France. Among the numerous Fellows, there were only Marian Coffin and Beatrix Farrand, Elizabeth Jane Bullard having died in 1916. Among the even more numerous regular members, there were twenty-five women, including Marjorie Sewell Cautley, Annette Hoyt Flanders, Martha Brookes Hutcheson, Helen Swift Jones, Louise Payson, Isabella Pendleton, and Eleanor Roche. Several distinguished women landscape architects were members of the ASLA but did not work on Long Island, including Rose Greely, whose sphere of operation was mostly in the Washington, D.C., area. The junior associates included four women, none well-known names. Women were poorly represented on both the standing committees and special committees.[75] After two and a half decades of progress by women landscape architects, the ASLA still had the face of an exclusive men's club.

The uncertain progress seen in the organization of the ASLA was also characteristic of the political environment in twentieth-century America. In 1920, after twenty-five years of effort and amendments to several state constitutions, the Nineteenth Amendment to the United States Constitution was passed. It was greeted with jubilation, although the immediate effects were rather anticlimactic.[76] There is no evidence that any of the eighteen women landscape architects discussed here was particularly interested in the right to vote, although, when granted it, they may have done so. Even apolitical women gained from the passage of the Amendment, at least indirectly. When women were given the right to vote, it opened up the possibility that they might deserve rights in other areas formerly assumed to be the exclusive prerogatives of men.[77] The gains of the 1920s and 1930s were eroded during the postwar period, an era of conservative backlash and reversal of many of the societal advances made in earlier years. Again, the women who were already practicing landscape architecture were not deterred by the change in climate, although it is impossible to know how many women were deterred by a repressive social culture.[78]

The climate shifted again in the next several years. In 1964, the Civil Rights Act made it illegal to discriminate against women in hiring, pay, or promotions. Although the Equal Rights Amendment, fifty years in the making, was passed by Congress in 1972, it fizzled out in 1977 after being ratified by thirty-five of the thirty-eight states needed to make it law.[79]

None of these gains happened automatically or even easily. The faculties of graduate and professional schools in the late 1960s and early 1970s—those who controlled the admissions process—consisted almost exclusively of men of an older generation, who often found it hard, or refused to try, to adjust their thinking to the changing times. Women applicants were met with quizzical looks and not-so-subtle queries about their marital and reproductive plans. Once admitted, a woman's commitment to the profession was repeatedly questioned and was always assumed to be less than a man's. To some extent, this sort of reaction was understandable. Graduate and professional schools invest a great deal in their students, whom they hope will be the future of their professions. They want some assurance that students will stay the course. Ironically, the Vietnam War may have provided some assurance that women would persevere. Sometimes, men dropped out of graduate and professional schools at the age of 26 when they were no longer subject to the draft, while the women doggedly hung on.

Within the architecture and landscape architecture professions, three organizations emerged in 1973 with the goal of supporting women: Women Architects, Landscape Architects, and Planners (WALAP) in Boston; Alliance of Women in Architecture (AWA) in New York; and the Organization of Women Architects (OWA) in San Francisco. While significant efforts were made by these groups, bureaucratic roadblocks were thrown up, and there was little in the way of concrete progress.[80]

In 1973, a key article on the status of women in the profession of landscape architecture was published in the *ASLA Bulletin*.[81] At this time, while there were a number of women studying landscape architecture, they were still not very visible in the ranks of the profession and certainly not in the ASLA. By 1981, the ASLA had formed a Committee on Women in Landscape Architecture, which published a compendium of thirty-seven tables of statistics, focusing on things such as demographics, income, practice settings, and benefits.[82]

In 1983, Darwina L. Neal, the author of the 1973 article and a landscape architect with the National Park Service, became the first woman president of the ASLA. In the same year, a full report was published on a national survey of career patterns among women landscape architects.[83] In 1972, only 5 percent of ASLA full and associate members were women. By contrast, in 1982, women were 7.7 percent of full members, 23.3 percent of associate members, and 6 percent of prospective members (it is unclear how these last were defined). Surprisingly, in 1982, there were only 6,647 male and female landscape architects on the ASLA mailing list, which probably also included the names of the prospective members. The ASLA has always had a fairly expensive dues structure. When prospective members were asked why they did not join, most cited cost.

About two-thirds of the women landscape architects were under thirty-five; many were married but not parents. Strangely, both female students and women practitioners reported that they knew little about the profession before starting to study it.[84]

Of the women surveyed, most of the practitioners and students felt satisfied with the core curriculum subjects they had studied in school (i.e., drafting, graphics, design, and plant materials), although the current students wanted more instruction in plant materials, writing, business management, public speaking, and computer technology. (The last, of course, was still a new area for most landscape architects.) Nearly all of the full-time practitioners had experienced discrimination from employers or professional colleagues and especially from contractors and nonprofessional workers who refused to follow their directions.[85]

Up to this point, we have discussed landscape architecture exclusively, but there is a closely related and more recently defined profession called landscape design. Landscape designers generally study in landscape design programs of which there are several throughout the country associated with various colleges and universities, which may or may not also offer landscape architecture programs. Most often, the designers receive certificates rather than degrees. Unless, they work in a landscape architect's office for a number of years (ten in Massachusetts), holders of these certificates cannot sit for the registration, or licensure, examinations held by forty-six of the states. They can't call themselves landscape architects, which most do not see as a problem, and they can't put an official registration stamp on their drawings.[86]

How important is it to be a registered landscape architect? It depends on the state. The state (any state) can regulate only matters that affect public health, safety, and welfare. The state has no jurisdiction whatsoever over aesthetics. Registration means just that the landscape architect has a certain minimal competence in the technical aspects of the profession. In most states, the registration of landscape architects is a relatively recent phenomenon, Ohio, for example, initiating it in 1965. Today, only New Hampshire, Vermont, North Dakota, and Colorado do not regulate the profession. In some states, including California, landscape designers are restricted to preparing planting plans and must avoid anything having to do with hardscape.[87] In Massachusetts, within the restrictions of building codes and zoning laws, there is very little they cannot do.

Since the 1983 survey of career patterns in the profession, the fortunes of women landscape architects have improved dramatically, although statistics are generally not sorted by gender. There are, for example, no longer any men-only or women-only offices. Some states have designated women-*owned* businesses, which can be an advantage in securing government contracts. A look around most landscape architecture offices, however, reveals a rather even distribution of male and female faces. In many classrooms, including Harvard's Department of Landscape Architecture, women predominate.[88] Discrimination by employers, colleagues, and employees appears to be non-existent, although women who supervise construction crews are sometimes still patronized.[89] A glance at the profession overall, as it stands in the first decade of the twenty-first century, is revealing. The United States Department of Labor Statistics indicates that there are 17,130 landscape architects in the country, a figure that must have been derived from the 2000 federal census.[90] (There is no separate statistic for landscape designers.) One hundred and five years after its founding, the total membership of the ASLA stands at about 14,000, of whom 2,000 are student and 100 corporate members. There are 502 Fellows, 9,312 full members, and 1,216 associate members. In addition, there are 550 affiliate members, many of whom may be landscape designers. (Landscape designers, even more than landscape architects, tend to feel that ASLA membership is not critical to their careers.) It is estimated that there are at least as many landscape architects practicing who do not belong to the ASLA as members, bringing the total to about between 24,000 to 28,000.[91]

By most standards, the profession appears to be flourishing. Beatrix Farrand, Martha Brookes Hutcheson, Marian Coffin and their successors would be astonished by the American Society of Landscape Architecture meetings of today, crowded with both men and women. They would marvel at the many landscape architecture and landscape design programs open to both genders, where women frequently outnumber men. Theirs were the first steps that made possible the advantages now enjoyed by all women in the profession. As Hutcheson put it, the eighteen women in this book "held high the torch" for later generations.

APPENDIX

PROJECTS ON LONG ISLAND
BY WOMEN LANDSCAPE ARCHITECTS

* Projects discussed and/or illustrated in this book.

Note: All of the projects listed in this Appendix were not necessarily carried out or, if carried out, may not still be extant. If the current (2008) status of a project or site is known, that information is given here.

If an archive of drawings or other materials exists for a landscape architect, it is indicated below her name. Even if there is no repository specific to a landscape architect, projects by many of the women are represented in the photograph collections of the Long Island Studies Institute and the Garden Club of America glass slide collection at the Smithsonian Institution, Washington, D.C. In addition, many of the Long Island projects listed here were published in such periodicals as *Landscape Architecture*, *Country Life in America*, *House and Garden*, and *House Beautiful*, as well as the American Society of Landscape Architects, New York Chapter, *Work of Members*, for the years when it was published, 1931–34, and *American Landscape Architect*, 1929–1932.

Beatrix Jones Farrand
1872–1959

Repository: College of Environmental Design Documents Collection, University of California, Berkeley.
* Percy Chubb Residence, Rattling Spring, Dosoris. 1900. No longer extant.
* Mrs. Roswell Eldridge Residence, Great Neck. 1903–30. A small park is on the site.
* Edward F. Whitney Residence, Oyster Bay. 1906–14. No longer extant.
  Mrs. A. T. Mahan Residence, Quogue. 1908.
  William Bayard Cutting Residence, Westbrook, Oakdale. 1910. The general layout of this property was done by Frederick Law Olmsted Sr. and survives as a state park.

Beatrix Jones's walled flower garden was probably never carried out.
Mrs. Philip W. Livermore Residence, Jericho. 1911. There are only two drawings for this project, which may not have been carried out.
Sherman Flint Residence, Islip. 1912. There is only one drawing for this project—a topo by a civil engineer. It is likely that nothing came of this commission.
* C. Oliver Iselin Residence, Wolver Hollow, Brookville. 1913–14. Farrand designed a rose garden and other gardens for this property. Several other landscape architects worked here, including Olmsted Brothers (1925–46). The house is extant. It is not clear whether Farrand's work was carried out.
* Mrs. George D. Pratt Residence, Killenworth, Glen Cove. 1913–14. Farrand prepared plans for a garden. James Greenleaf and Olmsted Brothers also worked here. The house is no longer extant.
* Straight Improvement Company (Willard D. and Dorothy Whitney Straight, later Mr. and Mrs. Leonard Elmhirst—the former Mrs. Straight), Old Westbury. 1914–32. The property was originally called Elmhurst, then renamed Apple Green. The house is no longer extant, but the foundations of the Chinese garden are said to remain.
  Thomas Hastings Residence, Bagatelle, Old Westbury. Ca. 1915. Built for a partner in the architectural firm of Carrère & Hastings. The house is extant.
* S. Vernon Mann Residence, Grove Point, 19 Harbor Road, Great Neck. 1918–30. The house is said to be extant, but Farrand's landscaping apparently no longer is.
* Theodore and Edith Roosevelt Headstone, Young's Cemetery, Oyster Bay. Ca. 1919. Extant.
* Otto Kahn Residence, Oheka, Cold Spring Harbor. 1919–28. Delano and Aldrich's house and their water garden layout, done in association with Olmsted Brothers, survive. The gardens by Farrand are no longer extant.

William Adams Delano Residence, Muttontown Corners, Syosset. 1921. Delano designed the plot plan for his property himself; Farrand annotated a blueprint of it and made planting plans for a flower border. It seems unlikely that her ideas for this project were carried out or even fully developed. The house is extant.

Mrs. Richard Derby, The Old Adam House, Lexington Avenue, Oyster Bay. 1921. The 1878 house by Potter and Robertson is extant. Farrand did only one drawing, a preliminary sketch for the grounds, and nothing may have been carried out.

* Edward S. Harkness Residence, Weekend, Manhasset. Ca. 1921.

* Great Neck Green, Great Neck. 1922–32. Executed. Little remains of Farrand's design.

* Great Neck Green Public Library, Great Neck. Ca. 1925. Not executed.

D. H. Morris Residence, Glen Head. 1925.

* Percy Pyne Residence, Rivington House, Roslyn. 1925–29. Farrand's plans were carried out. The house is extant, but the present status of the landscaping is unknown.

* Harrison Williams Residence, Oak Point, Bayville. 1928–29. This property, including the two gardens designed by Farrand from initial sketches by Delano and Aldrich, no longer survives.

* S. Vernon Mann, Jr. Residence, King's Point, Nassau County. 1920. Not extant.

Dr. J. C. Ayer Residence, Glen Cove. Undated. The property is no longer extant.

Mrs. Douglas W. Paige Residence, Bellport. Undated.

Projects by Farrand Outside Long Island for Long Island Clients:

Headstone for Quentin Roosevelt and Hamilton Coolidge, France (exact location unknown). Ca. 1918.

* Dartington Hall, Ltd., Totnes, South Devon, England. 1933. The property is extant. Some of Farrand's work is said to remain.

Churston Development Co., Dartington Hall, Totnes, South Devon, England. 1934.

Michael Straight Residence, Alexandria, Virginia. 1942. This was apparently carried out. Mr. Straight is deceased, and it is not clear if anything remains of the Farrand landscaping.

Martha Brookes Brown Hutcheson
1871–1959

Repository: Morris County Park Commission, Morristown, New Jersey. (Contains no plans for any of Hutcheson's Long Island commissions.)

* Mrs. Robert Bacon Residence, Oldfields, sometimes called Old Acres, Westbury. 1904–10; 1913; 1920; 1926. Hutcheson designed a large garden and a smaller garden for Mrs. Bacon, as well as paths connecting her house with those of other members of her family. Shipman also worked on this property, but the extent of her involvement is unknown. The Bacon property is no longer extant.

Julien T. Davies Residence, Great River. 1907.

* Mrs. Payne Whitney Residence, Manhasset. 1907. This seems to have been a minor project.

* Frederic B. Pratt Residence, Poplar Hill, Glen Cove. 1910–11. The house is extant.

* Harold I. Pratt Residence, Welwyn, Glen Cove. 1911; 1913. Hutcheson designed the west garden at Welwyn. Other work was done by Olmsted Brothers, James L. Greenleaf, and the Pratts themselves. The house is extant as a holocaust museum. The property as a whole survives as Welwyn Preserve. The outlines of Hutcheson's west garden—but not her planting—remain.

Mrs. Charles R. Tiffany Residence, Oyster Bay. 1911–12.

* Mrs. Daniel Lord Residence, Sosiego, Lawrence. By 1923. The Lord house was extant in 1981, but the surroundings had been subdivided.

Hobart Porter Residence, Lawrence. Undated.

David Bows Residence, Brookville. Undated.

Marian Cruger Coffin
1876–1957

Repository: Henry Francis du Pont Library, Henry Francis du Pont Winterthur Museum, Winterthur, Delaware. This is a very complete collection of photographs of Coffin's work, but contains plans for only one of her Long Island projects.

* Edward E. Sprague Residence, Flushing. 1906. Status unknown.

* William Woodin Residence, East Hampton. 1916. The house is extant. The status of landscaping is unknown.

* Charles H. Sabin Residence, Bayberryland, Shinnecock Hills, Southampton. 1919. The house and some landscaping were extant in 2002. Both were demolished in 2005 for an organic golf course, not built as of April 2008.

Henry Benkard Residence, Oyster Bay. Ca. 1919.

* J. Harry Alexandre Residence, Glenhead. Ca. 1920. Status unknown.

* Winter Cottage at the Marshall Field III Residence, Caumsett, Lloyd Neck. The Winter Cottage is extant but Coffin's plantings are not.

* Edward F. Hutton and Marjorie Merriweather (Post) Residence, Hillwood, Wheatley Hills. 1921–22. The house and most of the major garden spaces remain, although the plant materials have changed. It is part of the C. W. Post campus of Long Island University. Rehabilitation of the house was currently in progress (2006), with landscape restoration to start when the architectural work is complete.

* Albert B. Boardman Residence, Wind Swept, Southampton. 1923. No longer extant.

* Henry Francis du Pont Residence, Chesterton House, Southampton. 1924–28. House is extant.

* Childs Frick Residence, Clayton, Roslyn. 1925. Formal (Colonial) garden, spring garden, azalea garden, and zodiac garden. The house is extant as a museum. The formal garden was partially restored 2001–3.

* W. W. Benjamin Residence, Crossways, East Hampton. Ca. 1928.

* Irving Brokaw Residence, Mill Neck (Oyster Bay). Ca. 1930. The house is extant. It is unclear how much of this property Coffin laid out and also whether anything remains.

Agnes F. Keyes Residence, Greencote, Southampton. 1942–49.

* James Blackstone Taylor Residence, Oyster Bay. Undated.

Henry W. Bull Residence, Smithtown. Undated.

* Eric MacDonald Residence, Penrhyn, Southampton. Undated.

* W. Allston Flagg Residence, Westbury. Undated.

Ellen Biddle Shipman
1869–1950

Repository: Ellen Shipman Collection, Rare and Manuscript Collections, Carl A. Kroch Library, Cornell University, Ithaca, New York. The library contains plans and photographs but no correspondence. The undated projects are generally not documented by plans but, instead, were taken from a list of projects prepared by Shipman's assistant.

* William P. T. Preston Residence, Longfields, Jericho. 1913.

* Herbert L. Pratt Residence, The Braes, Glen Cove. Ca. 1913–14. Shipman's work consisted only of a construction drawing for a drying yard. The house is no longer extant.
* Miss Julia Fish Residence, Greenport. 1916.
* Mrs. Meredith Hare Residence, Pidgeon Hill, Huntington. 1916. Charles A. Platt. The house is no longer extant.
* Lewis Cass Ledyard, Jr. Residence, Syosset. 1917. House, 1914, by Charles A. Platt. The house is extant.
* C. Oliver Iselin Residence, Wolver Hollow, Brookville. 1917. The house is extant.
  A. M. Hegeman Residence, Southampton. Ca. 1917.
* Mary and Neltje Pruyn Residence, Jones Road, East Hampton. 1919. The house is extant, and some outlines of the landscape design may be seen, but none of Shipman's plantings.
* A. Ludlow Kramer Residence, Picket Farm, Westbury. 1920. The house was demolished.
  Maidstone Club, East Hampton. 1922.
* Mrs. Robert L. Bacon Residence, Old Acres, Westbury. 1920s. Earlier gardens by Hutcheson. The property is no longer extant.
  Julian Peabody Residence, Westbury. 1924.
* Philip Gossler Residence, Topsfield, Wheatley Hills. 1925. J. Randolph Robinson was the previous owner; the subsequent owner was Edward F. Hutton. The house is now part of the C. W. Post College campus. Shipman's terraces survive, and the university plans to restore the plantings from her plans at Cornell.
* Lansing F. Reed Residence, Windy Hill, Lloyd Harbor. 1925. House, 1924, by Charles A. Platt. The house is extant.
  Carl J. Schmidlapp Residence, Mill Neck. Mid-1920s.
* Sir Samuel Agar Salvage Residence, Rynwood, Glen Head. 1926. The house is extant, and is now called Villa Banfi. There was later landscape work on the site by Innocenti and Webel. The house, teahouse, dovecote, and Shipman's garden spaces remain, but not her plants.
* Ellery S. James Residence, Southampton, 1926. (Attribution.) The house is extant.
  J. Averell Clarke Residence, Westbury. 1927.
  Richard S. Emmet Residence, High Elms, Glen Cove. Ca. 1929.
* Franklin B. Lord Residence, Cottsleigh, Syosset. Ca. 1929. The house is extant.
* George DeForest Lord Residence, Overfields, Syosset. Ca. 1930. The house is extant.
  Mrs. Walter E. Maynard Residence, Jericho. Ca. 1930. Shipman's plans for this site were probably not carried out, although the house is extant.
  Mrs. E. J. Plumb, Dering Harbor, Shelter Island. 1937.
  Mrs. Willis Delano Wood Residence, Fort Hill House, Lloyds Neck. Ca. 1928. (Also worked on by Olmsted Brothers.)
  W. H. Jackson Residence, West Hills. 1941.
  Edward F. Hutton Residence, Brookville, 1942.
  Mrs. Edwin Gould Residence, Oyster Bay. 1945.
  Julian Peabody Residence, Huntington. 1945.
  August Belmont Residence, Syosset. Undated.
  Anson Burchard Residence, Locust Valley. Undated.
  Leslie Bushnell Residence, Oyster Bay. Undated.
  Paul Cushman Residence, Syosset. Undated.
  Arthur Davis Residence, Mill Neck. Undated.
  John W. Davis Residence, Locust Valley. Undated.
  George R. Dyer Residence, Roslyn. House, 1909 by Charles A. Platt. The landscape is undated.
  Frederick E. Guest Residence, Roslyn. Undated.
  Parker Handy Residence, Glen Cove. Undated.
  Henry Harriman Residence, Jericho. Undated.
  F. T. Hepburn Residence, Locust Valley. Undated.
  B. B. Jennings Residence, Glen Head. Undated.
  John P. Kane Residence, Matinecock. House by Beers & Farley. Louise Payson also worked on this. Undated.

William C. Langley Residence, Westbury. Undated.
John B. Morris Residence, Roslyn. Undated.
Hugh A. Murray Residence, Wheatley Hills. Undated.
* Herbert L. Pratt Residence, The Braes, Glen Cove. Laid out by James Greenleaf, 1912. Shipman's work is undated. The house is no longer extant.
L. M. Richmond Residence, Sunninghill, Glen Head. Undated.
Kermit Roosevelt Residence, Oyster Bay. Undated.
R. Penn Smith Residence, East Williston. Undated.
F. S. Smithers Residence, Glen Cove. Undated.
Glenn Stewart Residence, Locust Valley. Undated.
Mrs. Eugene Taliaferro, Oyster Bay. Undated.
A. M. White Residence, Oyster Bay. Undated.
William Zinsser Residence, Great Neck. Undated.
William J. Matheson Residence, Lloyds Neck. Undated.
Henry T. Peters Residence, Islip. Undated.
Charles Lane Poor Residence, Dering Harbor, Shelter Island. Undated.
Philip Ruxton Residence, East Hampton. Undated.
* Eleanor Swayne Residence, Red House, Shinnecock Hills. Undated. The house is by Grosvenor Atterbury.
Florence M. Towle Residence, Dering Harbor, Shelter Island. Undated.
Francis M. Weld Residence, Lloyd Harbor. Undated. House, 1911, by Charles A. Platt.

Ruth Bramley Dean
1889–1932

Repository: None.
* Miss Fannie Mulford Residence, Hempstead. By 1917. The status is unknown.
* Arthur G. Schieren Residence, Beachleigh, Great Neck. 1917, 1921. House by Aymar Embury II. The house is extant.
* Mrs. George Gales Residence, Great Neck. 1922. Aymar Embury II, architect. The status is unknown.
* Mrs. Monroe Douglas Robinson Residence, Syosset. 1924–25. Status unknown.
* Harbor Acres, Hempstead, for Vincent Astor, 1926. With Aymar Embury II. This was a subdivision plan for a complete community. The roads appear to have been laid out, but most houses on the site are much later. Because of the Depression, only four houses were built.
* Henry Hall Residence, Smithtown. 1928.
* George Roberts Residence, Furtherfield, East Hampton. 1930. (Finished by Lamson.) The house and some of the grounds are said to remain.
* Aymar Embury II and Ruth Dean Embury Residence, East Hampton. 1930. House remodeling by Aymar Embury II. The house is extant, and general outlines of the garden remain but none of Dean's plantings.
* The Guild Hall, East Hampton. 1930. The building, designed by Aymar Embury II, is extant, as is the Ruth Dean Sculpture Garden.
* Ellis L. Phillips Residence, Lauriemore, Plandome. 1932. Flower garden, 1933. The house and pieces of a wall are extant. Nothing remains of Dean's garden.
  Free Library, East Hampton. nd. Aymar Embury II, architect, 1910–11. (Attribution.) The building is extant.

Annette Hoyt Flanders
1887–1946

Repositories: Sophia Smith Collection, Smith College, Northampton, Massachusetts, holds copy slides of Flanders's slide collection, mostly of her own work. The originals are in a private collection in Wisconsin. The Collection also holds photographs, photographs of plans, and one original drawing from another source. Wisconsin Architectural Archives, Milwaukee, Wisconsin, holds drawings for two projects in Wisconsin. The University of Illinois at Circle Campus, Chicago, Special Collections holds some of her 1934 correspondence relating to the Century of Progress Exhibition in Chicago.

* Myron C. Taylor Residence, Underhill Farm, Locust Valley. This was done in association with Vitale, Brinckerhof, and Geiffert. 1921–22. The house is extant and serves as headquarters for the Episcopal Diocese of Long Island. The status of the landscape is unknown.
* Mrs. Benson Flagg Residence, Apple House, Brookville. Early 1920s. The status is unknown.
* E. Mortimer Barnes Residence, Manana, Glen Head. 1924. Garden, house terrace, pergola, dovecote. The house is extant. The status of the landscaping is unknown.
* F. C. Demarest Residence, Rockville Center. Ca. 1925. The status is unknown.
* Vincent Astor Residence, Cloverley Manor, Port Washington. Ca. 1925. The house is extant with extensive acreage. The status of Flanders's garden is unknown.
* Mr. and Mrs. Charles E. F. McCann Residence, Sunken Orchard, Oyster Bay. 1927–32. House, Ca. 1914, by George B. de Gersdorff. Playhouse by James W. O'Connor. The French gardens and several other gardens were designed by Flanders. The house, playhouse, and portions of the grounds are in two separate ownerships. Part of Flanders's landscaping around the house remains. Only truncated remains of part of the French Gardens are visible.
* Mr. and Mrs. Thompson Ross Residence, Great Neck. 1929. Rock garden. The status is unknown.
* William R. Simonds (formerly Russell) Residence, Southampton. 1929–30. The status is unknown.
* Mr. and Mrs. Charles E. Van Vleck, Jr. Residence, Ballyshear, Southampton. By 1929. Blue Garden, East Lawn, Rose Garden, Perennial Walk, Magnolia Terrace. (Two gardens designed about 1915 by Rose Standish Nichols were partially retained by Flanders.) The house, as well as some of Flanders's and some of Nichols's work, is said to survive.
* Mr. and Mrs. John W. Kiser Residence, Southampton. 1929–30. Sunken garden. The house remains. Some of the landscaping survives, but there have been alterations by later owners.
* Mr. and Mrs. Lewis Cass Ledyard, Jr. Residence, Syosset. By 1931. Terrace garden, woodland garden, cutting garden and pool. Flanders made changes to a garden originally designed by Charles Platt with planting design by Ellen Shipman. The house is extant. The status of the landscaping is unknown.
* Mrs. Patrick Valentine Residence, Southampton. By 1932. Rose and Heliotrope Garden. The status is unknown.
* Mr. and Mrs. Warren S. Crane Residence, East View, Cedarhurst. By 1932. The house is extant.
* Mr. and Mrs. DeLancey Kountze Residence, Roslyn. By 1932.
* Mr. and Mrs. George S. Olds Residence, Great Neck. By 1932.
* Dr. and Mrs. T. Lawrence Saunders Residence, Westbury. By 1932.
* Mrs. Arthur Peck Residence, Cedarhurst. By 1934. House by Bradley Delehanty.
* Garden for a Schoolteacher, Forest Hills Gardens, Queens. By 1934. The client has not been identified.
* A "Jardin Potager in the Period Manner," for Mr. Henry Leuthardt. 1938. This was prepared for Leuthardt's exhibition in the 1939 World's Fair, Flushing. It is no longer extant.
* Sketch Plan for a "House of Jewels." (Project.) ca. 1938. This was also intended for the 1939 World's Fair, Flushing.
* Mr. and Mrs. Montague Flagg Residence, Upper Brookville. nd. The house is extant.

Mary Rutherfurd Jay
1872–1953

Repository: College of Environmental Design Documents Collection, University of California, Berkeley.

* Howard C. Sherwood Residence, Setauket. 1909. The house remains as a SPLIA property. Jay's landscaping is not extant and may never have been carried out.
* George S. Wickersham Residence, Cedarhurst. 1914. The status is unknown.
  H. W. Cannon Residence, Huntington. 1915.
  Mrs. John T. Livington Residence, Woodmere. 1915–16.
  Mrs. H. T. S. Green Residence, Hewlett. 1920–21.
  The C. Oliver Iselin Residence, Wolver Hollow, Mill Neck. Before 1931. Jay installed a garden that had been designed by Mrs. Iselin. The house is extant.

Rose Standish Nichols
1872–1960

Repository: Papers of the Nichols-Shurtleff Family, 1780–1953, Schlesinger Library, Radcliffe Institute for Advanced Study, Harvard University, Cambridge, Massachusetts; Archives, Boston State House; Rose Standish Nichols House. (None of these collections contains Standish's office archives, although there are some financial records that may be relevant.)

* Charles B. MacDonald Residence, Ballyshear, Southampton. By 1915. F. Burrall Hofmann Jr., architect. The grounds were later worked on by Flanders. The house and some landscaping are said to be extant.

Louise Payson
1894–1977

Repository: University of Maine, Orono.

Edward Streeter Residence, Great Neck. 1923. House by Almus Pratt Evan.
* Mr. and Mrs. Charles S. Payson Residence, Manhasset. 1927. House by Delano and Aldrich. The house is extant in religious use. The status of the plantings unknown.
Kenneth Phillips Residence, Woodmere. 1927.
W. Scott Blanchard Residence, Hewlett Bay Park. 1928.
* Mr. and Mrs. John P. Kane Residence, Matinecock. 1929. House by Beers and Farley. Ellen Shipman also worked on this. The house is extant.
Mrs. Charles H. Russell Residence, Northport. 1929.
Mr. and Mrs. C. Perry Beadleston Residence, Hewlett. 1930.
Mrs. William Averall Harriman Residence, Sands Point, Port Washington. 1930. James W. O'Connor, architect.
Mrs. Albert Franke Residence, Lawrence. 1931.
Mr. and Mrs. Alexander M. White, Jr., Laurelton, Oyster Bay. 1936. House by Kimball and Heusted.
Gerald Warburg, Jericho. 1937.
Phillip Gossler Residence, Westbury. Undated.
Whitman Residence, Cedarhurst. Undated.
Mr. and Mrs. Lewis Weeks, Cedarhurst. Undated.

Marjorie Sewell Cautley
1891–1954

Repository: Marjorie Sewell Cautley Papers, Rare and Manuscript Collections, Carl A. Kroch Library, Cornell University; Avery Architectural Library, Columbia University, New York City; Phipps Garden Apartment Archives, New York City. (Avery has drawings for phase 1 of Phipps Garden Apartments, Sunnyside, New York, and Radburn, Fair-

lawn, New Jersey; The Phipps Archives have blueprints and some other materials for phase 2 of Phipps Garden Apartments.)
* Sunnyside Gardens, Queens, New York City. 1924–28. With Clarence Stein and Henry Wright. The buildings are extant. Unclear if anything remains of Cautley's landscaping.
* Phipps Garden Apartments, Queens, New York City. 1931 and later. With Clarence Stein and Henry Wright. The buildings are extant. The grounds were restored beginning in 1995 by R. Terry Schnadelbach of Gainesville, Florida.

Isabella Pendleton
1891–1965

Repository: None known.
* Garden for Pendleton's uncle in Nassau County. Ca. 1923. The uncle and the property have not been identified.
* Mrs. Percy Chubb Residence, Glen Cove. By 1924. Spring Garden. (1900 terraced garden by Farrand.) The property is no longer extant.
* Mrs. Howard Whitney Residence, Glen Cove. By 1925. Formal garden. This is no longer extant.
* Henry Balthusan Residence, Mill Neck. By 1927. Formal garden. The status is unknown.
* Paul D. Cravath Residence, Locust Valley. By 1931. House by Bradley Delehanty. The house is extant. The status of the grounds is not known.
* Herbert L. Pratt Residence, The Braes, Glen Cove. By 1931. Iris garden, no longer extant.
Mr. and Mrs. C. Oliver Iselin Residence, Wolver Hollow, Mill Neck. By 1931. Garden. The house is extant.
Mrs. Walter James Residence, Eagles Beak, Cold Spring Harbor. By 1931. Terraced hillside and pool. This is not extant.
Roadside Planting on Long Island. nd. Probably no longer extant.

Eleanor Roche
1892–1975

Repository: No design archive has been located, but the Roche-Leake family has family papers and other documents.
* Jackson A. Dykman Residence, Glen Cove. By 1930. Roche transformed a vegetable garden into a flower garden. The status is unknown.

Mary Deputy Lamson
1897–1969

Repository: Some of Lamson's correspondence about the Cambridge School is in the Cambridge School Archives, Sophia Smith Collection, Smith College. This contains no Lamson office archives.
* George Roberts Residence, East Hampton. Begun by Ruth Dean in 1930. Work on the residence continued until about 1941. The house is extant, and the grounds are said to be partially extant.
* Van S. Merle-Smith Residence, Oyster Bay. 1936.
Joseph Ramée Residence, East Hampton. By 1941.

Nellie Beatrice Allen
CA. 1874–1961

Repository: A limited number of plans are in the Rare and Manuscript Collection, Carl A. Kroch Library, Cornell University. There are none relating to Long Island.

* Clifford H. McCall Residence, Apaquoque Road, East Hampton. Ca. 1927.
* Mrs. Isabel Dodge Sloane Residence, Brookmeade, Locust Valley (Lattingtown). By 1936. Vitale and Geiffert laid out the original garden. Allen designed herbaceous borders for the property.
* Parterre Garden in Honor of Lowthorpe School, 1939 World's Fair, Queens, New York City. Allen worked on this with Constance Boardman. It is no longer extant.

Helen Elise Bullard
1896–1987

Repository: Limited archives at the Rare and Manuscript Collection, Carl A. Kroch Library, Cornell University. The archives include specifications for some Long Island properties, but no plans or photographs.
* Brooklyn State Hospital, Creedmoor Division, Queens. 1930. Specifications. The building is extant; the status of Bullard's tree and shrub planting is unknown.
* Central Islip State Hospital, Islip, 1930s. Specification for Infirmary Building. This facility closed in 1996, although some buildings remain, in poor condition.
Bullard worked for the Long Island State Park Commission, beginning 1933: Projects included:
* Scented plantings at the Bath Houses, Jones Beach and shrubbery along sections of the Southern State and Grand Central Parkways, both discussed in this book and unlikely to have survived and landscaping of the Montauk Parkway, also unlikely to have survived. After 1938, Bullard worked for New York City Park Department in charge of all plantings at the 1939 World's Fair, Flushing, Queens, discussed in this book. Some of the trees planted under her direction may survive as part of Flushing Meadows Park.

Helen Swift Jones
1890–1982

Repositories: Smith College Archives; Cambridge School Archives, Sophia Smith Collection, Smith College; Fairfield Historical Society, Fairfield, Connecticut; Adelphi University Archives. None of these contains her office archives.
* The Levermore Elms and Garden, Adelphi College (now University). 1930. The elms have either been removed to make space for later buildings or have died.

Janet Darling Webel
1913–1966

Repositories: Some information in the Smith College Archives and the Cambridge School Archives, Sophia Smith Collection, Smith College.
* Jennings Residence, location unknown, but possibly in Long Island. 1956.
* Pool, Richard F. Coons Residence, Oyster Bay. 1960–63. Status unknown.

Alice Recknagel Ireys
1911–2000

Repository: Cambridge School Archives and Alice Ireys Collection, Sophia Smith Collection, Smith College, Northampton, Massachusetts.
* Lakeside Plantings at the 1939 World's Fair, Queens, New

York City. While employed by Charles N. Lowrie. The lake survives. The plantings probably have not.

* Kate and Henry Sturgis Residence, Cedarhurst. 1945–57.

* Robert and Ethel Blum Residence, Winter Harbor, New Hyde Park. 1951–63.

* Garden of Fragrance for the Blind, Brooklyn Botanical Garden. 1952–55. Extant. Ireys also did other work for the Brooklyn Botanical Garden.

* William S. and Barbara Paley Residence, Kiluna Farm, Manhasset. 1962–72. Subdivided. Ireys's pool is extant with some modifications but is not accessible, since it is now in a gated community.

* Mr. and Mrs. Howard Phipps, Old Westbury. 1971–81, 1992–97. Ireys created a Japanese garden and new entrance. The property is extant.

Planting Plan for Edward Fuller Wing, Long Island College Hospital, Brooklyn. 1965–75.

New Drive and Entrance, Polytechnic Preparatory Country Day School, Brooklyn. 1965–75.

Planting Plan, Shelter Island Library, Shelter Island. 1965–75.

Planting Plan, Flatbush Congregational Church, Brooklyn. 1975–85.

Planting Plan, Garden City School, Garden City. 1975–85.

Planting Plan, Garden City Historical Society, Garden City. 1975–85.

Design, Construction and Planting for Japanese Demonstration Garden, Old Westbury Gardens, Old Westbury. 1975–85. This probably does not survive.

Planting Plan for Perennial Garden, Planting Fields Arboretum, Oyster Bay. 1975–85. This probably was not executed.

Planting Plan for Garden, Plymouth Church of the Pilgrims, Brooklyn. 1975–85.

Planting Plan for Library Garden and Terrace, Poly Prep Country Day School. Brooklyn. 1975–85.

Mae L. Wien Cutting Garden, Brooklyn Botanical Garden. 1988.

Ireys designed many other private projects on Long Island, mostly 1950s–80s. Plans for many of these exist at Smith.

NOTES

PREFACE AND ACKNOWLEDGMENTS

1. Laura Wood Roper, *FLO: A Biography of Frederick Law Olmsted* (Baltimore and London: The Johns Hopkins University Press, 1973) and Charles E. Beveridge and David Schuyler, eds., *The Papers of Frederick Law Olmsted, Volume 3: Creating Central Park 1857–1861* (Baltimore and London: The Johns Hopkins University Press, 1983) are the two key sources.

2. This may seem an exaggerated statement, but, with the exception of Rose Standish Nichols, all of the women in this book had offices at one time or another in the New York City area, although many received their education in the vicinity of Boston or at land-grant colleges in the East or the Midwest. Important landscape practices were, of course, growing up in other parts of the country, but New York, and Long Island, in particular, was still seen as the place where the action was. It was certainly where the greatest concentration of money was.

3. A woman who did not come to my attention until recently was Barbara Capen, who graduated from Lowthorpe School in 1935 and who redesigned the plantings in the walled garden at Old Westbury Gardens in Old Westbury, probably in the 1970s. See Jane Alison Knight, "An Examination of the History of the Lowthorpe School of Landscape Architecture for Women in Groton, Massachusetts, 1901–1945," a thesis presented to the faculty of the graduate school of Cornell University in partial fulfillment of the requirements for the degree of Master of Landscape Architecture, August 1986, 187. Barbara Capen appears in a group photograph on this and other pages of the Knight thesis. By 1946, Capen was working in the New York office of Mary Deputy Lamson. See Mary Deputy Lamson, *Gardening with Shrubs and Small Flowering Trees* (New York: M. Barrows and Company, Inc., 1946, page 8). Capen rarely published her work and did not belong to societies such as the American Society of Landscape Architects. I am grateful to Howard Phipps of Old Westbury for information about her work at Old Westbury Gardens. Horticulturist Richard Weir of Cornell University also remembers her activities there. The only published project by Capen that I have found is an herb garden for an unidentified client in New Jersey. See Faith H. Swanson and Virginia B. Rady, *Herb Garden Design* (Hanover and London: University Press of New England, 1984), 56–57.

4. A most important master's thesis had been written on Flanders by Patricia Louise Filzen, which is discussed fully in chapter 7. However, this fine thesis remains unpublished and known to only a small number of people.

CHAPTER 1
A New Profession for Women

1. Mary Bronson Hartt, "Women and the Art of Landscape Gardening," *The Outlook* 88 (March 28, 1908), 694–704. The women who had small local practices include Elizabeth Jane Bullard of Bridgeport, Connecticut and Annette McCrae; the latter designed landscapes primarily for railroad companies in the west and midwest.

2. Clarence Fowler, "Three Women in Landscape Architecture," *Alumnae Bulletin of the Cambridge School of Domestic and Landscape Architecture* 4, no. 2 (April 1932), 7–12.

3. Farrand, Ibid., 7.

4. Hutcheson and Coffin, Ibid., 8–12.

5. Judith B. Tankard, *The Gardens of Ellen Biddle Shipman* (New York: Sagapress, Inc., in Association with The Library of American Landscape History, Inc., 1996), 7–9, 11–28, 155.

6. Henry Atherton Frost, "The Cambridge School of Architecture and Landscape Architecture, Reminiscences," 1943, 9, typescript, Smith College Archives, Smith College, Northampton, Massachusetts.

7. Hutcheson, in Fowler, "Three Women," 9.

8. M. D., "Ruth Dean: A Brief Sketch of Her Life," *Bulletin of the Garden Club of America*, no. 1, Fifth Series (January 1933): 52.

9. I.(ris) A.(shwell), "Annette Hoyt Flanders: A Biographical Minute," *Landscape Architecture* 37, no. 2 (October 1946), 29–30.

10. Rebecca Warren Davidson, "The Spirit of the American Garden: Landscape and Cultural Expression in the Work of Martha Brookes Hutcheson," *Journal of the New England Garden History Society* 4 (Spring 1996), 22, note 6; Frances Drewry McMullen, "Ruth Dean, Landscape Architect," *The Woman's Journal* 14, no. 6 (June 1929): 25.

11. Nell Walker, "Marjorie Sewell Cautley," in Charles C. Birnbaum and Robin Karson, eds., *Pioneers of American Landscape Design* (New York: McGraw Hill, 2000), 47–49.

12. Daniel W. Krall, "Were they Feminists? Men Who Mentored Early Women Landscape Architects," a paper presented in a conference called "A Century of Women: Evaluating Gender in Landscape Architecture," University of California, Berkeley, November 8, 2002. I am grateful to Professor Krall for allowing me to read this paper prior to publication in the conference proceedings.

13. Farrand, in Fowler, "Three Women," 7.

14. Hutcheson and Coffin, Ibid., 8–12.

15. Margaret Henderson Floyd, "Architectural Education and Boston to 1899," in Margaret Henderson Floyd, ed., *Architectural Education and Boston* (Boston: Boston Architectural Center, 1989), 1, 10–12; Kimberly Alexander, Ph.D., "Guy Lowell and Landscape Architecture at MIT," manuscript article, nd, kindly provided by Dr. Alexander.

16. H. W. Gardner, '94, "The Course in Landscape Architecture," *The Technology Review* 5, no. 1 (January 1903), 1–7; Caroline Shillaber, *Massachusetts Institute of Technology, School of Architecture and Planning, 1861–1961: A Hundred Year Chronicle* (Cambridge, Massachusetts: MIT, 1963), 34–43; Alexander, "Guy Lowell," 8; Cynthia Zaitzevsky, "Education and Landscape Architecture," in Floyd, ed., *Architectural Education and Boston*, 30–31; and Davidson, *Images and Ideas*, 201–8, and Eran Ben-Joseph, Holly D. Ben-Joseph, and Anne C. Dodge, "Against all odds: MIT's Pioneering Women of Landscape Architecture," Massachusetts Institute of Technology, School of Architecture and Planning, City Design and Development Group, November 2006, available at LandArch@MITlow.pdf. The last article is a very valuable contribution, although the authors repeatedly state that Marian Coffin received a degree, which is not indicated on her transcript. For degree recipients, such as Edna Stoddoud, the transcript generally reads: "Recommended for the degree S.B.," and the title of the thesis is given.

17. This information comes from the MIT transcripts of Hutcheson and Coffin and from those of some of the "regular" students, both male and female, that I examined.

18. The first wave of this transformation was felt in Harvard's School of Architecture, when, in 1937, Walter Gropius instituted philosophical and technical approaches that he had pioneered at the Bauhaus in Germany. See John Coolidge, "Harvard's Teaching of Architecture and of the Fine Arts, 1928–1985," in Floyd, ed., *Architectural Education and Boston*, 59–65.

19. Quotation from the Land-Grant College Act of 1862, introduced by Senator Justin Smith Morrill of Vermont. Even the country's smallest state, Rhode Island, received 90,000 acres of land for its two senators and one congressman.

20. www.uky.edu/CampusGuide/land-grant.html. Other information about the land-grant system may be found at www.avu.edu/~exten/about/land.htm.

21. www.answers.com/topic/university_of_Massachusetts-amherst.

22. Frederick R. Steiner and Kenneth R. Brooks, "Agricultural Education and Landscape Architecture," *Landscape Journal* 5, no. 1 (Spring 1986), 19–32.

23. http://en.wikipedia.org/wiki/Cornell_University.

24. Daniel W. Krall, "Visions of Outdoor Art: One Hundred Years of Landscape Architecture Education at Cornell," book manuscript summer 2005), passim. I am grateful to Professor Krall for allowing me to read his comprehensive study in manuscript.

25. Ibid., 168, and Chapter VII: "Landscape Design and Coeducation," np.

26. Ibid., Chapter 7, np. Cites Davis to Richard C. Drinker, December 2, 1914 (Coll. 21/25/137, Box 5).

27. Ibid., Chapter 7, np. Cites Bryant Fleming to M. R. Getman, May 6, 1913 (Coll. 21/25/137), Box 4.

28. Ibid., np.

29. Helen Elise Bullard, "Journal," Entry of January 28, 1918, Cornell Archives. As a student, Bullard excelled in planting courses, and planting continued to be her strength in her career.

30. Krall, "Visions," Chapter 7. Cites RWC to Warren Manning, March 31, 1917 (Coll. 21, 25/137, Box 11). As will be seen in chapter 8, Cautley worked for Warren Manning for a time after graduating from Cornell.

31. Helen Elise Bullard, Transcript, Cornell University Registrar's Office.

32. Krall, "Visions," 189; "Cornell's Farrand," *Time* XIII, no. 24 (June 17, 1929): 54. The *Time* article implied that Livingston Farrand was offered the presidency of Cornell in part because the Trustees were so enchanted by his wife. Daisy Farrand was also the first president of the Ithaca Garden Club, and a peony was named after her ("Mrs. Livingston Farrand").

33. Krall, "Visions," 189.

34. *State Campus News* VII, no. 1 (February 1954): np. For Daisy Farrand, see also Elizabeth Wells, "Remembering Margaret Carleton 'Daisy' Farrand," September 1988, Rare and Manuscript Collections, Carl A. Kroch Library, Cornell University; "A Daisy Farrand Story," *The Cornell Plantations* 34, no. 4 (Winter 1978–1979), 61; and Elizabeth Anne Thomson '85, "Daisy's Garden," *Cornell Alumni News* 86, no. 9 (May 1984), 16–21. The last article is illustrated with photographs of Daisy and her garden, and there also appear to be loose photographs of the garden in the Cornell archives.

35. Tankard, *Shipman*, 18, 29–46.

36. Hartt, "Women and the Art of Landscape Gardening," 695.

37. "Miss Beatrix Jones' Vocation: She Does Landscape Gardening of All Kinds, from the Ground Up," *New York Sun*, October 31, 1897, p. 5, col. 3. (Farrand preferred to call herself a "landscape gardener" rather than a landscape architect.)

38. *Bar Harbor Record*, May 11, 1904. This article was excerpted from the *Rockland Star*. I am grateful to Earle G. Shettleworth, Jr., Director of the Maine Historic Preservation Commission, for a copy of this article.

39. *New York Sun*, October 31, 1897.

40. Janis P. Stout, *Willa Cather: The Writer and Her World* (Charlottesville and London: University of Virginia Press, 2000), 29–33, 39. Although this biography obviously focuses on Cather, these pages provide a good account of the New Woman. The New Woman phenomenon is often identified with the women's suffrage movement, which concluded with the passage of the Nineteenth Amendment to the United States Constitution in 1920. However, the New Woman phenomenon seems to have had many manifestations of which the drive toward women's suffrage was the most important but not the only one. In 1943, Henry Atherton Frost wrote: "We grew up in a period when women were more and more assuming responsibilities outside their homes. Their struggle for equal suffrage meant simply to us that they wanted to vote, and we who did not vote if to do so was inconvenient marveled at their tenacity. . . . A study of the period will show that there was a certain unrest among women, a desire to broaden their horizons and their activities. This has been developing gradually." (Frost, "The Cambridge School," 8–9.) There is no evidence that any of the women in this book were particularly active politically.

41. Clipping from an unidentified newspaper, dateline Bar Harbor, Maine, August 17, 1896, Scrapbook and Clippings File, Library of the Arnold Arboretum, Jamaica Plain, Massachusetts.

42. Quoted in Hartt, "Women and the Art of Landscape Gardening," 703. Farrand rode a bicycle (in which outfit she frequently supervised landscape construction in her early years), played golf and tennis, hunted, and fished. It should be noted that male landscape architects, including Olmsted, were not immune to the fatigue caused by constant train travel.

43. Coffin in Fowler, "Three Women," 12.

44. Coffin, quoted in Hartt, "Women and the Art of Landscape Gardening," 701–2.

45. M. D., "Ruth Dean," 52; Frances Drewry McMullen, "Ruth Dean, Landscape Architect," *The Woman's Journal*, June 1929, 25.

46. Ashwell, "Annette Hoyt Flanders," 30.

47. Farrand, in Fowler, "Three Women," 7.

48. Jane Alison Knight, "An Examination of the History of the Lowthorpe School of Landscape Architecture for Women in Groton, Massachusetts, 1901–1945," A Thesis Presented to the Faculty of the Graduate School of Cornell University in Partial Fulfillment of the Requirements for the Degree of Master of Landscape Architecture, August 1986.

49. Daniel W. Krall, "The Landscape Architect as Advocate: The Writings of Elizabeth Leonard Strang," *Journal of the New England Garden History Society* 11 (Fall 2003), 12–21.

50. Krall, "Visions," np. No reason was apparently given for this exclusion, but the fact that Lowthorpe could not grant degrees may have been a consideration.

51. Valencia Libby, "Jane Haines' Vision: The Pennsylvania School of Horticulture for Women," *Journal of the New England Garden History Society* 10 (Fall 2002), 44–52. See also www.fsm-pls.sxu/ambler/news.

52. Ibid.

53. Mildred B. Bliss, "An Attempted Evocation of a Personality," *Landscape Architecture* 49, no. 4 (Summer 1959): 222.

54. M. D., "Ruth Dean," 52.

55. *House and Garden* (January 1950), biographical summary in Table of Contents.

56. Transcript, Annette Hoyt, Smith College Archives, Smith College: "In Memoriam, Annette Hoyt Flanders," *Smith Alumnae Quarterly*, August 1946, 216.

57. Hutcheson, in Fowler, "Three Women," 8–9.

58. Coffin, Ibid., 11.

59. Nancy Fleming, *Money, Manure & Maintenance, Ingredients for the Successful Gardens of Marian Coffin: Pioneer Landscape Architect, 1876–1957* (Weston, Massachusetts: Country Place Books, 1995), 12, 98. Fleming says that this exhibition was at the Arden Galleries, but two newspaper articles place it in the Studio Guild Gallery. See an untitled clipping from the *New York Sun*, January 27, 1942, and "Flower Paintings," *New York Herald Tribune*, January 25, 1942 (Artists' Files, Art and Architecture Reading Room, New York Public Library).

60. Ellen Shipman, Garden Note Book, manuscript, nd (assembled ca. 1945), np, Ellen Shipman Collection, Rare and Manuscript Collections, Carl A. Kroch Library, Cornell University, Ithaca, New York.

61. Hartt, "Women and the Art of Landscape Gardening," 699.

62. Ibid., 697.

63. Ibid., 697–9.

64. Quoted in Anne Petersen, "Women Take Lead in Landscape Art," the *New York Times*, Sunday March 13, 1938, Section VI, p. 5, col. 7.

65. Hartt, "Women and the Art of Landscape Gardening," 699.

66. Ibid., 704.

67. Dorothy May Anderson, *Women, Design, and The Cambridge School* (East Lafayette, Indiana: PDA Publishers Corp., 1980): 105.

68. Some examples are Gasworks Park in Seattle, Washington, by Richard Haag (1971); Freeway Park, also in Seattle, by Angela Damadjieva of Lawrence Halprin's firm (1976); and the John F. Kennedy Memorial Park, Cambridge, Massachusetts, by Carol R. Johnson (1987). The last is located on the Charles River on the former site of a trolley storage yard for the Massachusetts Bay Transportation Authority.

69. Diana Balmori, "Campus Work and Public Landscapes," in Diana Balmori, Diane Kostial McGuire, and Eleanor M. McPeck, *Beatrix Farrand's American Landscapes: Her Gardens and Campuses* (Sagaponack, New York: Sagapress, Inc., 1985), 127–96; Martha Brookes Hutcheson, A list of her professional record made by Hutcheson as part of her application for Fellowship in the American Society of Landscape Architects, Archives of the Morris County Park Commission, Morristown, New Jersey; Fleming, *Money*, 58–69; and Tankard, *Shipman*, 167–74.

70. An exception is Ruth Dean, who died in her early forties. Because she died suddenly, it is often assumed that she died of a heart attack. I have not been able to locate her death certificate and cannot confirm this. (For non-relatives, vital records are very difficult to obtain in New York State.)

71. Sandra Lueder and Jeannette Oppedisano, "True Grit: Entrepreneurial Women Beating the Odds of Life Expectancy," *Studies in American Historical Demography* (New York: 1995), 1–14. The authors identify certain personality traits that might have contributed to these women's success and, presumably, to their longevity: hardiness (resistance to negative effects on health of stressful events); resiliency; self-efficacy (an individual's belief in her capacity to perform specific tasks); and adversity quotient (similar to resiliency). Psychological studies are cited.

72. Ibid., Table 1, np. The only design professional included in the Oppedisano and Lueder study was the California architect Julia Morgan, born the same year as Beatrix Jones Farrand, although Farrand lived two years longer.

73. Elizabeth Meade, "Martha Brookes Hutcheson, 1872–1959, a Biographical Minute," *Landscape Architecture* 50, no. 3 (Spring 1960): 182.

CHAPTER 2
Beatrix Jones Farrand 1872–1959

1. Max Farrand was the youngest of three brothers, all of whom were academics. The eldest, Wilson, was the headmaster of Newark Academy in Newark, New Jersey, a position his father Samuel had held before him. Wilson Farrand was also the clerk and a life trustee of Princeton University. We have already met the middle brother Livingston in chapter 1. Because of his sister-in-law Daisy, Max Farrand may well have had an interest in landscapes and gardens even before he met Beatrix. See "Cornell's Farrand," *Time* XIII, no. 24 (June 17, 1929): 54.

2. See Cynthia Zaitzevsky, "A Career in Bud: Beatrix Jones Farrand's Education and Early Gardens," *Journal of the New England Garden History Society* 6 (Fall 1998): 14–31. This article sums up what I was then able to find out about Farrand's early life and education. I have referred to her as Jones before her marriage and Farrand after. When I have made general statements about her life and career, I have referred to her as Farrand.

3. (Beatrix Jones Farrand), *Reef Point Gardens* Bulletin 1, no. 17 (1959), in Beatrix Farrand, *The Bulletins of Reef Point Gardens* (Bar Harbor, Maine: The Island Foundation, 1997): 112–14. This is a two and one-half page autobiographical account written by Farrand in the third person in 1956, three years before her death (hereafter cited as Autobiographical Account). For a time, Farrand's father had a bookbinding business in New York City, but, for most of his life, he followed no business or profession. See Shari Benstock, *No Gifts from Chance: A Biography of Edith Wharton* (New York: Charles Scribner's Sons, 1995), 30.

4. Diane Kostial McGuire, "Sermon on The Mount: Edith Wharton's Influence on Beatrix Jones Farrand," *Journal of the New England Garden History Society* I (Fall 1991): 10–17; Susan Child Design, LLC and Cynthia Zaitzevsky, Ph.D., *Cultural Landscape Report for The Mount*, (Lenox, Massachusetts: Edith Wharton Restoration, Inc., 2006), chapters 2 and 3.

5. In 1919, Wharton went to live permanently in France. See also Edith Wharton, "Gardening in France," in Daniel Bratton, ed., *Yrs. Ever Affly: The Correspondence of Edith Wharton and Louis Bromfield* (East Lansing, Michigan: Michigan State University Press, 2000), 135–39. The original is in the Beinecke Library, Yale University. Eleanor Dwight, *Edith Wharton: An Extraordinary Life* (New York: Harry N. Abrams, Inc., Publishers, 1994), 211–60; Child and Zaitzevsky, Cultural Landscape Report for The Mount, chapter 5. The original letters are in the Edith Wharton Papers, Yale Collection of American Literature, Beinecke Library, Yale University. Farrand's side of this correspondence has not survived. Wharton's two French residences were Pavillon Colombe just north of Paris and Château Ste-Claire on the Riviera. One was primarily a summer and the other a winter home.

6. Percy Lubbock, *A Portrait of Edith Wharton* (New York and London: D. Appleton-Century Company, Inc., 1947; reprint ed., New York: Kraus Reprint Co., 1969): 184.

7. Quoted in Mildred B. Bliss, "An Attempted Evocation of a Personality," *Landscape Architecture* 49, no. 4 (Summer 1959): 218. Beatrix apparently called Cadwalader "uncle," which has led to considerable confusion about the relationship.

8. Zaitzevsky, "A Career in Bud": 16. These young women received all of their education from tutors, in contrast to today when tutors or tutoring services are hired to provide *remedial* education in subjects that students may be failing in school.

9. Eleanor M. McPeck, "A Biographical Note and a Consideration of Four Major Private Gardens," in Diana Balmori, Diane Kostial McGuire, and Eleanor M. McPeck, eds. *Beatrix Farrand's American Landscapes* (Sagaponack, New York: Saga Press, Inc., 1985), 14–15.

10. Mrs. Winthrop Chanler, *Roman Spring* (Boston: Little, Brown and Company, 1934): 269. Mary Cadwalader Jones first met Henry James in 1883 but established a lasting friendship with him around 1900, the same time that her sister-in-law Edith did. Edith and Teddy Wharton, Mary Jones, and Beatrix frequently visited James at Lamb House in Rye, Sussex, England. The importance of Mary Cadwalader Jones's friendship to James has recently been recognized in the collection of his letters to her in Susan E. Gunther, ed. *Dear Munificent Friends: Henry James's Letters to Four Women* (Ann Arbor: The University of Michigan Press, 1999). James destroyed nearly all of his incoming correspondence, including that from Mary Jones. During his two American trips, James also stayed with the Whartons at The Mount.

11. Autobiographical Account, 112.

12. Bliss, "Evocation," 218. Sargent intensely disliked the term "landscape architecture," and even what he saw as overemphasis on design at the expense of attention to plants made him edgy. This somewhat contradictory attitude is best understood by studying an exchange of correspondence between Sargent and the garden writer Louisa Yeomans King, which has been published by Virginia Lopez Begg in "Influential Friends: Charles Sprague Sargent and Louisa Yeomans King," *Journal of the New England Garden History Society* 1 (Fall 1991), 38–45.

13. "Beloved pupil," Bliss, "Evocation," 220.

14. Farrand, quoted in Fowler, 8.

15. Ibid.

16. Robert W. Patterson, "Beatrix Farrand, 1872–1959: An Appreciation of a Great Landscape Gardener," *Landscape Architecture* 49, no. 4 (Summer 1959): 216.

17. Farrand in Fowler, 8.

18. Beatrix Jones, "Book of Gardening," 1893–95, College of Environmental Design Documents Collection, University of California, Berkeley. I have discussed this notebook and the 1895 trip in detail in "A Career in Bud," 16–22. In her Autobiographical Account (p. 112), Farrand wrote that this trip had included Holland, but there are no entries on Dutch gardens in this notebook.

19. Mary Cadwalader Jones, *European Travel for Women: Notes and Suggestions* (New York: Macmillan, 1900): 45.

20. *New York Sun*, October 31, 1897, p. 5, col. 3.

21. Farrand in Fowler, "Three Women," 8.

22. Farrand, Autobiographical Account, 112.

23. Cynthia Zaitzevsky, research in progress on Chiltern.

24. Beatrix Farrand to Mildred Barnes Bliss, July 7, 1922, Beatrix Farrand File, Dumbarton Oaks Garden Library, Washington, DC; "A List of Beatrix Jones' Work, compiled by her," In *Beatrix Jones Farrand (1872–1959): An Appreciation of A Great Landscape Gardener*, nd, privately printed.

25. Beatrix Jones to Max Farrand, undated note (Spring or Summer 1913), Reef Point Gardens Collection, CED, University of California, Berkeley, np. Berkeley (MSS III.3).

26. McPeck, "A Biographical Note," 26–31. The lych gate is no longer there, and it is unclear if it was ever constructed.

27. Zaitzevsky, "A Career in Bud," 24–27.

28. "History of the Cathedral of St. Peter and St. Paul," Private Record of Henry Y. Satterlee, undated typescript, Archives of the National Cathedral, Washington, DC, 25.

29. Ibid., 26; Jane Brown, *Beatrix: The Gardening Life of Beatrix Jones Farrand, 1872–1959* (New York: Viking, 1995): 232, n. 7, cites Suzanne K. Miller, letter to the author, November 7, 1991; Beatrix Farrand to Mildred Barnes Bliss, April 7, 1947, Beatrix Farrand File, Dumbarton Oaks Garden Library. According to Brown, the Glastonbury stones, which consisted of 23 cubes, 18 inches and 20 inches, arrived in June 1899. They were used to construct the Glastonbury Cathedra, designed by Robert W. Gibson, architect of the Cathedral Girls' School, and fabricated by C. Flannery, stonemason, in 1901. The cathedra was first installed in the Little Sanctuary and eventually moved into the Main Sanctuary. Farrand mentioned to Mrs. Bliss that she had been able to obtain the stones through the kindness of the authorities at Wells. The National Cathedral and Glastonbury Abbey were both dedicated to Saints Peter and Paul.

30. Henry Y. Satterlee, D.D., LL.D., *The Building of a Cathedral* (New York: Edwin S. Gorham, nd.), 51–52.

31. Beatrix Farrand to Mildred Barnes Bliss, February 28, 1947, Beatrix Farrand File, Dumbarton Oaks Garden Library.

32. Norman T. Newton, *Design on the Land: The Development of Landscape Architecture* (Cambridge, Massachusetts: Harvard University Press, 1971), 387–88.

33. Bliss, "An Attempted Evocation," 218.

34. Henry James to Mary Cadwalader Jones, from Lamb House, September 26, 1912, James Family Papers, Houghton Library, Harvard University.

35. Charles Moore, *The Life and Times of Charles Follen McKim* (Boston and New York: Houghton Mifflin Company, 1929): 299.

36. Autobiographical Account, 113. In 1914, Farrand designed the grounds of Mrs. Pyne's residence in Princeton.

37. Ibid.; Benstock, *No Gifts*, 289. When Max Farrand's sister-in-law, Daisy Farrand, heard of the romance early in 1913, she went to the Princeton campus, without identifying herself, to watch Beatrix directing workmen. She came to the conclusion that "If that lady really wants Max, she'll get him." See Brown, *Beatrix*, 102.

38. Autobiographical Account, 113. Beatrix Jones became engaged, probably in 1895, to an Irish barrister, but later broke it off. This was the older son of John Pentland Mahaffy of Trinity College, Dublin. (*New York Times*, May 28, 1905, part 4, p. 11, col. 6). In 1897, she told a *New York Sun* reporter that she didn't think a "young woman dedicated to her profession could afford to marry at all." (*New York Sun*, October 31, 1897, 5, col. 3.)

39. Henry James to Beatrix Jones, from Lamb House, October 24, 1913, James Family Papers, Houghton Library, Harvard University.

40. Benstock, *No Gifts*, 289–90; Brown, *Beatrix*, 104–5. *Bar Harbor Record*, December 24, 1913, 2. While heavy on clergy, the ceremony, which was held in the morning room of the Jones house, seems to have been short on guests: Max Farrand's mother was also ill; he had no best man; there were no attendants or ushers; and there was no reception. Both of Farrand's brothers were absent from the ceremony.

41. Edith Wharton to Beatrix Farrand, January 18, 1914, Edith Wharton Collection, Beinecke Library, Yale University. The Farrands' marriage coincided almost exactly with the Whartons' divorce.

42. Eolia is a Connecticut State Park overseen by the State's Department of Environmental Protection. Both Farrand's work and that of an earlier Harkness landscape firm, Brett & Hall, have been restored. I am grateful to Mark Darin of the Connecticut State Parks for this information. Alice Orme Smith, who worked in Farrand's office on both Eyrie and Dumbarton Oaks recalled that Farrand kept track of time spent by her assistants by setting aside shoe boxes, one for each client into which her draftswomen would put slips indicating how many hours they had worked on each project. See Dona E. Caldwell to Director, Documents Collection, College of Environmental Design, Berkeley, January 25, 1992, "Summary of Holdings for Alice Orme Smith," Fairfield Historical Society, Fairfield, Connecticut.

43. Patterson, "Beatrix Farrand," 218.

44. Farrand in Fowler, "Three Women," 8.

45. Autobiographical Account, 113.

46. Diane Kostial McGuire, "Beatrix Farrand's Contribution to the Art of Landscape Architecture," in Diane Kostial McGuire and Lois Fern, eds., *Beatrix Jones Farrand (1872–1959): Fifty Years of American Landscape Architecture* (Washington, DC: Dumbarton Oaks, 1982), 40–41, 46.

47. Autobiographical Account, 113–14; Michael M. Laurie, "The Reef Point Collection at the University of California," in *Beatrix Jones Farrand (1872–1959)*, 11–20.

48. Autobiographical Account, 114. Farrand died on February 27, 1959 of a heart condition. See undated clipping from the *New York Herald Tribune, Artists' Files, Art and Architecture Reading Room*, New York Public Library. The "smaller quarters," Garland Farm in Eden, Maine, near Bar Harbor, survive. The house and Farrand-designed plantings are being restored by the Beatrix Farrand Society. Plans are underway to turn Garland Farm into an educational program similar to what Farrand had planned for Reef Point.

49. Robert W. Patterson, "List of Clients and Projects, from Surviving Account Books," 1985. I am very grateful to Earle G. Shettleworth, Jr., Director of the Maine Historic Preservation Commission, for supplying me with this list and other information about Patterson. Under Farrand, Patterson listed John D. Rockefeller, Jr. (the Eyrie), David Rockefeller, Potter Palmer, Morris McCormick, Vance McCormick, Gerrish Milliken, and others. These were some of Farrand's most distinguished Maine clients, most of them on Mount Desert Island. See also Robert Whiteley Patterson, Entry, *Harvard Class of 1927, Fiftieth Anniversary Report* (Cambridge, Printed for the University, 1977), 546–48.

50. "Percy Chubb Dies on Train in Canada," *New York Times*, June 16, 1930, 21, col. 5.

51. Eleven plans for the Chubb garden out of a total of at least 47 survive at Berkeley. I am very grateful to Marion Smith Drake of Hastings-on-Hudson, New York, for information on the Chubb family. Mrs. Drake is the daughter of Peter Smith, the Chubbs' gardener. I am also grateful to Mr. and Mrs. Percy Chubb of Bernardsville, New Jersey for information about the family and for locating Mrs. Drake.

52. (Beatrix Jones), Notes on her projects prior to her marriage to Max Farrand, nd (ca. Spring/Summer 1913), np. Berkeley (MSS.III.3), hereafter cited as "Jones, Notes."

53. Ibid.

54. See www.saddlerock.org/history.html.

55. Jones, Notes, np. By "head," Jones probably meant ego.

56. Ibid. Jones had appendicitis in early June 1903. See Benstock, *No Gifts*, n. 77, 138, 494.

57. Ibid.

58. "Edward Farley Whitney," obituary. *New York Times*, February 10, 1928, 23, col.5; "E.F. Whitney's Niece His Chief Beneficiary," *New York Times*, February 29, 1928, 17, col. 4.

59. Jones, Notes, np.

60. (illegible) Pyncheon, Oyster Bay, "Land of Edward Whitney, Oyster Bay—Home Lot 6.83 acres," ink on linen, surveyed Spring 1901, updated March 19 and April 10, 1906. (Berkeley)

61. Jones, Notes, np.

62. Diana Balmori, Entry on Beatrix Farrand, in Robert B. MacKay, Anthony K. Baker, and Carol A. Traynor, eds., *Long Island Country Houses and Their Architects, 1860–1940* (New York: W. W. Norton, 1997): 164.

63. SPLIA files.

64. Jones, Notes, np.

65. Ibid.

66. Ibid.

67. McPeck, "A Biographical Note," 40. For the Straights, see also Michael Straight, *After Long Silence* (New York: W. W. Norton & Company, 1983), 13–24.

68. SPLIA, Archives.

69. McPeck, "A Biographical Note," 40–41; Brown, *Beatrix*, 106–8; Balmori, Entry on Beatrix Farrand, in MacKay, Baker, and Traynor, eds., *Long Island Country Houses*, 164.

70. Farrand was extremely protective of her clients' privacy and almost never published her private projects. In the annual American Society of Landscape Architects, *Illustrations of the Work of Members* (1931–34), she generally published only her university work, but the illustration in fig. 2.10 was published in the 1931 volume. See American Society of Landscape Architects, *Illustrations of Work of Members* (New York: The House of J. Hayden Twiss, 1931), np.

71. Anne Baker to Beatrix Farrand, November 17, 1924. Vertical files for Willard Straight, Old Westbury, Reef Point Gardens Collection, Documents Collection, College of Environmental Design, University of California, Berkeley. Anne Baker worked for Farrand from 1924 to 1938. Apparently with Farrand's blessing, she also ran an independent practice from Farrand's address. See H. S. J., "Anne Baker, July 18, 1890–February 16, 1949. A Biographical Minute," *Landscape Architecture* 40, no. 1 (October 1949), 34–35. The vertical files at Berkeley consist of photographs, notes, and correspondence with nurseries that are filed separately and aren't wrapped up with the plans. They exist for only some of the larger projects.

72. McPeck, "A Biographical Note," 44. I am grateful to Mac Griswold for information about the Chinese garden foundations. The file on the Straight project at Berkeley is called "Straight Improvement Co.," implying that, at some time, the Straights intended to subdivide at least part of their property. There are, however, no subdivision plans in the file, and this cannot have had anything to do with the 1951 subdivision.

73. The supplementary drawings include 16 plans by New York City architect S. Gage for remodeling the house between 1925 and 1927 and seven plans by Wm. H. Lutton Co. of Jersey City, New Jersey, for a service building and a proposed greenhouse. In 1929, Farrand designed part of the grounds of S.Vernon Mann, Jr., which was apparently near his father's property.

74. MacKay, Baker, and Traynor, eds., *Long Island Country Houses*, 510.

75. Clive Fisher, *Hart Crane: A Life* (New Haven, Connecticut: Yale University Press, 2002): 269.

76. Thesea M. Collins, *Otto Kahn: Art, Money & Modern Times* (Chapel Hill, North Carolina: University of North Carolina Press, 2002): 1.

77. Ibid., 156–87.

78. Ibid., 84, 8.

79. Richard Guy Wilson, Entry on Delano and Aldrich, in MacKay, Baker, and Traynor, eds., *Long Island Country Houses*, 138, 506.

80. *Portraits of Ten Country Houses Designed by Delano and Aldrich* (1922), pl. 18. In the Delano and Aldrich archives at Avery Library, Columbia University, there is an undated plan by the Florentine-born landscape architect Feruccio Vitale for the Kahn property, which proposed an impressive false perspective just below the terrace and continuing to the southern end of the landscape. This project was not carried out and probably dates from before the involvement of Olmsted Brothers, since there is no trace of the water gardens done by them with Delano and Aldrich.

81. Undated, unsigned memo, vertical files for the Kahn project, Berkeley.

82. Field visit by the author and Robert B. MacKay, February 2002.

83. Farrand also designed a burial plot for the Harknesses in Woodlawn Cemetery, New York City, probably between 1929 and 1933.

84. www.saddlerock.org/history.html

85. Vertical files, Great Neck Green, Berkeley.

86. Ibid.

87. The League of Women Voters of Great Neck, *This is Great Neck* (Great Neck, Long Island, New York: 1975), 28–30.

88. Vertical files, Percy R. Pyne II, Berkeley.

89. Balmori, Entry on Beatrix Farrand, in MacKay, Baker, and Traynor, eds., *Long Island Country Houses*, 165. Balmori attributed this plan to Farrand, but it is signed by Delano and Aldrich.

90. For the extremely elaborate planting plan of the rock garden, see Brown, *Beatrix*, 130–33.

91. While this way of arranging group gardens was not typical of Farrand, it was also unlike the site plans produced by Delano and Aldrich for numerous other properties on Long Island. See Wilson in MacKay, Baker, and Traynor, eds., *Long Island Country Houses*, 133, 136, 138, 141, and 143. It is possible that this array of specialty gardens was the choice of the owners.

92. SPLIA Archives.

93. There seemed to be no information on this property at rediscov.com/Olmsted. The Williams project may not have been entered yet into this database, since this is an ongoing process. The Olmsted National Historic Site in Brookline, Massachusetts is closed indefinitely, so I was not able to review plans, photographs, etc. However, if the firm was active at a site for only one year, it generally means a limited involvement.

94. Michael Young, *The Elmhirsts of Dartington: The Creation of an Utopian Community* (Boston: Routledge & Kegan Paul, 1982): 110.

95. Straight, *After Long Silence*, 37–42.

96. Brown, *Beatrix*, 150–51; Laurence J. Fricker, "Dartington Hall, Devonshire, England," in McGuire and Fern, eds., *Beatrix Jones Farrand*, 75–84; Reginald Snell, *From The Bare Stem: Making Dorothy Elmhirst's Garden at Dartington Hall* (Devon Books in association with the Dartington Press, 1989), 34–36.

97. Brown, Beatrix, 150–51. For the quote, see Fricker, "Dartington Hall," 85.

98. "Dartington Hall, Feb. 4, 1933. Plants liked by Mrs. Elmhirst," vertical files, Berkeley.

99. Ibid. Notes taken February 17, 1933.

100. Beatrix Farrand to Dorothy Elmhirst, summer 1939. Quoted in Fricker, "Dartington Hall," 85.

101. Many of these are illustrated in Fricker, "Dartington Hall," pls. 2–6.

102. Diane Kostial McGuire, "Introduction," in McGuire and Fern, eds., *Beatrix Jones Farrand*, 5.

103. Dartington Hall, Bench Study #13, nd.

104. Dartington Hall, Bench Study #5, nd.

105. This, of course, is a hypothetical scenario, but something very like this must have happened.

106. Beatrix Farrand to Leonard and Dorothy, June 27, 1933. Vertical files, Job 861, Berkeley.

107. There is one drawing for this project at Berkeley.

108. Quoted in Eleanor M. McPeck, "Beatrix Jones Farrand: The Formative Years, 1890–1920," in McGuire and Fern, eds., *Beatrix Jones Farrand*, 28. McPeck cites an unlabeled and undated newspaper clipping in the vertical files of the Frances Loeb Library, Harvard Graduate School of Design. This clipping can no longer be located.

109. Quoted in Fricker, "Dartington Hall," 95–96. Mrs. Elmhirst wrote this as an obituary on Farrand in Dartington Hall's "News of the Day," no. 2156 (March 13, 1959), original in Dartington Hall Archives.

CHAPTER 3
Martha Brookes Brown Hutcheson 1871–1959

1. Martha Brookes Brown Hutcheson, Application for Fellow Membership to the American Society of Landscape Architects, October 29, 1934, Martha Brookes Hutcheson Collection, Morris County (New Jersey) Park Commission, Fosterfields Living Historical Farm, Morristown, New Jersey (hereafter Hutcheson, Application for Fellow Membership).

2. Sharon M. Doremus, "Martha Brookes Hutcheson," in Joan N. Burstyn, ed., *Past and Promise: Lives of New Jersey Women* (Syracuse, New York: Syracuse University Press, 1997), 155–57. This entry was based on an interview with Hutcheson's daughter and contains some inaccuracies about the landscape architect's early life. See also the will of Ellen D. Brookes Brown of Fern Hill, Burlington, Vermont, November 25, 1921, with three codicils, dated May 31, 1927, September 2, 1929, and March 6, 1933 (Hutcheson Collection). The Brown children were Douglas, Martha, Herbert P., Elliot G., and Elsie.

3. Marriage between Martha Brookes Brown and William Anderson Hutcheson, October 12, 1910, Vital Records, State of Vermont, filed October 13, 1910. See also Rebecca Warren Davidson, *Images and Ideas of the Italian Garden in American Landscape Architecture* (Ann Arbor, Michigan: UMI Dissertation Services, 1994): 327. A photograph of the wedding party at Fern Hill may be found in Hutcheson, *The Spirit of the Garden* (reprint ed., 2001), Introduction by Rebecca Warren Davidson, fig. 2, ix. The original is in the Hutcheson Collection, with a diagram identifying everyone in the photograph. The styling of the wedding announcement (in the name of "Mrs. Brookes Brown") indicates that Martha's parents were divorced and that her father had died (Hutcheson Collection).

4. Martha Brookes Hutcheson to Clarence Fowler, October 28, 1931, Hutcheson Collection. Hutcheson noted that this was her corrected copy, with additions, of a rough draft of October 19, 1931. The draft does not differ in content from the version of Hutcheson's account published in Fowler, "Three Women," 8–9.

5. Martha Brookes Hutcheson, "Notes on Fern Hill, Burlington, Vermont," and, Typescript, Version 1, page 1, Hutcheson Collection.

6. Ibid.; Hutcheson, Application for Fellow Membership. There are a number of photographs of Fern Hill in the Hutcheson Collection. Biographical information on Dr. John Pomeroy and John Norton Pomeroy is found in W. S. Rann, ed., *History of Chittenden County, Vermont* (Syracuse, New York: D. Mason and Co., Publishers, 1886), 258–60; Abby Maria Hemenway, ed., *The Vermont Historical Gazetteer* (Burlington, Vermont: Miss A. M.

Hemenway, 1888), 478, 727–29; Hamilton and Child, eds., *Gazetteer and Business Directory of Chittenden County, Vermont* (Syracuse, New York: The Journal Office, August 1882), 147–48. John Norton Pomeroy's property appears on the 1857 Walling Map and the Beers 1869 Map of Chittenden County. The latter map clearly shows the footprint of his house. There are a few discrepancies between Hutcheson's accounts of Fern Hill and other sources, probably due to her young age at the time her mother acquired the property. I am grateful to Virginia Lopez Begg, Andover, Massachusetts, Rebecca Warren Davidson, Princeton, New Jersey, and the staff of the Morris County Park Commission, Morristown, New Jersey for information about Martha Brookes Hutcheson. I am also indebted to the Vermont Historical Society, Montpelier, Vermont; the Bailey/Howe Library, Special Collections, University of Vermont, Burlington, Vermont; and the Probate Court, Chittenden County, Burlington, Vermont, for assistance in reconstructing the history of Fern Hill.

7. Hutcheson in Fowler, "Three Women," 9.

8. Hutcheson, Application for Fellow Membership. For Nicholls, see Rebecca Warren Davidson, Introduction to Martha Brookes Hutcheson, *The Spirit of the Garden* (Amherst, Massachusetts: University of Massachusetts Press, reprint ed., 2001), x, n. 9, xxvii.

9. Hutcheson in Fowler, "Three Women," 9.

10. Ibid.

11. Henry Atherton Frost, "The Cambridge School of Architecture and Landscape Architecture—Reminiscences," 1943, Manuscript, Smith College Archives, Smith College, Northampton, Massachusetts, 9.

12. Ibid. Brown was almost thirty when she entered MIT, hardly a "child."

13. Hutcheson in Fowler, "Three Women," 9. Hutcheson misremembered the year she entered MIT. In her Application for Fellow Membership, she stated that she studied at MIT, starting in 1900–1, through 1903. The Office of the Registrar at MIT has information on Hutcheson for three semesters only, although she may have taken some courses in the spring of 1902, on which she was not graded.

14. Doremus, "Hutcheson," 155. Martha's father remains a shadowy figure, but he might have died about this time and left her a bequest, although a divorce seems to have occurred earlier.

15. Frost, "The Cambridge School," 9. MIT was then located on Boylston Street in Boston's Back Bay, not in Cambridge.

16. The often-repeated statement that women could not receive degrees from MIT simply because they were women is not true. Women—including at least two in the landscape architecture program—could and did receive degrees if they took the required courses and satisfactorily completed a thesis.

17. Hutcheson in Fowler, "Three Women," 10.

18. Hutcheson, Application for Fellow Membership. Hutcheson is not listed as a Landscape Architect or Landscape Gardener in the Boston City Directories, Business Directory, for the years 1902–7. A "Statement Regarding Professional Methods and Charges" in the Hutcheson Collection, dated 1905, lists her as "Martha Brookes Brown, Landscape Gardener," at 60 Chestnut Street, Boston. Sources vary as to the length of her practice in Boston. Undoubtedly, in addition to funding her tuition, the small bequest paid for the expenses involved in setting up her Boston office and for her European study trip.

19. Hutcheson quotation from class notes of 1903, *MIT Alumni Bulletin*, May 1959, vii, Smith College Archives, Smith College, Northampton, Massachusetts; Martha Brookes Brown Hutcheson to Mrs. Florence Ward Sterns, Librarian, Massachusetts Institute of Technology, School of Architecture, April 7, 1936, Hutcheson Collection. This was in response to a query about her professional activities and those of her classmates.

Edna Dwinel Stoddard graduated from MIT with an S.B. degree in 1903. Stoddard was born January 4, 1881, the daughter of Orrick H. Stoddard, 4 Thwing Street, Roxbury (Boston),

Massachusetts. She prepared at Boston Girls High School. Stoddard had an excellent record at MIT, with many Cs, the highest grade then given (Office of the Registrar, MIT). Her thesis was "A Country Estate on the Maine Coast"; her thesis statement and one drawing are extant in the Rotch Architectural Library and the MIT Museum, respectively. Stoddard's thesis statement and one drawing were also published. See E. D. Stoddard, "A Country Estate," *The Technology Review* 5, no. 1 (January 1903), 27–30. In his brief introduction on Stoddard's "programme," Guy Lowell indicated that the proposed estate was on Long Island, not on the Maine coast.

Stoddard probably worked as Hutcheson's assistant until the latter closed her office in 1912. Between 1912 and 1918 and again in 1930, Stoddard taught a course in landscape architecture as part of the botany department of Smith College. If she ever practiced independently after leaving the Smith faculty in 1918, there seems to be no record of it. Stoddard married Arthur Ramseyer in 1918, apparently ending her active involvement in landscape architecture, except for the one additional year teaching at Smith. They seem to have had no children. Stoddard died December 20, 1958 as the result of an automobile accident. [Class Notes of 1903, *M.I.T. (Alumni Bulletin)*, May, 1959; Anderson, *Women, Design and the Cambridge School*, 57.] Stoddard's class of 1914–15 is illustrated on page 67 of this book. Stoddard is probably the mature woman standing second to left, wearing a dark suit and with dark hair parted in the middle.

20. Martha Brookes Hutcheson, *The Spirit of the Garden* (Boston: *The Atlantic Monthly Press*, 1923), 11, 20–23, 70–71, 122–24, 190, 198–99.

21. Hutcheson, Professional Record, part of her application for Fellow membership (hereafter Hutcheson, Professional Record). A four-page report on the Maudesleigh Estate was also made as part of her application. Unfortunately, the plans and photographs that accompanied it have not survived, although some were published in *The Spirit of the Garden*.

22. I am grateful to Wendy Pearl of the Massachusetts Conservation and Recreation Department, State Parks and Recreation Division, for this information.

23. Hutcheson to Frank Chouteau, August 2, 1935 and June 16, 1936. Quoted in Catherine Evans, Landscape Architect, National Park Service, *Cultural Landscape Report for Longfellow National Historic Site, Volume I: Site History and Existing Conditions* (Boston: National Park Service, North Atlantic Region, Division of Cultural Resources Management, Cultural Landscape Program, 1993), 63–64. Cites HABS Collection, Archives of the Society for the Preservation of New England Antiquities, Boston. Old photographs but no plans have survived in the Hutcheson Collection. The Longfellow garden at Craigie House was also published in *The Spirit of the Garden*, 104–5, 154–58.

24. Evans, Cultural Landscape Report for Longfellow National Historic Site, 71–73; Tankard, *The Gardens of Ellen Biddle Shipman*, 192.

25. Hutcheson, *The Spirit of the Garden*, 26–27, 52, 73, 89, 143–47, 194–97.

26. Virginia Lopez Begg, "Martha Brookes Hutcheson (1871–1959)" in Charles A. Birnbaum and Robin Karson, eds., *Pioneers of American Landscape Design* (New York: McGraw-Hill, 2000), 188–192; Denise Royle and Jean-Marie Hartman, "Martha Brookes Hutcheson and Her Influence on the American Landscape," Proceedings of the Council of Educators in Landscape Architecture, nd., ms. in the Hutcheson Collection, 6–7. For the Woman's Land Army, see Davidson, Introduction to Hutcheson, *The Spirit of the Garden* (reprint ed., 2001): xv.

27. Martha Brookes Hutcheson, "The First Quarter Century of the Garden Club of America as Seen by an Old Member," *Bulletin of the Garden Club of America*, no. 7, Sixth Series (January 1938), 26–27.

28. Ibid., 30–31; Royle and Hartman, "Martha Brookes Hutcheson," 7–9.

29. Hutcheson, Application for Fellow Membership. "Are Our Garden Clubs to Progress in Unison or Die of the Inertia of the Commonplace?" was published in *Bulletin of the Garden Club of America*, no. 4, Third Series (July 1925), 21–24.

30. Hutcheson, "The First Quarter Century," 31; Royle and Hartman, "Martha Brookes Hutcheson," 7–10.

31. Hutcheson, Application for Fellow Membership. The dates of most of these lectures are not given.

32. *Landscape Architecture* 18, no. 6 (April 1928): 249.

33. Meade, "Martha Brookes Hutcheson," 181.

34. Hutcheson, *The Spirit of the Garden*, ix–x.

35. Ibid., 44, 78, 96–103, 130–36. These photographs include some very interesting construction views.

36. A detailed and perceptive discussion of *The Spirit of the Garden* is found in Davidson, *Images and Ideas*, 322–62.

37. Hutcheson, Professional Record.

38. Ibid.

39. Helen Lefkowitz Horowitz, *Alma Mater: Design and Experience in the Women's Colleges from Their Nineteenth-Century Beginnings to the 1930s* (Amherst, Massachusetts: University of Massachusetts Press, 1993), 328–39.

40. Buell Hueston, Boonton, New Jersey, "Noted Native Daughters: Martha Brookes Hutcheson," typescript, nd., Hutcheson Collection. This apparently was to be an article in a series. The typescript is heavily annotated by Hutcheson, who crossed out "Native" and put in "Adopted." Another vivid impression of Martha's personality is a poem in the Hutcheson Collection entitled "October 12, 1910," written by Harry Marquand, a close friend. It emphasizes Hutcheson's volubility and includes the lines: "But anybody here seen Matty?/ She'll talk when she is dead."

41. Meade, "Martha Brookes Hutcheson," 181–82.

42. Davidson, *Images and Ideas*, 330.

43. Hutcheson, *The Spirit of the Garden*, 24–25, 88, 160, 161, 204, 206, 207.

44. Hutcheson, Professional Record; Steven Bedford, Entry on John Russell Pope, in MacKay, Baker, and Traynor, eds., *Long Island Country Houses*, 359.

45. Hutcheson, Professional Record.

46. In a later publication, this smaller garden is called the "Italian garden." See Augusta Owen Patterson, "Mrs. Robert Bacon's Westbury Garden," *Town and Country* (August 1926), 44–47. See also *Famous Gardens Selected from Country Life* (New York: Country Life—American Home Corporation, 1937): 68, top. The other gardens illustrated on the Bacon property do not appear to be Hutcheson's work.

47. This garden is also illustrated in Hicks Nurseries, "Home Landscaping," 1924, 30.

48. Aerial photograph in Hicks Nurseries, "Home Landscaping," 1924, 3. Numerous watercolors of the Bacon property by Amy Cross illustrate this and other Hicks catalogues. It is impossible to tell whether these show Hutcheson's work. These gardens are also described in the Patterson article and, by 1926, included a children's garden on one path and a wild garden along another. For the Bacon property in 1931, see *Bulletin of the Garden Club of America*, July 1931, 47–48.

49. Ibid.

50. Tankard, *The Gardens of Ellen Biddle Shipman*, 194. The Shipman Collection at Cornell has no plans for the Bacon property, but the Bacons are on Shipman's client list. I am grateful to Ms. Tankard for this information. The photographs in the Patterson article may show some of Shipman's work or possibly work done by Mrs. Bacon on her own.

51. Hutcheson, Professional Record. There are photographs of this property in the Hicks Nurseries Glass Plate Collection, Westbury, Long Island.

52. Ibid.; Pratt family tree provided by SPLIA.

53. Mosette Glaser Broderick, Entry on Babb & Cook, Babb, Cook & Willard, Babb, Cook & Welch, in MacKay, Baker, and Traynor., eds., *Long Island Country Houses*, 59.

54. Hutcheson, Professional Record; Pratt Family Tree.

55. Hutcheson, *The Spirit of the Garden*, 40–42; Hutcheson, Professional Record.

56. Hutcheson, Professional Record.

57. *Bulletin of the Garden Club of America*, no. 16, Fourth Series (July, 1931): 35.

58. Hutcheson, *The Spirit of the Garden*, 30–33, 106, 112, 152, 200–201; Inventory of drawings, photographs, and planting lists for the "Pratt Estate" (Job number 3120) kindly provided by the Frederick Law Olmsted National Historic Site, Brookline, Massachusetts. The kinds of plans listed in the inventory seem to indicate that, between 1906 and 1909, Olmsted Brothers prepared the initial layouts for Welwyn, Poplar Hill, and the George Pratt place in Glen Cove. They seem to have also prepared plans for a rose garden for Welwyn. Between 1934 and 1936, Olmsted Brothers also prepared subdivision plans for the entire Pratt compound, including the grounds of a mausoleum. Given the size of the present Welwyn Preserve, it seems unlikely that the subdivision plans were carried out. Olmsted Brothers seems to have done a general layout of the entire Pratt compound.

59. Broderick, Entry on Babb, Cook & Willard, in MacKay, Baker, and Traynor, eds., *Long Island Country Houses*, 61.

60. Hutcheson, Professional Record.

61. Ibid. In connection with the tour in 1931, the Garden Club of America described the situation at Welwyn a little differently. According to this report, only the west garden had been designed by Hutcheson and that, during her illness, Greenleaf installed only the background planting with Mrs. Pratt grouping the trees. Throughout Welwyn, much overall planting was done by Mrs. Pratt. Mr. Pratt also "surveyed the vegetable garden, the greenhouse terrace, and the perennial border." See *Bulletin of the Garden Club of America*, July 1931, 34, 37.

62. Lewis and Valentine Archives, SPLIA. At least one source attributed the garden at Welwyn to both Greenleaf and Hutcheson. See Elsa Rehman, *Garden-Making* (Boston: Houghton Mifflin, 1926): 71. The west garden at Welwyn is illustrated in *Famous Gardens*, 26, top. The other Welwyn gardens illustrated are not Hutcheson's work.

63. Hutcheson, *The Spirit of the Garden*, 31.

64. Ibid., 33.

65. Rena Tucker Kohlman, "Things Old and New in Sun-Dials," *Country Life in America* 45, no. 4 (February 1924): 43.

66. I am grateful to Alexandra Wolfe for this information.

67. Hutcheson, Professional Record; Hutcheson, *The Spirit of the Garden*, 22, 58, 134, 136–37, 220.

68. Hutcheson, The Spirit of the Garden, 220.

69. Anne H. Van Ingen, SPLIA, Building-Structure Inventory Form for the D. D. Lord house, 20 Westover Place, Lawrence, NY, April 17, 1981. Attached to this form is a photocopied detail of the Beers Comstock *Atlas of Long Island*, 1873, which shows the Lord house on extensive acreage but without the artificial pond that Hutcheson wrote had been added in the late 1880s. (Small bodies of water are indicated elsewhere on the map.)

70. Hutcheson in Fowler, "Three Women," 11.

CHAPTER 4
Marian Cruger Coffin 1876–1957

1. Warren Hunting Smith, "Memoir of Marian Coffin," in *Gardens Designed by Marian Cruger, Landscape Architect, 1876–1957, Memorial Exhibition of Photographs of 17 Gardens* (Geneva, New York: 1958, reprint ed., 1983), Courtesy of the Geneva Historical Society, Geneva, New York, 1–2 (hereafter Smith, "Memoir"); Nancy Fleming, *Money, Manure & Maintenance: Ingredients for Successful Gardens of Marian Coffin, Pioneer Landscape Architect, 1876–1957* (Weston, Massachusetts: Coun-

try Place Books, 1995), 8–9. For biographical information about Warren Hunting Smith, see note 19 below.

Other studies of Coffin include Jeanne Marie Teutonico, "Marian Cruger Coffin, The Long Island Estates: A Study of the Early Work of a Pioneering Woman in American Landscape Architecture," submitted in partial fulfillment of the requirements for the degree Master of Science in Historic Preservation, Graduate School of Architecture and Planning, Columbia University, 1983, 27; and Valencia Libby, "Marian Coffin (1876–1957), The Landscape Architect and The Lady" in *The House and Garden* (Roslyn, New York: Nassau County Museum of Fine Arts, 1985): 24.

After the publication of *Money, Manure & Maintenance*, Smith wrote to Fleming informing her that, although Coffin's mother's calling cards were inscribed "Mrs. Julian Ravenel Coffin," her husband's middle name was something much more ordinary like "Ross." (Warren H. Smith to Nancy Fleming, February 23, 1995, in Nancy Fleming, "Update on Information about Marian Coffin," nd.) The Geneva Historical Society, Geneva, New York has a notice of Marian Coffin's father's death that reads: "Coffin—In this city on the 25th instant, in the 38th year of his age, Julian Rose, son of the late Thomas Aston Coffin; of Charleston, S. C. Notice of funeral hereafter." Another notice reads: "Julian R. Coffin died at Mrs. Cruger's May 25, 1883, 5:25 P.M." The sources of these notices are not known.

2. Smith, "Memoir," 1; Fleming, *Money, Manure & Maintenance*, 8.

3. Ibid.; Smith, "Memoir," 2. See also "Pioneer Among Women Landscape Architects," a newspaper clipping on microfilm at the Loeb Library, Harvard Graduate School of Design: VF NAB 205 Cof (source unknown). While this unsigned article contains some interesting information, there are too many obvious errors for it to be considered reliable.

4. Coffin in Fowler, "Three Women," 11.

5. Smith, "Memoir," 3; Fleming, *Money, Manure & Maintenance*, 8–9. A lovely undated photograph of Mrs. Coffin and a teenaged Marian is in the collection of the Geneva Historical Society.

6. Coffin in Fowler, "Three Women," 11.

7. Ibid., 11–12. Coffin's preparatory studies were sufficiently complete and rigorous that she was able to enter the program at MIT as a sophomore. (MIT, Office of the Registrar.) In this case, Marian Coffin's tutoring in mathematics was "remedial."

8. Fleming, *Money, Manure & Maintenance*, 9; Coffin in Fowler, "Three Women," 12; Fleming, "Update." Frances Ropes was born July 23, 1883, the daughter of Willis H. Ropes, 114 Federal Street, Salem, Massachusetts. She prepared at Salem High School. She was admitted to MIT as a regular student and may have studied previously at Radcliffe College or have been admitted to Radcliffe. Ropes received her S.B. from MIT in June 1904. She had a record of predominantly Cs and Ps and her thesis was "A Design for a Marine Park for Salem Neck." There is no indication that she ever practiced. (MIT, Office of the Registrar, Transcript of Frances Ropes.)

9. Coffin in Fowler, "Three Women," 12.

10. Transcript, Marian Cruger Coffin, January 1901 through October 1903, MIT, Office of the Registrar. A list of the courses that Coffin took, with the professors who taught them, may also be found in Teutonico, "Marian Cruger Coffin: The Long Island Estates," 111–12. Although it is not so indicated on the transcript, the courses that Coffin took repeatedly were probably increasingly difficult. It should be noted that, during this period, leaving a college program without a degree did not involve any stigma of "dropping out."

11. Fleming, *Money, Manure & Maintenance*, 12–13.

12. Ibid., 15.

13. Ibid., 20. Coffin received the Gold Medal for the design of the grounds of the Mr. and Mrs. Edgar Bassick property in Bridgeport, Connecticut, and for the Mr. and Mrs. J. Morgan Wing property in Millbrook, New York, as well as for "other distinguished work well known to the members of the Jury." Gold Medal certificate, Collection of the Geneva Historical Society, Geneva, New York.

14. Fleming, *Money, Manure & Maintenance*, 22; Marian Cruger Coffin, "Letter to the Garden Club of America," *Bulletin of the Garden Club of America*, no. 4 (May 1920), 58–59.

15. "Marian C. Coffin, Designed Estates," *New York Times*, Monday, February 4, 1957, p. 19, col. 3; H. B. W., "Marian Cruger Coffin, September 27, 1876–February 2, 1957, A Biographical Minute," *Landscape Architecture* 47 (April 1957), 431–32.

16. Fleming, *Money, Manure & Maintenance*, 58–94, 114–117.

17. Ibid., 20–24.

18. Ibid., 95; Smith, "Memoir," 4–5. According to Smith, at her parties Coffin mixed together students, faculty, old New Haven families, and visiting celebrities. Coffin, a lovely woman, attracted male attention, but her mother once commented that "Marian's beaux are either eighteen or eighty."

19. Warren Hunting Smith received his B.A. from Yale College in 1927 and his Ph.D. in English literature from Yale University in 1931 (Yale University, Registrar's Office). Born in 1905, he died on November 22, 1998. For over fifty years, Smith edited the letters of the English writer Horace Walpole (1717–97) at Yale University's Sterling Library. See Mel Gussow, Obituary, Warren Hunting Smith, *New Haven Register*, November 27, 1998, Courtesy of the Yale University Registrar's Office. Among Walpole's writings was the highly influential *The History of the Modern Taste in Gardening* (New York: Ursus Press, reprint ed. 1995), a classic book on gardening that Coffin must have known.

20. Fleming, *Money, Manure & Maintenance*, 95–97. I am pleased to acknowledge many conversations with Nancy Fleming. Fleming also told me about Coffin's enthusiasm for golf, an interest that, like Farrand, she picked up in Scotland (Fleming, "Update"). Coffin's trip to Scotland took place in 1895.

21. Smith, "Memoir," 6, 8.

22. Clippings from the *New York Herald Tribune*, January (25 or 27), 1942, Artists' Files, Art and Architecture Reading Room, New York Public Library.

23. Fleming, *Money, Manure & Maintenance*, 97–98.

24. Ibid., 99–107.

25. Marian Cruger Coffin, *Trees and Shrubs for Landscape Effects* (New York: Charles Scribner's Sons, 1940).

26. Ibid., 1.

27. Ibid., 156.

28. Smith, "Memoir," 7; Fleming, *Money, Manure & Maintenance*, 23.

29. Smith, "Memoir," 8.

30. Smith, "Memoir," 3. Coffin is not mentioned in any of the biographies of Edith Wharton.

31. Fleming, *Money, Manure & Maintenance*; Marian Cruger Coffin, "Where East Meets West: Visit to Picturesque Dalmatia, Montenegro and Bosnia," *National Geographic Magazine* 19, no. 5 (May 1908), 309–44.

32. Fleming, *Money, Manure & Maintenance*, 95, 97.

33. Ibid., 107.

34. Smith, "Memoir," 9.

35. Ibid., 108; Warren Hunting Smith to Nancy Fleming, February 28, 1995, in Fleming, "Update." Smith was present at the burial.

36. Warren H. Smith to Nancy Fleming, February 28, 1995, in Fleming, "Update."

37. Fleming, *Money, Manure & Maintenance*, 40, 108. The manuscript of *Seeing Eye* was sent to many publishers but was considered impractical for postwar home gardeners without staff.

38. Marian Cruger Coffin, "A Suburban Garden Six Years Old," *Country Life in America* 21, no. 8 (February 15, 1912), 19–22, 64, 66–67, photographs by W. H. Wallace. The Sprague

garden was also illustrated in Ruth Dean, *The Livable House: Its Garden* (New York: Moffat Yard, 1917), 72, 75, and in Elsa Rehmann, *The Small Place: Its Landscape Architecture* (New York and London: G. P. Putnam's Sons, 1918), 107–17.

39. Guy Lowell, *American Gardens* (Boston: Bates and Guild, 1902).

40. Coffin, "A Suburban Garden Six Years Old," 19–21. A rear lot earmarked for a later building site was left unimproved.

41. Ibid., 22, 64, 66; Dean, *The Livable House: Its Garden*, 72; Rehmann, *The Small Place*, 107–17.

42. Rehman, *The Small Place*, xi.

43. Clay Lancaster, Robert A. M. Stern, and Robert Hefner, *East Hampton's Heritage* (East Hampton, New York: Ladies' Village Improvement Society, 1996), 112–13, 192. The photograph on page 112 was taken by Samuel Gottscho, apparently in 1916, and credited to Gottscho-Schleisner. This collection was broken up within the past ten years or so and given to three or possibly four institutions. The Library of Congress, Prints and Photographs Division has two registers of Gottscho's negatives. These registers show that Gottscho made five negatives of the William H. Woodin property on July 9, 1927. The Library of Congress does not have these negatives or prints from them (Gottscho negatives numbered 7501–7505), and I have not been able to locate the original of the photograph located on page 112 of *East Hampton's Heritage*, which I have illustrated as Figure 4.5. (Library of Congress, Prints and Photographs Division, e-mail to author, March 16, 2006).

44. Augusta Owen Patterson, *American Homes of Today* (New York: The MacMillan Company Publishers, 1924), 231, 237, 342; P. H. Elwood, *American Landscape Architecture* (New York: Architectural Book Publishing, 1924), np; Teutonico, "Marian Cruger Coffin," 54–66; Michael Adams, Entry on Cross & Cross, in MacKay, Baker, and Traynor, eds., *Long Island Country Houses*, 124.

The Sabin property was also published in Geoffrey Holme, ed., *The Studio Year-Book of Decorative Art* (Leicester: the Studio, Ltd., 1922), 166–67. There is also a postcard of it in the East Hampton Public Library.

45. Eugene Clute, "Relating the House to the Landscape," *Country Life in America* 60, no. 6 (April 1927), 42–43.

46. Rena Tucker Kohlman, "Things Old and New in Sun-Dials," *Country Life in America* 40, no. 4 (February 1924): 42.

47. Smith, "Memoir," 10.

48. Fleming, *Money, Manure & Maintenance*, 35–36.

49. Teutonico, "Marian Cruger Coffin: The Long Island Estates," 61–63, figs. 23–40.

50. This new golf course is covered voluminously on the Internet. See especially libizblog.wordpress.com/2007/12/07/. The course recycles rain water and is otherwise environmentally friendly.

51. Elsa Rehmann, "Engaging a Landscape Architect," *House and Garden* 38, no. 4 (October 1920), 40, 78, 82, 84. Except for the illustrations, there is little in this article specifically about the Alexandre garden.

52. Ibid., Caption to photograph on page 82.

53. Fleming, *Money, Manure & Maintenance*, 21–22.

54. I have written about the overall planning of Caumsett and about the role of Olmsted Brothers there in my entry on the Olmsted firm in MacKay, Baker, and Traynor, eds., *Long Island Country Houses*, 328–30.

55. Daniel P. Higgins, "Business and Management in the Practice of Architecture: Their Application in Coordinating Office and Field Forces in the Development of the Estate of Mrs. Marshall Field," *The American Architect* 133, no. 2543 (April 20, 1928): 502. The entire issue is devoted to the Field property.

56. Olmsted Brothers to John Russell Pope, October 2, 1924, Olmsted Associates Records, Job #7359, Manuscript Division, Library of Congress, Washington, DC.

57. Lisa Sclare and Donald Sclare, *Beaux-Arts Estates: A Guide to the Architecture of Long Island* (New York: Viking Press, 1980): 138; Teutonico, "Marian Cruger Coffin: The Long Island Estates," 67–88.

58. Sclare and Sclare, *Beaux-Arts Estates*, 138.

59. "The Gardens of Edward F. Hutton, Roslyn, New York, Marian C. Coffin, Landscape Architect," *House and Garden* 45, no. 5 (May 1924), 82–83. This article has pictures only, with no text except for the captions.

60. Much of the information about the Hutton gardens given here comes from Coffin's captions on her photographs at Winterthur.

61. Smith, "Memoir," 9. Coffin probably meant "shadeloving."

62. Leon Henry Zach, "Texture in the Garden," *Landscape Architecture* 28, no. 3 (April 1938): 156; Hugh Findlay, "Trees," *Country Life in America* 64, no. 4 (August 1933): 36.

63. Agents for the En-Tout-Cas Company, "The Problem of Placing The Tennis Court: A Bird's-Eye View of Six Successful Solutions," *Country Life in America* 58, no. 3 (July 1928): 38, Photographs Courtesy of H. A. Robinson, Co., Inc.; Advertisement for En-Tout-Cas in American Society of Landscape Architects, *Work of Members*, 1933, 159.

64. The aerial photograph of the Hutton property that illustrates "The Problem of Placing The Tennis Court" cited in the previous note seems to show a small open space above (to the east) of the tennis court but nothing that looks at all like a topiary garden. The space is encircled by a thick belt of trees.

65. For the condition of the Hutton landscape in 1983, see Teutonico, "Marian Cruger Coffin: The Long Island Estates," 78–82.

66. Information from Ken Mensing, LIU, December 2007.

67. The first Boardman house in Southampton is illustrated in *Architectural Record* 40, no. iii (September 1916), 266–71. See also Carol A. Traynor, Entry on Hill and Stout, in MacKay, Baker, and Traynor, eds., *Long Island Country Houses*, 209, 486. I am also grateful to SPLIA for more information on Polhemus and Coffin, including Polhemus's obituary: "Henry M. Polhemus, Retired Architect," *New York Times*, December 23, 1970. The architect Coffin does not appear to be related to Marian Coffin.

68. Fleming, *Money, Manure & Maintenance*, 22. Cites Coffin to du Pont, December 17, 1925, Winterthur.

69. Ibid., 36–37; Teutonico, "Marian Cruger Coffin, The Long Island Estates," 89–104; Valencia Libby, "The Formal Garden at Clayton" in *The House and The Garden* (Roslyn, New York: Nassau County Museum of Fine Arts, 1985): 31.

70. For the landscape of Clayton before the Coffin interventions, see William H. Browne, C.E., "Topographical Map of Property belonging to Frick Estate at North Roslyn," April 1919, illustrated in Teutonico, "Marian Cruger Coffin: The Long Island Estates," Chapter 5, fig. 6.

71. Libby, "The Formal Garden at Clayton," 31.

72. Ibid., 31–33; "A Georgian Garden Near New York," *Architecture* 65, no. 4 (April 1932): 210. (The second citation consists of a photograph only, no text.)

73. Teutonico, "Marian Cruger Coffin: The Long Island Estates," 96–99.

74. Libby, "The Formal Garden at Clayton," 33.

75. Charles E. Beveridge and Carolyn F. Hoffman, *The Master List of Design Projects of the Olmsted Firm, 1857–1950* (Boston: National Association for Olmsted Parks, in conjunction with the Massachusetts Association for Olmsted Parks, 1987): 116. American Society of Landscape Architects, New York Chapter, *Yearbook and Eighth Annual Exhibition*, 1931. Irving Brokaw was a figure skater who also wrote an influential book on skating.

76. American Society of Landscape Architects, New York Chapter, *Yearbook and Seventh Annual Exhibition*, 1930.

77. American Society of Landscape Architects, New York Chapter, *Yearbook and Eighth Annual Exhibition*, 1931.

78. Coffin in Fowler, "Three Women," 12.

CHAPTER 5
Ellen Biddle Shipman 1869–1950

1. Tankard, *The Gardens of Ellen Biddle Shipman*, 5, 9.

2. Ibid., 6–7.

3. Ellen Shipman, Garden Note Book, nd (assembled c. 1945), np, Ellen Shipman Collection, Rare and Manuscript Collections, Carl A. Kroch Library, Cornell University, Ithaca, New York (hereafter Cornell).

4. Tankard, *The Gardens of Ellen Biddle Shipman*, 6–7.

5. Shipman, Garden Note Book, Cornell.

6. Ibid.

7. Tankard, *The Gardens of Ellen Biddle Shipman*, 7. There is no information about whether she made a social debut.

8. Helen Lefkowitz Horowitz, *Alma Mater*, 95.

9. Tankard, *The Gardens of Ellen Biddle Shipman*, 7–8; Transcript of Ellen McGowan Biddle, 1892–93, Radcliffe College Archives, Schlesinger Library, Radcliffe Institute for Independent Study, Cambridge, Massachusetts. The fall-term half of the course that Shipman completed was taught by Dr. Herbert Nichols and stressed psychology (then still taught in the philosophy department) and logic.

10. Tankard, *The Gardens of Ellen Biddle Shipman*, 9.

11. Ibid., 11–16; Alma M. Gilbert and Judith B. Tankard, *A Place of Beauty: The Artists and Gardens of the Cornish Colony* (Berkeley and Toronto: Ten Speed Press, 2000); Susan Faxon Olney et al., *A Circle of Friends: Art Colonies of Cornish and Dublin* (Durham, New Hampshire: University Art Galleries, University of New Hampshire, 1985); Marion Pressley and Cynthia Zaitzevsky, *Cultural Landscape Report for the Augustus Saint-Gaudens National Historic Site* (Boston: National Park Service, 1993); and William Noble, "Northcote: An Artist's New Hampshire Garden," Journal of the New England Garden History Society 2 (1992), 1–9.

12. Tankard, *The Gardens of Ellen Biddle Shipman*, 12, 26; Ellen Shipman, "How I Teach My Own Children," *Ladies Home Journal* 28, no. 14 (September 1911): 60. There is another article by Ellen Shipman in this issue: "Window Gardens for Little Money," 30.

13. Shipman, Garden Note Book, Cornell; Tankard, *The Gardens of Ellen Biddle Shipman*, 18–21.

14. Shipman, Garden Note Book, Cornell.

15. Tankard, *The Gardens of Ellen Biddle Shipman*, 18–21, 26–35.

16. Tankard, *The Gardens of Ellen Biddle Shipman*, 2, 28, n. 38, 205. Cites Ellen Shipman to Gertrude Eisendrath Kuh, c. 1942, quoted in Mary Elizabeth Fitzsimons, "Outdoor Architecture for the Midwest: The Modern Residential Landscapes of Gertrude Eisendrath Kuh, 1935–1977," M.L.A. Thesis, University of Minnesota, January 1994, 18.

17. Tankard, *The Gardens of Ellen Biddle Shipman*, 29–46; Keith N. Morgan, *Charles A. Platt: The Artist as Architect* (Cambridge and New York: MIT Press/Architectural History Foundation, 1985), 75, 203.

18. Tankard, 47, cites Shipman, *Garden Note Book* (a section that is not at Cornell but in a private collection).

19. Ibid., 53; Shipman, Garden Note Book, Design Chapter, 2, 7 (private collection).

20. Ibid., 53, 56.

21. Ibid., 57–61.

22. Ibid., 28.

23. Ibid., 73–74.

24. Ibid., 74–76.

25. Judith S. Hull, Guest Curator, *A Century of Women Landscape Architects and Gardeners in Pittsburgh* (Pittsburgh, Pennsylvania: The Heinz Architectural Center and the Carnegie Museum of Art, Pittsburgh, 1996), 9–11, 16–17.

26. Shipman, Garden Note Book, Cornell.

27. Tankard, *The Gardens of Ellen Biddle Shipman*, 77–78.

Shipman generally sent former employees on their way with her blessing when they left to start their own offices, but in 1945, she interpreted the departure of Frances McCormic, long-term office head, chief draftswoman, and modelmaker, as desertion. McCormic won a prize in 1926 for modelmaking at the Lowthorpe School but interrupted her studies after Shipman made her a job offer. Most of the women went on to have highly successful independent careers, including Agnes Selkirk Clark, who was particularly active in the town of Fairfield, Connecticut, where she lived, and surrounding towns. She often worked with her husband, an architect. (Finding Aid to the Landscape Architecture Collection of the Fairfield Historical Society.)

28. Elsa Rehmann, "Engaging a Landscape Architect," *House and Garden* 38, no. 4 (October 1920), 40, 78, 82, 84.

29. Tankard, *The Gardens of Ellen Biddle Shipman*, 78–80.

30. Ibid., 87–108; "Mrs. Robert Brewster's Garden at Mt. Kisco, New York, Designed by Ellen Shipman," *The Garden Magazine* 38, no. 10 (October 1923), 92–93; "Two Gardens at Mount Kisco, New York, Ellen Shipman, Landscape Architect," *House Beautiful* 50, no. 11 (March 1924): 256. Ethel B. Power, "A Blue-Ribbon Garden: The Garden of Ms. Holden McGinley," *House Beautiful* 73, no. 2 (March 1933): 88.

31. Tankard, *Gardens of Ellen Biddle Shipman*, 116–18; 183–88. The English garden was restored about ten years ago.

32. Warren Manning to Frank and Gertrude Seiberling, 1928, Archives, Stan Hywet Hall, Akron, Ohio.

33. Tankard, *The Gardens of Ellen Biddle Shipman*, 129–31, 160–66. Hurricane Katrina caused significant damage to Longue Vue in 2005.

34. Ibid., 153–56.

35. Ibid., 176–77.

36. "Mrs. Ellen Shipman, Famous Landscape Architect, Thrills Hearers," *Winston-Salem Journal*, October 8, 1932, 7, cols. 1 and 2.

37. Tankard, *The Gardens of Ellen Biddle Shipman*, 155–56.

38. Some other sections of the Garden Note Book, such as those quoted in notes 20 and 21, survive either at the Saint-Gaudens National Historic Site, Cornish, New Hampshire or were discovered by Judith B. Tankard in 1994 and remain in private hands. See Tankard, *The Gardens of Ellen Biddle Shipman*, 176, note 5, page 212. Tankard is preparing all surviving sections of the Garden Note Book for publication.

39. Ibid., 175–76.

40. Ibid., 177–79.

41. Ibid., 181.

42. Ibid., 189, 213.

43. All references to the holdings at Cornell are excerpted from a catalogue of the Shipman Collection, Cornell.

44. Ibid. A beautiful aerial view of The Braes by Aiglon Aerial Photos is illustrated in Philip H. Elwood, Jr., *American Landscape Architecture* (New York: Architectural Book Publishing, 1924), nd. The landscaping that appears in this aerial seems to be by Greenleaf. For The Braes, see also *Bulletin of the Garden Club of America*, no. 16, Fourth Series (July, 1931): 35.

45. Tankard, *The Gardens of Ellen Biddle Shipman*, 67–69. It is possible that Miss Fish was a relative of Shipman's mother.

46. Jeanne Marie Teutonico, Entry on Ellen Biddle Shipman, in MacKay, Baker, and Traynor, eds., Long Island Country Houses, 386–87. In 1921, Mrs. Hare invited Paramount Pictures to perform "Peter Ibbetson" in her garden for the Film Mutual Benefit to aid the American Committee for Devastated France. See "The Garden of Mrs. Meredith Hare at Pidgeon Hill, Huntington, L.I.," *The Garden Magazine* (January 1922): 241.

47. *Bulletin of the Garden Club of America*, July, 1931, 43.

48. Ibid., 39; "C. Oliver Iselin, Noted Banker, Dead," *New York Times*, January 2, 1932 (Courtesy SPLIA); Gay Wagner, SPLIA, Building-Structure Inventory Form, C. Oliver Iselin estate, Oyster Bay, January 1981 (Courtesy SPLIA); and MacKay, Baker, and Traynor, eds., Long Island Country Houses, 504, 508.

49. Tankard, *The Gardens of Ellen Biddle Shipman*, 70–72; "The Garden in Good Taste: Miss Mary Pruyn, East Hampton, Long Island," *House Beautiful* 40, no. 11 (March 1924), 236, 253–54. An obituary for Mary Pruyn was published in the *East Hampton Star* on December 23, 1943; one for Neltje Pruyn appeared in the same paper on June 16, 1949. A third sister, or at least a relative, may have been Mrs. Marshall Field III, whose maiden name was Ruth Pruyn. See MacKay, Baker, and Traynor, eds., *Long Island Country Houses*, 497. The family was of Dutch origin and leading citizens of Albany, New York. In 1881–82, H. H. Richardson designed a monument for Robert Hewson Pruyn in Albany Rural Cemetery. See Jeffrey Karl Ochsner, *H. H. Richardson: Complete Architectural Work* (Cambridge, Massachusetts: The MIT Press, 1982): 266.

50. Fletcher Steele, ed., *House Beautiful Gardening Manual* (Boston: *Atlantic Monthly*, 1926): 10.

51. Tankard, *The Gardens of Ellen Biddle Shipman*, 95, 111; "The Garden of A. L. Kramer, Esq., Westbury, Long Island," *House Beautiful* 40, no. 1 (March 1924): 255; "Garden of Mrs. A. L. Kramer at Westbury, L.I.," *Garden Magazine* 39, no. (April 1924), 128–29; Mary P. Cunningham, "Design in Planting," *House Beautiful*, 56 (October 1924): 325.

52. Monica Randall, *The Mansions of Long Island's Gold Coast* (New York: Rizzoli, 1984), 94–96; MacKay, Baker, and Traynor, eds., *Long Island Country Houses*, 507.

53. *Garden Magazine & Home Builder*, 40 (October 1924): 91. Shipman's first plan for Gossler's grounds in New Canaan was not a success, but her second, executed scheme, which was considerably simpler, was a fine achievement.

54. "House of Philip Gossler, Wheatley Hills, Long Island," *Architecture* 56, no. 6 (December 1926), 383–88; Steven Bedford, Entry on John Russell Pope, and Teutonico, Entry on Ellen Shipman, in MacKay, Baker, and Traynor, eds., *Long Island Country Houses*, 359–60, 388; Sclare and Sclare, *Beaux-Arts Estates*, 144–47.

55. Sclare and Sclare, *Beaux-Arts Estates*, 144, 147; MacKay, Baker, and Traynor, *Long Island Country Houses*, 519. Long Island University has put the restoration of the Gossler landscape on hold for the time being. (Ken Mensing, of e-mail to author, January 24, 2008.) In 1942, Shipman was asked to do some design work for Mr. and Mrs. E. F. Hutton in Westbury (not Wheatley Hills). It is unclear whether this was the former Gossler place or yet another E. F. Hutton residence. There are drawings for this project at Cornell.

56. "Rynwood, House of Samuel A. Salvage, Esq., Glen Head, New York," *Architectural Forum* 53, no. 1 (July 1930), 51–85; *Famous Gardens*, 89; Anna Lee Spiro, Entry on Roger H. Bullard, in MacKay, Baker, and Traynor, eds., *Long Island Country Houses*, 87, 91–92. In 1922, Bullard designed the Maidstone Club in East Hampton, apparently with Shipman's assistance, but there are no plans or photographs for this project at Cornell, so this attribution cannot be confirmed. See Clay Lancaster and Robert A. M. Stern, *East Hampton's Heritage* (New York: W. W. Norton, 1982), 106–7.

57. Tankard, *The Gardens of Ellen Biddle Shipman*, 132–37; Teutonico, Entry on Ellen Biddle Shipman, in MacKay, Baker, and Traynor, eds., *Long Island Country Houses*, 388–89.

58. "Long Island Shows a Varied Garden," *House and Garden* 70, no. 10 (October 1936): 89.

59. Tankard, *The Gardens of Ellen Biddle Shipman*, 137.

60. Innocenti and Webel, Undated plan for Villa Banfi, Tankard files.

61. Society of Architectural Historians, 2002 Annual Domestic Tour to Long Island. Villa Banfi was visited on October 14, 2002. The approximate date for the Innocenti and Webel plan was provided by a representative of Villa Banfi.

62. Keith N. Morgan, Entry on Charles A. Platt, in MacKay, Baker, and Traynor, eds., *Long Island Country Houses*, 354; Susan C. Faxon, "Forces of Change: The Transformation of the Campus, 1900–1932," in *Academy Hill: The Andover Campus, 1778 to the Present* (Andover, Massachusetts: Phillips Academy and New York: Princeton Architectural Press, 2000), 101–43.

63. Teutonico, Entry on Ellen Biddle Shipman, in MacKay, Baker, and Traynor, eds., *Long Island Country Houses*, 387.

64. MacKay, Baker, and Traynor, eds., *Long Island Country Houses*, 519.

65. Roger H. Bullard, "A House Especially Designed for the Dunes of East Hampton," *Arts and Decoration*, 31, no. 6 (October 1929), 68–70, 112, 170; Lancaster and Stern, East Hampton's Heritage, 105–6.

66. Christopher E. Miele, Entry on Beers and Farley, in MacKay, Baker, and Traynor, eds., *Long Island Country Houses*, 68–70, 509.

67. Catalog of the Shipman collection, Cornell.

68. Morgan, *Charles A. Platt*, 30–35.

69. Shipman, Garden Note Book, Cornell.

CHAPTER 6
Ruth Bramley Dean 1889–1932

1. Information from the 1900 Census for Wilkes-Barre, Pennsylvania, National Archives, Washington, DC. The exact date of Dean's birth is not known. The Federal censuses give only the month of birth, and Luzerne County, of which Wilkes-Barre is the county seat, has no birth records prior to 1893. Dean's three older sisters were Ada B. Dean, born August 1873, an elocutionist; Emma A. Dean, born August 1881; and Martha E. Dean, born October 1884, a student. The Deans lived on Carey Avenue in Wilkes-Barre. I am very grateful to Eve F. W. Linn of Carlisle, Massachusetts, for sharing her information and insights about Dean with me.

Dean's obituaries (see below) also mention a brother, Alexander, who may have been born before Ada left home by 1900. Her obituaries give only the full married names of her sisters, not their first names.

See also Eve F. W. Linn, "Comfortable Haven: The Garden Idyll of Ruth Dean," unpublished paper, January 1993, Courtesy Eve Linn; Eve F. W. Linn, Entry on Ruth Bramley Dean, in Charles A. Birnbaum and Julie K. Fix, eds., *Pioneers of American Landscape Design II: An Annotated Bibliography* (Washington, DC: National Park Service, 1995), 40–44; Eve F. W. Linn, Entry on Ruth Bramley Dean in Charles A. Birnbaum and Robin Karson, eds., *Pioneers of American Landscape Design* (New York: McGraw-Hill, 2000), 79–81; "Mrs. Embury 2d Dies; Landscape Architect," *New York Times*, Friday, May 27, 1932 (Artists' Files, Art and Architecture Reading Room, New York Public Library). An article in the *East Hampton Star*, May 1932, repeats the information in the *Times*. Ruth Dean is buried in Cedar Lawn Cemetery, East Hampton, New York.

2. M. D., "Ruth Dean: A Brief Sketch of Her Life," *Bulletin of the Garden Club of America*, no. 1, Fifth Series (January, 1933): 52. The author of this article was probably Dean's sister Martha. However, at the time of Dean's death, all of her sisters were married, but none to a man whose last name began with "D." Since the census information does not give the maiden name of Dean's mother, it has not been possible to determine who her maternal grandfather was. Dean's mother's place of birth is listed as New York, presumably New York City, which makes the New England connection problematic but not impossible.

3. Ibid.

4. Frances Drewry McMullen, "Ruth Dean, Landscape Architect," *Woman's Journal* 14, no. 6 (June 1929): 25.

5. M. D., "Ruth Dean," 52.

6. Transcript of Ruth Dean, Office of the University Registrar, University of Chicago.

7. M. D., "Ruth Dean," 52; Transcript of Ruth Dean. According to the transcript, the Dean family was living at 34 Carey

Avenue, Wilkes-Barre, presumably the same address as at the time of the 1900 census.

8. Transcript of Ruth Dean. The certificate may have been something like the Associate of Arts degrees given today.

9. M. D., "Ruth Dean," 52; Robert E. Grese, *Jens Jensen: Maker of Natural Parks and Gardens* (Baltimore and London: The Johns Hopkins University Press, 1992): 227.

10. McMullen, "Ruth Dean," 25. According to her sister, Dean spent four years in Chicago, which presumably would have included her study at the University of Chicago, her work with Jensen, and her cartography employment. (M. D., "Ruth Dean," 52.)

11. Ibid.; "Mrs. Embury 20 Dies," *New York Times*, May 27, 1932. It is likely that Embury loaned Dean the money, or at least cosigned a note for her. In 1915, it would have been almost impossible for a woman to get a loan from a bank to start a business. Embury seems to have been a kind and thoughtful "boss" to all of his employees, who included other women after Dean left his office. See Aymar Embury II, Letter to the Editor about "the human element in the architect's office," *Pencil Points* 5, no. 4 (April 1924), 45–46.

12. From a list of Dean's work compiled in Linn, "Comfortable Haven," 43.

13. An extensive list of publications by and about Dean is given in Linn, Entry on Ruth Dean in *Pioneers of American Landscape Design II*, 42–44.

14. Ruth Dean, "Tubs and Gravel," *Country Life in America* 27, no. 1 (January 1915), 39–41; Ruth Dean, "Garden Walls," *Country Life in America* 27, no. 3 (March 1915), 59–61; and Ruth Dean, "Practical Plans for the Home Grounds VI, A Naturalistic Garden," *The Garden Magazine* 22, no. 23 (August 1915): 11. This was one of a series of articles by Dean, each one page long.

15. Aymar Embury II, Introduction to Ruth Dean, *The Livable House: Its Garden*, being Volume 2 of the Livable House Series edited by Aymar Embury II (New York: Moffat Yard and Company, 1917): ix.

16. Ibid., 37, 40, 45, 57, 76, 136, 137, 172; Susan L. Klaus, *A Modern Arcadia: Frederick Law Olmsted, Jr. and the Plan for Forest Hills Gardens* (Amherst, Massachusetts: University of Massachusetts Press, 2001).

17. Dean, The Livable House, Its Garden, 52.

18. Ibid., 84.

19. Ibid., 21, 93, 95, 97.

20. Ibid., 63.

21. Ibid., 96, 100. Shipman's double perennial borders for Julia Fish in Greenport, designed in 1916 and discussed in the previous chapter, were 240 feet long and about 6 ? feet deep (not quite on Jekyll's scale, but close).

22. Ibid.

23. Ibid., 100.

24. Ibid., 134, 151–53, 171; Anna Gilman Hill, *Forty Years of Gardening* (New York: Frederick A. Stokes Company, 1938), 127–37. The Hill garden in East Hampton is sometimes incorrectly attributed to Dean. Mrs. Hill had another property, Niederhurst, at Sneeden's Landing in Palisades, New York on the Hudson River, to which her book is largely devoted. In 1922–23, Marian Coffin revised the grounds at Niederhurst. See Fleming, *Money, Manure & Maintenance*, 115.

25. M. D., "Ruth Dean," 52. Dean apparently served in the Motor Corps of the National League for Woman's Service driving an ambulance, but whether this was in France or in the New York City area is unclear. In an article on the Corps, she describes only the New York City area activities. See Ruth Dean, "The Recognition of Women by the Army," *Country Life* 35, no. 3 (January 1919), 49–51.

26. A vivid evocation of the desolation toward the end and just after World War I, in that part of France north of Paris where Dean might have been working, is given in Edith Whar-

ton, *A Backward Glance* (New York: Charles Scribner's Sons, reprint ed., 1985), 362–63.

27. Linn, "Comfortable Haven," 21.

28. Ibid., 43.

29. "Mrs. Embury 20 Dies," *New York Times*, May 27, 1932. Vincent Astor had a house, Cloverley Manor, in Port Washington, Long Island, designed in 1922 by Delano and Aldrich, but a garden there was designed around 1925 by Annette Hoyt Flanders. See MacKay, Baker, and Traynor, eds., *Long Island Country Houses*, 482. Astor also had a city house at 130 East Eightieth Street designed by Mott Schmidt in 1927–28. This house, now the headquarters of the Junior League of New York, originally had a large garden, but what remains is suggestive of Dean's work. (Site visit by the author, June 22, 2002.) I am grateful to Derek Ostergard of Bard College for this lead.

30. Ruth Dean, "Landscape Architecture on a House Top," *Landscape Architecture* 40, no. 5 (May 1931), 18–20.

31. Peter Kaufman, Entry on Aymar Embury in MacKay, Baker, and Traynor, eds., *Long Island Country Houses*, 155–56.

32. Ibid.

33. Ruth Dean, "Developing a One-Acre Plot," *House and Garden* 56, no. 4 (October 1929), 108–9, 180.

34. McMullen, "Ruth Dean," *The Woman's Journal*, 24–25, 48.

35. The periodical seems to have been in existence under another name for about a dozen years previously.

36. McMullen, "Ruth Dean," 24.

37. Ibid., 25.

38. Ibid.

39. Linn, "Comfortable Haven, 22; Ellen Samuels, "Ruth Dean: How Her Garden Grew," *East Hampton Star* (March 1989), np.

Vera Poggi Breed (1890–1967), a descendant of a British governor of the Bahamas, was born in Elizabeth, New Jersey, and educated in Wales. Upon returning to the United States in the early 1920s, she applied for a job with Ruth Dean, who advised her to take the course in landscape architecture at Massachusetts State College (now the University of Massachusetts, Amherst). After completing the course in 1928–29, she was accepted into Dean's office. In 1931, she married architect Nelson Breed, with whom she frequently collaborated. Plans for fifty-one projects by Vera Poggi Breed have survived, most of them for projects located in Connecticut and New York State. See Donna Caldwell, "Biographical Sketch and List of Commissions," ms., Fairfield Historical Society, Fairfield, Connecticut, 1992. One of her extant projects is a sunken garden (1932) for Cora Weir Burlingham (daughter of American impressionist painter J. Alden Weir), now part of the Weir Farm National Historic Site in Ridgefield and Wilton, Connecticut. This was published in James Marston Fitch and F. F. Rockwell, eds., *Treasury of American Gardens* (New York: Chanticleer Press, 1956), 78, 173. Breed may have designed gardens on Long Island in her independent practice, but none have so far been identified.

40. McMullen, "Ruth Dean," 25.

41. Ibid.

42. Ibid.

43. Ibid., 48. The exclamation point is mine.

44. "Mrs. Embury 20 Dies," *New York Times*, May 27, 1932. At the time of Dean's death, her siblings were a brother Alexander Dean of Pittsburgh; a sister, Mrs. Dean Turpisch of Boston; a second sister, Mrs. George Hemstreet of Hastings-on-Hudson, New York; and a third sister Mrs. George Lownes of Sausalito, California. The first names of the sisters were not given in the obituary and thus cannot be matched up with the information in the 1900 census of Wilkes-Barre. Briefer obituaries appeared in the *New York World Telegram*, May 27, 1932; the *New York Sun*, May 26, 1932; and *Architectural Forum*, July 1932 (clippings in the Artists' Files, Art and Architecture Reading Room, New York Public Library). Because she died suddenly at a relatively young age, it is often assumed that she was stricken by a

heart attack. This cannot be confirmed, because Ruth Dean's death certificate has not been located.

45. Mary Lois Deputy Lamson, Alumnae Notes, Smith College/Cambridge School of Architecture and Landscape Architecture, February 15, 1935, Smith College Archives, Smith College, Northampton, Massachusetts.

46. Linn, "Comfortable Haven," 43. Dean archives have been persistently sought, not only by me but by Linn and other scholars. It is possible that they may yet turn up.

47. Dean, *The Livable House: Its Garden*, 85, 165.

48. "Beachleigh, Great Neck, Long Island, The Home of Mr. G. A. Schieren, Aymar Embury II, Architect, Ruth Dean, Landscape Architect," *Country Life in America* 33, no. 2 (December 1917), 62–63.

49. MacKay, Baker, and Traynor, eds., *Long Island Country Houses*, 522.

50. Dean, *The Livable House: Its Garden*, 53. Records at SPLIA indicate that a house for George Gales was designed about 1927 by Harrie T. Lindeberg in Lattingtown, not Great Neck. No Embury design for Gales is listed. The Lindeberg house must be a different one. See MacKay, Baker, and Traynor, eds., *Long Island Country Houses*, 498.

51. Architectural League of New York, *Yearbook and Thirty-seventh Annual Exhibition*, 1922; American Society of Landscape Architects, New York Chapter, *Yearbook*, 1926; "Mrs. George N. Gales' Long Island Garden," 46.

52. "The Spring Garden at Syosset, Long Island, Home of Mrs. Monroe Douglas Robinson," *The Garden Magazine* 41, no. 1 (March 1925), 46–47.

53. Ibid., 46.

54. Ibid., 47.

55. Astor's house is extant, and I have been told that the site is pretty much intact.

56. "At Harbor Acres: A Private Park for Country Houses, Port Washington, Long Island," undated folder, SPLIA files. Astor may well have lost money on the project, since he would have had to cover Dean's and Embury's design fees. Also, the land on which the houses were built (his land) was apparently thrown in for free.

57. Ibid. Plans and perspectives for two completed houses are shown in this folder. They have 3–4 bedrooms and 2–3 maids' rooms. One has a maids' dining room.

58. "Harbor Acres: The Unusual Country Life Community," undated booklet, SPLIA files. Neither this nor the previously cited publication include an actual subdivision plan. However, an "Amended Map of Property belonging to Vincent Astor, Esq., situated at Port Washington, L.I., New York," dated October 6, 1926, filed November 20, 1926, File No. 620 in the office of the Clerk of Nassau Country is cited in "Certificate of Incorporation and By-Laws of Bathing and Tennis Club," booklet, 15, SPLIA files. This plan was made by William H. Bowne, C.E.

59. Blank Contract of Sale, Harbor Acres Realty Corporation, 3, SPLIA files.

60. I am grateful for this information to Dr. Irmgard Carras, historian and resident of Harbor Acres.

61. I believe that the roads may be seen on Hagstrom, Nassau County Atlas, 1986, Plate 2, coordinates C and 5, just south of the IBM Country Club and north of a large tract of undeveloped land, probably Cloverley Manor.

62. Architectural League of New York, *Annual Exhibition*, 1928, np.; American Society of Landscape Architects, New York Chapter, *Fifth Annual Exhibition*, 1928, np.

63. McMullen, "Ruth Dean," caption to photograph on page 25.

64. *House Beautiful* 78, no. 7 (July 1936), 34–35; "Split Shingles in Early American Type of House, *Arts and Decoration* 36, no. 6 (April 1932): 46. See also MacKay, Baker, and Traynor, eds., *Long Island Country Houses*, 520; and Lancaster and Stern, *East Hampton's Legacy*: 200.

The exterior photograph in the *Arts and Decoration* article and an additional exterior photograph in the Mattie Edwards Hewitt collection at the Long Island Studies Institute show only extensive yew hedges at the front of the house and a few specimen trees at its rear and were obviously taken before the complete landscape design was installed.

65. Samuels, "Ruth Dean: How Her Gardens Grew," np.

66. Lancaster and Stern, *East Hampton's Heritage*, 139; Jeannette Edwards Rattray, *Up and Down Main Street: An Informal History of East Hampton and Its Old Houses* (East Hampton, New York: *East Hampton Star*, 1968), 139–41; Building-Structure Inventory Form, New York State Office of Parks and Recreation, October 23, 1972; Aymar Embury, Plans and Specifications for 223 Main Street, East Hampton, 1929 (The Pennypacker Long Island Collection, East Hampton Public Library).

67. Aymar Embury, quoted in Rattray.

68. "The Charm of Simplicity: The Garden of Mr. and Mrs. Aymar Embury II," *Country Life in America* 61, no. 5 (March 1932), 42–43; Leon Henry Zach, "Texture in the Garden," *Landscape Architecture* 27, no. 3 (April 1938), 154–60; "'Third House' at East Hampton," *Arts and Decoration* 39 no. 4, (May 1933), 44–45.

69. "An Old Long Island Town Gains a Guild Hall Done in Brick," *House and Garden* 61, no. 5 (May 1932), 70–71, with a photograph of Dean on page 33; Lancaster and Stern, *East Hampton's Heritage*, 218; Enez Whipple, *Guild Hall of East Hampton* (New York: Henry N. Abrams, Inc., 1994), 24–25.

70. MacKay, Baker, and Traynor, eds., *Long Island Country Houses*, 516.

71. Beatrice A. Tusiani, "A Complete History of Plandome Manor," Long Island Forum 44, no. 7 (July 1981): 138; Manhasset Chamber of Commerce, *Manhasset: The First 300 Years* (Manhasset, New York: 1980): 39.

72. American Landscape Architect 6, no. 5 (May 1932): cover. The path and beds probably continued symmetrically around the other side of the lawn.

73. Field visit by the author, February 24, 2002.

74. Lancaster and Stern, *East Hampton's Heritage*, 99–100. A plan published by Embury in the February 1913 issue of *The Brickbuilder* shows a conceptual scheme for a terrace with benches and flower beds in the angle between the two wings of the building.

75. M. D., "Ruth Dean," 52.

CHAPTER 7
Annette Hoyt Flanders 1887–1946

1. Ashwell "Annette Hoyt Flanders," 29–30; "Hoyt, Veteran Lawyer, Dies," *Milwaukee Sentinel*, Thursday, July 5, 1934, 1, 3; "Mrs. Hoyt, 86, Artist, is Dead," *Milwaukee Journal*, Wednesday, November 25, 1942, L-2. Mrs. Hoyt's paintings were exhibited in New York, Philadelphia, and Chicago, and one hangs in the building of the Daughters of the American Revolution in Washington, DC. For Mrs. Hoyt, see also an obituary of her daughter Annette in "Noted Garden Creator Dies," *Milwaukee Sentinel*, Saturday, June 8, 1946, T-3. In their last years, Mr. and Mrs. Hoyt lived with their other daughter, Constance Hoyt Powell, first in Stamford, Connecticut, and then in Cleveland Heights, Ohio, where Mrs. Hoyt died.

See also Patricia Louise Filzen, "Garden Designs for the Western Great Lakes Region: Annette Hoyt Flanders and Early Twentieth Century Women Landscape Architects," a thesis submitted in partial fulfillment of the requirements for the degree of Master of Arts (Landscape Architecture) at the University of Wisconsin at Madison, 1988, 45. This outstanding thesis has been a great help to me in this chapter, and I am very grateful to Ms. Filzen for also sharing her thoughts on Flanders with me over the phone.

2. Announcement of Annette Ladd Hoyt's marriage to Roger Yale Flanders in the *Milwaukee Journal*, June 15, 1913, 5, and in the *Smith Alumnae Bulletin*, Smith College Archives. Her sister, Constance, was her maid of honor. The wedding reception was held at The Shelter, the Hoyt summer house in Oconomowoc, Wisconsin, followed by dancing at the Oconomowoc Lake Club. The Milwaukee City Directory for 1914–15 lists Roger Y. Flanders's business address as the Pabst Building and his occupation as a lawyer. There were no children.

3. Anne Petersen, "Women Take Lead in Landscape Art," *New York Times*, Sunday, March 13, 1938, sec. 6, 5.

4. Transcript of Annette Ladd Hoyt and Biographical File on Annette Hoyt Flanders, Smith College Archives. For detailed descriptions of courses, see *The Thirty-third Official Circular, 1906–1907*, Smith College Archives. In lieu of a major, Smith students at this time were required to take related three-hour courses consecutively in their Junior and Senior years. Annette met this requirement in English and Elocution. They were also required to take at least one course in each semester of each of these years that was "distinctively different" from the related courses. Annette met this requirement by taking Economics, Zoology, and Chemistry. Smith College catalogs through 1908–1909 are at clio.fivecolleges.edu/smith/catalogs.

Ashwell in "Annette Hoyt Flanders" writes that Flanders initially wanted to pursue further studies in botany after college, but this seems unlikely since she took only two courses in botany at Smith (although the horticulture course was probably pivotal in drawing her toward her eventual career).

5. The early gardens that Flanders designed as contributions to charity have not been identified. She designed the grounds of the Maryland Avenue School in Milwaukee, but the date of this project or whether it was done pro bono is not known (Filzen, "Garden Designs," 116, 207). The Junior League of Milwaukee was not founded until 1916. Flanders may have either worked with another volunteer group or designed projects for charity on her own initiative.

6. Ashwell, "Annette Hoyt Flanders," 29–30; Transcript of Annette Hoyt Flanders, Office of the Registrar, the University of Illinois, Urbana-Champaign. The University of Illinois credited Annette not only with the courses she took at Smith but with three courses from Lake Forest College: History and Theory of Landscape Architecture; Plants and Planting Design; and Applied Landscape Design. The Lake Forest College Registrar's Office has no record of Annette's attendance there but has suggested that she may have been a student in a special program.

See also "Curriculum in Landscape Gardening," University of Illinois, College of Agriculture, *Handbook*, 1915–16, 185, reproduced in Filzen, "Garden Designs," 63.

The details of Flanders's wartime service are from the Archives of the University of Illinois at Urbana-Champaign. Marquette University has no record of Flanders's attendance, but the Registrar's Office keeps transcripts only of students who studied for degrees.

7. Ashwell, "Annette Hoyt Flanders."

8. Ibid. For Vitale and Geiffert, see Laurie E. Hempton, "Alfred Geiffert, Jr.," and "Ferruccio Vitale" in Birnbaum and Karson, eds., *Pioneers of American Landscape Design*, 132–35, 417–20. For Vitale, see also a monograph by R. Terry Schnadelbach, *Ferruccio Vitale: Landscape Architect of the Country Place Era* (New York: Princeton Architectural Press, 2001).

9. Schnadelbach, *Vitale*, 68–73.

10. Ibid., 163. Specific information about how Vitale and Flanders interacted is lacking, so it is unclear whether he was a mentor or merely an employer.

11. For Vitale's rationalistic design principles, which were related to the French beaux-arts philosophy of design espoused by Guy Lowell in the United States, see Ibid., 28–31. Schnadelbach coined the term *rationale* for the Italian version of this phe-

nomenon. I have chosen instead to use the English word "rationalism." (The Italian word is *razionalismo*.)

12. Ibid., 133. It is possible that Flanders designed projects on her own separately from Vitale, Brinckerhof & Geiffert, but none are known.

13. Personal communication, Terry Schnadelbach to author, April 24, 2002.

14. Filzen, "Garden Designs," 131.

15. Ashwell, "Annette Hoyt Flanders," 30; Annette Hoyt Flanders, "Annette Hoyt Flanders, Landscape Architect, Announces the Opening of an Office at Milwaukee," Milwaukee, 1942. It has been suggested that Flanders's move back to Milwaukee may have been influenced by her mother's illness (although her mother was then living in Cleveland Heights, Ohio) and by the onset of her own final illness. See Filzen, "Garden Designs," 134.

16. "A Plan to Aid Unemployment," *Horticulture* 11, no. 1 (January 1, 1933): 8. Under this unfortunately titled plan, landscape architects offered to give one free day of consultation or supervision to any property owner who would give ten or more unemployed men six days of work between January 1 and March 15, 1933. Obviously, only owners of very large properties could take advantage of this offer, especially during such a chilly time of year.

17. Annette Hoyt Flanders, "Landscape Design," *Bulletin of the Garden Club of America*, no. 8 (March 1938), 20–25.

18. "The Gardener's Calendar for July," *House and Garden* 44, no. 1 (July 1923): 76; "House & Garden's Own Hall of Fame," *House and Garden* 63, no. 6 (June 1933): 50.

19. Ashwell, "Annette Hoyt Flanders," 30. Unfortunately, unlike Dean, no one interviewed her on this occasion.

20. Annette Hoyt Flanders, *An Exhibition of Landscape Architecture* (New York: The Author, 1932), with a Foreword by Richardson Wright; "Landscape Architecture," *Bulletin of the Milwaukee Art Institute* (April 1932): 10.

21. "Finding Aid to the Helen Elise Bullard Papers, 1909–1987," Collection Number: 6501, Division of Rare and Manuscript Collections, Cornell University Library (hereafter Bullard Papers).

22. Leslie Rose Close, Entry on Annette Hoyt Flanders, in MacKay, Baker, and Traynor, eds., *Long Island Country Houses*, 169–70. See also Catherine R. Brown, "Women and the Land: A Biographical Survey of Women Who Have Contributed to Development of Landscape Architecture in the United States," nd, SPLIA Files.

23. Jane Alison Knight, "An Examination of the History of the Lowthorpe School of Landscape Architecture for Women, Groton, Massachusetts," A Thesis Presented to the Faculty of the Graduate School of Cornell University in Partial Fulfillment for the Degree of Master of Landscape Architecture," August 1986, 172, 180. Bell graduated from the Lowthorpe School in 1916, Richardson in 1932.

24. Herbert H. Cutler to Patricia Filzen, January 28, 1987, Annette Hoyt Flanders Papers, Sophia Smith Collection, Smith College, Northampton, Massachusetts (hereafter Flanders Papers).

25. Alice Upham Smith to Natalie B. Alpert, nd and November 4, 1976 (Flanders Papers).

26. Petersen, "Women Take Lead in Landscape Art."

27. Roper, FLO, passim.

28. Flanders, *An Exhibition of Annette Hoyt Flanders*; Annette Hoyt Flanders, "Sculptured Landscapes," *Arts and Decoration* 43, no. 4 (November 1935), 36–37, 52. Drawings for this project and for the Mr. and Mrs. W. Eric Passmore property in Milwaukee are located in the Wisconsin Architecture Archive, Milwaukee.

29. Ashwell, "Annette Hoyt Flanders." The Library of the University of Illinois at Circle Campus, Chicago, Special Collections, has some Flanders correspondence concerning *Good Housekeeping* and also the work at the Century of Progress, the

1933–34 World's Fair in Chicago. Flanders's Classic Modern Garden designed for this exhibition and sponsored by *Good Housekeeping* is illustrated in Architectural League of New York, *Fifty-first Annual Exhibition*, 1937.

30. Ashwell, "Annette Hoyt Flanders," 30.

31. Cutler to Filzen, January 28, 1987 (Flanders Papers).

32. Filzen, "Garden Designs," 108. The articles that Annette Hoyt Flanders published in *Good Housekeeping* (98, nos. 2–5) are "Coming! Design in Small Gardens," (February 1934), 53, 103; "Design in Small Gardens: Properly Planned, a Yard Becomes a Garden," (March 1934), 76–77, 233; "Design in Small Gardens: The Atmosphere of the Garden," (April 1934), 76–77, 244; and "The Value of Vistas in the Small Garden," (May 1934), 76–77, 154, 156. In 1939, Flanders published a garden plan for an imaginary client with an income in the range of ten to twenty thousand dollars. See "*Life* Presents Landscapes and a Garden Calendar for *Life's* House," *Life* 6, no. 12 (March 20, 1939), 24–26. Flanders's garden was a "modern" one, while Marianne Dean, Ruth Dean's niece, published a "traditional" garden. Frank Lloyd Wright was featured in the same article with a swimming pool that he wrote could be turned into a garden.

33. Patricia Filzen, Interview with Ronald Mattox, December 12, 1986 (Flanders Papers).

34. Annette Hoyt Flanders, "Under the Open Sky," *Arts and Decoration* 63, no. 2 (June 1935), 2–5; Annette Hoyt Flanders, "Hawaiian Symphony," *Country Life in America* 68, no. 4 (August 1935), 27–29; and Annette Hoyt Flanders, "Honolulu Garden," *House Beautiful* 77, no. 10 (October 1935), 60–61, 113–15. None of these articles illustrate Flanders's one known Hawaiian garden, that for Mr. and Mrs. Vernon Tenney in Honolulu (Filzen, "Garden Designs," 202).

35. Flanders, *An Exhibition of Landscape Architecture*, 1932.

36. Ashwell, "Annette Hoyt Flanders;" *Bulletin of the Milwaukee Art Institute*, April 1932; Schnadelbach, *Vitale*, 30.

37. Marianne Morgan Henry, Garden Club of Cleveland, "Notes. A Practical Course in Landscape Architecture," *Bulletin of the Garden Club of America*, no. 7, Sixth Series, January, 1938, 124.

38. Ibid., 122–23.

39. Ibid., 123.

40. Ibid.

41. Ibid., 123–25. A photograph of Flanders with a model of a small residential property is found in Petersen, "Women Take Lead in Landscape Art," 5. She seems to have routinely used models, instead of reserving them for unusually complex projects or cases where the client had a particular need for a three-dimensional presentation.

42. Filzen, Interview with Ronald Mattox, December 12, 1986 (Flanders Papers).

43. Annette Hoyt Flanders, "Landscape Design," *Bulletin of the Garden Club of America*, no. 8, Sixth Series, March, 1938, 20–25. In 1933, *Collier's* published an article on Flanders that quoted her at length. Her advice in this article was practical and was not presented abstractly as in the "Landscape Design" article. See Selma Robinson, "From the Ground Up," *Collier's* 91, no. 21 (May 27, 1933), 19, 26.

44. Ibid., 20.

45. Ibid., 21–24. A diagram illustrating this process on page 23.

46. Filzen, "Garden Designs," 136.

47. Schnadelbach, *Vitale*, 28–32.

48. Other people described her as a "prima donna," a difficult person, and someone who didn't like children. (See Filzen, Interview with Mary Kasten, November 18, 1986, Milwaukee, and Filzen, Interview with Mrs. Harriet Philsbury, November 21, 1986, Sister Bay, Wisconsin, Flanders Papers.) Flanders was a good friend of Kasten's mother and often stayed with the family. Still another person remembered her as "beautiful and cordial." (See Jane Silverstein Ries, FASLA, to Patricia Filzen, October 29, 1986, Flanders Papers.) Flanders never had children and apparently had little to do with them. Mrs. Kasten invited Flanders to stay at her home to allow her to catch up on rest and sleep, but the Kasten children frequently woke up the recuperating landscape architect.

49. Filzen, "Garden Designs," 106–7, 110–11.

50. Ashwell, "Annette Hoyt Flanders," 30.

51. Ibid.; "In Memoriam, Annette Hoyt Flanders;" "Noted Garden Creator Dies," *Milwaukee Sentinel*, Saturday, June 8, 1946, T-3; and "Mrs. Flanders is Dead Here," *Milwaukee Journal*, Friday, June 7, 1946, L-1. An additional obituary is "Mrs. Annette Flanders; A Designer of Gardens," *New York Herald Tribune*, Sunday, June 9, 1946, 46, col. 8; this obituary contains some errors. Flanders died from complications of breast cancer, from which she had suffered for four years. (Wisconsin State Board of Health, Bureau of Vital Statistics, Original Certificate of Death, Annette Hoyt Flanders, recorded July 9, 1946.) Funeral services were held at Immanuel Presbyterian Church, and she is buried in the Hoyt family plot in Forest Home Cemetery, Milwaukee.

52. Filzen, "Garden Designs," 199. Unfortunately, it has not been possible to locate any descendants of Flanders's Long Island clients who may have retained plans.

53. Because of Ms. Filzen's wish to have these materials available to scholars, with the help of her friend David Egan of the University of Wisconsin Arboretum, and through the kind intervention of Catha Rambusch and Chris Panos formerly of the Catalog of American Landscape Records, Wave Hill, New York City, this fortunate outcome took place in 2002–3.

54. This also occurred through the intervention of Catha Rambusch.

55. Filzen, "Garden Designs," 200–2.

56. MacKay, Baker, and Traynor, eds., *Long Island Country Houses*, 46, 526.

57. Annette Hoyt Flanders, "The Garden That Has Charm, Vitale, Brinckerhoff & Geiffert, Landscape Architects, Annette Hoyt Flanders, Associated," *Country Life in America* 42, no. 1 (May 1922), 67–69, quotation on page 67; Schnadelbach, *Vitale*, 118–23.

58. Flanders, "The Garden That Has Charm," 67.

59. Ibid.

60. Ibid., 69.

61. Ibid., 68. It is interesting that Shipman used the same altar image (see the quotation that ends chapter 5).

62. Ibid.

63. Annette Hoyt Flanders, "Tulips for the May Garden: A Design in which a Planting Scheme of Tulips is Laid Over the Herbaceous Pattern To Make a Prelude of Pink in Spring," *House and Garden* 44, no. 3 (September 1923), 74–75, 124. Oddly, in this second article, Flanders did not identify either the owner or location of the property.

64. Flanders, "Tulips for the May Garden," 74.

65. Ibid., 75.

66. Schnadelbach, *Vitale*, 119. The Frederick Law Olmsted National Historic Site is closed for construction, and I could not view the plans and planting lists that Olmsted Brothers prepared for Taylor. However, an internet source shows that there were only three plans—a paced survey and two planting plans, and some planting lists for Taylor (Olmsted firm number 7313)—all dated 1924. There are also three pieces of correspondence under the Olmsted Associates Records, Library of Congress, Manuscript Division. See rediscov.com/Olmsted.

67. MacKay, Baker, and Traynor, eds., *Long Island Country Houses*, 526.

68. "A Garden in Brookville, Long Island," *House and Garden* 49, no. 5 (May 1926), 112–13. The same photographs of the Benson garden, but no additional text, are found in Robert S. Lemmon and Richardson Wright, eds., *House and Garden's Second Book of Gardens* (New York: Condé-Nast Publications Inc., 1927), 20–21. The status of the Mrs. Benson Flagg house and garden is not known.

69. Flanders, *An Exhibition of Landscape Architecture*; American Society of Landscape Architects, New York Chapter, *Sixth Annual Exhibition of Work of Members*, 1929; American Society of Landscape Architects, New York Chapter, *Eighth Annual Exhibition of Work of Members*, 1931; "Estate of Mrs. Mortimer E. Barnes, Glen Head, Annette Hoyt Flanders," *American Landscape Architect* 7, no. 1 (October 1932): 2; Ellen Fletcher, Entry on Thomas H. Ellett, in MacKay, Baker, and Traynor, eds., *Long Island Country Houses*, 154–55, 484.

70. Illustrated in a modern 35 mm color slide of a 1930s hand-tinted glass slide, Flanders Papers.

71. "A Little Garden under Big Trees," *House and Garden* 49, no. 6 (June 1926): 198.

72. Wilson, Entry on Delano and Aldrich, in MacKay, Baker, and Traynor, eds., *Long Island Country Houses*, 143.

73. Flanders, *An Exhibition of Landscape Architecture*; Architectural League of New York, *Forty-first Annual Exhibition*, 1925; photographs in the Mattie Edwards Hewitt Collection, Long Island Studies Institute, Hofstra University; "Gardens and Stairways, Mystery and Grace. . . .," *Country Life in America* 62, nos. 4 and 5 (August–September 1932): 34. In 1986, the original pastel of the Astor garden was owned by Mrs. Harriet Philsbury, Sister Bay, Wisconsin, who also owned one of the porcelain models from the 1932 exhibition, and two Flanders dioramas. (Filzen, Interview with Philsbury, November 21, 1986, Flanders Papers.)

74. MacKay, Baker, and Traynor, eds., *Long Island Country Houses*, 482.

75. Gary R. Hilderbrand, ed., *Making a Landscape of Continuity: The Practice of Innocenti & Webel* (Cambridge, Massachusetts: Harvard University Graduate School of Design, 1997). A print of the Innocenti and Webel plan for Sunken Orchard is located in private hands.

76. Wendy Joy Darby, Entry on George B. de Gersdorff, in MacKay, Baker, and Traynor, eds., *Long Island Country Houses*, 125.

77. "Gardens: A Portfolio of Paintings by George Stonehill," *Fortune* 13, no. 2 (August 1933): 70; "Richest U. S. Women," *Fortune* 14, no. 5 (November 1936): 200; Mac Griswold and Eleanor Weller, *The Golden Age of American Gardens: Proud Owners, Private Estates, 1890–1940* (New York: Harry N. Abrams, Inc., 1991), 93, 106–8. Mrs. McCann did not inherit this money until after the death of her mother, which may have been about the time that she bought Sunken Orchard. The fortune was then split between Mrs. McCann, a sister, and a niece.

78. Nancy Curtis and Richard C. Nylander, *Beauport* (Boston: David R. Godine, 1990): 11.

79. Flanders, *An Exhibition of Landscape Architecture*; American Society of Landscape Architects, New York Chapter, *Sixth Annual Exhibition of the Work of Members*, 1929; "Bath House Architecture in Garden Design," *Country Life in America* 13, no. 6 (April 1928): 40; "Gardens on the Estate of Mrs. Charles E. F. McCann, Oyster Bay, N.Y.," *Country Life in America* 14, no. 2 (June 1928), 54–55; *House and Garden* 61, no. 3 (March 1932): 34 (a photograph of a pagoda hood over the front door of the house); Close, Entry on Annette Hoyt Flanders in MacKay, Baker, and Traynor, eds., *Long Island Country Houses*, 169.

80. Flanders, *An Exhibition of Landscape Architecture*; "As Though Direct from France comes this Long Island Garden to take the Year's Gold Medal," *House and Garden* 61, no. 6 (June 1932): 50–51. The French gardens were completed in four months. See "Gardens: A Portfolio," 70. Also see Darby, Entry on George B. de Gersdorff, in Mackay, Baker, and Traynor, eds., *Long Island Country Houses*, 125; field visit by the author, February 23, 2002. The subdivision of the McCann property began as early as 1942, shortly after the death of Mr. and Mrs. McCann. See Arthur W. Leach, Civil Engineer & Surveyor, "Topographical Map of the McCann property in the Inc. Village of Oyster Bay Cove," January 12, 1942 (SPLIA files).

81. Ibid.; Architectural League of New York, *Forty-seventh*
Annual Exhibition, 1932; American Society of Landscape Architects, New York Chapter, *Ninth Annual Exhibition*, 1932. My husband and I attempted to measure the remnants of the French garden in 2002, but there were too many breaks in the dimensions to come up with accurate measurements. The photograph of the knot garden in fig. 7.18 notes that all flowers were white. Darby, Entry of George B. de Gersdorff, in Mackay, Baker, and Traynor, eds., *Long Island Country Houses*, 125; field visit by the author, February 23, 2002.

82. Flanders, *An Exhibition of Landscape Architecture*; American Society of Landscape Architects, New York Chapter, *Seventh Annual Exhibition*, 1930; Architectural League of New York, *Forty-fifth Annual Exhibition*, 1930.

83. Annette Hoyt Flanders, Introduction to "Portfolio of Notable Landscape Architecture in America: 'Ballyshear,' the Estate of Mr. and Mrs. Charles E. Van Vleck, Jr., Southampton, Long Island, New York, Annette Hoyt Flanders, Landscape Architect," *American Landscape Architect* 3, no. 2 (August 1930): 10. This portfolio is heavily illustrated, but there is no plan of the property as a whole.

84. Close, Entry on Annette Hoyt Flanders, in MacKay, Baker, and Traynor, eds., *Long Island Country Houses*, 169–70; Christopher E. Miele, Entry on F. Burrall Hofmann, Ibid., 213; Ibid, 510; "Previews," New York City, nd, courtesy SPLIA.

85. Close, Entry on Annette Hoyt Flanders, in MacKay, Baker, and Traynor, eds., *Long Island Country Houses*, 170; Flanders, *An Exhibition of Landscape Architecture*; American Society of Landscape Architects, New York Chapter, *Eighth Annual Exhibition*, 1931. Helen Elise Bullard worked on this project with Flanders (Bullard Papers).

86. Notation on the envelope of a Mattie Edwards Hewitt photograph, LISI 28434.

87. Colors from notations on the envelope of the Mattie Edwards Hewitt photograph in fig. 7.25. Mr. Kisa was one of several businessmen who, in summer, commuted to their New York City offices via their private yachts. See *Country Life in America*, vol. 42, no. 3 (July 1922): 47. Helen Elise Bullard also worked on the Kiser project, in a supervisory capacity. After receiving her degree from Cornell in 1918, Bullard spent two years as a designer for a Ohio nursery, then spent an additional seven years as a designer for landscape architect Warren Manning in Cambridge, Massachusetts, so she was well prepared to take a position as second-in-command for Flanders. In the Bullard collection at Cornell, there are five pieces of correspondence from Flanders to Bullard, four dating from June and July 1929 and one undated, all relating to the Kiser property or the Simonds property. On June 22, 1929, she wrote to Bullard about the removal of subsoil from the Kiser property. Top soil was also to be delivered from Mr. Frankenback for extending a terrace. The pool that appears in fig. 7.25 was still under construction. Water lilies were about to be delivered for it. In an earlier letter (July 11), of which only the second sheet survives, Flanders directs Bullard to supervise the contractors doing brickwork at the Kaiser place. On July 17, 1927, Flanders instructs Bullard on how to charge and make contracts for new work while Flanders is working on her western projects. She ends this letter by saying: "I hope a whole lot of new work will come in while I am away." This, of course, is about three months from the stock market crash that ushered in the great Depression—which no one had anticipated. The undated memo seems to come from about the same time or even earlier and gives Bullard instruction about three Long Island properties and two others. Dorman, apparently a male employee, is to design and construct the Kiser job. Bullard is to be in charge of the Simonds job herself. The Van Vleck property was apparently under way. The two other projects—Shields and Bernheim—are to be done by Bullard herself, the former with Savage, apparently another male employee. Flanders also wants everyone to learn to use the dictaphone. These letters and memos are a rare example of inter-office communica-

tion that has rarely survived, not only for Flanders's practice but for nearly everyone in this book. They are commonplace in the voluminous correspondence files of the Olmsted firm.

88. Charles Smith, interview and site visit to the Kiser garden with Mac Griswold, November 28, 1987, in Griswold and Weller, *The Golden Age*, 108 and note 32, 364.

89. MacKay, Baker, and Traynor, eds., *Long Island Country Houses*, 507; Flanders, *The Architecture of Annette Hoyt Flanders*; American Society of Landscape Architects, *Eighth Annual Exhibition*, 1931.

90. Flanders, *The Architecture of Annette Hoyt Flanders*, 1932; MacKay, Baker, and Traynor, eds., *Long Island Country Houses*, 508.

91. A map of Valmay, dated December 13, 1935, shows the formal garden at the rear of the house and two other gardens: a formal garden with a sundial in front of the greenhouse and another (probably a kitchen garden) near the cold frames. (Copy, kindness of Joseph Tyree.) The Valentines also had a place in Oconomowoc, Wisconsin and undoubtedly knew Flanders from there. See Filzen, "Garden Designs," 46.

92. Flanders, *An Exhibition of Landscape Architecture*.

93. Ibid.; American Society of Landscape Architects, New York Chapter, *Seventh Annual Exhibition of Work of Members*, 1930; *American Landscape Architect* 4, no. 6 (June 1931), Cover; Zachary Studenroth, Entry on Bradley Delehanty, in MacKay, Baker, and Traynor, eds., *Long Island Country Houses*, 145, 492. In 1933, the house was named "Bride and Groom House of the Year" by *House and Garden*.

94. Flanders, *An Exhibition of Landscape Architecture*.

95. "A House and Garden in Dream and in Reality," *House and Garden* 67, no. 2 (February 1935), 54–55.

96. Ibid. An earlier (c. 1910) house for Arthur N. Peck in Woodmere designed by William Adams is discussed in MacKay, Baker, and Traynor, eds., *Long Island Country Houses*, 516. If this is the same Mrs. Peck, the play lawn would surely have been for her grandchildren.

97. Petersen, "Women Take Lead in Landscape Art," 5; Flanders, "Design in Small Gardens," 76–77, 233.

98. Flanders, "Design in Small Gardens," 76.

99. Since this is a freestanding house, it probably was not in the older part of Forest Hills Gardens, which has mostly row houses, semi-detached houses, and apartment buildings.

100. Flanders, *An Exhibition of Landscape Architecture*; Carol A. Traynor, Entry on Montague Flagg, in MacKay, Baker and Traynor, eds., *Long Island Country Houses*, 168, 497. See also Mardges Bacon, *Ernest Flagg: Beaux-Arts Architect and Urban Reformer* (Cambridge, Massachusetts: MIT Press, 1986), 6–10. No photograph of the Flagg cottage garden has been found.

101. Modern 35 mm color slide from a tinted 1930s glass slide, Flanders Papers.

102. Henry Leuthardt exhibited an "Espalier Garden" in the 1939 World's Fair. A comparison of fig. C.18 with a photograph of the executed garden seems to indicate that Leuthardt used Flanders's design, but she is not credited. See *Gardens on Parade: The Horticultural Exhibition at the New York World's Fair 1939*, Souvenir Book (New York: 1939), 14–15.

103. Royal Cortissoz, quoted in Richardson Wright, "Foreword" to Flanders, *An Exhibition of Landscape Architecture*.

CHAPTER 8
The Second Generation

1. Still another woman was Beatrice Morgan Pruyn Goodrich, who designed the grounds of the George C. Clarke property on Ram Island, Southampton. There are several photographs by Richard Averill Smith of this garden at the Long Island Studies Institute, dated 1935–36. Biographical information about Goodrich has not been located. I am grateful to Joseph Tyree for information about the Clarke property.

2. *Who Was Who in America* 3 (Chicago, Illinois: The A. N. Marquis Co., 1963): 446. The MIT Registrar's Office has no record of Jay's attendance, which probably means she went the tutoring route. Her brother Pierre Jay, a banker, died in 1949. See Bulletin of Yale University, *Obituary Record of Graduates of the Undergraduate Schools Deceased During the Year 1949–1950*, Series 47, no.1 (1 January 1951), 17–18. For his sister, see "Mary Rutherfurd Jay, 81, Landscape Architect, Dies," *New York Herald Tribune*, October 4, 1953, and "Miss Mary R. Jay, Garden Authority," *New York Times*, October 5, 1953 (both in the Artists' Files, Art and Architecture Reading Room, New York Public Library). In 1900, Jay lived with her mother at 29 Waverly Place, New York. See "What is Doing in Society," *New York Times*, Wednesday, January 26, 1900, p. 7. There is a slim chance that descendents of Jay's four nieces (listed in the *Obituary Record*) might have further information about her life and career.

3. "Garden Architecture as a Career," *Christian Science Monitor*, December 30, 1924, Jay Clipping Album No. 3, Reef Point Gardens Collection, Berkeley.

4. Ibid.

5. Ibid.; Mary Rutherfurd Jay Project List, Mary Rutherfurd Jay Collection, Reef Point Gardens Collection, Berkeley.

6. *Who Was Who in America*, 3, 446. Additional information is located in the finding aid to the Jay Collection at Berkeley, which cites the original entry in *Who's Who in America*, 25, 1948/1949.

7. Ibid.

8. Ibid.; *House and Garden*'s Modern House, Francis Keally, Architect, New York, Mary Rutherfurd Jay, Landscape Architect, New York, in Architectural League of New York, *Forty-fifth Annual Exhibition*, 1930.

9. Project List, Mary Rutherfurd Jay, Reef Point Gardens Collection, Berkeley; P. H. Elwood, *American Landscape Architecture* (New York: Architectural Book Publishing, 1924), np. Information on the Reese garden was kindly supplied by Heritage Landscapes, Charlotte, Vermont and Norwalk, Connecticut.

10. Mary Rutherfurd Jay, *The Garden Handbook* (New York and London: Harper & Brothers Publishers, 1931). During the Depression years, Jay also prepared "The Jay Family," a genealogical chart with more than 900 names (1935). (See *Who Was Who in America* 3, 446.)

11. Ibid., 195–251. In many other countries, there is no single "type" of garden but several, depending on period and sometimes on the geographical area of the country.

12. "Mary Rutherfurd Jay, 81, Landscape Architect, Dies," *New York Herald Tribune*, October 4, 1953; *Who Was Who in America* 3, 446. Jay's slides were converted to 35 mm and are in the slide collection, College of Environmental Design, Berkeley (not in the Reef Point Gardens Collection). Jay's scrapbooks documenting her extensive lecture tours are also at Berkeley. These contain correspondence with garden clubs in which, among other things, she asked that a member help with her delineascope (an early form of projector for lantern slides). There are also newspaper notices of her lectures, one of which remarked that she had a speaking voice of "unusual quality." I am grateful to Todd Gustavson, Curator of Technology at Eastman House, Rochester, New York, for information about the delineascope.

13. Mary Rutherfurd Jay Project List, Reef Point Gardens Collection, Berkeley.

14. Jay, *The Garden Handbook*, xiv. Also missing from the Berkeley list are plans for Jay's landscaping for *House and Garden*'s Modern House (1930) cited in Note 5.

15. Information from SPLIA.

16. Jay, *Garden Handbook*, 82–89, 221–22.

17. Mary Rutherfurd Jay Project List, Reef Point Gardens Collection, Berkeley. None of these properties is listed in MacKay, Baker, and Traynor, eds., *Long Island Country Houses*.

18. *Bulletin of the Garden Club of America*, 16, Fourth Series (July 1931): 39. Mrs. Iselin was one of the clients thanked by Jay

for allowing her to photograph (Jay, *Garden Handbook*, xiv), but no garden in the book is identified as Mrs. Iselin's.

19. MacKay, Baker, and Traynor, eds., *Long Island Country Houses*, 505.

20. Jay, *Garden Handbook*, xiv; MacKay, Baker, and Traynor, eds., *Long Island Country Houses*, 516.

21. Jay, *Garden Handbook*, 196–97.

22. Judith B. Tankard, "Rose Standish Nichols, A Proper Bostonian," *Arnoldia* 59, no. 4 (1999–2000), 25–32; Judith B. Tankard, Entry on Rose Standish Nichols, in Charles A. Birnbaum and Robin Karson, eds., *Pioneers of American Landscape Design* (New York: McGraw-Hill, 2000), 262–64; Gilbert and Tankard, *A Place of Beauty*, 88–90.

23. Quoted in George Taloumis, "Rose Standish Nichols: Sixty Years Ago She Organized the Beacon Hill Reading Club (1896)," an article as it appeared in the *Boston Globe*, September 16, 1956, np.

24. Gilbert and Tankard, *A Place of Beauty*, 56–63; Pressley and Zaitzevsky, *Cultural Landscape Report for the Saint-Gaudens National Historic Site*, volume 1. Augusta Saint-Gaudens was Nichols's aunt; Nichols was not related by birth to the sculptor.

25. Quoted in Taloumis, "Rose Standish Nichols."

26. Ibid.

27. Ibid.

28. Ibid.; Office of the Registrar, Massachusetts Institute of Technology, Transcript of Rose Standish Nichols, 1899. Nichols studied at MIT just before the landscape architecture option was introduced.

29. Rose Standish Nichols, *English Pleasure Gardens* (New York: MacMillan, 1902).

30. Guy Lowell, *American Gardens* (Boston: Bates and Guild, 1902); Frances Duncan, "A Cornish Garden," *Country Life in America* 13, no. 5 (March 1908), 507–8; Gilbert and Tankard, *A Place of Beauty*, 90–93.

31. Boston Directory, Boston Business Directory, 1903, 2075. She was also listed the following year but then seemed to drop out of the Business Directory. We know nothing about how Nichols ran her office or who may have worked for her. It should be noted that the editors of the Boston Directory determined the business and professional categories under which people were listed, not the individuals themselves. Also, the Boston Directory included only the people or businesses who chose to be listed; it was not obligatory.

32. Taloumis, "Rose Standish Nichols"; Rose Standish Nichols, "A Newport House and Garden," *House and Garden* VII, no. 4 (April 1905), 188–94; Cynthia Zaitzevsky, Entries on the Miss Ellen Mason Estate, in William H. Jordy and Christopher P. Monkhouse, *Buildings on Paper: Rhode Island Architectural Drawings, 1825–1945* (Providence: 1982), 44–45, 134–35; Jeffrey Karl Ochsner, *H. H. Richardson: Complete Architectural Works* (Cambridge, Massachusetts: MIT Press, 1982): 276. Olmsted Brothers did further design work in 1919. The last entry on the Mason property in *Buildings on Paper*, which was co-authored with William H. Jordy, includes a 1923 account of the grounds, part of which describes the Olmsted Brothers' work, while part describes that of Nichols, which neither Professor Jordy nor I knew about at the time.

33. Nichols Family Papers, State House Library, Boston; and the Nichols-Shurtleff Papers, Schlesinger Library, Radcliffe Institute for Advanced Study, Harvard University, Cambridge, Massachusetts.

34. Rose Standish Nichols, *Spanish and Portuguese Gardens* (Boston: Houghton Mifflin, 1924); Rose Standish Nichols, *Italian Pleasure Gardens* (New York: Dodd, Mead, 1928).

35. Taloumis, "Rose Standish Nichols."

36. Taloumis, "Rose Standish Nichols." Nichols was much better known for her extraprofessional activities than as a landscape architect.

37. Tankard, Entry on Rose Standish Nichols.

38. John P. English, "Charles Blair MacDonald," *Dictionary of American Biography*, Supplement II. New York: Charles Scribner's Sons, 1958, 404–5. English described MacDonald as a man, "who moved, often with hauteur, in the highest financial and social circles. People either respected his dogmatic views or disliked him intensely" (Ibid., 405).

39. "Ballyshear," *Southampton Magazine* (Autumn and Winter, 1913), 28–33; "Mr. C. B. MacDonald's Home, Southampton, L.I.," in Samuel Howe, *American Country Houses of Today* (New York: The Architectural Book Publishing Company, 1915), 184–191; Christopher E. Miele, Entry on F. Burrall Hoffman, in MacKay, Baker and Traynor, eds., *Long Island Country Houses*, 213; Tankard, "Rose Standish Nichols, A Proper Bostonian," 29.

40. "Ballyshear," *Southampton Magazine*, 29; "Mr. Macdonald's Home," 191. The cryptomeria can be seen in "Portfolio of Notable Landscape Architecture in America: 'Ballyshear,' the Estate of Mr. and Mrs. Charles E. Van Vleck, Jr., L.I., NY," *American Landscape Architect* 3, no. 2 (August 1930): 17. They are also visible in Figure 7.19 in this book.

41. Elizabeth Igleheart, "Louise Payson, 1894–1977," *A Biographical Dictionary of Architects in Maine*, 7, 1995, np.

42. Ibid.

43. Ibid.; Jane Alison Knight, "An Examination of the History of the Lowthorpe School of Landscape Architecture for Women, Groton, Massachusetts, 1901–1945," (MLA thesis, Cornell University, 1986): 174.

44. Igleheart, "Payson." Cites a diary entry by Payson. Columbia appears to have no record of Payson's attendance. Again, she may have been a tutee rather than an enrolled student.

45. *Pencil Points* III, no. 3 (March 1922): 12.

46. Igleheart, "Payson."

47. Ibid.

48. "House & Garden's Own Hall of Fame," *House and Garden* 68, no. 6 (June 1933): 50.

49. Igleheart, "Payson." Cites an interview with Royce O'Donal.

50. Igleheart, "Payson."

51. Payson Collection, Special Collections, the University of Maine, Orono.

52. Information from Elizabeth Igleheart.

53. Igleheart, "Payson."

54. Ibid.

55. MacKay, Baker, and Traynor, eds., *Long Island Country Houses*, 515.

56. American Society of Landscape Architects, New York Chapter, *Work of Members*, 1934, np.

57. MacKay, Baker, and Traynor, eds., *Long Island Country Houses*, 506.

58. "Marjorie Sewell," in "New York Chapter," *Landscape Architecture* 45, no. 1 (October 1954): 40; Nell Walker, Entry on Marjorie Sewell Cautley, in Birnbaum and Karson, eds., *Pioneers*, 47–49; Cautley family, courtesy of Nell Walker, May 2002; Preface to Marjorie Sewell Cautley, *Garden Design: The Principles of Abstract Design as Applied to Landscape Composition* (New York: Dodd, Mead & Company, 1935): ix. See also Marjorie Sewell, "The Magic of Guam," *Atlantic Monthly* 111, no. 5 (May 1913), 649–52; William Emerson to John Kelly, Philadelphia Housing Authority, May 6, 1943; Genealogy sheet in the Marjorie Sewell Cautley Collection (No. 4908), Rare and Manuscript Collections, Carl A. Kroch Library, Cornell University, Ithaca, New York, hereafter cited as Cautley Collection. Barbara Sewell died in 1938 ("News Bulletin of Sewell and Cautley Families," nd [1938], Cautley Collection). For Helen, see "Helen Moore Sewell (1896–1957)," located at www.ortakales.com/illustrators/Sewell.html.

59. Walker, Entry on Cautley.

60. Ibid.

61. Marjorie Sewell, "A City Garden," *Architecture* 45, no. 4 (April 1922), 124–27.

62. Ibid.; Marjorie Sewell Cautley, "New Houses of Old Flavor," *Country Life in America* 42, nos. 2–6; 43, nos. 1–2 (June–December 1922), 62–63; 58–59, 68–69, 66–67, 70–71, 66–67, 68–69.

63. Cautley family, courtesy Nell Walker.

64. Walker, Entry on Cautley.

65. Patricia Cautley Hill, Early Memories of her Mother (1995), Cautley Collection.

66. Clarence Stein, *Toward New Towns for America*, with an Introduction by Lewis Mumford (Liverpool, England and Chicago, Illinois: The University Press of Liverpool, 1951): 21.

67. Walker, Entry on Cautley. See also Marjorie Sewell Cautley, "Planting at Radburn," *Landscape Architecture* 21, no. 1 (October 1930), 23–29 and Marjorie Sewell Cautley, "Landscaping the Housing Project," *Architecture* 72, no. 4 (October 1935), 182–86. For Sunnyside and Phipps Garden Apartments, Cautley was most likely a subconsultant to Wright and Stein. For Hillside Homes, a PWA project, she was commissioned directly by the federal government. See Cautley to H. A. Stevenson, editor, *Cornell Alumni News*, April 22, 1935, Cautley Papers.

68. American Society of Landscape Architects, *Transactions* III, 1922–26, np.

69. Marjorie S. Cautley, "A Group of Houses Planned and Planted as a Unit," *House Beautiful* 65, no. 1 (January 1929), 68–69.

70. Cautley to H. A. Stevenson, April 22, 1935, Cautley Papers; Walker, Entry on Cautley; Marjorie Sewell Cautley, "New Hampshire's Planned Park Projects," *American City* 49, no. 5 (May 1934), 43–45. For the Civilian Conservation Corps, see Norman T. Newton, *Design on the Land: The Development of Landscape Architecture* (Cambridge, Massachusetts: Harvard University Press, 1971), 576–95.

71. Cautley to H. A. Stevenson, April 22 and May 6, 1935 and lecture brochure, Cautley Collection. Seven lectures are listed and described in the brochure: Garden Design; Color Contrasts and Harmonies; Historical Styles; Planting Problems; Roadside Planting; Recreation in Public Parks and Private Gardens; and Cottage Homes of Scandinavia.

72. Patricia Cautley Hill, Early memories of her mother (1995), Cautley Collection.

73. Hill, Early memories of her mother. Catherine Dodd Cole Church later practiced in the Evanston, Illinois, area and died in 1988 in Kenilworth, Illinois (undated memo, "get obits," Cautley Papers). It is not known when Cole left the firm.

74. Alice Recknagel Ireys, Curriculum vitae, Ireys Papers, Sophia Smith Collection, Smith College, Northampton, Massachusetts.

75. Cautley to H. A. Stevenson, May 6, 1935, Cautley Papers.

76. Marjorie S. Cautley, *Garden Design: The Principles of Abstract Design as Applied to Landscape Composition* (New York: Dodd Mead, 1935).

77. Arthur W. Dow, *Composition* (New York: Baker Taylor Co., 1900, 3rd edition.)

78. Gerald R. Jamieson, M.D., Medical Director, Payne Whitney Psychiatric Clinic, to Helen Sewell, July 23, 1937, Cautley Papers. Her move to the state hospital in Greystone Park, New Jersey is also documented by several letters in the Cautley Papers. Neurasthenia was a diagnosis introduced in 1869 by a Dr. Beard. It was a syndrome of chronic mental and physical weakness and fatigue, thought to be caused by exhaustion of the nervous system. It was sometimes called "Beard's Disease." See *Dorland's Illustrated Medical Dictionary* (Philadelphia, Pennsylvania: W. B. Saunders Co., 1994), 28th edition, 1127. This seems to be an overly benign diagnosis for Cautley's major illness.

Pat Cautley was away at camp when her mother was first institutionalized. She came home to find her mother gone—but no explanation (Hill, Early memories of her mother).

79. Cautley family, courtesy of Nell Walker. Stein suffered from manic depression, now called bipolar disorder, and was no stranger to mental institutions. See Kermit Carlyle Parsons, ed., *The Writings of Clarence S. Stein: Architect of the Planned Community* (Baltimore, Maryland: Johns Hopkins University Press, 1998), xxviii–xxix, 360–361.

80. See note 55, above. Since she was applying for jobs in the public sector as an employee instead of as a consultant, it is understandable that the four-year gap in her work history would have caused concern, although she was apparently open with prospective employers about her hospitalization.

81. Plan in an unidentified newspaper article, Cautley Collection. This was a "proposed" development in wartime, and it is not known if it was ever executed.

82. Walker, Entry on Cautley, Marjorie Sewell, "Rehousing for Fuller Social Life," in "How Blighted Areas in Philadelphia and Boston Might be Transformed," *The American City* LVIII, no. 10 (October 1943), 47–48. During her remission, Cautley lived in New Hope, Pennsylvania, near Philadelphia.

83. Divorce Decree, Pennsylvania, Cautley Collection. The grounds for the divorce were "cruel and barbarous treatment, insults to person, DESERTION [sic]."

84. A. K. Stimson to Pat Cautley (daughter), October 2, [1944], Cautley Collection.

85. The correspondence between 1937 and 1950 in the Cautley Collection documents these moves. In the 1940s, at least two doctors examined Cautley, although neither of them used the term "neurasthenia." Dr. Lerner first saw her in 1945, and his report mentioned paranoia, blunting of affect, and her habit of secreting numerous papers on her person (Joseph Lerner, M.D., to George M. Miller, Esq., January 3, 1945, Cautley Collection). In 1949, she was seen by a Dr. Morton McMichael of Philadelphia, who advised no changes in her treatment unless she were to become "either markedly depressed or definitely agitated," when electroshock treatments might be advisable. See Morton McMichael, M.D. to Mrs. Hill (daughter), March 25, 1949, Cautley Collection. Dr. McMichael's comments seem to describe bipolar illness. To put Cautley's illness and treatments in context, see Gerald N. Grob, *The Mad Among Us: A History of the Care of America's Mentally Ill* (New York: The Free Press, 1994) and Robert Whitaker, *Mad In America* (Cambridge, Massachusetts: Perseus Publishing, 2002).

86. Cautley family, courtesy of Nell Walker.

87. These are located in the Cautley Collection at Cornell.

88. Cornell Alumni Records, Cautley Papers.

89. Genealogical sheet, Cautley Papers. Cautley died of breast cancer or, more likely, its complications (Cautley family, courtesy of Nell Walker).

90. Marjorie Sewell Cautley to Miss Fitzgerald, February 12, 1943, Cautley Collection. Ironically, at some point Randolph Cautley switched careers and became a social worker. (Nell Walker.)

91. Stein, *Toward New Towns*, 22.

92. Ibid., 21–31.

93. Cautley Collection, Box 2, Cornell.

94. Stein, *Toward New Towns*, 31. There were also American elms, which, needless to say, have succumbed to Dutch elm disease.

95. Ibid., 37–44.

96. Ibid., 74–85.

97. Ibid., 87.

98. Ibid., 87–88.

99. The plans were drawn by CDC (Catherine Dodd Cole). They were checked by Cautley (MSC) and approved by Stein (CS), which would seem to imply that, for this job, Cautley was a subconsultant to Stein.

100. Stein, *Toward New Towns*, 87.

101. Cautley Collection, Cornell.

102. Stein, *Toward New Towns*, 108–13. Avery Library has plans for Phipps, Phase I, but blueprints for Phipps, Phase II, are located in the archives of the Phipps Houses Groups, New York City.

103. R. Terry Schnadelbach, "Phipps Apartment Houses, Sunnyside, Queens, New York: The Landscape Architecture of Marjorie Sewell Cautley," Abstract of a presentation at the University of California (www.ced.berkeley.edu/events).

104. I am grateful to Wendy Lanning of the Tenacre Foundation in Princeton, New Jersey for the dates of Pendleton's birth and death. The names of her parents and her younger brother Elliot H. were found in the United States Census for Cincinnati, Ohio, 1910, at the National Archives Center, Waltham, Massachusetts.

105. *Vineyard Gazette* (Edgartown, Massachusetts), Friday, July 13, 1951, *Vineyard Gazette Library*. I am grateful to Eulalie Regan, Librarian, for all of the citations to this publication.

106. Jessie Ash Arndt, "Gardens Don't Just Grow: Miss Pendleton Perfects Her Art," *Christian Science Monitor*, Thursday, August 26, 1954, 10, cols. 1–6.

107. Susan E. Schnare to Judith Tankard, December 12, 1995, Judith Tankard files. I am grateful to Dr. Schnare and Ms. Tankard for sharing their information with me. Dr. Schnare did research in the minutes of the Cincinnati Garden Club.

108. *Christian Science Monitor*, August 26, 1954.

109. Knight, "An Examination of the History of the Lowthorpe School," 173; Schnare to Tankard, December 12, 1995.

110. Schnare to Tankard, December 12, 1995.

111. Isabella Pendleton, "Striking Perennial Combinations," *The Garden Magazine* 32, no. 2 (October 1920), 81–82.

112. Mrs. Frances King, *Pages from A Garden Note-Book* (New York: Charles Scribner's Sons, 1921): 103.

113. *Christian Science Monitor*, August 26, 1954.

114. Griswold and Weller, *The Golden Age*, 102; "The Iris Garden, Estate of Z. G. Simmons, Greenwich, Connecticut, Isabella Pendleton, Landscape Architect, and John C. Wister, L. A., Iris Consultant," *Architectural Record* 74, no. 2 (August 1933), 137–41; Susan E. Schnare and Rudy Favretti, "Gertrude Jekyll's American Gardens," *Garden History* 10, no. 2 (Autumn 1982), 149–67.

115. *Bulletin of the Garden Club of America* 38, no. 4 (July 1950): 117; *Christian Science Monitor*, August 26, 1954. Telephone conversation with William F. Menke, American Society of Landscape Architects, Swarthmore, Pennsylvania, May 29, 2002. I am grateful to Mr. Menke for lending me plans of this project.

116. *Vineyard Gazette*, April 1939; Tankard, *The Gardens of Ellen Biddle Shipman*, 145–47. Mrs. Greenough was a summer resident of West Chop on Martha's Vineyard.

117. Grace Tabor and Isabella Pendleton, "Suggestions for Roadside Planting" (New York: Long Island Chamber of Commerce, nd).

118. *Vineyard Gazette*, March 4, 1960.

119. "Found No Place Even in Europe to Compare with Vineyard in Paintable Features, Says this Artist," *Vineyard Gazette*, 1938.

120. "Death of Dr. Bowen—Vivid Personality will not be Forgotten—Noted as Economist," *Vineyard Gazette*, December 28, 1945. It seems apparent that Pendleton's personality was also vivid.

121. "Her Own Garden is Planned to Illustrate Landscape Gardening's Fundamental Law," *Vineyard Gazette*, July 27, 1937.

122. Ibid. Pendleton's hobbies at this time were swimming, sailing, and knitting. In the summer of 1937, she was knitting a hat, an evening dress, and a lounging robe for her husband!

123. "Death of Dr. Bowen," *Vineyard Gazette*, December 28, 1945; "Ezra Bowen, Artist, Economics Teacher," *New York Times*, December 28, 1945 (Artists' Files, Art and Architecture Reading Room, New York Public Library).

124. "Basic Points in a Successful Garden," *Vineyard Gazette*, April 10, 1954; Isabella Pendleton, "A House and Garden Built in Four Months: Moderate Garden Maintenance a Major Consideration," *Landscape Architecture* 39, no. 3 (April 1949), 117–19.

125. *Vineyard Gazette*, April 9, 1965.

126. Ibid. The exhibition, organized by students in the Landscape Architecture Department of Harvard's Graduate School of Design, and the book that resulted from it were among the first fruits of a renewed interest in Olmsted in the 1960s. See Julius Gy. Fabos, Gordon T. Milde, & V. Michael Weinmayr, *Frederick Law Olmsted, Sr., Founder of Landscape Architecture in America* (Amherst, Massachusetts: University of Massachusetts Press, 1968).

127. *Vineyard Gazette*, July 27, 1937.

128. *Christian Science Monitor*, August 26, 1954.

129. *Vineyard Gazette*, July 27, 1937.

130. *Christian Science Monitor*, August 26, 1954. For Farrand's similar approach, see Dorothy Elmhirst's description of Farrand at work at Dartington Hall, in chapter 2.

131. As told by George Yarwood, who knew Pendleton, to Susan E. Schnare, c. 1981.

132. "Famous for Gardens. Isabella Pendleton Bowen Won Distinction in Landscape Architecture," *Vineyard Gazette*, April 9, 1965.

133. Ibid. At the time of her death, she was a resident of the Tenacre Foundation, a Christian Science nursing facility in Princeton. She had also maintained her residence in New York City and also, despite her "farewell," in Edgartown (Will of Isabella Pendleton Bowen, Dukes County Probate and Family Court, Edgartown, Massachusetts).

134. *Vineyard Gazette*, June 4, 1965. An undated clipping in the library reported that Pendleton's nephew Gilbert MacPherson had won a seat in the Connecticut legislature as a representative from Lyme. This may have been an earlier husband of Martha Hunt Nickerson, who must have been Pendleton's brother's daughter.

135. Architectural League of New York, *Yearbook and Catalogue of the Annual Exhibition*, 1924.

136. The status of the Chubb garden is not known, but it is unlikely to have survived, given that the house and Beatrix Jones's garden are gone.

137. Architectural League of New York, *Yearbook and Annual Exhibition*, 1925.

138. MacKay, Baker, and Traynor, eds., *Long Island Country Houses and Their Architects*, 531.

139. Architectural League of New York, *Yearbook and Annual Exhibition*, 1927.

140. *Christian Science Monitor*, August 26, 1954. There seems to be confusion in this article about the date of the house.

141. Architectural League of New York, *Yearbook and Annual Exhibition*, 1932; *Country Life in America* 60 (May 1931), 47–51, and 64 no. 1 (September 1933): 38; *Residences Designed by Bradley Delehanty* (New York: Architectural Catalogue Co., Inc., 1939); *Bulletin of the Garden Club of America* 16, Fourth Series (July, 1931).

142. MacKay, Baker, and Traynor, eds., *Long Island Country Houses and Their Architects*, 492.

143. *Bulletin of the Garden Club of America*, no. 16 (July, 1931): 35.

144. "June is Iris Time," *Country Life in America* LXII, nos. 2–3 (June–July 1932): 42.

145. MacKay, Baker, and Traynor, eds., *Long Island Country Houses and Their Architects*, 518.

146. *Bulletin of the Garden Club of America*, no. 16 (July 1931): 39.

147. Ibid., 45.

148. MacKay, Baker, and Traynor, eds., *Long Island Country Houses and Their Architects*, 505.

149. Roy Leake, comp., "Memoirs, Correspondence, and Other Documents—Roche, Glorieux, Thierry," typescript, comp. 1987, Roche-Leake family.

150. Knight, "An Examination of the History of the Lowthorpe School," 174.

151. American Society of Landscape Architects, *Transactions* 3, 1922–26, np. Roche does not appear to have ever been a Fellow of the ASLA, although the Knight thesis states that she was.

152. Roche-Leake family.

153. Ibid.

154. Virginia Prince and Eleanor Roche, "El Laberinto: A Spanish Garden in the Neo-Classic Style," *Landscape Architecture* 24, no. 1 (October 1933), 5–15.

155. "A Winter Visit to Mediterranean Gardens," *Landscape Architecture* 24, no. 1 (October 1933): 59.

156. American Society of Landscape Architects, New York Chapter *Yearbook and Catalogue of Ninth Annual Exhibition*, 1932, np; American Society of Landscape Architects, New York Chapter *Illustrations of Work of Members*, 1932, np.

157. *The New York Sun*, Saturday, January 20, 1934 (Artists' Files, Art and Architecture Reading Room, New York Public Library).

158. Roche-Leake family. I do not know which specific Ford properties she may have worked on.

159. "Estate of Jackson A. Dykman, Esq., Glen Cove, L.I.," American Society of Landscape Architects, New York Chapter, *Seventh Annual Exhibition*, 1930, np; Eleanor Roche, "Where Beauty Supplanted the Utilitarian," *American Landscape Architect* 4, no. 3 (March 1931), 14–18.

160. Roche, "Where Beauty Supplanted the Utilitarian," *American Landscape Architect*, (March 1931), 14–18; American Society of Landscape Architects, New York Chapter, *Seventh Annual Exhibition*, 1930, np.

161. Patricia A. Leake (great-niece), e-mail to author, March 28, 2003.

162. Alice Leake (niece), e-mail to author, April 1, 2003.

CHAPTER 9
The Second Generation, II

1. Information from the Indiana University Archives, Bloomington, from the 1920 United States Census for Bemidji, Minnesota, National Archives Center, Waltham, Massachusetts, and from a Funeral Arrangement Data sheet, Burnett & Rockefeller, Red Hook, New York, located at the Gardner Earl Memorial Chapel and Crematorium, Troy, New York. I am grateful to J. Winthrop Aldrich, former Deputy Commissioner for Historic Preservation, State of New York for locating the last document. There is also considerable biographical information on the dust jackets of Lamson's books, *Gardening with Shrubs and Small Flowering Trees* (New York: M. Barrows & Company, 1946) and *Garden Housekeeping* (New York: Oxford Press, 1951).

2. Mary Deputy Lamson, *Gardening with Shrubs and Small Flowering Trees* (New York: M. Barrows & Company, Inc., 1946), 207–208.

3. Ibid., 208.

4. Indiana University Archives. The groundskeepers were William R. Ogg (about 1899–1934) and Milburn Beck (about 1902–50). D. M. Mottier and J. M. Van Hook were the faculty members on the Advisory Committee. Two other faculty members were also actively involved with the grounds: G. J. Pierce and Frank Marion Andrews.

5. The present arboretum at the University dates only from the 1980s.

6. Mary Lois Deputy to the Cambridge School of Architecture and Landscape Architecture, September 22, 1919; Mary Lois Deputy, Application to the Cambridge School of Architecture and Landscape Architecture, for the year 1920–21, both in the Archives of the Cambridge School of Architecture and Landscape Architecture, Sophia Smith Collection, Smith College, Northampton, Massachusetts (hereafter Cambridge School Archives).

7. Indiana University Archives. The personal qualities were: "manners, neatness, speech, principles, sincerity, and sufficient attainment in physical training to have won an I.U. sweater."

8. Mary Lois Deputy to Cambridge School of Architecture and Landscape Architecture, September 22, 1919, Cambridge School Archives.

9. Cambridge School Archives. (Frost was an architect, and it is possible that Mary Lois Deputy told him of her childhood interest in drawing houses.)

10. Indiana University Archives, *Alumni Quarterly*, October 1922, p. 666; April 1923, p. 411. I suspect that her father needed a director of physical education and drafted his daughter. No landscape projects in Bemidji by Deputy have been located thus far. Bemidji was then a logging town taken up in large part by an Indian reservation and seems unlikely to have offered many opportunities for a novice landscape architect.

11. Marriage announcement, November 5, 1926, Cambridge School Archives; Indiana University Archives. The couple lived in Woodside, Long Island for a time after their marriage.

12. Mary Deputy Lamson, Reports to the Cambridge School Alumnae Bulletin, February 15, 1935 and May 1942, Cambridge School Archives.

13. Mary Deputy to Henry A. Frost, February 18, 1935, Cambridge School Archives.

14. Mary Deputy Lamson, Report to the Cambridge School Alumnae Bulletin, February 15, 1935, Cambridge School Archives.

15. Mary Deputy Lamson to Henry A. Frost, February 18, 1935, Cambridge School Archives.

16. Henry Frost to Mary Deputy Lamson, May 17, 1935 and Mary Deputy Lamson to Henry A. Frost, May 21, 1935, Cambridge School Archives; Dorothy May Anderson, *Women, Design and the Cambridge School* (West Lafayette, Indiana: PDA Publishers Corp., 1980): 188.

17. Mary Deputy Lamson, Report to the Cambridge School Alumnae Bulletin, May 1942, Cambridge School Archives.

18. Dustjacket, Lamson, *Gardening with Shrubs*.

19. Margaret Olthof Goldsmith, *Designs for Outdoor Living* (New York: George W. Stewart, Publisher, 1941), 181, 242–43, 269–72; "Helen Hayes Reigns in a Garden," *House and Garden* 72, no. 8 (August 1937), 52–53.

20. Dustjacket, Lamson, *Garden Housekeeping* (1951).

21. Dustjacket, Lamson, *Gardening with Shrubs*.

22. An example is "Summer-Place Gardeners," *House Beautiful* 78, no. 5 (May 1936): 84.

23. *House and Garden* (January 1950), biographical summary in table of contents.

24. Lamson, "Foreword" to *Gardening with Shrubs*, 8. Her three assistants were Barbara Capen (see Preface note 3), Maud Sargent, and Romaine Carpenter.

25. Mary Deputy Lamson, *Gardening with Shrubs and Small Flowering Trees* (New York: M. Barrows and Company, Inc., 1946).

26. Ibid., 120–24.

27. Ibid., 207–12.

28. Ibid., 272.

29. Mary Deputy Lamson, *Garden Housekeeping* (New York: Oxford University Press, 1951): 3.

30. Dutchess County Registry of Deeds, Poughkeepsie, New York. In 1947, prior to the divorce, Lamson transferred full ownership of Briar Patch to Mary Lois. In 1967 and 1968, she sold the property, by then fifty acres, in two separate parcels but remained in a five-room house or apartment in nearby Red Hook. I am grateful to J. Winthrop Aldrich for looking up these deeds. At least one landscape project by Mary Lois after her mar-

riage to Cattell has been identified: the Mrs. H. Donald Baker residence in Greenwich, Connecticut (1954). See Gottscho-Schleisner Collection, American Memory (memory.loc.gov).

31. *Poughkeepsie Journal*, Sunday, December 21, 1969; Records of Gardner Earl Crematory in Troy, New York; Will of Mary Deputy Cattell, March 31, 1969, Dutchess County Registry of Probate, Poughkeepsie, New York. According to records at the crematory, Mary Deputy Cattell died of a coronary thrombosis. Her ashes are interred with those of her parents in Rock City Cemetery, Rhinebeck, New York, a small community cemetery associated with a Lutheran Chapel. Thanks are again due to J. Winthrop Aldrich for locating these records.

32. Mary Deputy Cattell's furniture and household effects were inventoried and assessed shortly after her death. One room served as an office and contained bookcases, a two-drawer filing cabinet, a few tables and chairs, a typewriter, and typing tables, but no drafting table or anyplace where plans could have been stored. Presumably, she got rid of these when she sold Briar Patch, if not earlier. According to the Funeral Arrangement Data sheet (Burnett & Rockefeller, Red Hook, New York), Mary Cattell was retired at the time of her death. (Will of Mary Deputy Cattell, administration.)

33. In "Bits and Pieces," formerly part of the catalog of Landscape Records in the United States, Wave Hill, The Bronx, New York, now in the library of the New York Botanic Garden, Bronx, New York.

34. Mary Deputy Lamson, "Cutting Gardens: How to Design Them for Continuous Yields," *House and Garden* 89, no. 4 (April 1946), 96–97, 161–65.

35. Ibid.

36. Ibid., 97, 161.

37. Ibid., 97.

38. Ibid., 96–97, 165.

39. Van Santvoord Merle-Smith, *The Village of Oyster Bay, its Founding and Growth from 1653 to 1700* (Garden City, New York: privately printed, distributed by Doubleday, 1953). This book, which was published ten years after Merle-Smith's death, was originally his M.A. thesis at Columbia. Merle-Smith was a member of the Seawanhaka Corinthian Yacht Club.

40. I am again grateful to Joseph Tyree for bringing this project to my attention.

41. Federal Census of 1880, Central Township, Franklin County, Missouri, National Archives Center, Waltham, Massachusetts.

42. See www.sos.mo.gov/archives/resources/bdrecords.asp.

43. See users.rcn.com/deeds/homestead.htm.

44. Judith B. Tankard, "Nellie B. Allen (Osborn)," in Birnbaum and Karson, eds., Pioneers, 3–6; Judith B. Tankard, "Nellie Beatrice Allen," in Charles A. Birnbaum and Lisa E. Crowder, eds., *Pioneers of American Landscape Design: An Annotated Bibliography* (Washington, DC.: National Park Service, 1993), 8–9.

45. Ibid.; Judith B. Tankard, "Women Pioneers in Landscape Design," *The Radcliffe Quarterly* (March 1993), 8–10.

46. Ibid.

47. Ibid.

48. "At the League Exhibit in 1938," *Landscape Architecture* 28, no. 4 (July 1938), 171–73.

49. Tankard, "Nellie Beatrice Allen," in Birnbaum and Crowder, eds., *Pioneers*, 9.

50. Tankard, "Women Pioneers in Landscape Design," *The Radcliffe Quarterly* (March 1993), 8–10.

51. Information from Judith B. Tankard.

52. "Mrs. Isabel Dodge Sloane Dead; Owner of the Brookmeade Stable," *New York Times*, March 11, 1962.

53. R. Terry Schnadelbach, *Ferruccio Vitale, Landscape Architect of the Country Place Era* (New York: Princeton Architectural Press, 2001), 132–35.

54. *Gardens and Gardening*, January 1, 1936: 14.

55. Information from Judith B. Tankard.

56. *The Horticultural Exhibition: Gardens on Parade* (New York: New York World's Fair, 1939): 42. No biographical information or other projects are currently known about Constance Boardman.

57. Ibid.

58. Federal Census, 1900 and 1920, for Schuylerville, New York.

59. Lynn Bjorkman and Arnold R. Alanen, "Bullard, Helen Elise," in Candice A. Shoemaker, ed., *Chicago Botanic Gardens Encyclopedia of Gardens, History, and Design* (Chicago and London: Fitzroy, Dearborn and London, Publishers, 2001), 208–9.

60. Transcript, Helen Elise Bullard, Office of the University Registrar, Cornell University. The Helen Elise Bullard Papers, Division of Rare and Manuscript Collections, Carl A. Kroch Library, Cornell University; also her course notebooks (Journals).

61. David Bullard, "Helen Elise Bullard, A Biographical Minute, June 28, 1896–November 4, 1987," unpublished ms., 1987, Bullard Papers.

62. Bjorkman and Alanen, "Bullard," 208.

63. Helen Elise Bullard to Robert Wheelwright (draft), nd (1924), Bullard Papers.

64. Letters from Flanders to Bullard concerning these projects are in the Bullard Papers and are discussed in Chapter 7.

65. Bjorkman and Alanen, "Bullard," 208–9.

66. Bullard Papers, Cornell University.

67. Her transcript was sent to NYU. See Transcript, Helen Elise Bullard, Office of the University Registrar, Cornell University. In 1934, her transcript was sent somewhere else, apparently for an engineering course, but the entry is not entirely legible.

68. Bullard Papers, Cornell University.

69. Ibid. Undated quote from her nephew David Bullard's Memorial Minute.

70. There is considerable Bullard family genealogy on the internet. A photograph of her gravestone may be found at freepages.genealogy.rootsweb.com.

71. Bullard Papers, Cornell University; Jean Lyon, "Leading Women in the Big Performance of Building a World's Fair on Flushing Meadows," *New York Sun*, Tuesday, October 19, 1937, "News of Women": 18; Anne Petersen, "Women Take Lead in Landscape Art," *New York Times*, Sunday, March 13, 1938.

72. Ibid.

73. New York State Office of Mental Health, "Creedmoor Psychiatric Center History." This may be found at www.omh.state.ny.us. Most likely, only male patients worked on the farm.

74. State of New York, Department of Public Works, Division of Architecture and Division of Engineering, "Specification of Labor and Materials Required for Landscape Work, Brooklyn State Hospital, Creedmoor Division, Queens, Long Island, New York," Specification No. 5907, Project No. 2337, March 12, 1930. This specification was made to accompany Plans 435 to 453, but these plans are not in the Bullard Collection at Cornell. "Light" use of Boston ivy is practically impossible, since its growth is very aggressive. Creedmoor still exists primarily as an outpatient facility. Some of the land has been sold off, including thirty-plus acres for three schools and eight-and-a-half acres for a gated, upper-middle-class subdivision. 174 acres of the site still belong to the hospital.

75. State of New York, Department of Public Works, Division of Construction, Department of Mental Hygiene, Specification of Labor and Materials for Infirmary Building, Building No. 95, Central Islip State Hospital, Central Islip, New York. This specification was accompanied by drawings nos. 44-101 and 44-102, which are not included in the Bullard Collection at Cornell. The Central Islip Facility, which was initially also a farm community, was closed in 1996, although some severely dilapidated buildings remain. See www.newsday.com/extras/lihistory.

76. Bullard, "Helen Elise Bullard."

77. Ibid. David Bullard does not explain what these duties consisted of.

78. State of New York, Long Island State Park Commission, Babylon, Long Island, "Contract Documents for Supplying Nursery Stock and Collected Plants at Southern State Parkway near Wantagh," March 1931. (Bullard Collection, Cornell.)

79. State of New York, Long Island State Park Commission, "Contract Documents for Planting Trees, Vines and Shrubs for Southern State Parkway, Nassau County, Long Island," January 1931. (Bullard Collection, Cornell.)

80. Ibid.

81. F. Scott Fitzgerald, *The Great Gatsby* (New York: Collier Books, MacMillan Publishing Company, 1980, first published in 1925): 23.

82. Francis Cormier, "Flushing Meadow Park: The Ultimate Development of the World's Fair Site," *Landscape Architecture* 19, no. 4 (July 1939), 170–71.

83. See Domenico Annese, "Gilmore David Clarke (1892–1982)," in Birnbaum and Karson, eds., *Pioneers of American Landscape Design*, 56–60.

84. David Gelernter, *1939: The Lost World of the Fair* (New York: The Free Press, 1995), passim.

85. A list of objects in an exhibit "Designing Women," New York City Parks Department, 1989, courtesy of Arnold Alanen, University of Wisconsin, Madison. The same exhibition list states that M. Betty Sprout, a New York Parks Department employee, designed gardens at the 1939 World's Fair, but Sprout's gardens are not identified. Alice Orme Smith, a graduate of both Smith College (1911) and the Cambridge School (1911, 1926), also designed gardens at the 1939 World's Fair. See George A. Yarwood "Alice Orme Smith, February 26, 1889–April 4, 1980), Fairfield Historical Society, Summary of Holdings, Fairfield, Connecticut, 5 May 1980.

86. Lyon, "Leading Women."

87. Petersen, "Women Take Lead."

88. Ibid.

89. Helen Elise Bullard, ms. untitled, nd (1949), np, Bullard Collection, Cornell.

90. Ibid.

91. Ibid.

92. Ibid.

93. Ibid.

94. Ibid.

95. New York World's Fair 1939 Incorporated, New York City, "Contract Documents for Tree Planting—Fall 1937 in Section I," Proposal No. 25, Supplement no. 1, June 16, 1937. (Bullard Papers, Cornell.) These documents are not signed but, if not written by Bullard, must have been closely supervised by her.

96. Helen Swift Jones, Transcript, Smith College Archives. See Helen Swift Jones, application to the Cambridge School of Architecture and Landscape Architecture, Sophia Smith Collection, Smith College, Northampton, Massachusetts. At the time of Jones's birth, Brooklyn was still an independent municipality, becoming, along with the rest of King's County, a borough of Greater New York in 1898.

97. Helen Swift Jones, Application to the Cambridge School, Sophia Smith Collection, Smith College.

98. Obituary, *Smith Alumnae Quarterly* (Winter 1983): 66.

99. Anderson, *Cambridge School*, 188.

100. Obituary, *Smith Alumnae Quarterly* (Winter 1983): 66.

101. *New York Times*, Sunday, March 18, 1938.

102. "Helen Swift Jones Landscape Architect, announces the removal of her office from New York City to Stamford, Connecticut." Card, nd, Cambridge School of Architecture and Landscape Architecture, Student Files, Sophia Smith Collection, Smith College; Ann H. Sievers, ed., "Landscape Architects from the Cambridge School," exhibition catalog, Smith College Museum of Art, Northampton, Massachusetts, May 10–September 30, 1984, np.

103. These are: Helen Swift Jones, *Small Gardens and Landscape Planting* (New York: W. H. Wise, 1939; later ed. 1941); Helen Swift Jones, *Gardens and Planting Plans* (New York: W. H. Wise, 1936); and Helen Swift Jones and E. J. D. Seymour, *Landscaping the Small Home* (New York: W. H. Wise, 1952).

104. Anderson, *Cambridge School*, 105.

105. *New York Times*, Sunday, March 18, 1938.

106. There appears to be no record of this project, and the present Stamford Museum is a new building.

107. Fairfield Historical Society, "Summary of Holdings on Helen Swift Jones (1889–1982)"; American Society of Landscape Architects, *Work of Members*, 1932, 1933, and 1934.

108. "Landscape Architect Leaves Foundation Bequest," Landscape Architecture Foundation, AGORA, Winter/Spring, 1983, 38.

109. Ibid.

110. Sievers, ed., "Landscape Architects..."

111. With the help of Michael Goodison of the Smith College Museum of Art, I located Carter F. Jones's heir, but she did not respond to my letter.

112. I am grateful to Eugene Neely, Archivist, of Adelphi University for this information and documentation.

113. Archives, Adelphi. By 1930, the founding partners of McKim, Mead & White had died, and the firm was led by a second generation of partners, William Mitchell Kendall and Lawrence Grant White. According to Leland Roth, after 1920, the firm "came to specialize in educational and medical complexes," which certainly fits the situation at Adelphi. See Leland M. Roth, McKim, Mead & White, *Architects* (New York: Harper & Row, 1983): 345.

114. McKim, Mead & White, Plan for Adelphi College, 1930. Adelphi University Archives.

115. Helen Swift Jones to Mrs. Harold M. Baily, October 29, 1930 and (Mrs. Baily?) to Helen Swift Jones, February 26, 1931, Adelphi Archives.

116. Helen Swift Jones to Mrs. Harold J. Baily, December 2, 1930, Adelphi Archives. It is possible that there was another plan by McKim, Mead & White, now lost, or that there was a plan by another architectural firm.

117. Helen Swift Jones to Mrs. Harold J. Baily, February 25, 1931, Adelphi Archives.

118. Oak Park Nurseries to Helen Swift Jones, February 27, 1931, Adelphi Archives.

119. The Forman Co. to Helen Swift Jones, May 8, 1931, Adelphi Archives.

120. Report of the Levermore Committee, November 1, 1932, Adelphi Archives.

121. Smith College Archives. Further Darling family information has not been forthcoming.

122. Janet Darling, Thesis Statement, 1937, Cambridge School Archives.

123. Wedding announcement, Cambridge School Archives (undoubtedly sent to Henry A. Frost). There were no children of this marriage.

124. Gary R. Hilderbrand, ed., *Making a Landscape of Continuity: The Practice of Innocenti & Webel* (Cambridge, Massachusetts: Harvard University Graduate School of Design, 1997): 62.

125. Janet Darling, "Good Architecture Makes Good Planting Look Better," *House Beautiful* 90, no. 7 (July 1948), 78–79.

126. "Mrs. Janet D. Webel, Landscape Designer," *New York Times*, April 12, 1966; "Janet Darling Webel, '34," *Smith Alumnae Quarterly* (November 1966): 68.

127. Hilderbrand, ed., *Making a Landscape . . .*, 114.

128. Ibid., 110.

129. Ibid., 62–65.

130. Information from Ireys's daughter.

131. Maida Goodwin, text of a talk about Ireys given at Smith College in April 2002.

132. Paula Deitz, "Alice Ireys, 89, Dies; Designed Elegant

Landscapes Bridging Traditions," *New York Times*, Sunday, December 17, 2000, L64. Irey's curriculum vitae is in the Alice Recknagel Ireys Papers, Sophia Smith Collection, Smith College, Northampton, Massachusetts.

133. Goodwin, talk.

134. Goodwin, talk.

135. Alice Ireys, Curriculum vitae. Lowrie's contract with the Fair and Ireys's time sheets for the project are also in the Ireys Papers. The lake seems to have already been dug by the time of Lowrie's contract.

136. ARI (Alice Recknagel Ireys), "Charles Nassau Lowrie, "A Biographical Minute on His Professional Life and Work," *Landscape Architecture* 30, no. 3 (April 1940), 123–24; Goodwin, talk.

137. Ireys, Curriculum vitae.

138. Goodwin, talk.

139. Goodwin, talk.

140. Goodwin, talk. Alice Recknagel Ireys, *How to Plan and Plant Your Own Property* (New York: M. Barrows & Co., 1967); Alice Recknagel Ireys, *Small Gardens for City and Country* (Englewood Cliffs, NJ: Prentice-Hall, 1978); Alice Recknagel Ireys, *Garden Designs*, Burpee American Gardening Series (New York: Prentice-Hall Press, 1991); and Alice Recknagel Ireys, *Designs for American Gardens* (New York: Prentice-Hall, 1991).

141. Ireys, Curriculum vitae.

142. Goodwin, talk.

143. Suzanne Bales, manuscript for an article on Ireys, Ireys Papers.

144. Maida Goodwin to Cynthia Zaitzevsky, e-mail, March 22, 2004.

145. Goodwin to Zaitzevsky, March 22, 2004; Deitz, "Ireys, 89."

146. Ireys, Curriculum vitae.

147. Ireys, Curriculum vitae. According to Lorraine Gilligan, Director of the Planting Fields Foundation, Ireys was interested in the restoration of the Blue Pool garden at Planting Fields (original landscape architect: Andrew Robeson Sargent), but her work was never implemented. She had planned to use Burpee seeds (Rachel Whiteside to Cynthia Zaitzevsky, e-mail, August 6, 2002).

148. Alice Recknagel to Mrs. Henry Sturgis, January 31, 1946; "Perennial List, Mrs. Henry Sturgis," January 30, 1946; Ireys Papers, Sophia Smith Collection, Smith College (hereafter Ireys Papers).

149. Alice Recknagel, "Plant List, Mrs. Henry Sturgis, Chauncey Lane, Cedarhurst," February 1946.

150. Alice Recknagel to Jackson & Perkins Co., April 1946, Ireys Papers.

151. Ireys to Mrs. Robert E. Blum, May 23, 1951; Ireys to George C. White, Bobbink and Atkins, East Rutherford, New Jersey, June 7, 1951; George C. White to Ireys, June 11, 1951; all in the Ireys Papers.

152. Ireys to Edwin C. Clark, Grant Park Construction Co., Inc., Lynwood, New York, February 5, 1954; Ireys to Mrs. Robert E. Blum, February 5, 1954; Ethel Blum to Ireys, February 13, 1954; Ireys Papers.

153. Hicks Nurseries to Mrs. Robert E. Blum, November 18, 1954, Ireys Papers.

154. Ireys, *How to Plan and Plant Your Own Property*, 55.

155. Robert E. Blum to Ireys, August 16, 1962; Ireys to Mrs. Robert E. Blum, August 20, 1962; M & A Landscape Service, Locust Valley, New York, to Ireys, April 30, 1963; Ireys Papers.

156. Press release, Brooklyn Botanic Garden, May 21, 1954; Ireys to George W. Avery, Jr., Brooklyn Botanic Garden, June 28, 1954.

157. Ibid.

158. Ibid.

159. Ireys, "Fragrance Garden, 1994," Ireys Papers; see also www.bbg.org/exp/stroll/fragrance.html.

160. David Grafton, *The Sisters: The Lives and Times of the Fabulous Cushing Sisters* (New York: Villard Books, 1992), 55–64, 118–20, 125–35.

161. Karen Morey Kennedy, Entry on Walker & Gillette, in MacKay, Baker, & Traynor, eds., *Long Island Country Houses and Their Architects*, 423–24.

162. Keith N. Morgan, Entry on Charles A. Platt, in MacKay, Baker, and Traynor, eds., *Long Island Country Houses*, 352; Keith N. Morgan, *Charles A. Platt: The Artist as Architect* (Cambridge, Massachusetts: The MIT Press, 1985): 249.

163. Grafton, *The Sisters*, 150, 152–53, 155–56.

164. Russell Page to Barbara Paley from Paris, October 1, 1960, Ireys Papers. Page gave Mrs. Paley very specific directions and said that he was drawing out a detailed plan of the pool.

165. Marina Schinz & Gabrielle van Zuylen, *The Gardens of Russell Page* (New York: Stewart, Tabori & Chang, 1991): 177. Page's papers are located in Belgium with limited access.

166. Zion and Breen, "Garden in the Woods," progress print, April 3, 1961, Ireys Papers.

167. Ireys to Mrs. Herbert E. Jones, December 4, 1985; Ireys, Report of Visit to Mrs. William Paley, March 12, 1961; Ireys to Mrs. William Paley, August 16, 1962; Ireys Papers. The Archives of American Gardens at the Smithsonian Institution have three photographs of the pool. Under "makers," they list Page, Ireys, and Innocenti and Webel (they do not list Zion and Breen). Innocenti and Webel apparently worked on the part of the grounds near the house. Information from Eleanor Weller.

168. Nan Fairbrother, "Secret Gardens," *Vogue*, December 1964, 256–59, with the photograph of Mrs. Paley by the pool by Horst; Ireys Papers; Ireys, *How to Plan and Plant Your Own Property*, after page 133.

169. Ireys to Mrs. William S. Paley, July 26, 1967, Ireys Papers.

170. Ireys, Plan for Sculpture Terrace, October 18, 1972, Ireys Papers.

171. Diana Shaman, "Last Major North Hills Estate Yields to Development," *New York Times*, nd (ca. 1996), Ireys Papers.

172. I am very grateful to Charla Bolton, formerly of SPLIA, who managed to locate this gated community, gain access to it, and photograph the pool. The property is not open to the public.

173. Hilderbrand, ed., *Making a Landscape of Continuity*, 50–53.

174. Documents in the Ireys Papers, Sophia Smith Collection.

175. Quoted in Deitz, "Ireys, 89 ...."

CHAPTER 10
A Look Backward and Forward

1. Doris Cole, *From Tipi to Skyscraper: A History of Women in Architecture* (Boston: I press, distributed by George Braziller, 1973): 38. Women began practicing architecture somewhat earlier than they began practicing landscape architecture. However, women in both professions followed similar career paths and encountered similar problems, so it is helpful to track a few early women architects as well. Also, the history of women architects is better documented than that of women landscape architects. A recent general survey of the social history of American women does not explicitly discuss architecture or landscape architecture but is valuable for context: Gail Collins, *America's Women: 400 Years of Dolls, Drudges, Helpmates and Heroines* (New York: William Morrow, 2003).

2. Several women are listed in Robert O. Jones, comp., *Biographical Index of Historic American Stained Glass Makers* (Raytoun, Missouri: Stained Glass Association of America, 2002). Jones also cites a doctoral dissertation by Betty Ann MacDowell,

"American Women Stained Glass Artists," Michigan State University, 1986. The women stained glass artists include: Maria Herndl (1860–1912), who designed a window or windows in the United States Capitol; Sarah Wyman Whitman (1842–1904), who designed the Phillips Brooks Memorial Window in the Trinity Church Parish House, Boston, the South Transept ("Brimmer") window in Memorial Hall at Harvard University, as well as several windows at the Fogg Academy in Berwick, Maine; and Margaret Redmond (1867–1948), who also designed several windows at Trinity Church, Boston, including two in the nave depicting Apostles and Evangelists. See also Erica E. Hirschler, "Women Artists at Trinity: Sarah Wyman Whitman and Margaret Redmond," in James F. O'Gorman, ed., *The Makers of Trinity Church in the City of Boston* (Amherst & Boston: University of Massachusetts Press, Published in Association with Trinity Church in the City of Boston, 2004), 152–73.

3. Erica E. Hirschler, *A Studio of Her Own: Women Artists in Boston, 1870–1940* (Boston: Museum of Fine Arts Publications, 2001). This group of women includes the artist/photographer Sarah Choate Sears, who took the photograph of Beatrix Farrand illustrated in Figure 2.1.

4. Harriet Beecher Stowe, *Household Papers and Stories* (Boston: Houghton Mifflin & Co., 1896), 188, 257. This book was first copyrighted and published in 1864.

5. Cole, *Tipi*, 48. A builder must have drawn up working plans and written specifications for Stowe's house, since an amateur cannot do these things.

6. Calvert Vaux, *Villas & Cottages* (New York: Dover Publications, Inc., 1970): 248. This is a reprint of the second (1864) edition of Vaux's book.

7. Cole, *Tipi*, 49.

8. Margaret Supplee Smith and Emily Herring Wilson, *North Carolina Women: Making History* (Chapel Hill, North Carolina: University of North Carolina Press, 1999), 137, 326, note 53.

9. Cole, *Tipi*, 52–56.

10. Olmsted to Mrs. William Dwight Whitney, December 16, 1890, Frederick Law Olmsted Papers, Manuscript Division, Library of Congress, Washington, DC.

11. Ibid.

12. Adriana Barbasch, "Louise Blanchard Bethune," in Ellen Perry Berkeley, ed., *Architecture: A Place for Women* (Washington, DC.: Smithsonian Institution Press, 1989), 15–23.

13. Louise Blanchard Bethune, "Women and Architecture," *The Inland Architect and News Record* 17, no. 17 (March 1891): 21.

14. Barbasch, "Louise Blanchard Bethune," 17.

15. Cole, *Tipi*, 73; Elizabeth G. Grossman and Lisa B. Reitzes, "Caught in the Cross Fire," in Berkeley, ed., *Architecture: A Place for Women*, 32–34.

16. An interesting parallel story is told in Despina Stratigakos, "Women and the Werkbund: Gender Politics and German Design Reform, 1907–1914," *Journal of the Society of Architectural Historians* 62, no. 4 (December 2003), 490–511.

17. Grossman and Reitzes, "Caught in the Cross Fire," 32–33.

18. Minerva Parker Nichols, "A Woman on the Woman's Building," *American Architect and Building News* 38, no. 385 (December 10, 1892): 169.

19. Grossman and Reitzes, "Caught in the Cross Fire," 32–33.

20. Barbasch, "Louise Blanchard Bethune," 17.

21. Downing Vaux to Nathan Barrett, January 24, 1900, American Society of Landscape Architects records, Library of Congress, Box 33, Letterbooks. I am grateful to Thaisa Way for this citation.

22. Ibid.

23. In 1876, an editorial in the *American Architect and Building News* asserted that, for women, "the work of superintending would probably be found too laborious and inconvenient and would certainly involve a change in fashion of raiment; and the preparation of large working-drawings would be almost equally awkward." See *American Architect and Building News* I, no. 40 (September 30, 1876): 313.

24. A discussion of this phenomenon, along with a photograph of a woman architect in a "reform dress," is found in Stratigakos, "Women and the Werkbund," 502–03. The information about the effect of the corset on lung capacity comes from the PBS documentary, "The 1900 House," where a spirometer was used to measure the lung capacity of the British amateur actress who played the 1900 woman. Corsets also displaced some of a woman's internal organs.

25. "Miss Beatrix Jones' Vocation," *New York Sun*, Sunday, October 31, 1897, Part II, 5, col. 3. "Bicycle suits" were frequently sailor suits.

26. Helen Elise Bullard, Journal Entry, December 3, 1917, Bullard Papers, Cornell. For clarity, I have added some commas where Bullard did not. It is difficult to understand how someone could have done surveying while wearing a muff.

27. Elizabeth MacPhail, *Kate Sessions, Pioneer Horticulturist* (San Diego: San Diego Historical Society, 1976); Carol Greentree, "Kate Olivia Sessions," in Birnbaum and Karson, eds., *Pioneers*, 343–44.

28. Bertha Yerex Whitman to Doris Cole, January 16, 1972, quoted in Cole, *Tipi*, 74.

29. Cole, *Tipi*, 75.

30. Daniel W. Krall, "The Illusive Miss Bullard: First Professional Woman Landscape Architect," *Landscape Journal* 2, no. 1 (2002), 116–22; Amy Brown, "Elizabeth J. Bullard," in Birnbaum and Karson, eds., *Pioneers*, 37–39; Arleyn Levee, personal communication with author, October 30, 2003.

31. Laura Wood Roper, *FLO: A Biography of Frederick Law Olmsted*, 421. Quotation from Olmsted to Mrs. William Dwight Whitney, December 16, 1890, Olmsted Papers.

32. Krall, "The Illusive Miss Bullard," 119.

33. Ibid., 120–21.

34. Harold A. Caparn, "The Founding of the American Society of Landscape Architects," *American Landscape Architect* IV, no. 1 (January 1931), 20–23. Caparn described Elizabeth Bullard as capable but very modest and self-deprecating. The last adjectives would describe few of the other women in this book.

35. Olmsted to John Charles Olmsted, February 25, 1894, Olmsted Papers.

36. It is likely that Olmsted had little contact with Mary and Beatrix Jones. He was not describing a house party. Biltmore House was not completed until 1895. Olmsted and the architect Richard Morris Hunt, who was also at Biltmore, were there to work. When at Biltmore, Olmsted stayed at one of the many estate houses. Beatrix and her mother may have stayed at another one.

37. Olmsted retired in September 1895, largely because of failing memory. Although he did not die until 1903, he spent his last years at McLean Hospital in Belmont, Massachusetts, the psychiatric division of Massachusetts General Hospital. He probably suffered from Alzheimer's Disease or a related condition. We have no idea how he might have responded if, during his active career, a woman had applied to him for a position.

38. Koenigsberg, "Van Rensselaer," 47. The situation seems to have worsened. In 1913, when the architectural firm of Lois Lilley Howe, Eleanor Manning, and Mary Almy was formed in Boston, it was reported that there were only three other women-owned architectural firms in the country: Julia Morgan in San Francisco (who designed eight hundred buildings); Florence Luscombe and Ida Annah Ryan, both MIT graduates, who had a partnership in Waltham, Massachusetts until World War I; and Anna Schenck and Marcia Mead in New York, who had a partnership from 1912 until Schenck's death in 1915. Howe, Manning, and Almy, all MIT graduates, practiced until 1937, designing mostly new and remodeled houses, some commer-

cial buildings, an exemplary public housing development in Boston, and Denny Place, a residential cul-de-sac that was part of the planned community of Mariemont, Ohio. Howe had also won second place in the competition for the Woman's Building at the World's Columbian Exposition in Chicago. See Doris Cole, *The Lady Architects: Lois Lilley Howe, Eleanor Manning and Mary Almy* (New York: Midmarch Press, 1990), 1–8. In 1913, many of the women in this book were practicing.

39. Norman T. Newton, *Design on the Land: The Development of Landscape Architecture* (Cambridge, Massachusetts: Harvard University Press, 1971), 385–92.

40. John Gruber, "Annette E McCrae," in Birnbaum and Karson, eds., *Pioneers*, 248–49. I again thank Thaisa Way, who has studied McCrae.

41. Sarah Lewis Pattee, "Landscape Architecture in American Colleges," *Landscape Architecture* XIV, no. 3 (April 1924), 171–77.

42. Ibid., 172–175.

43. Ibid., 177. Pattee wrote nothing about the Pennsylvania School of Horticulture for Women.

44. Henry Atherton Frost, "The Cambridge School of Architecture and Landscape Architecture—Reminiscences," typescript, 1943, 4, Cambridge School Archives, Sophia Smith Collection, Smith College. Brooks's side of the story is told in a letter she wrote, excerpted in Anderson, *Women, Design, and The Cambridge School*, 2–3.

45. Ibid., 6.

46. Ibid., 6–7. One of these women was Abby Christensen, who later taught at the Cambridge School. The others were Emily Gibson from Utica, New York, who didn't continue, a Miss Iasigi, described as a "Boston socialite," and Florence Luscomb, already practicing as an architect in Waltham, Massachusetts. See Anderson, *Women, Design and the Cambridge School*, 3, 13, 23.

47. Frost, "Reminiscences," 7.

48. Ibid., 7. Instead of going to Lowthorpe, Katherine Brooks Norcross continued at the Cambridge School and was awarded her certificate in 1919. She was granted an M.L.A. by Smith College in 1934. See Anderson, *Women, Design and the Cambridge School*, 53, 101, 102, fig. 8.2. The caption under this portrait of Katherine Brooks Norcross indicates that she had designed and lectured on gardens. By 1980, she was retired and living in Wellesley, Massachusetts. Unfortunately, no specific projects by Norcross on Long Island or anywhere else have been identified. She does not seem to have belonged to the ASLA or the Boston Society of Landscape Architects.

49. Frost, "Reminiscences," 8.

50. Ibid., 8.

51. Ibid., 8–9.

52. Ibid. For Marian Coffin at MIT, see chapter 4 of this book.

53. Frost, "Reminiscences," passim.

54. Ibid., 21–22, 41. Fletcher Steele, for example, did almost no nonresidential work.

55. Ibid., 36–37, 42.

56. Ibid., 40.

57. Henry Atherton Frost and William R. Sears, *Women in Architecture and Landscape Architecture* (Northampton, Massachusetts: Smith College, 1928), 18–21. In literature of this period, the terms "apprenticeship" and "internship" seem to be used interchangeably. A more accurate term today might be "entry-level professional." In Olmsted's era, apprentices were never paid and, today, college-age interns generally are not either. In 1928, especially after four years of college and three of professional school, they would have been paid but at a modest rate.

58. Ibid., 11–12.

59. Ibid., 25.

60. Ibid., 22.

61. Ibid., 28.

62. Anderson, *Women, Design and the Cambridge School*, 53–98.

63. Ibid., 99–101.

64. Ibid., 188.

65. Ibid.

66. Ibid., 157. There appear to be no Lowthorpe School archives at RISD.

67. Frost, " Reminiscences," 13.

68. Ibid., 11.

69. Ibid., 14.

70. Ibid., 15.

71. Ibid., 15, 24.

72. Ibid., 24.

73. Ibid., 37. Between 1919 and 1928, Frost had a woman partner, Eleanor Raymond, a graduate of Wellesley College and the Cambridge School, who, because of Frost's teaching responsibilities, carried much of the practice's load. After 1928, Raymond practiced on her own and also taught at the Cambridge School. Raymond, who lived to be one hundred and one, was made a Fellow of the American Institute of Architects in 1961. Her work was primarily residential and included three fine houses in Andover, Massachusetts and the first solar-powered house in the country. In her designs, she gave equal attention to the outside of the house, its interior, and the landscaping, which she seems to have designed on her own. See Doris Cole, Eleanor Raymond, *Architect* (Philadelphia: Art Alliance Press, 1981) and www.cr.nps.gov/nr/travel/pwwmh/ma50.htm.

74. Frost, "Reminiscences," 38. The women at the Cambridge School were not the only beneficiaries of Frost's nurturing teaching style; in 1940, Philip Johnson and Carter H. Manny, Jr., then in their first year of graduate level architectural study at Harvard, described Frost as "unfailingly helpful and *sympathique*." See Franz Schulze, *Philip Johnson: Life and Work* (New York: Alfred A. Knopf, 1994), 150.

75. American Society of Landscape Architects, "Membership List," *Illustrations of Work of Members* (New York: The House of J. Hayden Twiss, 1934), np.

76. Collins, *America's Women*, 304–26, 338–40.

77. Ibid., 371–96.

78. Ibid., 397–420.

79. Ibid., 443–46. See also Ellen Goodman, "Ironies of the Equal Rights Battle," *Boston Sunday Globe*, December 14, 2003, D, 11.

80. Judith Edelman, "Task Force on Women," in Berkeley, ed., *Architecture: A Place for Women*, 117–23.

81. Darwina L. Neal, "Status of Women in the Profession," *ASLA Bulletin* (July 1973), 7–14. As a result of this article and of widespread general interest in the subject, Dorothy May Anderson was asked to write a history of women in the profession. She declined but instead agreed to write an account of the Cambridge School, resulting in the book cited so frequently in these pages (Anderson, *Women, Design and the Cambridge School*, 9).

82. Committee on Women in Landscape Architecture, American Society of Landscape Architects, *ASLA Resource File, Women in Landscape Architecture* (Washington, DC.: The Committee, 1981).

83. Joan Iverson Nassauer and Karen Arnold, "The National Survey of Career Patterns Among Women in Landscape Architecture" (Washington, DC: American Society of Landscape Architects, 1983).

84. Ibid., 4–16. Many people, of course, "fall into" their professions.

85. Ibid., 17–21, 33.

86. I am grateful for much assistance with this section of the chapter from John F. Furlong, formerly Director of the Landscape Design Program of The Landscape Institute, Arnold Arboretum, Harvard University.

87. See www.clarb.org/licensure; www.latc.ca.gov/publicinfo/publicfaqs.htm.

88. During the 2003–4 academic year, women made up 90% of the Landscape Architecture Department at Harvard's Graduate School of Design. This is most likely a one-time phenomenon.

89. Heidi Kost-Gross, "A Conversation with Laura Solano," Perspectives in *Landscape Design and History* 20, no. 2 (Winter/Spring, 2003): 3. Solano was addressed as "little missy" by a contractor.

90. See www.bls.gov/oes/2000. Women appear not to have fared quite as well in architecture. In 1997, it was reported that only nine percent of the membership of the American Institute of Architects were women, and ten percent of licensed (i.e. registered) architects were women, although forty-two percent of students in M. Arch programs were women. There were 113,000 jobs in the field. For these statistics, see www.archvoices.org/index.cfm?pg+resource&s&s=women; John Morris Dixon, "A White Gentlemen's Profession?" *Progressive Architecture*, (November 1994), 55–61.

In 2002, there were almost one and a half million engineers in the country, including all specialties. Of these, 228,000 were civil engineers, the specialty most closely related to landscape architecture (see www.bls.gov/oco/ocos). There is a national Society of Women Engineers, which reports a membership of lightly under 18,000 (see www.societyofwomenengineers.org/members). There is another society of Women in Engineering (WIE), but information about its membership seems to be available only to members.

In spring 2004, Smith College granted degrees to twenty women engineers. Although, at MIT, thirty-four percent of engineering students are women, nationally only one in five engineering students are women, and the profession itself is ninety percent male. See Marcella Bombardieri, "At Smith, Engineer Pioneers to Graduate," *Boston Globe*, Saturday, May 15, 2004, B1-2.

91. I am grateful again to John Furlong for this information.

INDEX

A

Adams, Charles L., 78
Adler, David, 112
Alexandre, J. Harry, 85
Alger Museum, 16
Allen, Nellie B., 10, 14, 16, 226, *234,*
    234–35, 269
Allen, Sidney P., 234
Alliance of Women in Architecture
    (AWA), 262
Amawalk Nursery, 243
Ambler Junior College, 14
American Committee for Devastated
    France, 194
American Horticultural Society, 247
American Institute of Architects, 257,
    260
American Society of Landscape Archi-
    tects, 34, 63, 78, 112, 139, 164,
    222, 228, 234, 242, 247, 258,
    259, 260, 261, 262, 263
Ammann, O. H., 139
Anchor Post Iron Works, 53
Anderson, Dorothy May, 111
Applegreen (Straight Residence), *18,*
    42–46
Apple House (Flagg Residence), 168
Applewood (Flagg Residence), 191
Appleyard, Selina, 80
Architectural League of New York, 78,
    139, 164, 234, 242
Arnold Arboretum, 11, 34, 62, 78, 204
Ashwell, Iris, 164
Astor, Vincent, 139, 144, 151, 165, 174
Atterbury, Grosvenor, 81, 132, 220

B

Babb, Cook and Willard, 53, 65
Bacon, Robert, 64–65
Bacon, Robert L., 65
Bailie, Margaret, 49
Baily, Harold M., 243
Baker, Anne, 46, 53
Ballard, Richard C., 80
Ballyshear
    MacDonald Residence, 201–2
    Van Vleck Residence, 179, 182–86,
    202
Baltusan, Henry, 220
Banfi Vintners, 128
Barnes, E. Mortimer, 168, 172–73
Barry, Philip, 228
Bassick, Edgar W., 78–79
Bauhan, Alice, 164
Bayberryland (Sabin Property), 81–85
Bayville, Williams Residence, 53,
    56–57
Beachleigh (Schieren Residence), 141,
    144
Beers and Farley, 128
Bell, Margaret Eaglesfield, 164
Bemidji State Teachers College, 228
Benjamin, W. W., 103
Berry, Walter, 80
Bethune, Louise Blanchard, 257
Bethune, Robert Armour, 257
Biddle, Ellen Fish McGowan, 108
Biddle, Ellen McGowan. *see* Shipman,
    Ellen Biddle
Biddle, James, 108
Bing, Alexander M., 212

Black, Russell Van Nest, 212
Bliss, Mildred, 15, 34
Bliss, William H., 34
Blum, Ethel, 250, 251–53
Blum, Robert, 250, 251–53
Boardman, Albert B., 98
Boardman, Constance, 235
Bonbright, Mrs. Howard, 139
Bowditch, Ernest W., 200
Bowen, Catherine Drinker, 217
Bowen, Ezra, 217
Bowen, Isabella. *see* Pendleton, Isabella
The Braes (Pratt Residence), 114, 220
Breed, Vera Poggi, 140
Brokaw, Irving, 103–5
Brookes, Ellen Douglas, 60
Brooklyn State Hospital, 239
Brookmeade (Sloane Residence), 235
Brooks, Katherine, 259
Brookville
    Flagg Residence, 168, 191
    Hutton Residence, 92–93
    Iselin Residence, 116
Brown, Janet, 238
Brown, Joseph Henry, 60
Brown, Philip Marshall, 78
Bullard, David, 239
Bullard, Elizabeth A. Huggins, 238
Bullard, Elizabeth Jane, 258, 261
Bullard, Helen Elise, 10, 12, 13, 16,
    164, 226, *238,* 238–41, 258, 269
Bullard, John, 239
Bullard, Oliver Crosby, 258
Bullard, Roger H., 121, 128
Bullard, Thomas Everett, 238

Bullitt, William, 78
Bussey Institute, 192, 194
Butler and Corse, 111

C

Cadwalader, John Lambert, 32
California Institute of Technology, 15
Cambridge School of Domestic and
    Landscape Architecture, 11, 13,
    14, 62, 192, 226, 242, 244, 246,
    259–60, 261
Canning, Edward J., 162
Cannon, H. W., 196
Carrère and Hastings, 200
Cattell, Mary Lamson. *see* Lamson,
    Mary Deputy
Cattell, William W., 229
Caumsett (Field Residence), 85–92
Cautley, Marjorie Sewell, 10, 11, 12,
    13, 210–13, 246, 261, 268–69
Cautley, Randolph, 210
Cedarhurst
    Crane Residence, 191
    Peck Residence, *30*, 191, 199
    Sturgis Residence, 250, 251
    Wickersham Residence, 196
Cedarhurst (Peck Residence), *30*
Central Islip State Hospital, 239
Chandler, Professor, 78
Chappell, George S., 53
Chesterton House (du Pont Residence),
    98
Christie, Eleanor Hills, 111, 204
Chubb, Percy, 36–37. *see also* Dosoris
    (Chubb Residence); "Rattling
    Spring"
Church, Benjamin, 76
Civil Rights Act (1964), 261–62
Clark, Agnes Selkirk, 111
Clark, Louis Jocelyn, 111
Clarke, Gilmore David, 240
Clayton (Childs Frick Residence), 80,
    98, 100–103
Cloverley Manor (Astor Residence), *21*,
    144, 174
Codman, Ogden, 98
Coffey, Clara Stimson, 79
Coffin, Alice Church, 76
Coffin, Julian Ravenel, 76
Coffin, Marian Cruger, 10, 11, 16, *77*,
    257, 261
    accomplishments, 107
    clients and designs, 15, 78–105,
        266
    early life, 76
    education and professional develop-
        ment, 11, 12, 13, 14, 76–78
    personal life and qualities, 15, 79
    published works, 79, 80
Cold Spring Harbor
    James Residence, 220
    Kahn Residence, 46–49
Cole, Catherine Dodd, 212
Colorado Springs Fine Arts Center, 16
Colour Schemes for the Flower Garden
    (Jekyll), 116, 139
Columbia University, 34, 204, 260
Colwell, Elizabeth F., 79

Combs, C. C., 239, 240
Composition (Dow), 212
Connecticut
    Bridgeport, Bassick property, 78–79
    Fairfield, Eaton Residence, 242, 243
    Hartford, Avery Convalescent
        Home, 242
    New Canaan, Peats Residence, 222
    New London, Harkness Residence,
        35
    see also Greenwich, Connecticut;
        Westport, Connecticut
Coolidge, Hamilton, 53
Coons, Richard F., 244
Cooper, James Fenimore, II, 110
Copeland, Lammot du Pont, 79
Cornell University, 11, 12–13, 210,
    226, 238, 259
Cortissoz, Royal, 191
Cottage Gardens Company, 53
Cottsleigh (Lord Residence), 128–32
Crane, Hart, 46
Crane, Warren S., 191
Cravath, Paul D., 220
Croly, Herbert, 110
Cross and Cross, 53, 81, 98
Crossways (Benjamin Residence),
    103–5
Cunningham, Mary P., 111
Curtis, Ralph, 13
Cutler, Herbert H., 164

D

Dana, Maria Trumbull, 80
Darling, Bella Crawford, 244
Darling & Webel, 244
Davis, Dwight F., 85
Davis, E. Gorton, 12
Dean, Alexander S., 136
Dean, Emma, 136
Dean, Ruth Bramley, 10, 11, *20*, *136*,
    137, 228, 257
    clients and designs, 139, 140–59,
        267
    early life and family background,
        136
    education and professional develop-
        ment, 11, 14, 136–38, 139–41
    personal life and qualities, 15,
        139–40, 159
    published work, 138–39
Delahanty, Bradley, 191, 220
Delano and Aldrich, 47, 53, 144, 174,
    205
Delaware
    Greenville, Copeland Residence, 79
    Wilmington, Ross Residence, 79
    Winterthur, 79, 80
Delaware College, 15, 79
Demarest, F. C., 172–74
Deputy, Carrie G. Gault, 226
Deputy, Manfred Wolfe, 226
Derrick, Mrs. Robert, 139
Designs for American Gardens (Ireys),
    247
Despradelle, Desiré, 11, 200
Despuis, Professor, 200
Dewing, Maria, 110

Dewing, Thomas, 110
Dixon, Percival, 244
Dodge and Ames, 63
Dosoris
    Chubb Residence, *17*, *36*, 36–38
    Pratt Residence, 40, 42
Douglas, Graham, 229, 231
Dow, Arthur W., 212
Duke University, 16
Dunham, Carroll, 34
Dunham, E. K., 34
du Pont, Henry Algernon, 76
du Pont, Henry Frances (Harry), 76,
    78, 79, 80, 98
Dykman, Jackson A., 222–25

E

Eagles Beak (James Residence), 220
East Hampton
    Benjamin Residence, 103
    Douglas Residence, 229, 231
    Free Library, 159
    Gray Gardens, 139
    Guild Hall, 156–58
    James Residence, 128
    McCall Residence, 235
    Pruyn Residence, 116–21
    Ramée Residence, 231
    Roberts Residence, 154, 229–31
    Woodin Residence, 81, *84*
East View (Crane Residence), 191
Eaton, Sargent, 242
Eckstein, Isabelle Gibson, 216
Edgar, J. Clifton, 78
Eldridge, Louisa Udall Skidmore, 38
Eldridge, Roswell, 38, 53
Ellett, Thomas H., 172
Elmhirst, Dorothy, 56, 58
Elmhirst, Leonard, 46, 56
Embury, Aymar, II, 14, 112, 136, 138,
    139, 140, 141, 151, 154, 156,
    159
Emerson, William, 210, 212
England, Devonshire, Dartington Hall,
    56–59
English Pleasure Gardens (Nichols), 200
English-Speaking Union, 234

F

Farrand, Beatrix Jones, 10, 11, 14, 15,
    16, *33*, 63, 76, 78, 116, 257–58,
    261
    clients and designs, 15, *17*, 34,
        36–59, 265–66
    early life and family background,
        32–34
    education and professional develop-
        ment, 11, 34, 258–59
    personal life and qualities, 15,
        34–35, 36, 59
    work methods, 58–59
Farrand, Daisy, 13
Farrand, Livingston, 13
Farrand, Max, 32, 35, 36, 38
Faunce, Linus, 78
Field, Marshall, III, 85. *see also* Lloyd
    Neck, Field property
Filzen, Patricia, 166

Fish, Julia, 114. *see also* Greenport, Fish
 Residence
Fitzgerald, F. Scott, 240
Flagg, Benson, 168
Flagg, Montague, 191
Flagg, W. Allston, 105
Flanders, Annette Hoyt, 10, 11, *21, 22,
 23, 24, 25, 26, 27, 28, 29, 30, 31,
 162, 163,* 238, 242, 261
 clients and designs, 164, 166–91,
  199, 202, 267–68
 design principles, 165–66, 168
 early life and family background,
  162
 education and professional develop-
  ment, 11, 14, 162–65
 personal life and qualities, 11, 15,
  166
 published works and lectures, 164,
  165
Flanders, Roger Yale, 162
Fleming, Bryant, 12–13
Flushing, Sprague Residence, 78,
 80–81
Foster, Mary Pauline, 76
Fouilhoux, Andre, 240
Fowler, Clarence, 11, 34, 35, 60, 75,
 76, 98, 107
France, Paris, Bois de Boulogne
 Bagatelle garden, 40
Francis, Henry, 76
Francis, Louisa, 76
Frankenbach Nursery, 188
Frick, Childs, 98. *see also* Roslyn, Frick
 Residence
Frost, Henry Atherton, 62, 226–28,
 246, 259–60, 261
Furtherfield (Roberts Residence), 154

G
Gales, Mrs. George N., 144
Ganong, William, 162
Garden City
 Adelphi College, 243
 Garden City School, 250
 Library, 250
Garden City movement, 210–213
Garden Club of America, 62–63, 75,
 78, 112, 113, 164, 194, 234
*Garden Design: The Principles of Abstract
 Design as Applied to Landscape
 Composition* (Cautley), 212
Garden Designs (Ireys), 247
The Garden Handbook (Jay), 194–96
Garden Housekeeping (Lamson), 229
*Gardening with Shrubs and Small Flower-
 ing Trees* (Lamson), 228–29
Gardner, Harry W., 78
Gardner, Isabella Stewart, 78
Geddes, Norman Bel, 46
Gersdorff, George B. de, 174
Gill, Irving, 200, 258
Glen Cove
 Chubb Residence, 217–218
 Dykman Residence, 222–25
 Pratt Residences, 65–70, 114, 220
 Welwyn Preserve, 70
 Whitney Residence, 218–20

Glen Head
 Alexandre Residence, 85, *88*
 Barnes Residence, 168, *172–173*
 Iselin Residence, 40
 Salvage Residence, 121–31
Gold Medal for Landscape Architecture,
 139, 164, 177
golf courses, 201–2
Gossler, Philip, 121, 205
Gottscho, Samuel, 100–102
Great Neck
 Eldridge Residence, 38
 Gales Residence, 144
 Great Neck Green, 53–54
 Mann Residence, *19,* 46
 Olds Residence, 191
 Public Library, 53–54
 Ross Residence, 188
 Schieren Residence, *20,* 138, 141,
  144
 Streeter Residence, 205
 Thompson Ross Residence, *27*
Greely, Rose, 261
Green, H. T. S., 196
Greenleaf, James L., 40, 70, 111, 114,
 220
Greenport, Fish Residence, 114–16
Greenwich, Connecticut
 Chapman Residence, 194
 Croft Residence, 111
 Edgar Residence, 78
 Resor Residence, 216
 Simonds Residence, 216
Griswold, Mac, 188
Grove Point (Mann Residence), 46

H
Haines, Jane Browne, 14
Haldeman, Anne Bruce, 113
Hall, Henry J. S., 151
Harbor Acres, 144–52
Hare, Meredith, 114
Harkness, Edward S., 53
Harrison, Wallace K., 240
Hart, Charles M., 92
Hartt, Mary Bronson, 11, 13, 15
Harvard University, 11, 108, 259,
 260–61
Hastings, Thomas, 200
Havey, Ruth, 59
Hawaii, Honolulu, Tenney Residence,
 166
Hayden, Sophia, 12, 257
Hayes, Helen, 228
Head, Charles, 62
Healy, Harry G., 113
Hempstead, Mulford Residence, 138,
 140–141
Heritage Landscapes, 64
Hewitt, Mattie Edwards, 70, 110
Hewlett, Green Residence, 196
Hicks Nurseries, 46, 53, 65, 70, 251
Hill, Mrs. Robert C., 139
Hillwood (Hutton Residence), 80, 92–93
Hoffman, F. Burrall, Jr., 202
Horn, Milton, 179
How to Plan and Plant Your Own Property
 (Ireys), 247

Hoyt, Frank Mason, 162
Hueston, Buell, 64
Huntington
 Cannon Residence, 196
 Hare Residence, 116
 Library and Art Gallery, 36
Huntington, Annie Oakes, 204
Hutcheson, Martha Brookes Brown, 10,
 11, 12, 16, *60, 61,* 261
 accomplishments, 75
 clients and designs, 15–16, 62, 63,
  64–75, 266
 early life and family background,
  60, 62
 education and professional development, 11–12, 15, 60–62
 personal life and qualities, 62–64
 published works, 63
Hutcheson, William Anderson, 60
Hutton, Edward F., 80, 92, 121. *see also*
 Brookville, Hutton Residence

I
Ickes, Harold, 212
Illinois, Dwight, Smith Residence, 138
Indiana University, 226
Ingalls, Fay, 174
Innocenti and Webel, 128, 174, 244,
 254
Ireys, Alice Recknagel, 10, 212, *246,*
 246–54, 269–70
Ireys, Henry Tillinghast, III, 246
Irwin, Harriet Morrison, 256
Iselin, C. Oliver, 40, 116, 196, *197,
 198,* 199, 220

J
Jack, John G., 78
Jackson and Perkins, 251
James, Ellery S., 128
James, Henry, 34, 35
James, Walter, 220
Jay, Julia Post, 192
Jay, Mary Rutherfurd, 10, 11, 36, *192*
 clients and designs, 196–99, 268
 education and professional develop-
  ment, 11, 192–96
Jay, Peter Augustus, 192
Jekyll, Gertrude, 36, 116, 139, 166,
 196, 234, 235
Jensen, Jens, 14, 136, 138, 257
Jericho, Preston Residence, 114
Jones, Beatrix. *see* Farrand, Beatrix
 Jones
Jones, Frederic, 32
Jones, Helen J. Swift, 242
Jones, Helen Swift, 10, 14, 15, 164,
 242, 242–43, 260, 261, 269
Jones, Hettie Pamelia, 162
Jones, Lucretia, 32
Jones, Mary Cadwalader Rawle, 32, 34,
 35, 256, 257
Jones, Wallace T., 242
Jones Beach Bath Houses, 239

K
Kahn, Addie Wolff, 46–49
Kahn, Otto H., 46–49

Kane, John P., 205–9
Kentucky, Oxmoor, Bullit Residence, 78
Kiley, Dan, 244
Killenworth (Pratt Residence), 40–42
Kiluna Farm (Paley Residence), 250, 254
Kipsveen (McCall Residence), 235
Kiser, John W., 188
Klar, Ed, 254
Kohn, Robert D., 212
Kountze, DeLancey, 191

L
Lake Forest College, 162
Lambert, Jack, 79
Lamson, Frank Vernon, 228
Lamson, Mary Deputy, 10, 14, 140–41,
    226–31, 227, 260, 269
Landscape Architecture Foundation,
    242
landscape design, 262
Lattingtown, St. John's Church, 235
Lauriemore (Phillips Residence), 158,
    160–161
Lawrence, Lord Residence, 75
Lazarus, Annie, 132
Leake, Alice, 225
Ledyard, Lewis Cass, 114, 191
Lenox, Elizabeth, 242
Leonard, Elizabeth, 111
Lerner, Joseph, 212
Leuthardt, Henry, 31, 191
Leuthardt Nurseries, 191
Levermore, Charles H., 243
Lewis and Valentine, 70, 92, 172
Lindbergh, Anne Morrow, 228
The Livable House, Its Garden (Dean),
    138–39
The Livable House (Embury), 138
Livingston, John T., 196
Lloyd Harbor, Reed Residence, 128
Lloyd Neck, Field property, 85, 90–92
Locust Valley
    Cravath Residence, 220
    Kane Residence, 205–8
    Sloane Residence, 235–236
    Taylor Residence, 164, 166–71
Longfellow, Alice, 62
Longfellow, Henry Wadsworth, 62
Longfields (Preston Residence), 114
Long Island Nurseries, 53
Long Island State Park Commission,
    239
Lord, Daniel, 75
Lord, Franklin B., 128–32
Lord, George deForest, 128, 132
Louisiana, New Orleans, Stern Resi-
    dence, 112
Low, Mrs. Edward Gilchrist, 14
Lowell, Guy, 12, 15, 78, 80
Lowrie, Charles N., 246
Lowthorpe School of Landscape Archi-
    tecture, 11, 14, 63, 111, 164, 192,
    204, 216, 222, 226, 234, 259, 261
Lynch, R. S., 58

M
MacArthur, Charles, 228
MacDonald, Charles B., 179, 201–2

MacDonald, Eric, 105
Mahoney, Marion L., 12
Maine, Farrand in, 35, 36
Mañana (Barnes Residence), 168, 172
Manhasset
    Harkness Residence, 53
    Paley Residence, 250, 254
    Payson Residence, 205
    Whitney Residence, 65
Mann, S. Vernon, 46
Manning, Warren, 13, 111–12, 210,
    238
Marquette University, 11, 164
Martin, Willis, 63
Mason, Ellen, 200
Massachusetts
    Ashburnham, Miller Residence, 234
    Bridgewater town center, 250
    Manchester-by-the-Sea, 62
    Maudsley State Park, 62
    Milton, McGinley Residence, 111
    Weston, Hubbard Residence, 139
    Woods Hole, McGarrah Residence,
        139
Massachusetts Institute of Technology,
    11, 12, 13, 15, 62, 76–78, 192,
    257, 260
Maudesleigh (Moseley Residence), 62
McCall, Clifford H., 235
McCann, E. F., 174, 176–181
McCartan, Edward, 70
McCormic, Frances, 111, 112
McGarrah, Gates W., 139
McKim, Charles Follen, 35
McKim, Mead & White, 35, 243
McMasters, Marianne Dean, 140
McMullen, Frances D., 136, 138,
    139–40
McRae, Annette, 259
Merle-Smith, Van S., 231
Merriweather Post, Marjorie, 80, 92. *see
    also* Brookville, Hutton Residence
Michel, Michael A., 254
Michigan
    Grand Rapids, Lowe Residence, 111
    Grosse Point, Dean designs in, 139
Miller, William D., 234
Milliken and Bevin, 100
Mill Neck
    Baltusan Residence, 220
    Brokaw Residence, 103–5
    Iselin Residence, 196, 199, 220
Missouri Botanical Garden, 259
Mitchell, Ledyard, 139
modernist design, 226
Montauk Parkway, 239
Morgan, Julia, 210
Morrill Act (1862), 12, 258
Morrow, Dwight, 228
Mosely, F. M., 62
Moses, Robert, 15, 238, 239, 242

N
Nassau County Museum of Art, 80
Neal, Darwina L., 262
Nevins, Ethel D., 79
New Hyde Park, Blum Residence, 250,
    251

New Jersey
    Cranford, Crane Park, 250
    Englewood, Dean designs in, 139
    Fairlawn, Radburn, 210, 213
    Gladstone, Brady Residence, 138
    Merchiston Farm, 64
    Princeton, Brown Residence, 78
    Tenafly, 138, 210
    Trenton, Trent House, 216
New York
    Albertson, Clark Gardens, 250
    Bedford Hills, Righter Residence,
        242
    Fort Ticonderoga Pavilion, 78
    Long Island. *see specific township*
    Millbrook, Thorne Residence, 234
    Mount Kisco, Brewster Residence,
        111
    New Hamburgh, Reese Residence,
        194
    Nyack, MacArthur Residence, 228
    Rye, John Jay Homestead, *193*, 250
    Tuxedo Park, Garrison property, 34
New York City
    Bellevue Hospital, 60, 242
    Brooklyn Botanic Garden, Garden of
        Fragrance, 250, 253–54
    Hillside Homes, 210, 212, 246
    Hochschild Residence, 165
    Jay designs, 194
    Lincoln Center, 244
    Mount Vernon Hotel, 250
    New York Botanical Garden, 15–16,
        79
    Phipps Garden Apartments, 210,
        213
    St. Luke's Hospital, 222
    Sunnyside Gardens, 210, 211–13
    World's Fair (1939), 235, 237, 238,
        239, 240–41
New York Horticultural Society, 194
New York School for Applied Design
    for Women, 15, 60
Nicholas, Dorothy, 100, 103
Nicholls, Rhoda Holmes, 60
Nichols, Arthur, 200
Nichols, Elizabeth Homer, 200
Nichols, Minerva Parker, 257
Nichols, Rose Standish, 10, 11, 110,
    179, *200*, 200–202, 268
Nickerson, Martha Hunt, 218
Nijinsky, Vaslav, 46
Nineteenth Amendment, 261
Nolen, John, 15
Norcross, Katherine Brooks, 259, 260
Northern State Parkway, 239
North Shore Landscape Company, 243
Norton, Charles McKim, 64
Norton, Martha, 64

O
Oak Park Nurseries, 243
Oak Point (Williams Residence), 53, 56
Occidental College, 15
O'Connor, James W., 144, 174, 177
O'Donal, Royce, 204
Oheka. *see* Cold Spring Harbor, Kahn
    Residence

Oheka (Kahn Residence), 46–49
Ohio
    Akron, Seiberling Residence,
        111–12
    Chagrin Falls, White Residence, 111
    Oberlin College, 15
Old Acres (Bacon Residence), 64–65
Olds, George S., 191
Old Westbury
    Blum Residence, 250, 251–53
    Phipps Residence, 250, 254
    Straight Residence, 42–46
Olmsted, Frederick Law, 15, 18, 200,
    256–57, 258–59
Olmsted Brothers, 15, 34, 47, 56, 65,
    105, 116, 139, 168, 200
Organization of Women Architects
    (OWA), 262
Osborn, Davis, 234
Osborn, Pauline, 234
Overfields (Lord Residence), 132
Oyster Bay
    Coons Residence, 244
    McCann Residence, 22, 23, 24, 25,
        164, 165, 174–79
    Merle-Smith Residence, 231
    Roosevelt headstone, Youngs Memo-
        rial Cemetery, 53
    Taylor Residence, 105
    Whitney Residence, 38–41

P
Page, Russell, 254
Paley, Barbara, 250, 254
Paley, William S., 250, 254
Parmalee, James, 110
Parrish, Stephen, 110
Pattee, Sarah, 259
Patterson, Robert W., 35, 36
Payson, Edgar Robinson, 204
Payson, Harriet Estabrook, 204
Payson, Jeannette, 204
Payson, Louise, 10, 14, 111, 204–9,
    261, 268
Peabody, Wilson & Brown, 114, 121
Peats, G., 222
Peck, Arthur, 191, 199
Pendleton, Elliott Hunt, 216
Pendleton, Isabella, 10, 14, 216–20,
    261, 269
Pennsylvania
    Alleghany College, 250
    Bryn Mawr, Tiffany Memorial, 63
    Pittsburgh, Rose Residence, 138
Pennsylvania School of Horticulture for
    Women, 14
Philadelphia School for Design, 256
Phillips, Ellis L., 158, 160–161
Phipps, Howard, 250, 254
Phipps, Mary, 250, 254
Picket Farm (Kramer Residence), 121
Pidgeon Hill (Hare Residence), 116
Pierce, Winslow, 53
Plandome Manor, Phillips Residence,
    158
Platt, Charles, 13, 15, 65, 110–11, 128,
    132, 200, 254
Platt, Geoffrey, 112

Platt, William, 112
Pomeroy, David E., 139
Pomeroy, John Norton, 60
Pond, Bremer, 259, 260, 261
Pope, John Russell, 64, 85, 121
Poplar Hill (Pratt Residence), 65
Port Washington
    Astor Residence, 20, 165, 174, 175
    Harbor Acres subdivision, 144,
        150–152
Post, Charles W., 92
C. W. Post College, Long Island Univer-
    sity, 80, 93, 121
Pratt, Charles, 65
Pratt, Frederic B., 65
Pratt, Harold I., 65, 68–70, 235
Pratt, Herbert L., 114, 220
Pratt, John T., 70
Pray, James Sturgis, 259
Princeton University, 15, 35
Prosser, Mrs. Seward, 139
Pruyn, Mary, 116
Pruyn, Neltje, 116
public work, 10, 15, 53, 238, 239–40,
    241, 250
Pyne, Moses Taylor, 35, 53
Pyne, Percy R., II, 53

Q
Queens Village Nurseries, 53

R
Radcliffe College, 108–10, 260
Ramée, Joseph, 231
Randolph, Sarah, 15, 108
Rattling Spring (Chubb Residence),
    37–38, 218
Raynor, Seth J., 201
Recknagel, Harold S., 246
Recknagel, Rea Estes, 246
"Red House" (Swayne Residence), 132
Reed, Lansing P., 128
Reef Point Gardens, 36, 196
regulation of landscape architecture,
    262
Repton, Humphrey, 242
Resor, Stanley, 216
Rhode Island, Newport, Mason Resi-
    dence, 200–201
Rhode Island School of Design, 261
Rice, Winthrop Merton, 242
Richardson, Dolores Hoyle, 164
Richardson, H. H., 200
Rivington House (Pyne Residence),
    53
Roberts, George, 154, 229, 231
Robeson, Paul, 46
Robinson, J. Randolph, 121
Robinson, Monroe Douglas, 144
Roche, Auguste, 222
Roche, Eleanor, 10, 14, 204, 222,
    222–25, 261, 269
Roche, Sophie Agnes Glorieux, 222
Rockville Center, Demarest Residence,
    172, 174
Roosevelt, Edith Kermit, 53
Roosevelt, Quentin, 53
Roosevelt, Theodore, 53

Ropes, Frances, 78
Roslyn
    Frick Residence, 80, 98, 100–103
    Kountze Residence, 191
    Pyne Residence, 53
Ross, Daniel, 79
Ross, Thompson, 188
Royal Horticultural Society, 194
Ryan, Edgar E., 242
Rynwood (Salvage Residence), 121,
    123, 128–130

S
Sabin, Charles H., 81, 85–87
Saint-Gaudens, Augusta, 110, 200
Saint-Gaudens, Augustus, 110, 200
Salvage, Samuel, 121
Sargent, Charles Sprague, 11, 12, 34,
    78, 204
Satterlee, Henry Y., 34
Saunders, T. Lawrence, 191
Scheiner, James M., 79, 85, 103
Schieren, G. Arthur, 141, 144,
    145–146
Schnadelbach Associates, 213
Schryver, Edith, 111
Scott, Edgar, 34
Scudder, Janet, 65, 235
Sears, William R., 260
Sessions, Kate, 258
Setauket, Sherwood Residence, 196
Sewell, Barbara, 210
Sewell, Helen, 210
Sewell, Minnie Moore, 210
Sewell, William Elbridge, 210
Shelter Island
    Library (Ireys), 250
Sherwood, Howard C., 196
Shinnecock Hills
    Sabin property, 81, 85–87
    Swayne Residence, 132
Shipman, Ellen Biddle, 10, 11, 14, 15,
    62, 65, 108, 109, 204, 222
    clients and designs, 15–16, 111–12,
        113–32, 216, 266–67
    design characteristics, 111
    early life and family background,
        108
    education and professional develop-
        ment, 13, 108–11, 112–13
Shipman, Louis, 108, 110
Silliman, Benjamin, Sr., 76
Simonds, William R., 188
Simonds, Z. G., 216
Sloane, Isabel Dodge, 235
Small Gardens for City and Country
    (Ireys), 247
Smith, Alice Upham, 164
Smith, Charles, 188
Smith, Warren Hunting, 79, 80
Smith College, 162, 166, 228, 242,
    244, 258, 259, 260–61
Smithtown, Hall Residence, 151,
    152–54
Society for the Preservation of Long
    Island Antiquities, 196
Sorbonne, 11, 164
Sosiego (Lord Residence), 75

Southampton
    Boardman Residence, 98
    du Pont Residence, 80, 98
    Kiser Garden, 28
    Kiser Residence, 188, 238
    MacDonald Residence, 105, 201–2
    Simonds Residence, 188, 238
    Valentine Residence, *29,* 165, 191
    Van Vleck Residence, 179,
      182–186, 202
Southern State Parkway, 239–40
The Spirit of the Garden (Hutcheson),
    63, 70, 75
Sprague, Edward E., 80. *see also* Flushing,
    Sprague Residence (Coffin)
Sprout, Mary Elizabeth, 164
Steele, Fletcher, 121, 234
Stein, Clarence, 210, 212, 213
"Still Place" Cravath Residence, 220
Stoddard, Edna D., 62
Stone, Charles A., 166
Stowe, Harriet Beacher, 256
Straight, Dorothy W., 42, 46, 59
Straight, Michael, 59
Straight, Willard D., 42, *43, 44–45,* 46,
    59
Strang, Elizabeth Leonard, 12, 14,
    111
Streeter, Edward, 205
Stroh, Florence, 111
Studies of Trees in Winter (Huntington),
    204
Sturgis, Henry, 250, 251
Sturgis, Kate, 250, 251
Sunken Orchard (McCann Residence),
    174, 176–181
Swayne, Eleanor, 132
Syosset
    Ledyard Residence, 114, 191
    Lord Residence, 128, 132
    Robinson Residence, 144, 148,
      149

T
Tabor, Grace, 216
Taylor, James Blackstone, 105
Taylor, Myron C., 164, 166–168,
    169–171
Temple University, 14
Tenney, Vernon, 166
Thorn, Frederick G., 257
Thorne, Oakleigh, 234
Trees and Shrubs for Landscape Effects
    (Coffin), 79
Triggs, F. Inigo, 200
Trowbridge & Ackerman, 65
Trumbull, John, 76
Turner, Ross, 78

U
Underhill Farm (Taylor Residence),
    166, 169–171
University of California, 258
University of Chicago, 11, 15, 136
University of Illinois, 11, 162
University of Michigan, 259

V
Valentine, Patrick, 165, 191
Valmay Cottage (Valentine Residence), *29*
Van Acken Smith, David, 166
Vanderbilt, George W., 258
Van Vleck, Charles E. Jr., 179
Vassar College, 15, 259
Vaux, Downing, 257
Vaux, Calvert, 256
Vermont, Bennington College, 15, 63
victory gardens, 113
Villa Banfi, 128
Virginia
    Charlottesville, Stone property, 166
    Frederiscksburg, Devore Residence,
      112
    Middleburg, Foxcroft School, 79
Vitale, Brincherhoff & Geiffert, 14, 164,
    166
Vitale, Ferruccio, 164, 166
Vitale and Geiffert, 235

W
Waite, Richard A., 257
Walker, Hiram, 139
Walker and Gillette, 254
Ware, William Robert, 12, 34
Washington, D. C.
    Dumbarton Oaks, 35
    National Cathedral, 34, 234
Watson, Benjamin M., 11
Watson, Mrs. Benjamin, 200
Webb Institute of Naval Architecture, 220
Webel, Janet Darling, 10, 14, 226, 244,
    244, 269
Webel, Richard K., 244
Weber, Nelva, 164
Weekend (Harkness Residence), 53
Weir, William, 58
Wellesley College, 259
Welwyn (Pratt Residence), 65, 70–74
Westbury
    Bacon Residence, 64–65
    Flagg Residence, 105
    Gossler Residence, 205
    Kramer Residence, 121
    Saunders Residence, 191
Westport, Connecticut
    Lenox Residence, 242
    Ryan Residence, 242

West Virginia, Charleston, Davis Park,
    250
Wharton, Edith, 32, 35, 80, 261
Wheatley Hills, Gossler Residence, 121,
    124–127
White, Andrew Dickson, 12
Whitman, Bertha Yerex, 258
Whitney, Edward Farley, 38–39
Whitney, George, 65
Whitney, Howard, 218, 220
Whitney, Margaret Sargent, 39
Whitney, Payne, 65
Wickersham, George, 196, 197–99
Wiley, Cynthia, 246, 251
Williams, Harrison, 53
Wilmott, Ellen, 63
Wind Swept (Boardman Residence),
    98–99
Windy Hill (Reed Residence), 128
Winter Harbor (Blum Residence), 250,
    251, 253
Wisconsin, Milwaukee, Wright Residence,
    dence, 164
Wolver Hollow (Iselin Residence), 40,
    116, 196, 199, 220
Woman's Land Army, 63
Women Architects, Landscape Architects,
    tects, and Planners (WALAP),
    262
Women in Architecture and Landscape
    Architecture (Frost, Sears), 260
women landscape architects
    common characteristics of pioneers,
      10, 16
    education and professional development
      of pioneers, 10–13, 14–16,
      256, 257–63
    recent trends, 262–63
    sociocultural environment of pioneers,
      neers, 13–14, 15, 256–59,
      261–62
    see also specific designer
Woodhouse, Lorenzo E., 156
Woodin, William H., 81, 84
Woodmere (Peck residence), 199
Woolsey, Georgie, 257
Woolworth, Helena, 177
World's Columbia Exposition (1893),
    257
Wright, Charles W., 164
Wright, Frank Lloyd, 12
Wright, Henry, 210

Y
Yale University, 15, 35

Z
Zion and Breen, 254